Regulating and Supervising Investment Services
in the European Union

Regulating and Supervising Investment Services in the European Union

Yannis V. Avgerinos

First published 2003 by
PALGRAVE MACMILLAN
Houndmills, Basingstoke, Hampshire RG21 6XS and
175 Fifth Avenue, New York, N.Y. 10010
Companies and representatives throughout the world

PALGRAVE MACMILLAN is the global academic imprint of the Palgrave
Macmillan division of St. Martin's Press, LLC and of Palgrave Macmillan Ltd.
Macmillan® is a registered trademark in the United States, Untied Kingdom
and other countries. Palgrave is a registered trademark in the European
Union and other countries.

ISBN 1–4039–1204–1 hardback

This book is printed on paper suitable for recycling and made from fully
managed and sustained forest sources.

A catalogue record for this book is available from the British Library.

Library of Congress Cataloging-in-Publication Data
Avgerinos, Yannis V., 1975–
    Regulating and supervising investment services in the European Union /
Yannis V. Avgerinos.
      p. cm.
    Includes bibliographical references and index.
    ISBN 1–4039–1204–1 (alk. paper)
    1. Financial services industry–Law and legislation–European Union countries.
  2. Banking law–European Union countries. 3. Banks and banking–European Union
  countries–State supervision. I. Title.

KJE2188.A98 2003
332.1′094–dc21   2002193092

10 9 8 7 6 5 4 3 2 1
12 11 10 09 08 07 06 05 04 03

Printed and bound in Great Britain by
Antony Rowe Ltd, Chippenham and Eastbourne

Table of Contents

3   The Home Country Control Principle · **50**

8 Consolidating Financial Supervision   225

Foreword

Dr Avgerinos' main thesis asserts that the EU securities market needs for its completion and efficient and stable functioning to establish a single supervisory authority. This new institution could draw inspiration from the institutional structure of the European Central Bank in order to enjoy a significant degree of independence and accountability. The author comes to this conclusion after having examined systematically the EU's strategy in the banking and securities markets. He has also critically examined the principles of harmonisation of essential aspects of supervision, mutual recognition and the "home country control", which allow for the "single passport" to be applied. The book concludes that the EU's approach in the financial services area has not yet fulfilled all its declared objectives, in particular the provision of cross-border financial services.

The author argues that a number of recent factors are influencing European financial integration, to such an extent that they should point to a change of the institutional, regulatory and supervisory framework. In fact, the advent of the euro and the introduction of innovations have accelerated the pace of European financial integration. In response to these developments, the Lamfalussy process adopted by the EU institutions aims at speeding up adoption of securities regulation and in principle should be regarded as an improvement. However, the author believes that even these changes will not be able to meet the objectives because of the involvement of different national regulatory and supervisory authorities. He suggests that this process could be regarded, at best, as a building block towards the future European Single Securities Supervisor.

Dr Avgerinos argues that there are a number of factors pleading for the concept of a single supervisor for the European securities markets. First, the volume of European capital markets entails risks that systemic instability may expand across the financial sectors and countries. Second, capital markets are exposed to the international competition of stock exchanges, which have been the pools of raising capital. A single supervisory authority could render the system more credible than the current multiple and overlapping national regulatory and supervisory authorities. In fact, enlargement to ten new member states would add to the plethora of financial supervisors. The US experience with the federal supervisor of securities markets, the SEC, despite its recent problems, has overall a very positive record of achievements over the last seventy years; third, the ongoing European Convention and the ensuing reform of the Treaties may, if appropriately exploited, offer an opportunity for tackling the challenges coming from the securities markets.

The author's methodology is fundamentally legal but he frequently resorts to an economic or political analysis which broadens considerably the scope of his research. Dr Avgerinos' book is very relevant and timely. It is relevant because the completion of the legal, regulatory and supervisory framework in the European securities markets is of vital importance for the future of European financial integration. Until now, it has not achieved the same progress as the banking regulation that was based on the Second Banking Directive. For this reason, the recent proposal of the European Commission for a radical overhaul of the investment services directive, if and when it is adopted, would provide the fundamental regulatory framework for the investment firms and capital markets in Europe to operate efficiently and effectively. This regulatory measure and its companion directives on prospectus, market abuse and accounting standards, as well as the forthcoming capital adequacy directive, are the essential legal framework for ensuring protection for investors, increasing integrity of the capital markets and fostering competition.

The book is also timely because it comes in the aftermath of a major crisis in the US, which has shaken the very foundations of the world capital markets and has eroded investors' confidence on a global scale. In substance, it has questioned the premises on which rely the legal, accounting and supervisory structures of the US system. It has highlighted the need for a high degree of integrity and transparency for all the institutions which intervene, as gatekeepers, in the chain of capital raising, which includes the companies as issuers, accountants and auditors, investment banks, stock exchanges, analysts, lawyers, rating agencies, regulators and supervisors.

The book of Dr Avgerinos makes an excellent contribution to the ongoing debate of European academics, lawyers, practitioners and policy-makers. It focuses on the appropriate governance of European financial services. Some of these issues were discussed during the creation of the ECB. It is true that the euro provided a new policy set of mind, extending beyond the banking and into to the securities and insurance sectors. The European paradox is that the Eurozone is the only known monetary area where the conduct of monetary policy is assigned to a federal institution, whilst banking supervision is entrusted to national supervisory authorities. However, since it can not be excluded that the Eurozone could face risks of financial instability, any policy-making arrangements will need to involve other sectors and, thus, might relate to the system of financial supervisors. The examination of this broader issue falls outside the scope of this book. From this perspective, the rapprochement of rather differing supervisory approaches will be important. For instance, banking supervisors are mainly focused on stability of the banks and of the financial system, while securities supervisors' primary concern is the protection of investors. However, recent market developments show that systemic risks might stem also from the securities and the insurance sectors.

Any debate and relevant action regarding the issue of a system of European Financial Supervisors will focus on three fundamental criteria relevant for any institutional change and public policy choice. The first is the *subsidiarity* test, which implies that valid reasons of financial stability, consumer protection and competition efficiency should exist to allow the transfer of powers from the national supervisory authorities to a European System of Supervisors. In any federally regulated system, such as that of the US, the state supervisors of securities retain significant powers of enforcement, investigation and sanctions. Thus, decentralisation following an appropriate allocation of powers could render the system operational. The second criterion is *independence* of the institution, whose validity for the credibility and soundness of the financial system would require revision of the Treaty. Third, *accountability* is an essential condition for the transparency and control of the entire system.

The pace of any change and the timing for the fulfilment of the above conditions will undoubtedly vary, depending on a number of factors. The author very elegantly explains that any piecemeal approach towards a single financial supervisor for securities markets will not suffice to tackle major risks that could stem from a financial crisis. The Lamfalussy Report and its institutional edifice and political logic favour a rather evolutionary approach. They clearly imply that the current legal and institutional structures would have to demonstrate that they could deliver the desired results. In case they would not do so, the EU would have no other option but to move to the system of European Financial Supervisors. One could also happily try to imagine what could happen if these structures turned out to function smoothly and thus lay the grounds for a regulatory convergence at EU level. Would the end result not be the same? Market factors and political dynamics, especially with the revision of the Treaty pending, could provide more clarity on these issues. The wisest current approach would seem to suggest that, irrespective of the immediate decisions, any future constitutional revision should enshrine the enabling clauses that will allow the advance gradually to a new supervision system for all the financial sectors.

In this period of interesting regulatory changes coming up soon, the book of Dr Avgerinos will provide an essential and indispensable analysis and guidance for all those directly and even indirectly interested in this complex but fascinating area of law and economic activity. I praise the author's masterly treatment of the issues involved and wholeheartedly recommend the book to all potentially interested readers.

GEORGIOS ZAVVOS
Member of the Legal Service
European Commission, Brussels.
Former Member of the European Parliament

Commission europèenne, B-1049 Bruxelles/Europese Commissie, B-1049 Brussel – Belgium – Office: N-85 8/43.
Telephone: direct line (+32-2)299.56.59, switchboard 299.11.11. Fax: 296.53.29.
Telex: COMEU B 21877. Telegraphic address: COMEUR Brussels.
Internet: Georges.Zavvos@cec.eu.int

* Commission document protected pursuant to Article 4 of Regulation (EC) No 1049/2001 of the European Parliament and of the Council (OJ L 145, 31.5.2001, p. 43).

Preface

The genesis of this book has been influenced by the latest developments in European financial markets, which are driven by the integration of infrastructures, technological innovation and the fall of physical borders in the provision of investment services. This book was written during a time of unpredictable and unprecedented change in investment and financial services across the European Union (EU). It is striking, though, that this breathtaking evolution has not been complemented by analogous convergence of regulatory and supervisory practices. Although markets become global and services are provided at the convenience of a button, investment services regulation and supervision has not managed to overcome national borders. Instead, it remains local.

Research in financial services not only constitutes a highly exciting exercise but also is capable of providing glimpses into the future. Many issues discussed in this book are still evolving. Hence, a difficulty encountered when writing this text was that it needed continuous adjustment and updating. Manifold questions are raised daily, which have hardly received critical examination and response by regulators. However, the only constant prediction that this book makes today is that in less than ten years European financial markets will have changed beyond imagination. In turn, the institutional structure of EU investment and financial services regulation and supervision cannot and will not remain unchanged. The need for reform is evident, as this issue has recently moved beyond the purely academic domain to form the main subject of specific political debate. Indeed, in the last couple of years, the EU financial services policy environment and the response of national regulators, firms and individuals have shown a remarkable dynamism in this field. This has been initiated by the Commission's Financial Services Action Plan (FSAP) and has been given new impetus with the Wise Men Committee proposals and the introduction of the single currency. The seed has been planted but only time will reveal whether European policy-makers will best nurture European financial markets to yield a bountiful harvest.

Many people have contributed to the creation of this book, from the initial idea, to research and completion. In particular, I would like to acknowledge the most valuable help and advice received from George A. Walker of Queen Mary, University of London and Kern Alexander of University of Cambridge. Valuable support was also provided by Professor John Phillips and Professor Jan Dalhuisen, both from King's College, University of London. This project benefited substantially from discussions with financial services regulators, including Nigel Phipps and David Green of the Financial Services

Authority, Stavros Thomadakis, Chairman, and Eleftheria Apostolidou, Director of the International Office, both from the Capital Market Commission, Gregor Pozniak, Deputy Secretary General of the Federation of European Securities Exchanges and Christoph Crüwell of the *Bundesaufsichtsamt für den Wertpapierhandel*. The fruitful and inspiring discussions with financial law practitioners, including Gilles Thieffry of BNP Paribas, George Zavvos of the European Commission, Jane Welch of Financial Services (Europe), Eric Pan of Covington & Burling and Anil Raval of the Interactive Investor International, and with American academics, including Professor Howell Jackson and Professor Joseph Weiler, both from the Harvard Law School must also be acknowledged. I would also like to thank Paulina for being a valuable intellectual companion. My friends and colleagues from King's College, LSE and UCL, Prodromos Tsiavos, Edite-Izabella Ligere, Eleftheria Psaraki, Barbara Kondilis, Yannis Boudouris, Ashutosh Khanna, Carsten Zatschler, Lazaros Panourgias and Vasso Galanopoulou are thanked for their friendship, understanding and inspiration. Also, Annette Lee and Peter Niven for their substantive secretarial and administrative support. My final thanks go to the staff of Palgrave Macmillan and in particular to Stephen Rutt and Caitlin Cornish for their assistance, professionalism and patience during the publication process. Last, but not least, I am grateful to my colleague and mentor, Mads Andenas, Director of the British Institute of International and Comparative Law, for his guidance and encouragement in completing this book. Any errors, shortcomings or omissions are my responsibility.

A special acknowledgement should be reserved to the Arts & Humanities Research Board (AHRB) and to the Jean Monnet Program of Harvard Law School for their financial support. I also thank the British Institute of International and Comparative Law and the Financial Services Authority for accommodating me during my research. However, my deepest debt of gratitude goes to my family for their sustained encouragement and endless love during the process of my research.

Yannis V. Avgerinos
London, October 2002

Table of Acronyms

ADEX	Athens Derivatives Exchange
ADR	Alternative Dispute Resolution
All ER	All England Law Reports
ATS	Alternative Trading Systems
BAC	Banking Advisory Committee
BAWe	*Bundesaufsichtsamt für den Wertpapierhandel*
BCCI	Bank of Credit & Commerce International
BFS	Barings Futures Singapore
BIS	Bank of International Settlements
BVR	*Bundesverfassungsgericht*
CA	Court of Appeal
CAD	Capital Adequacy Directive
CAP	Common Agricultural Policy
CBR	Conduct of Business Rules
CEEC	Central & Eastern European Countries
CEPA	Center for Economic Policy Analysis
CEPR	Centre of Economic Policy Research
CEPS	Centre of European Policy Studies
CER	Centre for European Reform
CESR	Committee of European Securities Regulators
CMC	Capital Market Commission
CMLR	Common Market Law Reports
CMLRev	Common Market Law Review
Commission	European Commission
CPSS	Committee on Payments and Settlements Systems
CSD	Central Securities Depository
CUP	Cambridge University Press
DG	Directorate General
DGD	Deposit Guarantee Directive
EBLR	European Business Law Review
EC	European Community
ECB	European Central Bank
ECJ	European Court of Justice
ECR	European Court Reports
EEA	European Economic Area
EEC	European Economic Community
EEIG	European Economic Interest Grouping
EFC	Economic & Financial Committee
EFSA	European Food Safety Authority

EFSL	European Financial Services Law
EIB	European Investment Bank
ELJ	European Law Journal
ELRev	European Law Review
EMI	European Monetary Institute
EMU	Economic & Monetary Union
ERF	European Roundtable on Financial Services
ESC	European Securities Committee
ESFRC	European Shadow Financial Regulatory Committee
ESR	European Securities Regulator
ESSR	European System of Securities Regulators
EU	European Union
EuroCCP	European Central Counterparty
Euro.NM	European New Markets
FBD	First Banking Directive
Fed	Federal Reserve
FESCO	Forum of European Securities Commissions
FESE	Federation of European Securities Exchanges
FIDE	*Fédération Internationale pour le Droit Européen*
FMG	Financial Markets Group
FSA	Financial Services Authority
FSAP	Financial Services Action Plan
FSF	Financial Stability Forum
FSLR	Federal Securities Law Report
FSMA	Financial Services & Markets Act
FSPG	Financial Services Policy Group
FT	Financial Times
FTC	Federal Trade Commission
GDP	Gross Domestic Product
HL	House of Lords
HLSSC	High Level Securities Supervisors Committee
HMSO	Her Majesty's Stationery Office
IAIS	International Association of Insurance Supervisors
IAS	International Accounting Standards
IBA	International Bar Association
ICLQ	International & Comparative Law Quarterly
ICSD	Investor Compensation Schemes Directive
IFLR	International Financial Law Review
IGC	Intergovernmental Conference
IIE	Institute for International Economics
IMF	International Monetary Fund
IML	*Institut Monetaire Luxembourgeoism*
IOSCO	International Organisation of Securities Commissions
IPO	Initial Public Offering

ISD	Investment Services Directive
ISMA	International Securities Market Association
ITF	Internet Task Force
JCMS	Journal of Common Market Studies
JIBFL	Journal of Internatisonal Banking & Financial Law
JIBL	Journal of International Banking Law
JIBR	Journal of International Banking Regulation
JIFM	Journal of International Financial Markets
LLR	Lender of Last Resort
LQR	Law Quarterly Review
LTCM	Long-Term Capital Management
M&A	Mergers & Acquisitions
MLR	Modern Law Review
MoU	Memorandum of Understanding
NASAA	North American Securities Administrators Association
NASD	National Association of Securities Dealers
NASDAQ	National Association of Securities Dealers Automated Quotation
NCB	National Central Bank
OECD	Organization for Economic Cooperation and Development
OJ	Official Journal of the European Communities
OUP	Oxford University Press
PES	Parliament European Socialists
POP	Public Offering Prospectus
SBD	Second Banking Directive
SE	*Societas Europeae*
SEA	Single European Act
SEC	Securities & Exchange Commission
SFA	Securities & Future Authority
SIB	Securities & Investment Board
SLIM	Simpler Legislation for the Internal Market
SME	Small & Medium Enterprise
SRO	Self-regulatory Organization
SSS	Securities Settlement Systems
UCITS	Undertakings for Collective Investment in Transferable Securities
UK	United Kingdom
UN	United Nations
US	United States
USC	United States Code
WLR	Weekly Law Reports
WP	Working Paper
WTO	World Trade Organisation
ZEI	*Zentrum für Europäische Integrationsforschung*

Table of Cases

European Court of Justice

Germany

United Kingdom

United States

≪οὐκοῦν ἐν μὲν χρηά'των διοικήσει κρατοίη
ἀ'ν οχρήμασιν εὐπορωτέραν τὴν πόλιν ποιων;≫

Ξενοφών,Απομνημονενμά'των Δ, Κεφά'λαιο 6, παρά'γραφος 14

... in financial administration, then,
is not the better man he who makes the city wealthier?

Xenophon, *Memorabilia*, Book 4, Chapter 6, Section 14

Prologue

A. Subject and focus

This book deals with the regulation and supervision of investment services within the European Union (EU).[1] Recent developments in financial services at EU level as well as regulatory and institutional developments at national level constitute the subject and focus of this book timelier than ever. The question of the institutional structure of the EU investment services regulation and supervision has now moved beyond the purely academic domain to form the subject of specific political debate.

The aim of this book is to contribute to this debate by critically assessing the current supervisory regime of home country control in EU investment services with a view to drawing policy lessons and recommendations on more effective and efficient alternatives. In this light, it purports to make specific suggestions with regard to the institutional structure and the operational sphere of a central pan-European regulator, which will not be based on a purely legal domain.

B. The background

We live in an era of breathtaking change. Over the past dozen years, Europe has experienced a revolutionary change regarding investment and financial services. From the introduction of the euro and the creation of the European Central Bank (ECB) to the dominant appearance of financial conglomerates, complex financial products and the electronisation of securities markets, the revolution is more than evident.

The European securities industry has changed dramatically. This can be seen chiefly as the consequence of the globalisation of financial services in general. Developments, such as fast storage, transmission and processing of information, increasing consolidation and conglomeration and electronic commerce, cause institutions not only to reconsider their geographical structure, to move bulk processing to lower cost centres and to outsource, but also oblige them to adjust their management structures and traditions based on location and regional geography. Globalisation and the need to create an appropriate and efficient regulatory and supervisory framework of the global economy form part of the background to the current debate. More developments are to come in the future, which will require imaginative and innovative responses from supervisory authorities. The impetus for some of these changes can be sourced to the European Economic and Monetary Union (EMU). Yet, there are other powerful forces at work such as technological changes and new competitive dynamics.[2]

Moving to the regulatory sphere, one cannot ignore the considerable progress made over the last twenty years. The starting point for EU investment services regulation and supervision is that their regulatory and supervisory framework matters as a precondition for the objectives of financial stability, consumer protection and competition promotion. Supervisors acknowledge that consumers want fair, honest, orderly, effective and efficient financial markets. This is an important matter of public interest and regulators should take necessary actions to promote these objectives. Moreover, past and recent financial institutions' failures worldwide justify the attention currently given to the reinforcement, or even to the complete reform, of current regulatory and supervisory arrangements.

In keeping with the overall objectives of the EC Treaty, mainly the concepts of freedom of establishment (Articles 49–55 EC (former Articles 59–66)) and freedom to provide services (Articles 43–48 EC (former Articles 52–58)), the EU has been concerned to create an environment, in which all financial institutions within the EU and the European Economic Area (EEA) should be able to offer their services throughout the Union on the same, or a similar, supervisory foundation. Investment and financial services regulation is based on the Treaty objective of developing a common market.[3] The Internal Market in financial services, introduced by the European Commission's 1985 White Paper[4] constitutes part of a wider project to create a single market comprising 'an area without internal frontiers in which the free movement of goods, persons, services and capital is ensured'.[5] Accordingly, capital markets have been liberalised and integrated, their access has been freed, rules in all the fifteen Member States are more or less harmonised and services circulate freely all over Europe under the 'European passport' and homogenous prudential rules, all of which have resulted in a true European securities market carried within a single currency. These achievements are far from negligible. However, the cessation of any substantial developments during the last eight years – that is after the Investment Services Directive (ISD) and the Second Banking Directive (SBD)[6] – makes one wonder: could there have been more liberalisation and could it have been better?

Indeed, these developments have not been followed by increased financial cross-border flows, as one would expect. Regretfully, the European picture resulting from this restructuring process is not very clear. One thing, however, is certain: cross-border market integration remains very limited. In the five largest EU countries, only 4.25 per cent of the assets and 6.2 per cent of the liabilities were cross-border in 1996. Capital and financial service markets are also reflecting the deterioration of general business conditions: stock market capitalisation of domestic firms fell 3.8 per cent in 2000 compared to the previous year.[7] Moreover, the market share of branches and subsidiaries from other EU and EEA countries is still limited in most EU countries.

Towards the aforementioned evolving environment, the current structure of investment services supervision appears old-fashioned and anachronistic. Rules and provisions of the 1992 'new approach' are now becoming out of date and require a thorough overhauling. The current debate among academic scholars, EU institutions' and Member States' representatives and – lately – members of the Financial Services Policy Group (FSPG) and the Wise Men Committee, leaves a feeling that something is moving at European level in securities regulation. The Financial Services Action Plan (FSAP),[8] adopted by the Commission in May 1999, supports this assumption. Yet, supervision deliberately remains out of the agenda.

Admittedly, the task of investment services supervision is very different today from what it was a decade ago. With the loss of the local or domestic character of the securities markets and the cross-border provision of investment services, national supervisory authorities suddenly found themselves exposed to new problems and challenges. As a result of historic market structures, traditional administrative approaches and existing European constitutional realities, supervisors are often thinking (only) in terms of national jurisdictions. As markets change, inadequate supervision can jeopardise the stability of the European and world financial system, competition neutrality and consumer protection.

C. Formulation of the *problematique*

The development of regulatory and supervisory arrangements of investment services on a pan-European basis gives rise to several categories of problems, which will be addressed in this book. In light of the fundamental restructuring of European securities markets and the failure of regulatory responses, the basic nature and operation of modern supervisory and regulatory practices must now be reconsidered.

As envisaged in the European Commission's White Paper of 1985 and adopted by subsequent secondary EU law, European financial sector liberalisation is based on the three principles of minimum harmonisation, mutual recognition and home country control.[9] Following the failure of previous complete harmonisation efforts by the European Community, this approach has been seen as the most appropriate to achieve a single market and has been subsequently followed by financial services secondary legislation. Its advantages are obvious: mutual recognition allows products and services legally circulated in one Member State to be admitted to other Member States without being required to meet additional regulatory requirements. Costly duplications are thus theoretically avoided without the need for complete harmonisation of national legislation at Community level. Thanks to mutual recognition, not all sectors of the Single Market needed to be harmonised, or harmonisation has been restricted to the 'essential requirements'. Hence, minimum harmonisation of basic standards allows a certain degree of regulatory competition between Member States and accommodates flexibility, innovation, simplification and experimentation. Furthermore, and perhaps most important, EU policy and law making remains sensible to local and regional interests, while the maintenance of specific national characteristics is ensured.

Albeit their initial success, however, a debate has started in Europe regarding the current status of the principles and their applicability to modern financial institutions and markets. Especially acute are the problems arising from the latter principle of home country control, as originated and developed by the Basel Committee on Banking Supervision and the European Court of Justice (ECJ). The 1985 Internal Market Programme has created a complex web of harmonised EU rules and unharmonised national regimes while many exceptions apply to home country control.

Even in areas where harmonisation has been achieved, this should not be seen as an attempt to apply uniformity of laws and regulations throughout the Union. There remain differences in national laws implementing secondary legislation. Divergences can also be observed in the laws on the supervision of financial services providers. As a result, the focus has been concentrated on the determination of the respective supervisory roles of EU institutions and Member States on the one hand, and of home and host Member States on the other. The relevant investment services and other financial services directives hardly manage to face the challenge and solve the problem.[10] In addition, the principle of subsidiarity, as introduced by the Maastricht Treaty and set out in Article 5 EC (former Article 3b), has brought about a major shift in EU policy and law making. Ambiguous and controversial, this principle has impacted on the form, length and content of legislation and has the potential to undermine the full liberalisation of investment services and the integration of financial markets.

As a result of increased market integration, stimulated by the single currency, problems are emerging. The EMU is prompting a quantum leap in how financial institutions and markets are interpreted and it is expected to act as a catalyst to existing trends and stimulate a further integration of EU financial markets. However, while the existing body of European law, once fully in force, should allow the integration of these markets, a number of regulatory and institutional barriers are hampering the development and efficiency of their operations. Regulatory and supervisory divergences and the overlap of rules amount to legal and economic barriers. The cost they represent may hinder access to foreign markets and financial market integration. In response, the reforms, both regulatory and deregulatory in nature, are not coming easily and may occasionally threaten Member State's national policies.[11] A new potential for pan-European instability is generated, while the capacity of individual Member States to handle crises is reduced.

Simultaneously, Member States and EU institutions face an increased demand for further simplification and standardisation of the present structure of supervision, to ease pan-European operations. European investment firms and financial groups, active in different Member States, are currently faced with multiple supervisory techniques and costs. If cross-border financial sector consolidation raises fresh problems and needs to be stimulated in Europe, this issue will need to be tackled as well. Against this background, it is necessary to reassess the adequacy of home country control.

While the Treaty provides for the possibility of greater formal centralisation of banking supervision through the ECB,[12] it is not easy to make a similar case for investment services. What is currently 'desirable' is the creation of arrangements for cooperation and coordination between supervisors across various disciplines in Europe. Several committees have been established to promote regulation and supervisory coordination at the European level. The Forum of European Securities Commissions (FESCO), for instance, was created in 1997 to allow national securities supervisors to cooperate and align supervisory practices. On the other hand, the Commission has recently formed the European Securities Committee (ESC) and the Committee of European Securities Regulators (CESR), which has replaced FESCO. Yet, the capacity of these bodies remains weak and limited – if not non-existent – in terms of regulation and supervision.

In terms of general framework, the elements of effective financial supervision consist of the following:[13]

(a) identifying the appropriate supervisory objectives;
(b) establishing mechanisms that will achieve those objectives;
(c) monitoring whether the objectives are being achieved; and
(d) enforcing or taking other corrective action when there is a violation or lack of compliance with requirements.

In the securities industry, the arguments for a more integrated supervisory body are less persuasive than in banking, mainly due to asserted fewer disturbing related risks. However, as this book will discuss, risks are no longer divided according to sectors of the financial industry. The dialogue in investment services should not and cannot be less challenging or of minor importance. In line with further harmonisation of securities regulation, the most controversial issue appears to be home country control and the supervision of conduct of business rules. Although financial services directives endeavour to divide supervisory responsibilities between the home and the host state, there are some 'grey' areas and complex provisions, particularly when transgressions occur from the host Member State's regulatory regime.[14] This has led some commentators to argue for a pan-European mega supervisor to help overcome these barriers.[15] To support centralised control implies a belief that the sophistication of investment or financial services in general requires some level of regulation and supervision to ensure the necessary consumer confidence. Others find such an argument remote and would prefer a more harmonised regulatory background within the EU prior to such a big step.[16]

It is true that the development of a harmonised regulatory framework for EU investment services is less sophisticated than in the area of banking. This is partly justified by the fact that cross-border externalities associated with investment services have attracted less attention by public policy. Only during the last couple of decades has the EU (and the international community) taken action towards harmonisation to ease the cost and market-access obstructions as well as regulatory and supervisory concerns provoked by cross-border activity. It becomes evident today that an integrated pan-European securities market needs simultaneous and parallel action on a regulatory and supervisory basis, in order to ensure that consumers are protected on an equal and sufficient level and that standards of securities markets' transparency and efficiency are effectively implemented by all Member States. Regretfully, supervisors do not function in a social, political or economic vacuum.

As in banking, it may be that existing national securities supervisors need a step-change in the level of their coordination. Although Member States' securities commissions have been less active in terms of cross-border cooperation, the introduction of the euro served to concentrate minds. The response to the new environment was the creation of FESCO, through which national supervisors get together and agree mutually to bind themselves to a set of standards. The fact that FESCO does not have implementing powers, has led the Commission to create two new committees, which will – it is believed – contribute to the elaboration of EU securities regulation. In the future, any technical adaptation will not have to take the form of formal Directives' amendment, but will be decided by the 'comitology' Securities Committee without delay. The success of the new regulatory regime notwithstanding, this book will support the view that legislation is not the only thorn that hurdles the free provision of investment services in Europe and the advancement of securities markets to compete with global components. The major problem lies in supervision and in the efficiency of the principle of home country control.

The rapid integration of EU securities markets, the alliances and networks established due to technology, and the lacunae in the EU regulatory and supervisory framework have led many scholars to support the establishment of a European Securities Regulator, equivalent to the US Securities and Exchange

Commission (SEC). This book will show that such a prospect seems less and less remote at the moment.

D. The response

1. Three steps for effective supervision and two criteria for EU action

The logical method for defining the trade-off relationship between effectiveness of supervision and its costs is built upon a simple three-step axiom. The first step is the definition of the objectives and rationale for financial supervision in the EU. Second, the marginal analysis of the current home-country based supervisory arrangements in connection with the aforementioned objectives. If the current structure provides overall costs charged on market participants much higher than marginal benefits, so as to make the Internal Market and investment services unable to function and compete with other markets, the third step must follow: the examination of alternative arrangements and the possibility of transferring policy at a more centralised EU level. An analysis of the issue of Member State competence versus federal EU competence involves identifying the costs and benefits of each. Accordingly, action at EU level is justified by way of *two* criteria, complementary to one another:

(a) The absence of action at the European level might have negative consequences for the effectiveness of instruments envisaged by the Member States and/or be contrary to the requirements of the Treaty.

(b) Action at Community level would produce clear benefits by reason of its scale or effects compared with action at the level of the Member States.[17]

Noticeably, there are several arguments in favour of greater decentralisation of the regulatory and executive tasks in the Community system, such as subsidiarity, proportionality, sovereignty and lack of harmonisation. Some of these tasks have, since the inception of home country control, been assigned to national authorities. The EU, for its part, should investigate the most appropriate forms of decentralisation with a view to an efficient and effective execution of the Treaty objectives and tasks. This has to be conducted in parallel with another important concern in mind: the definition of the limits of decentralisation.

There are two contrasting ways decentralisation could be seen. First, decentralisation responds to the need for an authority free from all national leanings to elaborate technical viewpoints that are coherent and uniform at EU level (this is to be called horizontal decentralisation). Alternatively, much more flexible application of the rules is necessary, giving a greater margin of assessment according to local situations (this is to be called vertical decentralisation).[18] Within this analysis, the latter is represented by the home country control principle and the former by a pan-European Securities Regulator.

2. The need for a pan-European Securities Regulator

The case for a European Securities Regulator constitutes the centrepiece of this study. It is not disputed in this book that, as far as systemic stability is concerned, the integration model of home country control may have worked well so far.[19] It has failed, nonetheless, in delivering the full application of the principle of the free movement of investment services within the Community. *A fortiori*, the European supervisory and regulatory system, as it exists at present, cannot continue to be adequate for an increasingly integrated European financial market, given its evident weaknesses. Whereas financial services and providers function and consolidate on a cross-border and cross-sector basis, their supervision cannot remain local. Home supervisors increasingly find their task more difficult, as they try to extend their power to financial business conducted beyond their country. Host supervisors, on the other hand, become less informed about the firms and the markets as a whole, which limits their ability to take *ex ante* action and successfully address crisis situations.

Recent attempts by the European Commission to address and tackle the drawbacks of home country control have hardly faced a warm welcome by market participants, academics and the European Parliament. The proposed Wise Men regime not only raises serious doubts as to whether it will actually speed up securities regulation, but also is likely to create greater complexity, confusion and legal uncertainty. Yet, despite these suggestions, supervision remains out of the agenda, while developments cannot wait. Hence, this book will show that centralisation in supervision and more flexible regulation will be the only answer to the hurdles of inconsistencies and loopholes, systemic inflexibility, high transaction cost, problematic cooperation and coordination and EU's failure to speak with one voice at international negotiations.

Where the regulatory and supervisory divergence of home country control fails to deliver, centralisation appears to be the best solution for free and effective movement of investment services. When compared with the current fragmented plethora of regulatory and supervisory structures, it is not unlikely that centralisation will facilitate cross-border securities activities and therefore competition. Economics of scale and great power over individual regulated entities should make a EU securities supervisor more effective than national competent authorities. Its strength will be drawn from two defensive parameters: management control and market discipline. A centralised structure should improve the information flow and introduce, with the market's assistance, suitable measures to defend against risk and boost efficiency. In turn, the reduction in the national supervisors' responsibilities would permit more resources to be devoted to local and regional areas that remain within their supervisory power, increasing, thus, their effectiveness. At the end of the day, of course, the rationale of a pan-European solution will solidly stand on the better promotion of the supervisory objectives of financial stability, competition and consumer protection.

3. Putting an end to sectoral supervision?

Inevitably, bringing investment services supervision to the centre of the EU will raise significant questions about institutional structures and operation. Recent financial services consolidation and conglomeration trends make business sectors' division look blurred.[20] In response to these developments, many countries in Europe not only have readdressed the challenges presented by the new lines of business, but also have moved towards the creation of single or, at least, fewer national regulators in order to adequately supervise groups of growing size and complexity.[21] In other European countries, the supervisory structure is known to be under official review or informal debate.

These issues need be addressed, as the necessity for a pan-European supervisory arrangement may extend beyond the securities sector. However, it is not within the scope of this study to analytically examine all options or even to predict the ultimate structure that will guarantee financial stability, consumer protection and the efficiency of cross-border provision of financial services within the Union.

E. Approach and structure of the book

The subject matter of this book covers regulatory and supervisory aspects that concern investment services providers and market participants. Hence, the book distinguishes their approach from the regulation of securities markets, which is addressed merely superficially and in a supplementary way.

The success or failure of individual regulatory and supervisory structures and institutional designs seems to depend on so many factors – legal, institutional, political, economic, administrative – that an analysis that leaves some out seems incomplete, while one that considers all makes each structure unique. The methodological approach and discussion of this book fluctuates between classical legal theory, institutional economics, politics and economic analysis. The comprehensive analysis of legislative instruments and case law, the use of cost–benefit analysis (CBA), the substantive impact of institutional alternatives on different groups and the assumptions of the neoclassical equilibrium, on which the technique is founded, will help this book as means of determining policy at EU level. On the other hand, certain relevant factors, such as the politics behind the creation and administration of specific supervisory regimes, are treated in less detail.

With regard to current regulatory and supervisory structures, this book follows a normative approach.[22] It considers the rationale for supervision and not its causes. It discusses the problems associated with a view of conscientious regulators who are trying to do their job well. This differs from efforts to produce general causal theories explaining the origin of regulatory and supervisory programmes and their effects.

Traditionally, the function of the market has been to lower the cost of transactions for buyers and sellers. Applying economic analysis to financial regulation and supervision is the only way of identifying the root of the issue. In particular, CBA is a practical and rigorous means of identifying, targeting and checking the impact of regulatory and supervisory measures on the underlying causes of the ills, which regulators need to address.[23] In addition, institutional theory should identify key instrumental variables and the relationships among them to predict and understand current and future structures, whereas the political theories of neo-institutionalism and neo-functionalism will assist in identifying political behaviour in relation to institutional structures. It might be said, though, that the best way of organising regulation and supervision cannot be derived from theory. However, as this analysis will show, the costs and drawbacks associated with the current supervisory structure of EU investment services can be described as anything but theoretical.

The structure of the book is as follows. The purpose of the first chapter is to consider the rationale for financial supervision. Before addressing the issue of home country control and examining its efficiency within the European context, it will briefly summarise the reasons for financial supervision and its objectives. The latter will in turn provide a solid rationale for institutional reform and centralisation of investment services regulation and supervision. The second chapter analyses the Community efforts to create a single market in financial services, from the initial unsuccessful harmonisation idea to the 1992 internal market programme, the three principles of minimum harmonisation, mutual recognition and home country control and the Wise Men regime. Chapter 3 unfolds the principle of home country control as it emerged and as it functions within the Community by exploring its history and identifying its legal basis and the key responsibilities between the home and the host Member State. Chapter 4 focuses on the institutional design of the current regulatory and supervisory regime of EU investment services and on the actors behind the scene. The role and efficiency of the newly established committees that followed the Wise Men proposals will constitute the primary concern of this chapter. An assessment of the present regulatory and supervisory regime of home country control is provided in Chapter 5. The lack of efficiency and effectiveness in the current structure will assist this book in defining the need for institutional alternatives. Liberalisation has long been the desire of financial industries' regulators and consumers. However, significant structural and substantial difficulties together with supervisory gaps still persist and clearly inhibit the full application of the freedom of provision of financial services, as envisaged in the Treaty, while financial stability, consumer protection and undistorted competition are jeopardised. As an alternative, the need and rationale for creating a pan-European Securities Supervisor is considered in Chapter 6. This chapter endeavours to signal the ways – if any – in which the EU institutional structure might be changed and explains the reasons that constitute centralisation an inevitable necessity in order to remedy the problems of the current supervisory system and better promote the supervisory objectives. Chapter 7 makes suggestions with regard to the principal objectives, competence and tasks of the pan-European Securities Regulator as well as its relationship with Member States supervisory authorities and EU institutions. In order to assist its analysis, the chapter draws arguments from the institutional structure and substantial powers of other federal institutions, namely the European System of Central Banks and the US Securities and Exchange Commission. The specific trend of integrated cross-sector financial supervision is examined separately in Chapter 8 as a catalyst that is likely to define and influence future institutional arrangements at the Community level. Finally, the general conclusions of this book are drawn in the Epilogue. This unfolds the main chain of arguments in the preceding chapters and explains how the different parts of the book fit together.

Part I
Why Supervise?

1
The Objectives of Financial Supervision

A. Introduction

The purpose of this chapter is to consider the objectives of financial supervision.[1] Before addressing the issue of investment services regulation and supervision and examining its effectiveness and efficiency within the European context, a brief summary of the rationale for financial supervision is provided. Why does supervision have welfare benefits? Why supervise investment services at all? What is special about financial firms and markets and what is the relationship between supervisory objectives and institutional structures of supervision? The highlights of the purpose of an incentive-based legal and supervisory framework will assist the main aim of this book to identify the most suitable and less risk-taking supervisory structure within the EU area.

The fundamental premise of this chapter is that the legal and supervisory framework of the European investment and broader financial services matters as a precondition for stability, consumer protection and competition. As stated in Chapter 1, one of the main elements of effective supervision is the identification of the appropriate supervisory objectives. Supervisors acknowledge that consumers want fair, honest, orderly and efficient markets. This is an important matter of public interest and regulators should take necessary actions to promote these objectives. Moreover, past and recent financial institutions' failures worldwide justify the attention currently given to the reinforcement, or even to the complete reform, of current regulatory and supervisory arrangements.

This chapter is set out as follows. It begins with a brief explanation of the theoretical background for state interference in financial services regulation and supervision and the distinctions often made in supervision and in risk factor assessments. The third section is devoted to the objectives of supervision, while the fourth section briefly highlights additional key principles that must coexist in any given sound and efficient supervisory regime. The conclusions of this chapter are drawn in its final section.

B. Theoretical underpinning

Financial firms perform a highly distinctive role in ensuring the smooth functioning of economies. By acting as transformers of liquidity intermediating between liquid and illiquid assets, they are able to ensure that resources are allocated in an efficient manner. In so doing, they act to assess and cost risk. In an efficient market this would, in principle, optimise the risk–return trade-off.[2] In the real world, however, the smooth operation of the market is not always considered as self-evident. The classical economic justification for state interference in a market is that the market fails to allocate resources fairly and efficiently. In supervision, the supervisor must question which financial services' function is to be regulated or supervised, what the precise concerns are, what risks can be protected against; in other words the true objectives of such supervision in each instance and how they can most effectively be achieved.[3] These aspects have often been given too little weight – if not forgotten entirely – during the regime shifts that preceded financial crises in many countries.[4] Risk is central to the whole process of investing, and that should always be the primary concern of supervisors. Elroy Dimson, a British finance theorist, once remarked, 'if projects were riskless, there would be no problem (...) Risk means that more things can happen than will happen'.[5] In response to a clear need to tackle risk, investment services have been regulated for a long time in Europe. The need to protect covers both the investors, to whom the services are rendered, and the financial intermediaries, from which services are provided.

A second theoretical underpinning for public intervention in economic matters is traditionally based on the need to correct market anomalies. The financial system itself needs protection, for inadequate regulation and supervision can jeopardise the stability of the financial system and hamper innovation. Recent financial crises fully justify the rationale for supervision of the financial sector, while public interest is recognised as superior in quality and importance, and therefore privileged, in respect of the legitimate interests of other market participants.[6] In turn, economics of securities regulation and supervision must try to find a manageable trade-off between effectiveness with reference to the objectives analysed in the following paragraphs and efficiency in terms of costs imposed directly or indirectly on financial firms and other market participants. In defining a manageable trade-off the institutional structure of financial supervision within Europe plays a major role.

Usually, a distinction is drawn between prudential supervision of financial firms, such as capital adequacy rules, and supervision of financial markets, such as disclosure rules. Prudential supervision involves the imposition of controls designed to ensure that investors do not lose their money.[7] Market supervision involves the adoption and implementation of a disclosure philosophy to ensure that markets operate in a smooth and efficient manner. Altogether, however, the emphasis of modern supervision of the financial services industry is mainly on the service and the service provider, rather than the market *per se*.[8] This is justified by the very character of state-of-the-art securities markets, which now have the possibility to act and operate as services providers as well.[9]

Another distinction is traditionally made in risk-assessing factors. It is often alleged that different financial firms have contrasting operational characteristics and risk-assessing factors that underline the need for different regulatory responses.[10] This functional division has been based on the differences in risk factors for banks, investment firms and insurance companies. For instance, traditional banking involved the acquisition of long-term non-marketable credit, which is typically held on the balance sheet until maturity. On the contrary, investment firms experience rapid asset turnover as a result of their market making, underwriting and trading activities.[11] As such, the assets of investment firms mainly comprise marketable securities, which are quoted and transacted every day. Prudential supervision in insurance is mainly a matter of controlling asset–liability match. The asymmetry of contracts that exist in the banking sector does not arise in the securities sector, and thus the susceptibility to a loss of confidence is considered lower in the latter. As a result, systemic risk has been traditionally seen as an issue merely for banks, to a lesser degree for investment firms and not for insurance companies. This has had a direct impact on the need and objectives of regulation as well as on the ways and techniques of regulatory responses to risk.

Nonetheless, in the modern financial environment, it is no longer possible to separate sets of regulatory objectives, as there has been a progressive erosion of the traditional demarcation lines that have separated banking, investment and insurance business.[12] The importance of the regulation and supervision of investment services in Europe, for example, has been explicitly recognised by the ECJ in its first decision regarding investment services. It held in *Alpine Investments* that 'the trustworthiness of the financial intermediaries on whom investors are particularly reliant' was important to ensure investor confidence in securities markets.[13]

Moving a step forward, when we refer to supervision, the separation of its objectives is even more difficult, if not impossible, to be conducted.[14] The risk profile of investment firms, for instance, has changed with the practice of trading in derivative instruments, where the risk exposure can be much higher than in the primary business. In addition, the rapidly increasing importance of investment banks and fund managers as big players in financial markets means that their failure could impact on the whole financial system and have cross-border systemic effects. This can be easily noticed in the recent southeast Asia crisis with the failure of Peregrine Investments, the largest investment bank in the region,[15] as well as in the rescue of the almost default Long-Term Capital Management (LTCM) in the United States.[16]

Finally, in the European context, where universal banking was taken as a model in the SBD, investment banking has become increasingly fused with traditional banking and insurance business.

C. The objectives of supervision

The objectives of public sector intervention are perhaps the easiest to disentangle.[17] Yet, while a valid case can be made for regulating credit institutions, the rationale for regulating investment firms is considered by some commentators to be much less obvious.[18] As explained before, however, the following supervisory objectives should apply in any institution that provides financial services.[19]

A first objective of financial market regulation and supervision is to strengthen the macroeconomic and microeconomic stability of the financial system as a whole. Financial stability is a pure 'public good' in that it will not be produced by the operation of market forces. It translates into macro-controls over securities exchanges, clearing houses and settlement systems.

A second objective of financial supervision is transparency in the market and in financial undertakings and consumer protection. This is linked to the more general objective of information equilibrium and may be mapped into the search for 'equity in the distribution of information as a precious good' among operators.[20] As we shall see, however, this theme closely relates to the objective of financial stability and may overlap.[21] Confidence in the market in general lies at the root of both financial stability and consumer protection.[22]

A third objective of financial market supervision is the safeguarding and promotion of competition in the financial undertakings' sector. This relates to the free provision of services and the promotion of competition *per se* as well as to limiting potential destabilising excesses generated by competition itself. In the following, I shall take a closer look at these three objectives.

1. Financial stability

The first objective of financial supervision is financial stability. The objective of financial stability takes a broader view than merely the operation of individual financial institutions. Rather, it is focused on the health and ability of the financial system to weather shocks, with special regard to the likely impact of financial disturbances on the economy as a whole.[23] Markets are not perfect. Hence, it is in the interest of both the private and public sector to assess the risks and avoid financial market crises as much as possible, for they may entail enormous expenses for private industry and national economies. Besides the monitoring of individual undertakings, the financial system itself needs protection since the crisis of a financial firm may threaten the stability of the whole financial system to which the firm belongs or is linked with. With this respect, however, banks are no longer 'special' in the sense of being uniquely exposed to systemic risk, for their risks and exposures have become intermingled with non-banking financial business.[24] The supervisory objective of financial stability now extends to investment firms, equity and derivatives clearing and settlement systems and even insurance and fund management entities. Recent developed and emerging markets' crises confirm the scenario of systemic risk[25] and reveal shortcomings in their supervision.

Attention needs to be given to new sources of systemic risk, which may reside in the electronic order-matching systems or in clearing and settlement systems.[26] Moreover, technology and innovation have made it possible for many exchanges and trading systems to operate as commercial, for profit organisations, or even as financial firms. Thus, regulators should consider these arrangements not only in respect of the traditional supervision of trading but also in respect of any other responsibilities the operator of a market might have.[27]

The key to combat systemic and market risk is a proper financial supervision architecture. Modern supervisory arrangement should be set up in such a way as to avoid market collapses. Defaults of the past should serve as lessons for present and future regulators. But what constitutes a market collapse? Market collapse is a sudden loss of liquidity. A price cannot be set because of the risk of further price changes (market risk), asymmetric information (information monopoly risk), solvency of counterparties (credit risk), and the divergent interpretation of market rules and supervisory arrangements (regulatory and supervisory risk).

In this light, it would be useful to see what factors increase and what factors decrease the probability of market collapse and financial instability, as well as the relationship of these factors with supervisory arrangements. A major factor that increases such a probability is the correlation of markets (interlocking). This is especially evident in an integrated financial market, such as the European Single Market. Another factor may be the high volatility of securities markets. On the other hand, factors that reduce the probability of market collapse include the low cost of information on counterparty risk and market prices and the use of modern market and credit risk models.

Between these two extremes intervenes the regulatory and supervisory risk, which may have a major impact on the stability of a market, especially in a supranational context. Supervisory risk, which may be provoked by bad government policies, is the most critical for EU regulators at the present and will be the particular concern of this analysis. Frequently, in an international integrated market environment, such as the EMU or the EEA, certain trading systems and financial services providers operate across jurisdictional borders and thus lie under the supervision of more than one country. In such a case, it is extremely important that rules are specified and control tasks are divided between the authorities involved in a clear and undisputable manner.[28] Potential double regulation and blurred supervisory responsibilities between 'home' and 'host' countries[29] may easily increase the burden of compliance and confuse all parties involved, which threatens the efficiency and stability of the market. When two entities are separately authorised and controlled, supervisory authorities cannot be aware of the overall risk profile of the group. *Per contra*, properly defined regulation and properly allocated supervision will promote confidence and legal certainty, reduce cost, encourage liquidity and, therefore, result in the reduction of market risk.

Finally, even if modern regulatory and supervisory arrangements ensure a fairly low probability of market collapse or failure, there is a last dimension to this debate that needs to be considered: the risk versus the seriousness of the issue. While the probability of a failure of a financial institution may be very low, the occurrence of such an event would be serious and the cost would be extremely high, given the interdependence of global markets. Therefore, regulation and supervision to prevent systemic problems may be viewed as an insurance premium against 'low-probability–high-seriousness' risk.[30]

2. Consumer protection

The second objective of financial supervision is the protection of consumers. The contribution to the strengthening of consumer protection constitutes one of the activities and objectives of the EU as prescribed by the Treaty.[31] Accordingly, the aim of consumer protection is dealt with by the regulation and supervision of financial firms, and must rest on two pillars: first, establishment of the criteria for awarding licenses to conduct investment business (prudential supervision) and second, ongoing monitoring (transactional supervision). Consumer protection issues arise for two reasons: because an institution, where clients hold funds, might fail, or because of unsatisfactory conduct of business of a firm with its customers. Accordingly, public policy issues are raised, for consumers are not in a position to judge the safety and soundness of the institutions, with which they are dealing, or to assess their investment choices.

Prudential supervision looks into the health of individual financial firms. It puts more emphasis on analysing the firm's balance sheets with special regard to capital adequacy, market risk, credit risk, operational risk and other indicators of prudential soundness. It is necessary because of imperfect information, agency problems associated with the nature of financial firms' business and the affect of financial firms' behaviour on the clients' stake in the firm.[32]

Transactional supervision, on the other hand, relates more to the relationship between financial firms and their clients. It is more focused on aspects of consumer protection, such as rules of conduct, disclosure, integrity, honesty, fair business practice, the way financial services are marketed and on the 'fact that the value of financial product or service may only be determinable well after the point in time at which it is purchased'.[33] In this light, the importance of transparency of public information becomes critical in supervision. The goal of transparency and disclosure from the supervisory perspective is to improve financial firms' incentives for prudent risk-taking and thus reduce the probability of failure.[34] Moreover, increased disclosure of information is thought to be most influential with respect to the enhancement of market discipline.[35]

Nonetheless, the consumer protection objective of supervision is closely linked with other concerns: the gridlock problem and moral hazard. Gridlock can emerge when all firms know how they should behave towards customers but nevertheless adopt hazardous strategies because they secure short-run advantages and they have no confidence that competitors will not behave hazardously.[36] Furthermore, the moral hazard problem can emerge, as the inappropriate pricing of regulatory protection.[37] Moral hazard may have two dimensions. First, 'efficient' supervisory mechanisms and compensation schemes may induce consumers to be less careful in the selection of financial firms and even seek high-risk institutions to conduct business.[38] Second, financial firms may be induced to take more risk too, as consumers are protected in the event the institution fails. In both cases, risky institutions will be able to attract business with the same ease and on the same terms as more prudently run firms, thereby undermining financial market discipline and consumer protection.

Problems of consumer protection within the financial services field are more severe than in any other professions, because of the very nature of the service, the amount of money at risk and the opportunity for high principal–agent conflicts of interest.[39] The key issue is the extent, to which supervision can effectively and efficiently address consumer protection issues and reduce the probability of them occurring. Supervisors are responsible for regulating and monitoring the activities of financial firms in order to protect investors and ensure the integrity of markets. In this light, supervisors must be proactive, rather than reactive, in devising high quality supervision of the dynamic financial industry. In particular, they should promote transparency, timely access to relevant information and seek to ensure that consumers' assets are managed in their best interest. Moreover, they should concern themselves with understanding the control environment of each firm and satisfying themselves as to the adequacy of controls established.[40]

Within the EU context, it is important that the objectives of transparency and consumer protection do not conflict with the Treaty objective of free movement of services. Moreover, the choice of the level of consumer protection, currently conferred to each Member State, can no longer be defined by each country in a completely autonomous way, as cross-border integration and competition among firms and markets give rise to the well-known phenomena of regulatory competition and arbitrage.[41] It is thus crucial that, at the necessary EU political and supervisory level, consensus is agreed on the appropriate level of consumer protection. Finally, despite their differences and because of their complementary character, the allocation of prudential and transactional supervision should not be divided between different supervisory authorities. This is, however, one of the main drawbacks of the home country control regime currently dominating the provision of investment services between EU Member States. Does this problem suffice to necessitate alternative institutional responses? This issue is examined later in Chapter 5.

3. Competition promotion

The third objective for public intervention arises when there is a private sector monopoly, or a collusive and antisocial oligopoly. Article 3 of the EC Treaty clearly states that one of the objectives of the EU is to establish a 'system ensuring that competition in the internal market is not distorted'.[42] Proper supervision should be designed to detect manipulation and other unfair practices and to control the risk of monopolies in the financial market. Both financial and other related services, such as price and other information supply, trading, clearing, settlement and custody, need be offered in a competitive framework encouraged by modern supervision.[43] All in all, stronger competition in the financial sector should lead to easier access to and lower cost of funding and trading, which works to the advantage of both consumers and markets. Although most of the financial industry is ferociously competitive, several of the supporting systems and markets incorporate network economies and/or economies of scale.[44] In this light, public intervention should always be kept in minimum and reasonable terms, so as to ensure the balance between fair and open competition and efficient and low-cost operation.

A particular point of interest is whether EU rules of competition are applicable to certain industries, such as financial services. As early as in 1972, the Commission stressed its awareness that 'application of the competition rules must take into account of the peculiar characteristics of certain industries'.[45] The concern was mostly referring to banks, in lieu of the role played by their operations in the financial and monetary policy of the Member States. However, the *Züchner* judgement[46] of the ECJ came to solve the vagueness. In that case, the Court decided that banks are not beyond the scope of the rules of competition by reason of provisions of the Treaty concerning economic policy.[47] Although this decision arises in the field of banking, its reasoning is applicable to the securities field too, where the relationship between investment services and economic policy are much less obvious. Indeed, although the Commission's Directorate General (DG) Competition has not adopted a formal decision in this field until very recently,[48] it has shown its determination to take action with its involvement in many cases, such as the clearing of rules governing the functioning of European Association of Securities Dealers Automated Question (EASDAQ), the merger between stock exchanges[49] and the sorting out of a row between primary dealers and interdealer brokers after the International Securities Market Association (ISMA) had notified its rules.

Given the above, it may be alleged that competitive equality does not provide an independent justification for financial supervision, since the public interest may seem less evident.[50] Nevertheless, reliance on competition and the smooth functioning of market forces should and has become a major policy tool used for improving efficiency. Another concern is that, in such an innovative sector as financial services, competition can also be distorted by supervisors themselves, reacting differently, at different speeds, or in a different capacity, to new developments and trends. EU competition policy is also directed to public authorities, for the impact of state aid in the financial sector will increasingly be felt across the borders, as national markets are opened up, and could negatively affect the smooth operation of the Single Market.[51] In an integrated financial area, such as the EU Single Market, even if the rules are harmonised, supervisors' divergent powers may result in the inconsistent and ineffective implementation of these rules. This is particularly likely to happen in a fragmented supervisory regime, such as home country control. This issue, however, is analysed more deeply later in Chapter 5.

D. Key principles of financial supervision

It is not in the purposes of this chapter to analyse how prudential and ongoing supervision should be best conducted. However, a number of principles may be identified in the pursuit of a better supervisory structure. These principles directly derive from the aforementioned objectives, but will also flourish in the analysis conducted in the following chapters. First, proximity to the markets and financial undertakings. 'Proximity' here is not meant strictly in geographical terms. Rather, it implies that supervisors should always be alert to the introduction of new products and the generation of new risks, in order to assess and obtain the necessary information in time. Supervision should precede markets. Second, integrated markets require integrated supervision. Recent financial defaults have clearly indicated that continuous surveillance, information exchange and crises management cannot be efficiently conducted on an individual or simply cooperative basis. Third, to avoid competitive distortion, the principle must apply: 'same business, same risks, same regulations'. Fourth, regulatory and supervisory balance. The regulator needs to strike a subtle balance between regulation that supports the reputation and, thereby, attracts business and regulation that is so severe as to drive business out.[52] Fifth, globalisation and financial business consolidation require new tools for supervision. Where such developments are significant enough to lead to regime shifts and new operational structures, authorities need to ensure that they have a supervisory system in place that can cope with the inevitable mistakes that financial institutions will make as they learn how to operate in the new regime. Where appropriate, market discipline and self-regulation should be used as supervisory methods. Of final importance are transparency and accountability. Supervisors must always be subject to reporting requirements and democratic control, without calling into question their independence.

These principles have to coexist if a chosen regime is to fulfil its task efficiently. This is particularly important in periods of structural change, for instance Europe's current introduction of the single currency, where concerns are greater and financial institutions have to adjust to more integrated and competitive markets. As pointed out by Estrella, 'supervision needs to cover behaviour and cannot merely rely on limits and rules'.[53] Especially today, when markets are integrated and the risk of systemic loss shadows their stability, regulators and regulated have to work together for the common objectives. Supervision, thus, ought not to be strictly confined by rules and procedures of the past, but rather be a living process walking side by side with market developments.

E. Concluding remarks

The reasons that require a need for financial supervision composed the theme of this chapter. Supervisors supply regulatory and supervisory service, for which there is a consumer demand. Regulation and supervision is always about making judgements and trade-offs, particularly when considering costs and benefits. Combining the three objectives of financial stability, consumer protection and competition is hardly a simple task.

In the final analysis, the consumer is the ultimate criterion. Nevertheless, the issue arises as to whether regulation and supervision simply transfer benefits from one group to another, or whether there are gains to all stakeholders.[54] This, in turn, relates to the magnitude and distribution of costs and benefits and to the question whether supervision is a negative, zero, or a positive sum game. If supervision is a negative sum game, the costs exceed the benefits. In the case of a zero sum game, the group of benefits match exactly with the group of costs. Finally, there is the possibility that, suitably structured and operated, supervision can be a positive sum game.

The sum game test is particularly relevant to the EU supervisory structure of investment services supervision. All the aforementioned objectives lead to a further, final, rationale for supervision. Potentially substantial economies of scale can be secured through collective regulation and supervision of financial firms. The following chapters will endeavour to show that the costs of the current supervisory arrangements exceed its benefits. Therefore, the need for institutional and substantive reform arises as an urgent priority, in order to strengthen the Single Market and ease pan-European investment services operations. At the end of the day, it is a question of balancing the benefits of a higher degree of achieving objectives (effectiveness) and the costs that may go with this pursuit (efficiency).

Admittedly, there is no simple single institutional paradigm for implementing the objectives of supervision. The structure chosen often reflects decisions made in the past, usually implicitly rather than explicitly, about the objectives and the purpose of supervision. Also, the structure chosen often proves to be the one that incorporates the most key principles of supervision, briefly described here. Nevertheless, other equally significant factors, such as technological developments, consolidation and externalities should determine the 'ideal' regime. Especially in the context of the EU the problem of the appropriate investment services oversight is more complex as the scope of supervision and the role of regulators is limited by the Treaty. The following chapter will analyse the current regime of home country control while the subsequent ones will reveal these complexities and argue for simple solutions.

Part II
How to Supervise?

2

The Single European Market in Investment and Financial Services

A. Introduction

This chapter seeks to provide and analyse the international and EU framework that relates to the regulation and supervision of investment and financial services. Within this context, the EU forms the most complex and sophisticated single system of financial integration attempted to date. As seen and examined in the wider global economic integration process, the Single European Market in financial services has influenced and has been influenced by powerful international integration forces. Nevertheless, the Single Market project remains unique in the world history for its legal, political and socio-economic achievements and progress.

The establishment of a common market is the cornerstone of the EU and its Treaties.[1] For this purpose, the activities of the Community are to include the abolition, as between Member States, of obstacles to the free movement of goods, persons, services and capital and the approximation of the laws of Member States to the extent required for the functioning of the common market.[2] With respect to financial services, the original and subsequent aim of the Community was to establish a single market throughout the EU by introducing minimum harmonisation of the national laws of each Member State insofar as they concerned the establishment of financial institutions and the cross-border provision of services and the setting of common standards of prudential supervision. This target has been ambitious and it has been reached to a certain degree.

The success of the European financial market integration process notwithstanding, a number of structural and substantive difficulties remain with regard to the development and application of specific policies and law harmonisation efforts. Despite the far-reaching harmonisation of investment and financial services regulatory and supervisory rules, certain areas remain untouched and in others national differences continue to exist. These are individually analysed in the following paragraphs and chapters in their historical and socio-economic context.

This chapter examines the operation of the EU's internal market in financial services. It begins with some background material on the early global integration concerns and on the EU and its general program to create an internal market free of trading barriers. It then focuses more specifically on the liberalisation of financial services and on the development and application of the Single Market in investment and financial services. Finally, future policy developments are discussed, while some concluding remarks are presented in the final section of this chapter.

B. Global economic cooperation

The point of departure for the cooperation of national governments and the development of international organisations can be traced in the year following World War II. First, there was a move towards free trade. The task of fostering worldwide free trade liberalisation has been entrusted to the General Agreement on Tariffs and Trade (GATT), which was transformed in the 1990s into the World Trade Organisation (WTO).[3] The GATT/WTO has accomplished a considerable international tariff decrease and the elimination of many trade impediments.[4] Next there was a move towards convertibility of currencies and free capital movements, with exchange rates pegged to the US dollar. This task has been entrusted to the World Bank and the International Monetary Fund (IMF).[5] The combined task of these organisations was to ensure well-regulated international monetary relations (conference of Bretton Woods). This meant fixed exchange rates between currencies. The monetary and macroeconomic coordination schemes of the IMF and the Organisation of Economic Cooperation and Development (OECD) had worked well for several decades.[6] However, in the 1970s they could no longer cope with the emerging inconsistencies, and the Bretton Woods system collapsed.

C. European economic integration

In contrast to the basis of agreement of international organisations, integration goes deeper in the cooperation of countries and collective decision-making.[7] Economic integration, defined as a process of economic unification of national economies, has been going on all through European history.[8] Already during World War II, the pursuit of intensive economic integration was put on a political-idealistic footing.[9] In the 1950s and the 1960s, the discussion on economic integration was concentrated on international economic relations. In the 1970s and 1980s, the idea of economic integration quickly spread to the economics of the sectors of economic activity (agriculture, energy, services, manufacturing, transport) and to such aspects as market regulation, macroeconomic equilibrium, monetary control and regional equilibrium or social welfare. At the end of the 1980s and during the 1990s, the issue of monetary integration was central to the discussion on European economic integration.[10] At the beginning of the twenty-first century, extensive policy attention has turned to the integration of financial markets and economic unification as the inevitable corollary of the monetary union.

Since the immediate post-war years, it was thought that economic integration had of itself inevitable political repercussions. The linkage between economics and politics lies in the notion that once states are drawn to cooperate in one sector of the economy, there will be an inevitable spillover into other areas.[11] The influential declaration made by Robert Schuman, the then French Foreign Minister, on 9 May 1950 deserves to be quoted in full:

> Europe will not be made all at once, or according to a single plan. It will be built through concrete achievements which first create a de facto solidarity ... The pooling of coal and steel production should immediately provide for the setting up of common foundations for economic development as a first step in the federation of Europe (...) The setting up of this powerful productive unit, open to all countries willing to take part and bound ultimately to provide all the member countries with the basic elements of industrial production on the same terms, will lay a true foundation for their economic activities.[12]

It was clear that the architects of post-war integration had in mind some form of political unity among states on the European continent, or at least a settlement to provide for the integration of Western Germany into the West European mainstream and to prevent a return to Franco-German conflict.[13] Political unity, and therefore peace, would be the ultimate consequence of economic enmeshment. Besides Schuman, Jean Monnet, the 'father of the Community',[14] shows a remarkable influence over the development of the Community:

> I could not help seeing the intrinsic weakness of a system that went no further than mere co-operation between Governments (...) The countries of Western Europe must turn their national efforts into a truly European effort. This will be possible only through a federation of the West.[15]

The desire to secure a lasting peace was one of the main inspirations behind post-war European integration.[16] From that stage, the strategy and development of European integration and the emergence of supranational institutions provided a valuable site for the development and application of a number of general theories including federalism,[17] functionalism,[18] neo-functionalism,[19] neo-realism and neo-liberal institutionalism,[20] behaviouralism,[21] neo-federalism and new institutionalism[22] or multilevel governance analysis.[23] The clutch of theoretical accounts that emerged during the second half of the twentieth century offered rival narratives of why and how regimes of supranational governance emerged and created wider socio-economic and political synergies.[24] All these doctrines, however, remind us that, while Europe developed as a political and economic concept, it was above all 'a moral idea'.[25]

D. European market integration and liberalisation

1. The roots of market integration

One of the most predominant objectives of the Rome Treaty was the creation of a common market for economic activities.[26] This goal is laid down in the opening lines of the Treaty. Article 2 states that 'The Community shall have as its task, by establishing a common market (...) to promote throughout the Community a harmonious, balanced and sustainable development of economic activities'. One of the means to achieve this objective is 'the abolition, as between Member States, of obstacles to the free movement of goods, persons, services and capital'.[27] Another tool is 'the approximation of the laws of Member States to the extent required for the functioning of the common market'.[28]

The free movement of services appears in the Treaty of Rome as one of the foundations of the EEC, in the same way as the free movement of persons, goods and capital. Yet progress was for a long time minimal and was in stark contrast to the considerable development in international financial relations and the accompanying emergence of global financial markets.

After the Treaty of Rome was signed, the conception of international economic cooperation was still largely under the influence of the Bretton Woods agreements, GATT and the UN Charter. Although there was little interpenetration of financial markets, all these efforts show an awareness of interdependence, a political determination to promote cooperation and integration and an increasingly widespread acceptance of the need for common policies in international trade.

At the end of the 1960s, the Community had completed the customs union ahead of schedule and had established a Common Agricultural Policy (CAP). It therefore seemed time for a further move forward. In the financial services context, a committee, under the chairmanship of Professor Claudio Segré was appointed to investigate the problems posed by liberalising capital movements and the repercussions of integrating capital markets in Europe. The committee submitted a report in 1966.[29] The report considered the specific problems of each segment of the capital market and examined the obstacles to the movement of capital, which resulted from national rules and tax arrangements. It concluded that the links between the integration of capital markets and other important areas, such as budgetary and monetary politics and incentives to savings and investment, were not to be underestimated. Importantly, an integrated European capital market was seen as increasingly necessary not only to finance economic growth on better terms but also to foster the implementation of Community policies in other areas. Moreover, while the predominant focus of the Segré Report was on the integration of securities markets and the capital-formation process, it also examined the role of intermediaries. At this early stage, the Report made clear that financial firms were hampered by the varying rules and supervisory controls applicable to them across the Community.[30]

Immediately after endorsing the Segré Report, the European Commission tried to put before the Council a number of legislative initiatives aiming mainly to abolish the discrimination regarding the harmonisation of banking regulation and supervision, issuing and placing of securities, stock exchange listings and the acquisition of securities by financial institutions. At the same time, the European Council of December 1969 in the Hague reaffirmed the wish to move forward to EMU – an early example of deepening and widening the initial plan. After years of negotiations, however, the efforts turned out unsuccessful.[31]

From the late 1960s onwards, the attempts at liberalisation came to a standstill. The lack of progress in these early stages of Community action can be explained by a number of factors. First, the recession of the world economy during the oil crises in the 1970s, the existence of high inflation and low growth and employment in Member States' economies resulted in protectionist policies and less concern for the common market. Second, in most sensitive areas of Community policy, the Treaty required unanimity for secondary decision-making and legislation. Hence, attempts to adopt legislation concerning matters in which Member States traditionally have strong interests were very often likely to turn out fruitless. Third, as we shall see, financial systems, practices and laws varied – and continue to vary – widely across the Community, which makes every integration or harmonisation effort even more difficult. Indeed, as a consequence of the prevailing reluctance to open up national financial markets and the substantial variations in the national legislation, Community rules on the financial services sector were virtually absent until the mid-1970s.[32]

2. Development of the Internal Market Programme

2.1. The White Paper

It has been apparent for some time that the cost of the fragmentation of national economies and the disparities between national regulations are the main reasons for Europe's weakness vis-à-vis its foreign competitors. In the early 1980s, concern was widespread within the European Community that Member States were recovering very slowly, compared with the United States and Japan, from the recessions of the late 1970s. The conventional wisdom was that, even though tariff barriers among the Member States had been dismantled more than a decade earlier, non-tariff barriers and market fragmentation within the Community were major impediments to Community's economic growth.

Partly because of this view, new initiatives were proposed to reactivate the process of European integration in the first half of the 1980s. Being aware of the urgency and importance of the problem, the European Commission – under the auspices of Commissioner Lord Cockfield – prepared a White Paper on the Internal Market early in 1985, proposing a programme of measures for its realisation.[33] In course of several summits held before the issuance of the White Paper,[34] the European Council adopted the programme at its Milan Summit on 28 June 1985 and endorsed the Commission's commitment to complete the single market by 1992.

With the formulation of the Internal Market Programme, the EU institutions moved into top gear to drive forward an extraordinarily ambitious programme of legislation. The idea and concept behind the White Paper was threefold:

(a) to merge the (then) twelve national markets to form a single enlarged market,
(b) to create an expanding, dynamic market, and
(c) to ensure that such a market is flexible enough to channel human, material and financial resources towards the domains where they will be best used.

Lord Cockfield remarked that the Internal Market Programme was one of the most ambitious market research exercises ever undertaken.[35] In his account of the creation of the internal market, he regarded four elements of the method of setting out the goals as important as its adoption in Milan and the subsequent dynamism the project achieved.[36] The first was the setting out of a clear programme for achieving the internal market. The second was the 1992 deadline with its mobilising effect. A third consideration was giving the project some kind of 'philosophical framework' to capture the imagination of those affected. Finally, the emphasis placed upon the removal of barriers was regarded as getting to the root of the incomplete Single Market.[37] All these elements gave the White Paper and the subsequent Single European Act a unique impetus to achieve the goals of integration. The clear expectations of the White Paper were that the removal of non-tariff barriers would lead not only to sharper competition and, therefore, to a general improvement to factor productivity, but ultimately to increased investment by industry and services in order to take advantage of the economies of scale offered by the genuinely unified market.[38] In this light, consumers are the final beneficiaries of this integration process.

The Commission estimated that some 300 measures (later reduced to 282) would be needed to bring about the Single Market in a wide range of domains – financial services, public procurement, taxation, free movement of individuals, free movement of capital, monetary policy and so on. Some fifteen dealt with financial services.[39] The White Paper set forth a timetable for the enactment of each proposal that called for the entire program to be in place by the end of 1992. This deadline was subsequently incorporated in Article 8a EEC giving it a legal-constitutional dimension.

2.2. The three modules of the Internal Market strategy

The White Paper constitutes the product of a dramatic change in the political and legal climate within the Community. For a long time, harmonisation of national legislation was regarded as a natural prerequisite for the opening-up of markets. This approach had some notable successes, but also revealed its own weaknesses. Harmonisation is difficult to attain because of the frequently divergent local practices in different Member States. It constitutes a lengthy and uncertain exercise.[40] The scale of the Internal Market project and the number of measures required called for an alternative regulatory approach. As a result, the strategy finally adopted combined three modules, which have been characterised as the cornerstone of the Single Market: minimum harmonisation, mutual recognition and home country control. It is important to stress that these principles were not derived from basic Treaty provisions or ECJ's case law. As we shall see in the following analysis (especially on mutual recognition and home country control), their origin can be traced in the case law of the European Court in the late 1970s or early 1980s, but they should not be considered as legal rules or principles of Community law.

2.2.1. Minimum harmonisation.

The priority of the Community in the early 1980s was the liberalisation of its markets. What was then aimed was no more than the conditions, which were indispensable for that purpose, ensuring only the harmonisation of essential legislative measures. The principal difference between this 'new' strategy and the 'old' one was that Community legislation is granted only a residual role, merely providing minimum guarantees ensuring some measure of equivalence between the different national legal regimes.[41] Minimum harmonisation was regarded as fundamental for a number of reasons:

(a) Whilst the effect of mutual recognition may be the elimination of barriers to trade, it does not by itself create a sufficient unified market,
(b) General application of the mutual recognition principle with no attempt to harmonise may invite competitive deregulation and may lead to lower standards of protection, which would not be acceptable by Member States' authorities.[42]
(c) The imposition of minimum harmonisation might be seen as a result of the Commission's belief in the benefits of competition between regulatory frameworks.[43]

2.2.2. Mutual recognition.   Mutual recognition is based on the philosophy that goods and services emanating from one Member State should be freely allowed into other Member States. Accordingly, each Member State recognises the equivalence of corresponding measures taken in other Member States, even when there are divergences between these measures and its own legislation. The advantage of this principle is that it allows the variety of products and services within the Single Market to be maintained, while ensuring their free movement. By applying mutual recognition, economic operators are not forced to adapt their production to the technical specifications of the host Member State. They are able to continue to provide their product or service according to the technical specifications of the home country and use mutual recognition to market their product in – potentially – all fourteen other Member States.

Unlike harmonisation, mutual recognition does not involve the transfer of regulatory powers to the Community. Instead, at least in theory, it stimulates competition among national regulators, which should provide an efficient way of assessing the costs and benefits of different methods of regulation – and thus improving them, as well as increasing the range of choice for consumers.[44] Mutual recognition can only be applied in full provided that the most essential rules are harmonised. If a product or service meets the legal requirements of any Member State, then, subject only to those requirements meeting certain EU-wide minimum standards, there should be no restriction on that product or service being sold or provided throughout the Community. There is therefore a crucial link between harmonisation on the one hand and liberalisation on the other. If harmonisation is not established at a minimum level, then the mutual recognition principle does not work in practice.[45] As the previous chapter has shown, this is particularly relevant in financial services, for this sector is deeply dependent upon reliability and stability for the sake and protection of both consumers and the financial system as a whole. A second element for effective application of the principle of mutual recognition is the mutual trust and comity between Member States and national authorities, a crucial element that is usually taken for granted.[46] Advocates of mutual recognition often do not seem to realise how demanding the principle is.[47] It could, thus, be concluded that mutual recognition is not based on any consideration of the requirements of the financial markets, but rather on what might be termed a ruthless pragmatism.[48] As put by Steil, 'mutual recognition, as the Commission's White Paper made clear, was considered an inferior integration mechanism, made necessary only by Council obstructionism in the Commission's pursuit of common rules'.[49]

2.2.3. Home country control.   Once mutual recognition has been agreed as the governing principle for EU internal market regulation, there follows a need for a rule to determine which country's regulatory framework applies in particular cases.[50] Qualified as the most logical principle, home country control allows a service provider authorised in one Member State to carry on its activities in any other Member States without further authorisation either with the provision of cross-border services or by the establishment of a branch. In accordance with the general principles of the White Paper, the home Member State authorities have the lion's share of responsibility for regulating and supervising the service providers they have authorised. However, the Commission itself has weakened the applicability of the home country control rule by permitting an escape clause, under which the host country also has a right to regulate to the extent necessary to 'protect the public interest'.[51] The whole of Chapter 3 is devoted to the principle of home country control and its application in EU secondary law on investment services. As we shall see, in terms of prudential supervision, the keystone of the financial services directives is based on this principle.

2.3. The Single European Act (SEA)

Signed in February 1986 and entered into force on 1 July 1987, the primary objective of the SEA was to progressively establish an internal market within a five years period ending on 31 December 1992. The SEA owes its name to the fact that it reflects the wish to bring together in a single instrument, first, provisions amending the Treaties establishing the European Communities and, second, measures to strengthen European political and economic cooperation, making it one of the component elements of membership of the Community. Article 1 of the SEA states that 'the European Communities and European political cooperation shall have as their objective to contribute together to making concrete progress towards European unity'.

The amendments to the Treaty of Rome enacted in the SEA were aimed principally at improving the decision-making process within the Community and confirming in the Community's basic charter the underlying ideas of the earlier White Paper. First, the SEA extended the use of qualified majority voting (QMV) to most matters relating to the goals that have not yet been fulfilled.[52] Second, the European Parliament was given a more prominent position in the decision-making process.[53] Finally, and perhaps more importantly, Article 8a of the SEA, incorporated in Article 3(1)(c) EC Treaty, included a formal consecration of the Internal Market: 'The internal market shall comprise an area without frontiers in which the free movement of goods, persons, services and capital is ensured in accordance with the provisions of the Treaty'.[54]

Creating a single Internal Market has conferred a new dimension on the process of financial integration in Europe. There can be no question of a Europe without frontiers in the absence of free movement of capital and financial services. This was regarded as an essential complement to the other aspects of the Internal Market. Nevertheless, even though the freedom of establishment and the freedom to provide services established in the Treaty of Rome constitute immediately and directly applicable rights of which any natural or legal person may avail himself, their implementation has proved especially difficult in the financial services sector. The difficulty lies mainly in the fact that financial services are strictly regulated in all Member States on grounds of public interest.

Problematic implementation notwithstanding, the SEA constitutes an illustrative paradigm of a project-based approach of European integration. One of the reasons for its success was its apparent modesty: far from following the European Parliament's blueprint of a quasi-federal scheme, it limited itself to what was perceived by many as a minimalist programme of removal of non-tariff barriers.[55] The genius of the programme was that it devised a new regulatory strategy, which was sufficiently malleable both to facilitate Community legislation and to accommodate Member State fears about loss of autonomy and lack of sensitivity to local interests. This would gain a legal concept after the Maastricht Treaty made the principle of subsidiarity a cornerstone of European constitutional law (Article 3b, now Article 5 EC).[56] For this reason, the 1992 project was one of the 'few Community fields in which a consensus for more intensive Community actions was likely to emerge'.[57] A final significant point, which is further argued in the following chapters of this book, should be brought up herein: the passage of the SEA, which made major amendments to the Treaty, demonstrates that even this apparently cumbersome process can be completed with surprising rapidity when a sufficient political will exists.[58]

The Internal Market Programme, although intended to remove internal barriers, has had significant implications for other countries as well. For the most part these have been positive as third-country firms benefit from regulatory approximation and the application of the principle of mutual recognition.[59] The success of the Internal Market Programme has led to it being considered as a model for aspects of international trade. In particular, the GATS provides opportunities for countries to conclude agreements on the mutual recognition of qualifications, licences, regulations and other requirements with regard to the provision of services.

3. The single financial market and beyond

3.1. Financial services liberalisation

An integrated Single Market for financial services as envisioned in Article 14 EC Treaty (former Article 7a(2)) presupposes, *inter alia*, that all market operators and service providers have an unrestricted access to all parts of this market's territory, that is, that they can act within all Member States.[60]

In the context of this study, the globalisation of financial markets is of particular interest. It is the integration of financial markets at global scale that has increased the need for a single European market in financial services.[61] The Internal Market project created an impression of an enormously powerful entity ready to compete on equal terms in the global arena with Japan and the United States. Furthermore, other implications played an equally significant role. As pointed out by Zavvos, the strategy in the financial sector primarily focused on three areas: liberalisation of financial services, liberalisation of capital movements and monetary integration.[62]

In respect to European financial markets, the Commission's goal was to create the legislative framework that would allow greater integration of EU markets with the minimum sacrifice of the public policy interests of Member States in the areas of prudential rules, market stability and consumer protection. The original aim of the Community was to establish a Single Market in investment and financial services throughout the EU by introducing minimum harmonisation of the national laws of each Member State insofar as they concerned the establishment of financial institutions and the cross-border provision of services and the setting of common standards of prudential supervision. In spite, however, of the far-reaching harmonisation of investment services' regulatory and supervisory rules, certain areas remain untouched and in others national differences continue to exist. This state of affairs can be explained partly by the fact that EU rules are minimum rules, which leave the Member States free to require higher standards of their own financial institutions, and partly by the, difficulty of agreeing on common standards for certain aspects of investment services' regulation and supervision.[63]

In light of these hurdles, the Commission launched in 1987 a Communication to the Council dealing primarily with the liberalisation of capital movements, but also with the creation of a European financial area.[64] The Commission explained that even though the liberalisation of capital movements was prerequisite to the establishment of a financial area, this required also financial services to be liberalised.[65]

Certain provisions of the EC Treaty are particularly relevant from this standpoint. Of fundamental importance for the understanding of the European financial firms' possibility to provide cross-border investment services are the Treaty's basic right of establishment and freedom to provide services. The principles of unrestricted establishment and movement of services are set out in Articles 43 (former Article 52) and 49 (former Article 59) EC Treaty respectively, which are the fundamental provisions on the subject in the Treaty.[66] Furthermore, Article 48 (former Article 58) EC establishes national, non-discriminatory treatment for Member State companies and firms.[67] The fact that the two freedoms apply to investment and financial services is clear from *Commission v Italy*, where the ECJ confirmed that the protections to establish applied to restrictions imposed by Italy on firms dealing with transferable securities,[68] and from *Alpine Investments*, which concerned restrictions on the ability of financial firms to use cold-calling when providing services.[69] All these freedoms, therefore, constitute the legal basis for the regulatory measures taken in the Community to create a level playing field for actors in the financial services market.

The provision of services shall be distinguished from the concept of establishment, although the distinction is far from clear-cut.[70] As a rule of thumb, provision of services means the performance of tasks, in exchange for remuneration, by an establishment located in one Member State, insofar as those operations are not covered by other provisions of the Treaty.[71] What constitutes a service is mainly dictated by the temporary nature of economic activity. Where service providers move to another Member State, they are to pursue their activities there on a temporary basis.[72] In turn, the temporary nature of provision of services is to be determined in the light of its duration, regularity, periodicity and continuity.[73] Establishment, on the other hand, involves setting up permanently in a Member State other than the country of origin with a view to exercising economic activity.[74] Generally, the provisions governing establishment is to be relied upon for the setting up of a plant, office or similar establishment. If the presence in a Member State is permanent, then Article 43 EC applies rather than Article 49.[75]

Albeit their differences, it is obvious that the right of establishment and the right to provide services do not constitute an obsolete right to supply services in any Member State regardless of qualifications, educational background, professional conduct of business rules and so forth imposed by Member States themselves. Although the Treaty itself does not contain any provisions that deal with the restrictions that Member States may legally impose on foreign establishments, secondary legislation and the ECJ's case law have pursued a rather controversial route in their effort to provide guidance and definitions. The relevant analysis is provided later in Chapters 3 and 5.

3.2. *Investment services secondary legislation*

Moving specifically to the securities and investment services sector, the White Paper prescribed a number of secondary legislative measures to open up the European financial market. As part of its Single Financial Market Programme the EU has adopted a set of directives covering investment services. The ISD[76] has given non-bank financial firms the same opportunities for conducting investment business in the EU as credit institutions already enjoyed under the SBD,[77] while the Capital Adequacy Directive (CAD)[78] fulfils a similar function to the bank regulatory directives in providing a common framework for regulating investment firms, as well as the securities activities of banks and other financial institutions. As a result, any analysis of the investment services secondary legislation has to be viewed in the context of prior banking legislative provisions.

3.2.1. *The Investment Services Directive (ISD).* The ISD, which was adopted by the Council on 10 May 1993, is the most important directive in the single market course, as determined by the White Paper and the SEA.[79] It constitutes an instrument essential to the achievement of the harmonisation of securities regulation, from the point of view both of the right of

establishment and of the freedom to provide investment services. According to former Commission vice-president Sir Leon Brittan, the Commission's original draft proposal was far less detailed than the final product, which emerged from the political negotiation process. Not surprisingly, therefore, many key sections of the Directive constitute political compromises.

The ISD seeks to ensure that investment firms are subject to uniform standards of regulation throughout the Union by imposing common standards with which all Member States have to comply. The Directive establishes, *inter alia*, the 'European passport' in investment services for specialised investment firms,[80] which the SBD has created for banks.[81] The concept of the European passport is very simple. It enables firms, authorised in one Member State, to provide investment services in other Member States, either on a cross-border basis or by establishing a branch, on the basis of their home State authorisation. Consequently, there is no necessity for any additional license from the State in which the firm provides services.[82] Conversely, investment firms will not be able to provide any of those investment services unless it has been authorised by its home member state. This means that the legal risk of carrying on business in a country without a license is greatly reduced, at least for firms that have in place adequate compliance procedures.[83]

The market-opening provisions of the ISD are similar to those of the SBD, so that investment firms may establish branches and provide cross-border services throughout the EU, based on home country authorisation. However, the passport based on the home State authorisation is only acceptable if the minimum standards for home State authorisation are harmonised.[84] For this purpose the ISD stipulates certain operating conditions and requirements for the authorities of the home Member State to impose on firms and assigns to them the supervisory task.

Nevertheless, there are important derogations from the principle of home State regulation mainly in the areas of conduct of business rules and advertising, where the notion of 'public good' makes its appearance.[85] Accordingly, the host authorities are free to adopt whatever systemic rules and impose whatever conditions on individual authorisations they view as necessary under the guise of the 'protection of the general public good'.[86] These terms may occur as ambiguous and they will be examined in more detail in Chapter 5. At this point it is sufficient to mention the clear obligation that Member States should not be allowed to overrule main principles of EU law (e.g. free movement of services).

Beyond the European passport, there is a second regulatory route by which an investment firm may do business throughout the EU: the 'regulated market'. A firm being classified to have access to a regulated market that operates without the need for a physical presence, should be allowed to place its automated facilities in other Members States, without the need for any regulatory recognition other than that required by its home authorities.[87] A range of criteria set out in Article 1(13) are needed to be satisfied by an institution in order to be classified as regulated market.[88] Member States, on their part, are required by the Directive to abolish any national laws or market regulations, which limit the size of the membership of any exchange or market. Such laws and regulations would restrict the freedom, which has been granted by the ISD.

Taking the ISD as a whole, the provisions on cross-border branching and delivery of investment services as well as those dealing with the allocation of regulatory responsibilities between the home and host State, are essential ingredients of the harmonisation process and the direction towards a pan-European capital market. For this reason, home and host Member States are required to collaborate closely in order to discharge more effectively their respective responsibilities in the supervision of cross-border financial activities.[89]

The ISD is the cornerstone of EU legislative framework for investment firms and securities markets. In the seven years since it came into force, it has eliminated a first set of legal obstacles to the Single Market for securities. Nevertheless, as Chapter 5 will show, structural faults and substantive problems persist while new challenges have arisen. It is a common belief that the ISD needs modernisation to meet the demands of the new securities trading environment. Market forces, amplified by the single currency, are driving demand for an integrated financial market. Information technology is revolutionising business practices and paving the way for the emergence of a new generation of service providers. The drive to enhance performance, reduce costs and establish a pan-European presence is stimulating profound restructuring of the securities trading infrastructure. Proposals for mergers and alliances between exchanges are the most visible manifestation of these profound changes. Consolidation of clearing and settlement, which can substantially improve efficiency of European securities trading, is gathering pace.

To tackle these challenges and problems, the European Commission decided that it was time to update the ISD, as prescribed in its 1999 Financial Services Action Plan (FSAP). For this reason, it issued a Communication in November 2000 to define orientations and seek public comments for a substantive overhaul of the Investment Services Directive (ISD).[90] The Communication opens discussion on the modifications needed if the (ISD) is to reflect the many changes that are reshaping investment services business and securities markets. It focuses on two specific areas: (a) a fully operational single passport for investment firms,[91] and (b) appropriate regulatory framework for the trading infrastructure.[92]

Following the Communication and taking account of the responses it attracted, the Commission launched a round of consultation as an initial set of orientations for revision of the ISD in July 2001.[93] This extensive dialogue with interested parties is considered to be in line with the approach to financial services legislation agreed with the European Parliament and Council and based on the recommendations of the Wise Men Committee on the Regulation of European Securities Markets.[94] This consultation document provided first indications of the views of the Commission as to the possible structure and content of a modified ISD. A second and final consultation document was published in March 2002.[95] The Commission services made substantial changes to their initial suggestions as a result of the seventy-seven responses received to the first round of consultation.[96] Finally, an open hearing, which was held in Brussels on 22 April 2002, constituted the latest demonstration of the Commission's commitment to systematic consultation of the financial services industry and the public.[97]

3.2.2. The Capital Adequacy Directive (CAD).   On 15 March 1993 the Council adopted the Capital Adequacy Directive laying down the capital adequacy requirements for market risks of credit institutions and investment firms. Like the ISD, this Directive has been the subject of extensive negotiation and bargaining between national governments. When first submitted by the Commission on 30 April 1990, the intention was that the CAD would standardise the capital requirements to be met by investment firms by setting out the minimum requirement for the provision of initial capital by firms established in Member States, and the amount of capital to be held by those firms to cover risk arising from positions held in various financial instruments. This would have brought in a capital regulatory regime for investment firms similar to that established by the Solvency Ratio Directive and the Own Funds Directive for banks.[98]

During the negotiations, however, it became clear that, in the context of global financial markets, investment firms and credit institutions were competing directly with each other. In order to meet the conflicts of the negotiating parties, namely Germany and the United Kingdom, it was agreed that the CAD should include banks too.[99] Hence, in order to achieve a level playing field, there had to be common standards of regulation with regard to the provision of capital against certain market risk. Therefore, the scope of the CAD was extended to include market risk undertaken by credit institutions as well.

The CAD makes provision for market risk related to movements of equities, which had not been taken into account until then, and further provided that supervisors of universal banks could apply the non-bank capital requirements to the trading book part of their operations. Regarded as a necessary follow-up to the proposed ISD, discussed below, the CAD simply provides three innovations:

(a) it sets out minimum initial capital for investment firms and credit institutions;
(b) it monitors the position of these institutions and explains the way that their business and consolidated requirements should be valuated; and
(c) it offers definitions of credit institutions, investment firms and their capital.

The capital requirements of credit institutions and investment firms depend on the level of services they provide. Capital has to be put up against each of the various risks so identified.[100] The CAD provides detailed rules to calculate the required amount of own funds separately to cover the various market risks described in Annexes I–V to the Directive. Specific details as well as technical assessments, however, are not within the scope of this book. The recent amending Directive 98/31/EC mainly modified some definitions and added Annexes VII and VIII on Commodities Risk and Internal Models respectively.[101]

In November 1999, the European Commission launched a round of consultations on a new capital adequacy framework for banks and investment firms.[102] A second round was launched in February 2001 to be concluded by May of the same year.[103] The latter consultation document was designed to be read in conjunction with a similar consultation on the new Basel Capital Accord launched by the Basel Committee on January 2001, but also concentrated on issues where particular EU concerns need to be taken into account. The contributions would help shape the proposals for a new EU capital adequacy framework planned for the autumn of 2001. Nevertheless, following responses to its proposals to revise the 1998 Capital Accord, the Basel Committee has extended its timetable for revision and implementation of the new Accord to 2005, with an additional round of consultation in early 2002. In this light, the Commission decided to undertake a further round of consultations with interested parties in view of this postponement. In addition, it committed itself to adopt a proposal for amending the EU framework shortly after the finalisation of the new Capital Accord by the Basel Committee.

In contrast to the work conducted by the Basel Committee, the EU will base its approach to the new Accord in respect of relevant activities whether carried out by banks or investment firms. The Commission has previously welcomed the revision of the Basel Committee's proposals in respect of operational risk in particular the recalibration of this charge as compared with earlier proposals. Nonetheless, it believes that in respect of certain types of lower-risk investment firms the operational risk requirements of the new Basel Accord would be disproportionate to the risks of those firms. The Commission has thus to consider how best to modify the proposals.

In connection to the above, the Commission was planning to make a working document available in October 2002.[104] On the basis of this text the Commission and Member State supervisory authorities will continue and intensify their dialogue with industry and other interested parties. A third and final consultative document is scheduled to be published in early summer 2003. Finally, the Commission expects to present a proposal for a Directive in early 2004 to amend the existing CAD. This will ensure that the new Basel Capital Accord is implemented within the EU as regards both banks and investment firms in a coherent manner and in accordance with EU law.

4. The Financial Services Action Plan (FSAP)

The establishment of the 1992 Single Market Programme has provided a secure prudential environment in which financial institutions can trade beyond the national Member State. Nonetheless, the EU's financial markets remained segmented while business and consumers continued to be deprived of direct access to cross-border financial institutions and markets. This was considered a disappointing result, especially after the introduction of the single currency, which gave a new impetus and a unique window of opportunity to equip the EU with a modern financial apparatus and truly liberalised financial markets.

In recognition of the changing financial landscape, the Cardiff European Council of June 1998 invited the European Commission to table a framework for action to improve the single market in financial services. In response, the Commission published a Communication, which identified a range of issues calling for urgent action to secure the full benefits of the single currency and to create a single financial market.[105] The Communication emphasised the need for integrating financial services and markets, given the employment generating and growth potential of the financial services sector and the wide range of choices that would be available to consumers. A group of personal representatives of the Council of Economy/Finance Ministers (ECOFIN) and the ECB was then entrusted with the task of assisting the Commission in selecting priorities for action. The Financial Services Policy Group (FSPG) met on three occasions. Its deliberations, together with the consultation undertaken earlier for the Communication have assisted the Commission in developing a fresh perspective to its work. The Financial Services Action Plan (FSAP)[106] is based on the work of the FSPG and broadly reflects the spectrum of discussions that took place within it.

The FSAP contains key measures to deliver an integrated financial market. Three indications of priority for a single financial market are grouped around four categories: wholesale markets, retail markets, prudential rules and supervision and wider conditions for an optimal single financial market.[107] A framework plan, annexed to the FSAP, provides the detailed basis for this work, which builds on efforts undertaken in other formal or informal bodies.

The completion of the Action Plan is regarded as a significant and necessary condition for reaping the potential from the Union's financial markets. Its significance for the Single Market in financial services can be compared to the 1992 Programme for the Internal Market in general. Progress on the FSAP is monitored regularly by the Commission and the FSPG, which issues a report almost twice a year. The mid-term review of progress of 22 February 2002 on the FSAP underlined strongly that financial integration will bring real benefits for European citizens in terms of economic growth, employment and sustained prosperity.

The FSAP is now halfway through its timetable for implementation. The last report,[108] prepared by the FSPG, acknowledged a positive progress but also called for significant challenges to be completed by 2005. Until July 2002, 26 of the 42 original measures were finalised. This is a notable achievement but the measures in the remainder of the package are crucial. In March 2002 the Barcelona European Council reaffirmed the objectives of the Action Plan as a key priority of the Lisbon economic reform agenda and set clear deadlines for the adoption of eight specific measures.[109] In addition, it called for full implementation by 2005 and for every effort to be made to foster an integrated securities market and risk capital market (via completion of the Risk Capital Action Plan)[110] by the end of 2003. The informal meeting of ECOFIN ministers in Oviedo on 13 April 2002 gave further impetus to the process and recognised the need to step up its own efforts in order to complete the FSAP on time.

5. Future policy developments

The Single Market in financial services is recently developing at a pace that poses significant challenges to regulators, market participants and consumers. The Santer Commission, which took office in 1995, included strict enforcement of existing single market rules among its priorities.[111] This approach suited well the concerns of European businesses, which wanted to see the gains of the Single Market as soon as possible. With the Action Plan, the European Commission did much to deliver on this intention.[112] Romano Prodi, in his first speech to the European Parliament, stressed the need to move beyond a single market and single currency towards 'a single economy and single politics'.[113] The single currency has removed currency risk and enhanced price transparency throughout the eurozone. It has also allowed an increase in cross-border mergers and acquisitions and changed the philosophical strategy of investors, as there is a trend towards pan-European sectoral rather than Member State–based investment patterns. Globalisation and technological innovation have created new electronic banking and trading systems, which ease the provision of cross-border financial services. Moreover, alliances between securities exchanges and consolidation of financial services offer unlimited choice to consumers and additional competition between market operators. The single financial market is now widely perceived as a key contributor to the Community's objectives of growth, competitiveness and job creation.[114]

Nonetheless, so much more remains to be done. EU financial markets are still governed by fifteen different legal, regulatory and supervisory systems. Many other obstacles to cross-border activity, such as taxation, culture and language, result in some degree of segmentation in most sectors. Since financial services providers face numerous legal, regulatory and technical obstacles that hinder intra-Community trade and a level playing field within the EU, there is an undeniable need for concerted policy response.

However, the 2002 Internal Market Review monitors progress since the previous year.[115] What emerges is a mixed picture. The success rate for completing target actions stands at just over 50 per cent, which is about the same as in 2001. There have been some notable achievements but the overall pace of delivery is still too slow. The FSAP faces similar concerns,[116] which are also reflected by the need for further action in the Single Market in services, as identified in the 2002 Internal Market Strategy Report.[117]

Additionally, close examination of the bulk of the activity of the 1992 Internal Market Programme and the FSAP to achieve the relevant deadlines was focused on the legislative programme rather than on the follow-through, on designing rather than implementing policy rules. The impact on economic sectors provides proof of the slow pace of transposition and convergence of standards. This may have also had an impact on the equity culture of Europe. In the FSAP, the financial services industry was described as one of the economic sectors with the highest job creation potential. Today, only three years later, there are four major drivers of change and development in Europe: the Single Market, the single currency, enlargement of the Union and the impact of globalisation and new technologies. Despite this dynamic environment, however, banks and investment firms are dismissing thousands of highly qualified staff. For this reason, concerns have been raised, particularly from the European Parliament, whether European policy-makers should ask themselves about the justification of the original optimism and the initial plans deployed in the field of financial services.[118]

With respect to financial supervision, the FSAP sets as a goal to enable the EU to assume a key role in setting high global standards for regulation and supervision and to contribute to the developing of EU supervisory structures, which can sustain stability and confidence in an era of changing market structures and globalisation.[119] The prescribed steps have already been taken, in particular in the securities sector where the implementation of the recommendations of the Wise Men Committee is already taking place.[120] The new approach is based on a hierarchy of measures involving law making at two levels (essential framework principles and non-essential implementing measures), which is regarded as a sea change from the earlier harmonisation plans. The first requests for technical advice on implementing measures (in the Prospectus and Market Abuse areas) have been sent to the Committee of European Securities Regulators (CESR). New processes to ensure a full consultation of the market and consumers for the proposed ISD II are also underway at both the CESR and the Commission. The next phase, as it becomes clear from the outcome of the ISD II consultations, will involve a smooth transition to 'more' home country control, at least for sophisticated market participants that need less protection than retail consumers.[121]

In its Report to the ECOFIN Council on financial integration, the Economic and Financial Committee (EFC) concluded that Wise Men Committee approach for investment services and securities markets has an important role to play in the field of supervisory convergence.[122] The ECOFIN meeting of 7 May 2002 invited the Commission to bring forward as soon as possible its report on the appropriate arrangements that are needed to facilitate the consistent implementation and enforcement of regulation including supervisory practices, in line with the recommendations of the EFC's report. However, it may be too soon to judge and calculate the impact of the new approaches. More meetings, consultations and reports are likely to follow. All these initiatives are separately analysed in the following chapters.

E. Concluding remarks

A Single Market for financial services has been under construction since 1973. Making financial integration a priority objective instead of one subordinate to the smooth operation of the Single Market represented a major upheaval in the traditional thinking behind EU policies. This upheaval was seen as necessary since unification of the enlarged European market as a whole requires – at least – the free movement of services, goods, capital and persons and the elimination of physical, technical and legal barriers.

Following a number of post–World War II global economic cooperation initiatives, the Single Market project began in earnest in 1985 when Jacques Delors published his blueprint for creating a frontier-free Europe by 1992. Today, ten years later, the EU looks more ambitious. Creating not simply a duty-free area but an integrated European economic area constitutes an exacting task that requires efforts to achieve harmonisation, strict exchange-rate and general macroeconomic discipline and close coordination of economic and monetary policies.

The EU Single Financial Market programme is straightforward. Investment and financial activities are dealt with under the general Treaty provisions governing the twin freedoms of establishment and provision of services. The need for special treatment and individual regulatory reform of the financial sector has resulted in the adoption of specific programmes by the Community, with the White Paper and the SEA being the cornerstone of this effort. As early as the mid-1980s, the three modules of minimum harmonisation, mutual recognition and home country control have generally been seen as the best operational means of implementing rules on the free movement of goods and services and have been applied with positive results in a large number of industrial sectors, including financial services.

Nevertheless, only during the recent years has it become clear that the Single Market in financial services, which is regarded as critical for growth and job creation, is incomplete. Following the 1998 Cardiff European Council and the 1999 FSAP, a tidal wave of regulatory reform is currently under way. Containing key measures to deliver an integrated financial market by 2005, the FSAP is now halfway through its timetable for implementation of crucial regulatory packages. Admittedly, there have been some notable achievements but the overall pace of delivery remains slow.

Overall, the development of financial markets had tended to receive little or superficial political interest in the past. It has not attracted the interest it deserves on the basis of its macroeconomic importance. As we shall see, this has no doubt failed to affect the speed and magnitude of change. The recent efforts, however, clearly demonstrate that Europe is able to intensify the work further in the most crucial areas. The Single Financial Market remains possibly the most ambitious supply-side reform ever attempted anywhere in the world. Europe, however, has enormous potential, which is waiting to be unleashed. Its ability to realise that potential will depend on the willingness of EU leaders to embrace and pioneer change. One of the main points of this book and its following chapters is that work has to continue with the current regulatory and supervisory arrangements and their reform. Accordingly, the following chapter specifically focuses on the regulatory and supervisory principle of home country control and its application in the Single European Market in investment and financial services.

3
The Home Country Control Principle

A. Introduction

This chapter unfolds the concept of home country control as envisaged and applied by the European Commission and Member States. What were the initial concerns faced by European leaders, what were the underlying considerations and principles that led to this approach, how did it evolve and what were the issues stemming from its application? As indicated before, the original aim of the Community was to establish a Single Market in investment and other financial services throughout the EU by introducing minimum harmonisation of the national laws of each Member State insofar as they concerned the establishment of financial institutions and the cross-border provision of services and the setting of common standards of prudential supervision. In this effort, the overall objectives of the EC Treaty should be kept, in particular the concepts of freedom of establishment and freedom to provide services.[1]

This chapter begins with an overview of the conceptual background, which lies behind the principle of home country supervision. The third section describes the supervisory concerns and the approach that was ultimately adopted by the European policy-makers and legislators. The fourth and the fifth sections are devoted to the origin, legal basis and the content of home country control, as well as to the issues deriving from its application in EU secondary law. Finally, the last part draws the main conclusions of this chapter.

B. Conceptual background

The starting point of the concept of home country control is the gradual liberalisation of global financial markets, which has given a great impetus to cross-border financial services transactions. Hence, investment services transactions with cross-border elements may be subject to various national laws and supervision depending on the point of contact with the different jurisdictions. Accordingly, the global nature of securities business gives rise to difficult questions to be faced by national supervisors. Should their supervision apply to foreign financial undertakings operating in their country but not to the foreign branches of home institutions (the national treatment principle), or should it extend to the foreign branches of domestic firms incorporated in the same country as the regulator (home country control principle)? Moreover, to what extent should national supervisors be responsible for the supervision of foreign subsidiaries of domestic institutions?

Nowadays, financial markets supervision requires far more than knowledge of the domestic economy and markets; it requires an ability to analyse and legislate for risks incurred in different and diverse markets and an ability to negotiate common principles and standards with other national supervisors, so as to ensure equal protection of consumers and equal supervisory treatment in increasingly integrated and competitive international and domestic markets.[2] Several national or international supervisory regimes have emerged in response to the liberalisation of international financial markets. In theory one can speak of three models of regulation and supervision of financial institutions, which provide financial services beyond their home borders: (a) a completely harmonised framework of standards between the domestic and the host country, (b) supervision by the home country and (c) supervision by the host country. However, as it will be shown subsequently, these models do hardly share the same legal and theoretic context.

The interdependence between global markets calls for international supervisory coordination and harmonisation. Harmonisation has been the prevailing method of regional organisations, such as the EEC in the 1970s and the North American Free Trade Agreement (NAFTA), as well as the key objectives of international organisations, such as the Basel Committee,[3] the International Organisation of Securities Commissions (IOSCO) and the International Association of Insurance Supervisors (IAIS). Although the latter are considered 'gentlemen's agreements' with no legally binding effect, they are increasingly viewed as important mechanisms for promoting convergence and harmonisation of national regulations.[4] Harmonisation of regulatory and supervisory standards requires unanimity, detailed specification and a need to continuously adjust to technical progress. Hence, this makes implementation, enforcement and monitoring by two or more countries more costly. Harmonisation in theory is about the content of rules in a special field of regulation. Where financial institutions expand their business beyond their country of incorporation, it is the task of the supervisors of the home and the host country to agree in detail on specific common rules, which will characterise their *content-of-rule* relationship. Whenever a consensus is not possible, their relationship acquires a different dimension, it becomes a *conflict-of-rule* relationship.

When one country, the home or the host, imposes its own control on financial undertakings, the issue is not about the content of rules. It is about the conflict of rules, which country's regulation will prevail and which country's regulator will ultimately have the power of supervision. The country of origin represents one line of conflict, while the country of provision of services the other. Cross-border business and integration of financial markets mean that it is increasingly difficult to apply supervision according to national boundaries. Legislators of some countries have tried to combat the problems of internationalisation of the markets by means of a strategy of applying national rules outside their territorial boundaries. The problem with that approach was the likelihood that other countries, affected by what they see as the extraterritorial application of legislation, would be offended and refuse to assist or even block the activities of the regulators in question.[5] Additionally, inherent in that approach lies the danger of allowing the application of two sets of rules, the home and the host, which, if contradictory, could completely hinder the cross-border flow of capital and provision of services.

Cooperative agreements between supervisory authorities are likely to provide solutions to these problems, supplemented by essential harmonisation. However, the power of the host country to impose justified or unjustified restrictions driven by economic and non-economic policies may weaken the sufficiency of cooperation. Then, a greater degree of harmonisation becomes necessary. A prototype paradigm has been developed by the Single Market Programme of the EU with regard to financial services, although the European regulator has not yet achieved full harmonisation of regulatory standards, but instead has relied on supervision by national authorities. This paradigm is examined in the next section.

C. The EU paradigm

1. Supervisory concerns

As envisaged in the Rome Treaty, the fundamental objective of the EU is the 'abolition, as between Member States, of obstacles to the free movement of goods, persons, services and capital'.[6] In the context of financial services, certain provisions of the Treaty are particularly relevant, such as the provision allowing for the right of establishment in a Member State other than the home State,[7] the freedom to provide services throughout the EU[8] and national, non-discriminatory treatment for Member State companies.[9]

The liberalisation of financial services has initiated the free movement of financial undertakings and the opening-up of financial markets at a pan-European level. However, the integration of EU securities markets and the establishment of cross-jurisdiction investment services may inevitably leave open the potential application of the legal system of not only the country, where the services originate, but also of the state, where the services are provided.[10] To keep the overall objectives of the Treaty, in particular the fundamental freedoms of establishment and of provision of services, the EU decision-making bodies were concerned to create a financial services environment, in which all credit and investment institutions within the EU should be able to freely offer their services on the same or similar regulatory and supervisory grounds.

In order to create such an environment, without vesting all supervisory power in a pan-European regulator, what could be required was either full harmonisation of the supervisory rules of all Member States, or minimum harmonisation of essential authorisation and supervisory standards, accompanied with recognition by each Member State of the adequacy of the rules of the others, insofar as the authorisation and supervision of financial institutions is concerned. The former approach would eliminate any differences between national rules and the possibility of regulatory arbitrage[11] and, thus, ensure that competition between financial institutions is carried out on a common EU foundation. The latter regime, on the other hand, although it does not entirely exclude the potential for distorting regulatory competition, is more perceptive, takes account of the Member States' national idiosyncrasies and serves the principle of subsidiarity.[12] But what was the European leaders' choice?

2. The three-tier *loci* of financial supervision

Despite initial proposals and the failure to create a single market in financial services on the first basis mentioned above, the European Commission has chosen the more pragmatic and flexible solution of the second approach, namely the minimum harmonisation of certain standards and mutual recognition.[13] This has confined legal requirements to broad regulatory objectives, which may be met by compliance with the technical specifications formulated by the specialised standards-setting institutions, thus enabling the EU to recognise multiple standards as equivalent.[14] As a supplement and medium to tackle the problems and to facilitate cross-border investment business transactions, EU law has introduced the principle of 'home country control' by way of Directives, which complete the Commission's Single Market.

As described in Chapter 2, the principle of home country control was introduced for the first time by the European Commission's White Paper of 1985,[15] as a basic pillar of the 1992 Internal Market Programme. It took many years for the Member States and the EU decision-making bodies to agree on what the appropriate level of regulation and supervision should be. Hence the White Paper marked a dramatic change of approach in the way in which liberalisation across Member States' frontiers was to be achieved.

The premise of the new approach involved three steps. First, the imposition of common minimum standards in every Member State. Second, the application of the principle of mutual recognition or 'European passport'. Finally, the introduction of the principle of home country control, as a corollary of mutual recognition.[16] Since its adoption, the principle has not only been followed, but also has became a basic pillar in building the financial services Directives and particularly the SBD, the ISD and the Third Generation Insurance Directives.[17]

As envisaged in the Single Market Programme, the legal methodology of the home country control principle involves the horizontal imposition of three supervisory rules:

(a) *The harmonised Community rules.* The financial services directives have introduced and established common minimum standards for financial firms, allowing thus, mutual recognition of the regulatory standards between Member States. The minimum standards have largely reflected a reaction against too detailed harmonisation attempts of the past and a desire to establish common rules and competitive equality insofar as regulatory requirements were concerned. Generally speaking, they include standards that the European regulator thought too important to be drafted and supervised by national rules and the national competent authorities.

(b) *The home country rules.* The principal purpose and meaning of the home country control principle is that the home Member State is conceded the primary role of authorising and regulating its own providers of financial services and supervising its own regulated markets. Under the financial services directives, the home country is the Member State, in which a credit institution or investment firm is incorporated and authorised. The rationale behind the supremacy of the home State's control is its special relationship, which it enjoys with the financial institutions incorporated within its borders.

(c) *The host country rules.* Despite the primary role of the home State, the Single Market financial services directives seem to depart from the originally envisaged scope of the principle and hardly allow the home country to enjoy an exclusive power of control on credit institutions and investment undertakings. When the latter wish to establish a branch or offer cross-border services in another Member State, they have to comply with the marketing, liquidity or everyday conduct of business rules of that host Member State.[18] Under the financial services directives, the host country is a Member State, other than the home State, in which a credit institution or an investment firm operates. Certain less significant supervisory powers are conceded to the host State, for it is that State's market, in which foreign financial institutions operate, and that market's rules should commonly apply to all financial services providers, domestic and foreign. However, the power of the host country to impose supervisory rules, which may hinder the freedom of cross-border services, is not without limits. As early as in 1974, in *Dassonville*,[19] the ECJ tried to place host country's rules under scrutiny and establish a criterion in order to examine their lawfulness and compatibility with the Treaty provisions.[20]

Despite their initial purpose, practice has shown that the twin principles of home country control and mutual recognition, as implemented by EU secondary legislation, have not been supplemented by a clear allocation of responsibilities in times of crisis and a mechanism to ensure that all financial institutions operating in Europe have an effective supervisory authority.[21] Not only have the limited cross-border provision of financial services and intra-Community flow of capital covered the initial triumphal voices of the Single Market liberalisation programme, but also the current regime has shown a legal, structural and practical lacuna in times of crises, as in the Bank of Credit & Commerce International (BCCI) case.[22]

The grey responsibilities between the home and the host Member State have resulted in the duplication of control in many cases, which significantly hinders the cross-border financial business of financial institutions and undermines the Single Market programme itself. This has an especially negative effect in a new European market with a single currency, a major change of asset allocation patterns and an increasing demand for euro-wide investment products. Especially in investment business, host country control is wider than in banking, which limits the liberalising effects of the directives. As a result, investment firms may be subject to overlapping or conflicting rules of conduct between the home and the host country. Before examining in detail the content and parameters of the home country control instrument, the next section explores its origin and legal status within the Community.

D. The origin and legal status of the principle

In any attempt to interpret and analyse a principle, which is originated by primary or secondary EU legislation, it is significant that its nature and legal thesis in Community law be identified. This section purports to address the following questions: what is the position of the home country control principle in EU law and what is its relationship with the freedoms of the Treaty? How has the ECJ approached the principle and how much significance and legal weight has it attached to it?

1. Secondary law and the international regime

As described before, the definition and birth of the home country control principle lies in the provisions of the Commission's White Paper of 1985. Since that stage, the principle has been explicitly – but not crystal clearly – adopted by investment and financial services directives, which have used it as a vehicle to facilitate the Single Internal Market. However, its origins can be traced in earlier legal documents of the mid-1970s and early 1980s, especially in the sphere of banking law, as well as in the jurisprudence of the ECJ.

With regard to banking services, the principle has been announced as an objective in the Preamble to the First Banking Directive (FBD).[23] At the international level, the Basel Committee has set out a set of principles, which were adopted by the countries represented in the Committee. In 1975, the Committee recommended that the supervision of the solvency of domestic banks' foreign branches should primarily be a matter for the 'parent' authority, which would also take account of the exposure of their foreign subsidiaries and joint ventures in light of their parent banks' moral and other commitments.[24] Later, in the Basel Concordat of 1983,[25] it was further stated that adequate supervision of banks' foreign establishments calls not only for an appropriate allocation of responsibilities between parent and host supervisory authorities, but also for contact and cooperation between them.[26] With regard to insurance services, the Schwarz report of 1971 has already made a suggestion in this direction.[27]

2. The ECJ and overview of its case law

A footprint of the principle has been identified by the European Court a few years before the White Paper, in a case that did not relate to the Treaty free movement of services doctrine, but to the free movement of goods. The home State supervision principle emerged in the *Cassis de Dijon* doctrine of the *Rewe-Zentral* case in 1979.[28] Hence, by permitting investment firms to operate throughout the EU under the same conditions as in their home State, this new approach allowed them in theory to obey one single set of regulations. However, the fact that the ISD, following the example of the SBD, permits host supervisory authorities to subject foreign undertakings to some of their own rules makes the home country control and mutual recognition principles less obvious.[29]

The secondary EU legislation in the field of financial services is general in form and reflects many uneasy compromises. Where Member States are unable to agree on harmonising measures on supervision, the ECJ is left to play an increasingly important part in the interpretation and application of the Treaty freedoms and directives. In exercising its powers of judicial review, the Court is often called upon to settle questions of a constitutional nature or of major economic significance.[30]

The ECJ consists of fifteen Judges assisted by eight Advocates General.[31] These are appointed by common accord of governments of the Member States and hold office for a renewable term of six years. They are chosen from jurists whose independence is beyond doubt and who are of recognised competence. The Judges select one of their number to be President of the Court for a renewable term of three years. The President directs the work of the Court and presides at hearings and deliberations. The Advocates General, on the other hand, deliver in open court and with complete impartiality and independence opinions on the cases brought before the Court.[32]

The European Court may sit in plenary session or in chambers of three or five judges.[33] It has its own registry and administrative infrastructure, which includes a large translations and interpreting service since the Court has to use all the official languages of the EU in the course of its work.[34] Its responsibility is to ensure that the law is observed in the interpretation and applications of the Treaties establishing the European Communities and of the provisions laid down by the competent EU institutions. To enable it to carry out that task, the Court has wide jurisdiction to hear various types of action and to give preliminary rulings.[35]

The Court has to state the law, even when it is badly drafted: normally it will interpret it rather than strike it down.[36] After the *Cassis de Dijon* decision, a series of ECJ cases tried to interpret the directives and the home country control principle itself, but the Court found itself ill-equipped to draw the line and divide the supervisory responsibilities between the home and the host Member State. It is noticeable that even in judgements concerning directives, the European Court begins its consideration by giving priority to Treaty provisions and its own case law rather than those of the directives.[37] The following paragraphs identify the relevant cases of the European Court, which have tried to analyse the home country control principle and to give answers regarding its nature and function.

In the first case, *Rewe-Zentral*,[38] the German company Rewe intended to import to Germany a consignment of '*Cassis de Dijon*' originating in France for the purpose of marketing it in Germany. It applied to the *Bundesmonopolverwaltung* for authorisation to import the liqueur and the monopoly administration informed it that, because of its insufficient alcoholic strength, the liqueur did not have the characteristics required in order to be marketed within Germany. The Court of Justice was convinced that the German restrictions created an indirect obstacle to imports and were covered by the prohibition of Article 28 EC Treaty (former Article 30).[39] Consequently, it found no reason why, provided that a good is produced and marketed in one Member State, it should not be introduced into any other country.[40] In other words, the home country control principle is applied in that any product imported from another Member State must, in principle, be admitted to the territory of the importing (host) Member State if it has been lawfully produced, that is, conforms to rules and processes of manufacture that are customarily and traditionally accepted in the exporting (home) country, and is marketed in the territory of the latter.

Before the decision in *Cassis*, the Court decided whether measures having equivalent effect are being subject to an extended discrimination or full effects doctrine in *Dassonville*.[41] This ruling was concerned with the validity of a Belgian requirement that goods bearing a destination of origin could only be imported in the host country if they were accompanied by a certificate from the government of the home country confirming their right to designation. Dassonville, a wholesale in business in France, had imported Scotch whisky into Belgium. Although the goods in question were duly imported into Belgium on the basis of the French documents required and cleared for customs purposes as 'Community goods', the Belgian authorities considered that these documents did not properly satisfy the objectives of Belgian law. This was because the goods were not accompanied by the required certificate. The Court held that

> the requirement by a Member State of a certificate of authenticity which is less easily obtainable by importers of an authentic product which has been put into free circulation in a regular manner in another Member State than by importers of the same product coming directly from the country of origin constitutes a measure having an effect equivalent to a quantitative restriction as prohibited by the Treaty.[42]

The concept of measure having equivalent effect is not so easy to define, given that the restrictive effect on imports and exports deriving from such a measure is only indirect and given the multiplicity of measures, which can tend to produce an effect of this nature. The Commission has had the opportunity to define this concept in the performance of its task conferred on it by Article 211 (former Article 155) of the Treaty.[43] Directive 70/50/EEC, in particular, abolished measures that applied equally to domestic and imported products and that hindered imports or made importation more difficult or costly than the disposal of domestic products (Article 2), and measures, where their 'restrictive effect on the free movement of goods exceeds the effects intrinsic to trade rules' (Article 3). Also, the ECJ judgement in *Donckerwolcke* expresses the settled legal view of the Court on the meaning and scope of the prohibition on measures having an effect equivalent to quantitative restrictions on imports. These include, *inter alia*, 'all trading rules enacted by Member States which are capable of hindering, directly or indirectly, actually or potentially, intra-Community trade'.[44]

The 'equivalent effect' principle has been confirmed in the Court's case law, although with minor variations. For instance, the term 'trading rules' does not usually appear nowadays and the Court sometimes speaks of obstacles 'to imports between Member States' rather than 'intra-Community trade'. In any event, it is clear from this formula that one must look to the effects of a measure rather than to its aims, in deciding whether it falls under Article 28. Notwithstanding the importance of *Dassonville* in terms of judicial policy construction, however, this judgement was not concerned with the lawful production and marketing of foreign products in the host country. This was conducted in *Cassis*. Therefore, while *Dassonville* was concerned with the nature of the restriction or prohibition, *Cassis* moved to considering the equivalence of the protection provided by the home country rules.[45] For the first time, *Cassis* confirmed that Article 28 covers measures applying in the same way to domestic and imported goods ('indistinctly applicable' measures). While the significance of the *Cassis* judgement may not have been immediately apparent by the Commission and Member States, the Commission recognised later the potential value of the decision to reactivate its integration policy in Europe.

The Court's interpretation in *Cassis* has induced the Commission to move even further and elaborate the principles of home country control and mutual recognition before fully adopting them in the White Paper of 1985. In its Communication of 1980,[46] it set out a number of guidelines including, *inter alia*, that a Member State may not prohibit the sale in its territory of a product even if it is produced according to technical or quality requirements that differ from those imposed on its domestic products.[47] This means that where a product 'suitably and satisfactorily' fulfils the legitimate objective of a Member State's own rules,[48] the importing (host) country cannot justify prohibiting its sale in its territory by claiming that the way it fulfils the objective is different from that imposed on domestic products.

A similar approach was reached a few years later in *Coditel*,[49] in the context of industrial property rights, reflecting another aspect of Article 30 EC Treaty (former Article 36).[50] In that case, the Court recognised that intellectual property rights in a film could be protected against a television showing of that film transmitted from another Member State (home). Advocate General Reischl concludes his opinion with the statement

> if a company holding the exploitation rights in a cinematographic film (in one Member State) enters into a contract granting a company in another Member State, for a fixed period, the exclusive right to exhibit that film, such a contract is not to be regarded as incompatible with Article 81 EC (former Article 85) if the circumstances are such that, without exclusivity, no license could be found for the territory in question.

With respect to services, the home country control principle was examined more recently by the ECJ in *Säger*,[51] by raising the essential question, whether Article 49 EC Treaty (former Article 59) entitles a company established in another Member State (home) to provide a certain service[52] for undertakings established in Germany. In his Opinion, Advocate General Jacobs states

> it does not seem unreasonable that a person establishing himself in a (home) member-State should as a general rule be required to comply with that State in all respect.

And he continues,

> It is less easy to see why a person who is established in one member-State (home) and who provides services in other (host) member-States should be required to comply with all the detailed regulations in force in each of those States.[53]

The European Court followed a similar approach in *Commission v Germany*,[54] which dealt with direct insurance affected through intermediaries.

In that case, Germany was justified in requiring insurance undertakings established in their home Member State to comply with its authorisation requirements insofar as they were necessary to ensure the protection of policyholders and insured persons.[55] Nonetheless, the Court held that such authorisation was not justified, in case insurance firms were required to duplicate conditions already met in their home States,[56] confirming in general once again the principal supervisory power of the home country.

One year after *Säger*, the *Cassis de Dijon* test was re-appraised in the *Keck* cases.[57] In its judgement,[58] the European Court confirmed the approach of the Advocate General and decided that, in the absence of harmonisation of legislation, obstacles to free movement of goods, which are the consequence of applying, to goods coming from other Member States (home) where they are lawfully manufactured and marketed, rules that lay down requirements to be met by such goods, constitute measures of equivalent effect prohibited by Article 28 EC Treaty (former Article 30). In other words, the host State's rules that impose restrictions to intra-Community trade are prohibited if the goods are lawfully produced and marketed in the home Member State. In contrast, and according to the *Cassis de Dijon* test, obstacles to free movement are to be accepted only insofar as the aim of the host State's legislation concerned is to satisfy 'mandatory requirements' justified in Community law and is also necessary to attain, and is proportionate to, the aim in view.[59] It may be observed herein that these mandatory requirements do not necessarily coincide with restrictions expressly permitted by Article 28, that they may only be invoked in favour of national measures, which are genuinely non-discriminatory,[60] and that, as has later appeared, the list is not closed.[61]

The division of supervisory powers between the home and the host Member State was further investigated by the ECJ in *Alpine Investments*,[62] the first case before the Court to deal with investment services. The case involved the proceedings brought by an 'introducing broker' company challenging the restrictions imposed on it by the Dutch Ministry of Finance regarding unsolicited telephone calls (cold-calling) offering commodities futures. The investment firm alleged that the ban on cold-calling was contrary to Article 49 EC Treaty (former Article 59) and prevented it from marketing its services to clients in other Member States. However, its arguments were not justified by the Court.

At the time of the judgement, there was no directive yet applicable to the marketing of investment business. Even if the ISD were implemented, it is not clear whether cold-calling would fall under its provisions. *A fortiori*, it is not clear whether the ISD passport applies to commodities derivatives.[63] Nonetheless, *Alpine Investments* raises a major issue. Even if one hypothesises that the investment services directives are applicable, the home country supervision principle does not cover the marketing of investment business and rules of conduct. This task is conceded to the responsibility of the host Member State, which has the power to govern the form and content of such marketing, in consonance with the 'general good' notion.[64] Here lies the contribution of the *Alpine Investments* case. It analyses the complex issues arising from the general good application of the Court's jurisprudence relating to Article 49 EC Treaty. On the other hand, it hardly confirms that the host State's control on rules of conduct excludes that of the home State. Indeed, the Court held that the provisions of the Treaty on the freedom to provide services impose obligations not only on the host Member State but also on the home Member State, if the services are provided to persons established in another Member State.[65] This is hardly surprising in view of the importance attributed by the Court to the free movement of services. To this end, it is justifiable that the home Member State may want to control the rules relating to investment services marketing and investment firm's conduct for reasons of public interest and consumer protection.[66] *Ad hoc*, the *Alpine Investments* judgement has failed to cover the lacunae of the ISD and offer a solution to the interpretation of the home country control principle. In the own words of Advocate General Jacobs,

> it is not entirely clear from the directive (ISD) how responsibility is divided between the authorities of the home State and the authorities of the host State.[67]

Finally, the home country control principle was examined in brief in the recent case *Germany v Parliament and Council*.[68] The principle was part (not the most important, though) of the grounds of action brought by Germany for the annulment of Directive 94/19/EC on deposit guarantee schemes (DGD)[69] in banking.[70] More specifically, as an alternative to its principal claim of the legal base of the Directive, Germany argued that the obligation the Directive imposes on a Member State to accommodate branches wishing to supplement the guarantee offered by their home State is contrary to the principle of home country control and infringes the principle of proportionality. It submitted that at the time the Directive was adopted, the Community legislature was already bound by the principle of home State supervision, which was designated in the Commission's White Paper of 1985 and in the SBD. If the supplementary deposit guarantee were adopted, then the tasks of banking supervision, auditing and guarantee of deposit would no longer constitute exclusive responsibility of the home State authorities, which would make the Community depart from its previous practice without stating reasons, in contrast to ECJ case law.

In response to Germany's arguments and confirming the Opinion of Advocate General Leger, the Court clearly held that, since home country supervision is not a principle laid down by the Treaty, the Community legislature is entitled to depart from it, provided that it did not infringe the legitimate expectations of the individuals concerned. In any case, the Advocate General indirectly questioned whether the challenged Directive actually departs from the home country control principle. He alleged that, in consonance with the Preamble to the Directive,[71] credit institutions do remain subject to the supervision of the home State, so that the contested departure from the rule seems to be limited to the specific situation, where the host Member State offers a branch a higher guarantee than that offered by the home Member State.[72]

3. Application of EU secondary and case law

References to the principle of home country control have been well documented, but often in such way that gives the impression that it forms one of the major principles set forth by the Rome Treaty.[73] However, the Court in *Germany v Parliament and Council* simply and clearly recalls that such a principle is not set out in the Treaty, but only in secondary legislation. Although the Advocate General admits that nobody questions that home country control has been the guiding principle in the harmonisation of the financial services sector,[74] the Court found unproved that Community legislation has laid down and adopted the principle in the sphere of banking law with the intention of applying it systematically to rules that fall within that sector in the future.[75] Such a decision comes in conformity with the constitutional legal position of EU primary law and the relevant subordinating role of black-letter law.

The home country control principle should not be applied systematically as the *de facto* principal rule subordinating all other principles in the financial services field.[76] It is not included in the general principles of the Treaty, but instead it is a concept defined and illustrated only by secondary law and subjected to jurisdictional review. It becomes obvious that EU secondary law, namely the directives, compose an exemption from the Treaty area, where the freedoms of establishment and provision of cross-border financial services are supported by intangible bases. Secondary legislation hardly plays the role of a supreme and *de jure* legitimate regulation; instead it acts as a framework law subject to the judicial control of the European Court.

One has, thus, to wonder: given its importance, why has the principle not been included in the Treaty provisions adopting the policies of the EU and its guiding principles?[77] Perhaps the Community legislator did not find it necessary to make a global statement about the universal precedence of the principle. Perhaps the Community legislator wanted to give the principle a retrospective character, rather than to suggest its application in future EU legislation. Subsequently, the principle's application or departure from it should be justified with great caution, as the EU legislator and the European Court have found themselves ill-equipped to interpret the principle and clarify the borders between home and host country supervisory responsibilities. The following section examines in detail and analyses the home country control principle.

E. Home country control and investment services

The publication of the White Paper in 1985 and the subsequent adoption of the SEA have marked the beginning of a new era in the field of investment services. The adoption of substantial equivalence and principal home country supervision has drastically altered the EU programme. Immediately apparent has been the drafting and adoption of investment services directives emanating from a difficult negotiation process between the Member States.

The EU investment services directives clearly adopt the grant of a single authorisation valid throughout the EU and the application of the home Member State supervision.[78] This means that the home Member State is conceded the primary role of authorising and regulating its own investment firms and supervising its own regulated markets. However, the directives hardly allow the home country to enjoy an exclusive power of control on investment undertakings. When the latter wish to establish a branch or offer cross-border services in another Member State, they have to comply with the marketing and everyday conduct rules of that host Member State.[79] The following paragraphs will commence a more detailed analysis on the division of roles between the supervisory authorities of the home and the host country.[80]

1. Supervisory responsibilities of the home Member State

As it becomes obvious from the White Paper and the third recital to the ISD, the European Commission has chosen to adopt a minimalist approach: initially it did not endeavour to create a single pan-European supervisor; it merely considered the efficiency of essential harmonisation to secure the mutual recognition of authorisation and prudential supervision systems. To this end, the sole responsibility to authorise and prudentially supervise investment firms lies in the hands of the home supervisor.[81] This does not mean, however, that the host Member State has no role to play.[82] Its competence will be discussed later. First, this section critically notes the responsibilities of the home country.

1.1. Authorisation – conditions for taking up business

The authorisation conditions and procedure are at the heart of the ISD's investment services regime in terms of both its primary market integration scope and its complementary financial stability and consumer protection objectives. Broadly speaking, the home Member State is made responsible for ensuring that the investment undertaking, those directing the firm and those with a major shareholding are suitable to undertake, or to be involved with a firm that deals with investment business.[83] In order to reach a view on the integrity, suitability and financial soundness of an investment firm and grant permission to take up business, the home supervisor obviously requires certain key information. The ISD lays down a number of specific minimum criteria that must be satisfied by an investment firm seeking authorisation to provide investment services, and that it must continue to meet thereafter. These standards are supplemented by others prescribed by the post-BCCI Directive.[84] All together, they compose the minimum requirements for assessing the fitness and propriety of an applicant undertaking, or for assessing subsequent alterations to business activities or personnel.

The ISD sets out four basic criteria for authorisation to be granted: capital requirements, competence of the directors, operations programme and identity of shareholders. Nonetheless, beyond the capital requirements and requirements for qualifying shareholders, the ISD does not seek to prescribe and harmonise detailed standards for fitness and propriety of the firm at the initial authorisation stage of the home country supervision.[85]

1.1.1. *Capital requirements.*

Regarding the nature of the investment undertaking, this is obliged to have sufficient initial capital.[86] This concept seems to have been obtained from the FBD. A natural reaction to this provision would be the discussion of what the sufficient initial capital requirement should be. The details of this discussion are left to the context of the Capital Adequacy Directive (CAD).[87]

As the capital requirement constitutes 'a minimum', it does not hinder the Member States from imposing higher, more stringent standards to the investment institutions, which they authorise. However, the mutual recognition principle does not permit Member States to impose these higher standards to firms authorised in another State, but wishing to do business within their borders.

1.1.2. *Competence of directors.*

Article 3(3) of the ISD provides that the home competent authorities must ensure that the individuals who direct the investment undertaking are of sufficient good repute and are sufficiently experienced. This provision comprises a very valuable tool of consumer protection. What is important for supervisors is to actually know who runs the business, which would allow them to take action against the individuals without having to discipline the whole firm. On the other hand, problems may be imposed by the fact that the ISD does not clarify the test of who is experienced and of 'good repute'.

The same Article imposes the so-called four-eyes principle in the firm's management. Accordingly, the direction of an undertaking's business must effectively be decided by at least two individuals satisfying the above conditions. The rationale of such a provision is to control potential misconduct of business by one of the directors, hoping that it would be prevented by the other. Regretfully, the ISD does not seem to distinguish between the responsibilities that each of the directors should have, or the role that they should play. Should they have equally divided management responsibilities? What if one of them is a 'shadow' director and the firm is literally run by the other?

In any circumstances, the ISD allows supervisors to waive this obligation and grant authorisation, in case of an individual trader or a one-person company and in accordance with the firm's articles of association and home Member State's national laws. Naturally, such a firm should be still in a position to satisfy the other fit and proper conditions prescribed by the Directive.

With regard to natural persons, in order to be considered as investment firms, the ISD requires a number of additional criteria to fulfil, as set out in Article 1.[88] In particular, where a firm has only one proprietor, he/she must make provision for the protection of investors in the event of cessation of business following death, incapacity or other similar event.

1.1.3. Operations programme. The third requirement, necessary for the undertakings authorisation, is the programme of operation, which must be included in every application for authorisation and that sets out, *inter alia*, the types of business envisaged and the organisational structure of the firm concerned.[89]

1.1.3.1. Type of business. The ISD does not specify what the type of business requirement should comprise. In a paper prepared by FESCO in April 1999,[90] the competent authorities of EEA countries agreed that the firm's business plan should at least include:

(a) basic information on the investment firm itself. In particular the legal and any other trading name used or to be used by the firm, the address of its registered or head office, any previous names and the names of directors, senior managers and qualifying shareholders;

(b) information on the investment services to be provided by the firm, either in the home or the host State, including relevant core and non-core services covered by Sections A and C of the Annex to the ISD;

(c) information on the way the firm plans to provide its services, so that competent authorities can monitor its soundness and fitness;

(d) information on the products and financial instruments, with which the firm will be involved, as prescribed by Section B of the Annex to the ISD;

(e) information on the regulated markets, in which the firm will be active, on its proposed client base and on whether it will be engaged in trading for its own account. It should be noted that not all investment undertakings are allowed to trade for their own account. The criteria is set out in Articles 3(1), 4 and 5 of the CAD;

(f) financial plans and projections. The agreed minimum requirement for the financial plan will usually cover the proposed first year of business. However, certain competent authorities may request more information either on a routine basis or under exceptional circumstances, taking into account the nature of the proposed business and risks involved. On the other hand, national supervisors should recognise that projections cannot always be an accurate indicator of appropriate capital adequacy requirements. To this end, the relevant capital requirements prescribed by the CAD will act as minimum standards; and

(g) information on the source of funding for the business and an indication that funding will be sustained. This requirement is extremely important for the operational propriety of small and medium firms, which are new to the market, while it can serve other purposes such as money laundering liabilities.

It deserves notice that the ISD does not include any continuing requirement for the investment firm to notify the home State of any changes to the operation programme or business profile, which it submitted with its initial application for authorisation.[91] In this context, the question arises, whether an existing firm, which moves into a new type of investment business, would need to ask for a new authorisation for that business. The first paragraph of Article 3 implies that a new authorisation is necessary, as it needs to specify the investment services provided by the firm. Whereas that is the case, however, the regulator should already have assessed the nature of the firm and its capability of taking up the new business. *Ad hoc* a shorter and more simplified authorisation procedure should be expected to take place.

1.1.3.2. Organisational structure.　Once again, Article 3(4) of the ISD is mute regarding the definition and explanation of the organisational structure that an investment undertaking must fulfil before being granted authorisation. In terms of firm's structure, it is accepted that such information will include details of the management structure, division responsibilities and operational procedures, as well as details of any proposals to 'outsource' functions or business, including proposed legal agreements with the providers of the outsourced services and procedures to monitor their performance.

According to the FESCO paper,[92] the disclosure of organisational structure should also comprise internal controls and systems for the monitoring and control of risks.[93] This will include arrangements such as 'Chinese Walls' for the segregation of front and back office and for monitoring employees and personal transactions. If such an interpretation were valid, then a major conflict would arise between the responsibilities of the home and the host Member State, which could jeopardise the efficiency of the home country control principle in general.

In terms of group structure, the home State is required to apply the conditions of the post-BCCI Directive[94] and authorise its supervisor to seek and identify the ultimate control of the applicant firm and its detailed structure/family tree. In addition, the home supervisor will have to regard the information that is required in order to perform its function as lead supervisor, solo supervisor or supervisor of a subgroup, in accordance with the CAD and the Banking Codified Directive.[95] In case an applicant investment firm is part of a group, which is supervised by another Member State on a consolidated basis, the home supervisor will endeavour to consider the kind of reliance that may be placed on that supervision in fulfilling its own obligations. On the other hand, in case an applicant firm is a subsidiary or sister company of an investment or credit institution authorised in another Member State, the home supervisor will have to consult the other Member State beforehand on the authorisation.[96] These provisions clearly reveal the intentions of the Commission to strengthen the stability and integrity of the financial system within the EU and reinforce the power of national regulators.[97]

1.1.4. Identity of shareholders.   Finally, in order to grant authorisation, the competent authority of the home State must be informed of the identity of the shareholders or members that have qualifying holdings and of the amounts of those holdings.[98] When the Directive makes provision of 'qualifying holding', it means any

> direct or indirect holding in an investment firm, which represents 10 per cent or more of the capital or of the voting rights, or which makes it possible to exercise a significant influence over the management of the investment firm, in which that holding subsists.[99]

Nevertheless, the second paragraph of Article 4 goes beyond the identity of the shareholders and, as with the directors, requires that the national authorities be satisfied as to the fitness and suitability of the shareholders or members of the firm. Again this provision plays a very important role in protecting consumers, who need to be certain of the sound and prudent management of the investment firm, to which they have entrusted their investment.

In particular, each supervisor should obtain information such as the qualifying shareholders' identity, complete work history and relevant experience, professional qualifications, educational background and information on his/her financial integrity, any criminal record, previous civil cases or even disciplinary sanctions. In most Member States, misleading or inaccurate information constitutes criminal offence. Nonetheless, in the Member States where it is not criminal offence, such behaviour may still be grounds for failing the fit and proper test and lead to refusal of authorisation.

One may ask however: what if a qualifying shareholder is not involved in the management of the firm? Is he still required to prove his competence to the supervisory authorities? As prescribed in Article 1(10) of the ISD, supervisors are mainly interested in those individuals or legal persons that actually influence the management of the firm. Consequently, shareholders that influence the management are required to disclose personal information and prove their competence, even if they hold less than 10 per cent of the firm's shares. To this end, it is logical to assume that qualifying shareholders are not required to pass the fit and proper test, as far as they do not get involved in the management of the investment firm.

In order for such a regime to function, it is conceivable that home State supervisors will not rely completely on the information attached to the application by investment firms, which wish to start business. It is vital that supervisors develop an information network, in order to assess the fitness and propriety of investment firms at application stage and thereafter. The benefits in supervisory authorities having a close relationship with law enforcement and other regulatory authorities are invaluable. Such cooperation, however, will inevitably reflect the extent to which authorities possess such information, always being in accordance with the professional secrecy obligations and 'gateways' of information exchange set out in the relevant directives.[100]

1.2. Prudential supervision

Besides the authorisation requirements, the home country control principle also requires that home prudential supervision be carried out and conditions be met during the whole operation period of investment firms. The ISD specifies the supervision task of the home Member State by laying down continuing information requirements and specific minimum prudential rules, which are to be imposed on investment firms 'at all times'.[101] The ISD's single market mechanism, therefore, extends beyond home country control and mutual recognition of authorisation to ongoing regulation and includes mutual recognition of the quality and suitability of supervision by the authority of the home Member State.

1.2.1. What is prudential supervision?
In accordance with the objectives of financial supervision analysed in Chapter 1, the prudential supervision of financial firms should primarily 'set minimum standards for market participants and provide consistency of treatment for all similarly situated intermediaries. It should also reduce the risk to investors of loss caused by negligent or illegal behaviour or inadequate capital'.[102] Prudential rules are concerned with risk management. They address the solvency of individual investment firms and they cover broader financial stability issues and safety and soundness policies.[103] Nonetheless, these rules should not be expected to remove risk from the market place, but they should ensure that there is proper management of that risk. Therefore, the link between risk and supervision is particularly critical in defining and imposing prudential rules. As developed further in this book, this link should constitute the most significant concern addressed by European regulators and policy-makers.

1.2.2. Continuing information requirements.
After being authorised to commence investment business, investment firms are required to comply with the conditions imposed in Article 3(3) of the ISD, throughout their operation

existence. These conditions involve the capital adequacy and the directors' fitness and propriety requirements. Regarding the former, the ISD quotes the CAD and adopts its continuing requirements, including, *inter alia*, adequate own funds, monitoring and control of large exposures, valuation of positions for reporting purposes and defaults in case of repurchase and reverse repurchase agreements or securities lending and securities borrowing transactions.[104] As pointed out before, the ISD is silent on whether investment undertakings need or need not notify their supervisors of any pragmatic or potential changes in their operation programme or business profile.

1.2.3. Information regarding qualifying holdings.   Under Article 9 of the ISD, anyone considering to acquire, directly or indirectly, a qualifying holding, representing at least 10 per cent, in an investment firm or making an investment firm a subsidiary, must first notify its supervisory authority, regarding the acquisition and the size of the intended holding. But this is not the only prerequisite; in view of the protection of the investment firm and its customers, the potential mega-shareholders have to substantially prove to the home State supervisory authority that they are suitable to provide the firm with a fit and sound management. In addition, it is obvious that change of control of an investment enterprise plays a very significant role in the fate of the firm itself.

On the other hand, major acquisitions or disposals are very likely to initiate the suspicion of regulators. Unlike in banking, where the central bank speaks the final word through its Lender of Last Resort (LLR) role, in the securities business, investment firms do not have the luxury of relying on institutions that would cover their losses in case of default. Supervisors, therefore, prefer businessmen who are credible, have 'deep pockets' and can sufficiently provide background capital in a crisis situation. Consequently, the requirements imposed by supervisors will resemble those provided for the actual qualifying shareholders or member of the investment undertaking,[105] although the ISD does not reveal how far the investigation should go. But what happens if the requirements imposed by supervisors are never met? In case the potential shareholder fails to satisfy the home competent authority of his/her suitability, the authority has up to three months from the date of the notification to oppose the shareholder's plans. If it does not oppose the plans, it may fix a deadline for its implementation.[106]

Similar provisions apply for the case where actual qualifying shareholders plan to dispose or reduce, directly or indirectly, their holding. With a difference: the shareholders who wish to give away part or their whole qualifying holding must inform the home supervisors of merely their act and its size.[107] The fact that they are qualifying shareholders reveals that the competent authorities have already been informed and satisfied of their competence to influence the firm's running. Even if they have not done so, the ISD requires the investment firms themselves to disclose any acquisition or disposal of holding in their capital that causes shareholdings to exceed or fall below the qualifying or 'control' thresholds.[108]

1.2.4. Drawing up of prudential rules.   The ISD assigns to home Member States the task of setting out prudential rules for investment firms. Article 10 of the Directive contains special organisational duties, which relate not only to the management level of the firm but also to subordinated operating structures. In light of those general principles of organisation, it deserves mention that the ISD does not contain extensive procedures for actual implementation. These are found at national level. At first sight, the individual prudential rules appear to be simple. Upon closer observation, however, certain important issues look more trivial.

First, the investment undertakings are required to have sound administrative and accounting procedures, control and safeguard arrangements for electronic data processing and adequate internal control mechanisms.

Second, the investment firms should make adequate arrangements for instruments and funds belonging to investors, with a view to safeguarding the latter's rights. The segregation of clients' funds from the firm's capital is a significant *ex ante* measure of defence against potential failure of the investment firm. What is important here, but complex at the same time, is to define the critical point at which clients' capital ceases belonging to the investor and is transferred to the ownership of the firm and vice versa. The fact that Member States have different settlement systems and ways of handling clients' funds, raises the enquiry, whether the drawing of these rules should be conceded to the home State, or be included in the conduct of business rules responsibility of the host State. Is it functional for investment firms commencing business in one Member State to have different fund arrangements according to their home supervisory authority's prudential rules?

Third, the firms are required to keep the records of executed transactions. An important tool in the prudential supervision of firms and markets, designed to protect investors and ensure market confidence, is the establishment of an 'audit trail' of securities transactions. Such a record would be in position to reveal the transaction of a particular security by a particular undertaking on a particular market. In this way, home country authorities could monitor compliance with the prudential rules covered by the financial services Directives, as well as with national rules. Although the competent authorities are offered the discretion to choose the length of the records' maintenance, the ISD makes no reference of the place in which they must be kept or the specific information that must be kept.

Finally, firms must be structured and organised in such a way, as to minimise the risk of clients' interests being prejudiced by conflicts of interest. Conflicts can exist either between the firm and its clients or between clients.

Regarding the latter, a significant question arises: should firms be required to adopt for themselves a structure that keeps conflicts to a minimum?

Or should rules be designed in such a way as to ensure that investors are sufficiently informed of the potential relevant conflicts and are free to make their own decision as to the action they should take? Relevant to the first enquiry, a second comes to our minds: to what extent does the organisational structure of an investment firm influence the way that conflicts of interest are handled? The revolutionary changes in European securities markets have introduced considerably higher competition both at national and supranational levels. This has given firms the ability to organise themselves in a way that was most beneficial and efficient, but has also brought with it an increase in the conflicts of interest faced by firms undertaking investment services.

On the other hand, inevitable doubts do arise as to the ability to impose rules relating to the management and disclosure of conflicts of interest. Is it an area of supervision that can be left exclusively to the home Member State, or should the host Member State include it in its conduct of business rules? And beyond that: what prevents us from interpreting the rules of 'records keeping' or 'investor funds arrangements' as 'prudential' and not as 'conduct of business'? Do these rules not cover the everyday business between the investment firm and its clients? These responsibility conflicts, which are left unclear between Articles 10 and 11 of the ISD, will be discussed later in Chapter 6.

1.3. Notification requirements

The greatest benefit that the White Paper and the ISD provide in the Single European Market is the European passport, which gives financial firms the possibility to travel across their home country's borders and commence investment business in any other Member State by the establishment of branches or cross-border services. The procedure to obtain the passport resembles that of the SBD regarding credit institutions.[109] Although investment firms do not have to obtain a second authorisation from the host Member State under the mutual recognition principle, they are subject to notification procedures, which have to be addressed to the home State authorities. Accordingly, under Articles 17 and 18 of the ISD, investment firms are obliged to notify the supervisors of the activities on the list they intend to conduct. This obligation immediately raises the question whether a new notification procedure is needed every time the investment firm intends to extend its activities in the host Member State. A literal interpretation of the provision would point to the positive. In contrast to banking, where subsequent alterations in the firm's strategy on its foreign business ought to be of inferior importance,[110] investment firms are explicitly obliged to file a new written notification every time they change their operations programme.[111] Whether this obligation results in additional burdens on the investment firms' right to provide free cross-border services seems obvious.

Even though this solution might appear to be the most appropriate and useful from the national supervisors' point of view, it should not be ignored that the notification procedure should be construed in accordance with the ECJ's case law regarding the permissible restrictions on the free provision of services in the interest of the general good. This assessment will take place later in Chapter 5. At this point, it is sufficient to observe that the basis of this examination has to reflect the approach the Court employed in *Cassis de Dijon*: a financial firm should be permitted to provide services beyond its home country borders unrestricted, unless limitations adopted in the general good holds otherwise.[112] This assessment is supported by a number of the Court's rulings on services.[113]

Regretfully, the text of the ISD does not give guidance on the legal nature and the purpose behind the notification requirement. It could be argued that the notification procedure was introduced with a view to satisfy the host supervisors that the financial firm has a valid authorisation from the home country. Such purpose would fall within the ambit of acceptable restrictions on the right to provide services.[114] A further reason that might be stemming from Article 17(4) ISD is to facilitate the host authority in indicating the conditions, including the rules of conduct, under which, in the general good interest, investment services must be carried on in its territory.

In addition, the Directive remains silent on the issue of potential consequences if the service provider fails to inform the home State of its intentions or if the host supervisors do not receive notification from the home authorities. It is unclear how stringent such an obligation can be on the ability of the host authorities to inhibit the financial firm from commencing business within its territory unless it has notified its intentions. In this context, it would be useful to make a distinction between establishing a branch and providing cross-border services.[115]

1.3.1. Establishing a branch.

Any investment firm wishing to establish a branch within another Member State must, in addition to the authorisation conditions just described, communicate some information to the home Member State.[116] These particulars should include:

(a) the Member State or States, in which the firm plans to establish the branch;
(b) an operation programme setting out the type of business and the organisation of the branch envisaged;
(c) the address of the branch and the names of the individuals responsible for its management.

Regarding the latter, the present drafting of the ISD leaves unclear whether notification has to be given only for the first branch that a firm sets up in another Member State, or whether similar notification is required for all potential subsequent branches. Here we should perhaps make a distinction.

Certain items, such as the type of business and the operation programme approved by the home supervisory authorities, do need to be duplicated. On the other hand, the host competent authorities should expect to receive information about the organisational structure and the managers responsible for each branch.

Another confusing matter is whether a firm is required to notify the home or host authorities if it intends to cease operating a branch in the jurisdiction of the host State. The wording of Article 17(6) allows for changes to be notified, without specifying whether it covers cessation of activities of the branch. It rather implies that the firm should notify through writing the competent supervisors in case of modification or extension of its activities.

After receiving all the necessary information, the home competent authority shall communicate it to the host authority within three months and inform the investment firm accordingly.[117] In case the home Member State refuses to send the information to the host State, it must give reasons for its refusal within three months of the receipt of the particulars. As in every similar case, refusal or failure to reply is subject to judicial review by the courts of the home Member State.

The ISD allows a branch to be established two months after the notification has reached the host State competent authority.[118] However, what is important here is the fact that the host Member State does not appear to have any power to hinder an investment firm from setting up a branch. Even if it is clear that the branch will not be able to comply with the host State's conditions, such as the conduct of business or capital adequacy rules, the host supervisory authorities do not have the ultimate word in the establishment of the branch or the continuation of its business. Whether it would be desirable for the host Member State to have such a power or not is not within the scope of this chapter.

1.3.2. Establishing cross-border services.   The reasonably extensive notification requirements for banks and for investment firms wishing to establish a branch are not applied to investment firms, which undertake cross-border business. Since in this case there is no physical existence of the investment firm in the host Member State, it is obliged to notify their home competent authority only of the Member State, in which it plans to do business, and of the operation programme, stating in particular the investment activities included in the Annex to the ISD, which it intends to provide.

In contrast to the establishment of branch, the time between receiving of information by the home State and forwarding it to the host State is limited to one month. This means that the investment business can directly start business after the relevant information is sent to the host supervisors.[119] But what justifies such a difference?

It is noticeable that no distinction is made in the ISD between conduct of business rules that are to be applied to firms doing cross-border business and firms doing business through a branch.[120] As a result, the host competent authorities will have the same responsibilities for supervising rules regardless of the geographical location of the investment firm. To this end, it would be more appropriate to have the same notification requirements for branch services and cross-border services. In addition, another distinction should be made here regarding the investment firm's clients, whether they are retail or professionals. This issue, however, is discussed in more detail later in Chapter 5.

1.4. Drawing up of list of regulated markets

For the purposes of mutual recognition, the ISD gives every Member State the responsibility of drawing up a list of the regulated markets, for which it is the home Member State and which comply with its regulations.[121] In that list, Member States indicate the markets they have chosen to designate as 'regulated markets' for the purposes of the Directive. Together with the relevant rules of procedures and operation of the markets, the list is communicated to all Member States and the Commission. The list of 'regulated markets' is published in the Official Journal of the European Communities (OJ)[122] and is updated regularly.

As far as the definition of a 'regulated market', the ISD gives its own version.[123] Regulated is the market for the instruments listed in Section B of the Annex to the ISD, which:

(a) appears in the list drawn up by Member States;
(b) functions regularly;
(c) is regulated regarding its operation, its conditions for access, its conditions governing admission to listing (if the Admissions Directive is applicable) and its conditions for trading of financial instruments (if the Admissions Directive is not applicable); and
(d) requires compliance with all reporting and compliance requirements laid down by Articles 20 and 21 of the ISD.

Regretfully, the definition of the Directive has hardly proven to be a helpful instrument and problems have emerged from it. In a report conducted by the Commission for the Council in 1998,[124] Italy and Spain reported difficulties in applying the definition of the ISD. In particular, the Italian and Spanish supervisory authorities have looked into the implication of a transaction, whereby commodity derivatives as well as financial instruments referred to in Section B of the Annex to the ISD are traded on a regulated market established in another Member State and appearing on the list referred to in Article 16. The derivative instruments in question are not listed in the Annex and the market segment in which they are traded consequently does not figure among the regulated markets of Article 16. Does such a market segment qualify for the mutual recognition established by EU legislation or not? Unfortunately, the Commission believed that the problems faced by Italian and Spanish authorities did not call into question the way in which the definition is worded and did not see any reason for amending that definition.

Similar problems indicate that there are a number of areas in which, for the maintenance of public confidence in regulated markets, fuller and more explicit regulatory standards are needed. Changes in the market environment, driven by technological advances, electronic trading, cross-membership stock exchange agreements and alliances, the increase in cross-border securities transactions and the launch of the euro, are revolutionary and the consequences for market structure and market regulation are likely to be profound.

These issues raise significant issues for the competent authorities of Member States and have induced them to agree on common standards for regulated markets. FESCO, in consultation with the Federation of European Securities Exchanges (FESE), has agreed and published these standards, which elaborate the definition of 'regulated market' by adding detail to, and supplement the ISD requirements for regulated markets.[125] To this end, the competent authorities will introduce these standards in their regulatory objectives and, when possible, in their respective country's rules.

2. Supervisory responsibilities of the host Member State

The drafters of the ISD did not intend to formulate the principles of home country control and mutual recognition so as to grant financial firms complete freedom from the supervisory reach of the host Member State. The latter is explicitly given a complementary but significant jurisdiction. In particular, the responsibilities of the host supervisor include the drawing up of the conduct of business rules, the provision of access to regulated markets and other requirements often imposed on financial firms.

2.1. Drawing up of Conduct of Business Rules (CBR)

When the initial text of the ISD was proposed by the Commission back in early 1989, there was no mention in it of CBR to be adhered to by investment firms.[126] It was only during the course of negotiations between the Member States and the Commission in the Council of Ministers that some Member States felt that the proposed Directive lacked a sufficient degree of investor protection.

Pursuant to Article 11(1) of the ISD, the Member States must 'draw up rules of conduct which investment firms shall observe at all times'. CBR are in general the provisions setting out the standard of conduct expected from those engaged in the investment business and regulating the good market relationship between the investment undertakings and their clients.

The Directive harmonises Member State's CBR to a certain extent.[127] It is obvious that a detailed common designation of minimum CBR at EU level does not exist.[128] Nevertheless, the rules, which are left to the Member States to draw up at national level, must implement at least the seven principles set out in the same provision of the Directive.[129] These principles, some of which display similarities with principles laid down in a Commission's Recommendation concerning a European code of conduct relating to transactions in transferable securities,[130] stem from the international principles of conduct elaborated by the technical committee of IOSCO.[131]

The very absence of harmonisation in CBR partly reveals that an approach based on home country control could not be achieved. Instead, as stated in the ISD, the implementation of these CBR remains the responsibility of the Member State, in which a service is provided.[132] In addition, the host Member State is not only vested to draw up CBR but also to supervise compliance with them within its territory. As a result, rules of conduct seem to remain mostly a matter for the host Member State.

2.1.1. CBR as a regulatory issue. It may be suggested that the lack of common pan-European CBR implies that the issue of these rules is not so important for the European regulator. More significant could be, for instance, capital adequacy rules, especially because of their increased awareness of systemic risk.[133] *Ad hoc*, essential requirements regarding capital adequacy had to be set at the EU level.[134]

Yet, CBR should not be considered less significant.[135] EU regulators agree that, especially in times when offerings are oversubscribed and trading volumes arc particular high, certain rules are needed in order to ascertain the fair treatment and protection of consumers.[136] Rules of conduct form an important part of the regulatory framework governing the operation of financial firms. At the end of the day, they constitute the game play of everyday investment services transactions, they satisfy transparency requirements and they ensure the smooth relationship between financial undertakings and their clients. As such, CBR are more specifically dealt with in the ISD than in the SBD and seem to remain a regulatory matter of the host Member State. This draws heavily on the fact that they are more specifically described in Article 11 ISD than the prudential rules of Article 10. However, as Chapter 5 will show, they are not clearly separated from the prudential rules, which are essentially issues of the home Member State.

Nevertheless, there is dispute about the legal nature of rules of conduct – is it a supervision (public law) or a contract (private) law rule? – which, however, is irrelevant to the key issues. It is clear that the supervisory authority can impose compliance with the code of conduct, and the ISD makes it equally clear that any client can sue individually on the basis of the code asking for compliance with it or for damages.[137]

2.1.2. Unlimited CBR? With respect to CBR, the question arises whether the current system is fully compatible with the principles of free movement of business and services and of market unity, as laid down by the EC Treaty. The ISD is ambiguous with regard to the question whether the host Member State may only impose CBR justified by the general good.[138] More than one interpretation is possible. First, it could be suggested that the competent authorities of the host Member State are given a *carte blanche* to impose rules of conduct on investment firms of other Member States. The second opinion, on the contrary, would contend that the host country may only impose rules of conduct subject to a justification and proportionality test under the limitation of the general good principle.

This issue has been well documented.[139] If one adopts the first reading, there is little to prevent the host Member State from enacting rules of conduct, which officially are supposed to implement the aforementioned principles but, *de facto*, serve other micropolitical or economic purposes.[140] This would restrict host States' national markets from the free provision of services and make life harder for foreign investment firms[141] counter to Article 59 EC Treaty.

Following a growing body of opinion,[142] it is clear that the second reading should be adopted, not only because of the duty to interpret the ISD in conformity with the EC Treaty, but also in an objective-driven approach of the Directive, the objective of which is the achievement of an internal market in investment business.[143] However, in order to explain the reasons for such an allegation, one should first look into the provisions of the ISD, the background of the Directive and the case-law of the ECJ relating to the general good principle and the freedom of the provision of services.

2.2. *Access to regulated markets*

The second task vested in the host Member State is to provide financial firms with access to regulated markets, which operate under its supervision. According to the ISD, the host Member States shall ensure that investment firms, provided they are lawfully authorised by the supervisory bodies of their home State, can become members of or have access to the regulated markets and the clearing and settlement systems provided for the members of such markets.[144]

It would appear from the wording of Article 15(3) that securities exchanges would continue to be free to require their members to be separately incorporated, or at least to have a physical presence in the Member State where the exchange is located. While this may be the case where a physical presence is still required to deal on a trading floor, it should be borne in mind that where a market makes use of an electronic trading system, it may be possible to allow membership of an exchange even when a firm has no physical presence.[145] Indeed, although the draft proposal of the ISD did not take into consideration the increasing use of telecommunication in securities trading, the final body of the Directive did include a provision that allowed membership without physical presence.[146] To this end, in order to facilitate cross-border investment services, the home Member States are obliged to allow host States' regulated markets to establish and provide facilities within the home States' territories. Although the 'remote access' rule protects the investment firm's free provision of cross-border investment services in general, it is 'popularly viewed as the European "single passport" for screen-based trading systems'.[147]

The rules included in the provisions of Article 15 reflect a number of Decisions by the European Commission, where the rules of commodities exchanges were examined in light of Article 85 EC Treaty.[148] Clearly the rationale of these rules is to eliminate the obstacles that limit the freedom of investment services providers to operate across their home country. However, the rationale could be questioned at a theoretical level, considering that the required openness of regulated markets may run against the interest of each member to share the benefits of the investments made in an exchange with a limited number of other members.[149]

Finally, in connection to membership lies the requirement that investment firms shall comply with capital adequacy rules imposed by home Member States according to the CAD.[150] Nevertheless, the host State is given the power to impose additional requirements exceptionally, only in respect of matters not covered by the CAD.

2.3. *Compensation schemes*

The ISD and the Investor Compensation Schemes Directive (ICSD)[151] expressly acknowledge that an important aspect of their harmonising activity is investor protection.[152] To this end, the ICSD has introduced investor compensation schemes in all Member States and has harmonised their minimum standards in analogy with the related banking field. As mentioned before, the home country control principle has been chosen for the compensation schemes, but in a modified version.[153] Accordingly, the home country supervisor provides the cover for the compensation scheme, which applies to investment firms and their branches set up in other Member States.[154]

However, where there are disparities between the home and the host compensation schemes, the modified version of the home country control principle is applicable. Then the host Member State acquires a more significant responsibility in two cases. First, if the host State's schemes are more generous than those of the home, then the branch of the investment firm may voluntarily join the host scheme in order to supplement the cover of the home scheme.[155] Secondly, until 31 December 1999, when the level and scope of the home State's schemes where superior to those of the host State, the latter were the maximum an investor was entitled to. The meaning of this provision was that the host country could determine the maximum cover it would provide to the investors within its territory, while the latter could not benefit from the more generous schemes of the investment firm's home country.

It is obvious that such a complex sharing of responsibility between the home and host country's compensation schemes means complex mechanisms for allocating liability[156] and reveals once more the underlying drawbacks of the current home country control regime. The directives themselves seem to realise these problems and have already placed these provisions subject to future reassessment by the Commission.[157]

2.4. Direct intervention by the host Member State

The areas where the host country authorities may intervene in the business activities of investment firms using the European passport are outlined in Article 19 of the ISD. This Article allows direct communication, reporting requirements and enforcement powers by the host Member State.

When foreign investment firms operate in a host Member State through a branch, the supervisory authorities of that host State may require periodical reports on their activities for statistical purposes,[158] or other information in discharging their responsibilities in the conduct of monetary policy and in the conduct of supervision under the ISD.[159]

Article 19 deals with the problem of refusal of the investment firm to comply with the rules of the host State, and lays down the procedures that the host country is required to follow in such a case.[160] The procedure involves four steps of action by the supervisory authorities of the host State. First, authorities shall require the firm to put an end to its irregular behaviour. Second, the failure of the investment firm to take the necessary actions implies a consultation process with the supervisors of the home State, which are obliged to adopt at the earliest opportunity all the appropriate measures and report them to the host State. However, if the home State measures are inadequate or the undertaking persists with its infringements, the host authorities may pursue the third step and prevent the investment firm from initiating any further transactions within the host State. In the exercise of these supervisory powers, host authorities are required to communicate to the home country all the measures taken involving penalties and restrictions. Moreover, all measures of the home and the host State must be justified and communicated to the investment firm concerned and be subject to the right to apply to the courts.[161]

This procedure, and especially the consultation with the home State before any direct action by the host authorities, raises considerable difficulties and questions regarding the current regime. If one accepts the argument that the host Member State should have regulatory and supervisory responsibilities over investment firms that operate within its territory, it is necessary to ensure that the host State has the ability to properly enforce its rules, while keeping the home State informed.

Modern financial markets are very complex and fast moving. To this end, it is not only important for the supervisor to have an understanding of the financial market as a whole, but also to realise that the slightest delay in the imposition of necessary measures may endanger the financial position of investors and undermine the smooth operation of the market. If an investment firm fails to comply with the standards of the host country, the latter cannot afford to consult the home competent authorities and wait for their response. Even if that response occurs 'at the earliest opportunity', Article 19(5) acknowledges the possibility that the home Member State may not take the appropriate action or may not take any action at all.[162]

Even the fourth step taken by the host supervisors does not seem to resolve the problem: in case of emergencies, the host authorities may take any precautionary measures to protect consumers and market participants, which have to be communicated to the Commission and the other Member States. The problem lies in the possibility that the Commission may instruct the host State to amend or abolish these measures, after consulting all relevant competent authorities. In dealing with securities markets, decisions have to be made by authoritative supervisors in short notice in order to protect consumers and market participants. Supervisors cannot be expected to have the necessary authority if they know that their decisions may be finally overturned.[163]

3. Cooperation

In order to facilitate its operation and implementation, the current supervisory regime of home country control, with all its imperfections and modifications calls for a compulsory cooperation between the home and host countries. In order to facilitate supervision, information exchange and cooperation is envisaged between the supervisory authorities and liquidators, auditors, law enforcement and other regulatory authorities of the home and the host Member States. The European Commission has extended these provisions on the exchange of confidential information and has imposed an obligation on statutory auditors and bodies involved in liquidation and bankruptcy to inform regulators of irregularities in the affairs of investment and generally financial undertakings.[164] Nonetheless, exchange information remains subject to the conditions of professional secrecy.[165] The need for enhanced cooperation is discussed in more detail in Chapter 6.

F. Concluding remarks

This chapter provided an overview of the main characteristics of the principle of home country control. Following the failure of initial harmonisation efforts, the European policy-makers have chosen the more pragmatic and flexible approach of home country control and mutual recognition of minimum standards. This regime was thought to constitute the best means of liberalisation of European financial markets and the free provision of services on the one hand, as well as to take more account of national idiosyncrasies and to serve the principle of subsidiarity on the other.

If one looks at the regulatory function of the securities directives, it becomes clear that the principle of supervision by the competent authorities of the home Member State only refers to prudential control. To this end, prudential supervision of investment intermediaries is, in principle, the exclusive competence of the home country and the rules of this country apply. On the other hand, the host country seems to retain responsibility of everyday CBR between the investment firms, which operate within its territory, and their clients. Although certain aspects of cross-border investment services supervision are harmonised by EU law, other areas of competent authorities responsibility are not clearly separated between the home and the host country. Inevitably one has to face the questions: what is the magnitude of home country control imperfections? Do these constitute an obstacle to the fundamental Treaty freedoms? Shall an enhanced home country control regime offer the best solution, or shall we endeavour to find a new structure of EU financial services supervision? And, how far can the home country control principle go?

The ECJ has found unproved that EU legislation works on the principle of home country supervision in the field of investment and financial services law with the intention of subordinating in a systematic way all other rules in that field. Whatever the principle can do, it sits uneasily in the EU financial regulation system and it cannot by itself rectify the EU investment services supervision structural problems. To this end, if the developing and restructuring of European financial services sector demands a new and more challenging approach by EU regulatory and supervisory authorities, there is no legal obstacle that hinders the abandonment of the current home country control regime and the adoption of a better solution. However, in order to examine and argue for or against such a possibility, this book must first pursue a detailed review of the current institutional framework of EU investment services supervision and a critical assessment of the home country supervisory regime. These are conducted in Chapters 4 and 5, respectively.

4
The Institutional Design

A. Introduction

Following the presentation and examination of the supervisory regime of home country control, this chapter turns to the actors behind the scene and sets the investment services policy process of the EU in its institutional context. Research in investment services regulation and supervision has tended to concentrate on defining appropriate objectives and standards and on issues related to efficiency in their operation. Only during the past couple of years have questions on institutional structures received increasing attention and have become a major issue of policy and public debate.[1] The primary reason for this attention is more than obvious. Almost ten years after the 1992 EU 'big bang', it is a common belief that the 'new regime' of financial regulation and supervision has not delivered the benefits envisaged by its creators.

The structure and power allocation between individual institutions in the national, EU or international financial arena determine, in fundamental ways, regulatory and supervisory behaviour. This is one of the basic arguments of the political theory of 'new institutionalism', which emerged as a leading perspective and as a rebellion against behaviouralism in the mid-1980s, an era when institutions became firmly established as areas of scientific investigation in the study of politics, European integration and international relations.[2] The point neo-institutionalists insist on, is that institutions matter, as they determine political, economic and legal outcomes in ways that are often crucial.

This view is supported by this chapter. The overview of the *fora*, in which regulators and supervisors of the European securities sector meet, will explain the origins, tasks and composition of the various institutions and groups. Nevertheless, it is not within the scope of this chapter to examine in detail the policy process of EU securities regulation and supervision. Rather, it will briefly focus on the institutional structure of decision-making and supervision within the Union and comment on its efficiency. The following analysis encompasses the relevant national and international institutions, as well as those created by the EU Treaties. Furthermore, new trends include the emergence of committees, as envisaged by the Commission and the Lamfalussy Group.

Looking beyond the Union's borders, influencing and developing EU financial regulation is not exclusively for Community bodies and Member States. In many respects, and in reaction to the internationalisation of the financial sector, several international standard-setting bodies have been established, notably the Basel Committee on Banking Supervision, the International Organisation of Securities Commissions (IOSCO) and the International Association of Insurance Supervisors (IAIS). In order to promote the level playing field between financial intermediaries of different nationalities and to avoid, if possible, undesirable regulatory arbitrage, these bodies have realised a significant harmonisation of financial regulation. Nevertheless, there remains work to be done by the aforementioned organisations, as well as by the IMF and the Financial Stability Forum (FSF).

Of course, EU harmonisation of financial regulation is more far-reaching than the international *fora*. However, the EU legal framework leaves some discretion to Member States for interpretation and implementation into national legislation, which may negatively influence and undermine the competitive equilibrium. As we shall see later, although the existing prudential and transactional regulation framework may not need a radical overhaul, there is a pragmatic need for a more streamlined, flexible and faster legislative approach to respond to the fast moving environment of financial integration and to the new risks arising as a consequence.[3]

Accordingly, the following section begins by highlighting the origins and the role of international non-legislative organisations. The third section briefly sketches the broad contours of the EU securities policy process and the institutions through which it is articulated, while the fourth section briefly considers some constitutional concerns stemming from the present structure. The last section offers the main conclusions of this chapter.

B. International non-legislative initiatives

1. Worldwide supervisory cooperation

Europeanisation and globalisation are intertwined. Albeit their participation in European groupings, Member States take part in many other international organisations, an important factor that shapes EU policy. Although the integration of financial markets has turned the world into a twenty-four-hour global market, supervisory rules and enforcement mechanisms are still largely organised on a national basis. The major coordinating groups, like the G10 (Group of Ten industrialised countries), may cover the most important financial centres but there are no continuous universal mechanisms for coordination of supervisory policies among national regulators. With respect to financial regulation and supervision, there are three main supervisory groupings working at the international level: the Basel Committee on Banking Supervision, which was formed in 1974, the IAIS established in 1994, and the IOSCO, which, in its present form, dates from 1990. All these bodies share common characteristics, as they provide a forum for supervisors to get to know each other, exchange information and set standards. For this reason they formed in 1996 the Joint Forum on Financial Conglomerates to facilitate information exchange between financial services supervisors of homogeneous and heterogeneous sectors, while they also constitute founding members of the recently established FSF.

2. The Group of Ten and the Basel Committee on Banking Supervision

Within the context of the G10 it is customary for the Central Bank Governors to meet regularly at the premises of the Bank of International Settlements (BIS). The G10 was formed in the early 1960s within the context of the International Monetary Fund (IMF).[4] Like the IMF, the informal G10 grouping discussed economic and monetary matters but did not go into aspects of prudential supervision. The IMF's mandate has remained purely monetary in nature, but the G10 ventured into the area of banking supervision. Ten years after its emergence in 1964, banking failures with international spillovers led the G10 into discussing international cooperation and coordination concerning supervision. The G10 central bank governors have set up a number of advisory groups, which meet at different intervals and report to them. Among these, the Basel Committee on Banking Supervision takes a prominent place.

The Basel Committee, established at the end of 1974, meets regularly four times a year. It has about thirty technical working groups and task forces, which also meet regularly.[5] The Committee's members come from Belgium, Canada, France, Germany, Italy, Japan, Luxembourg, the Netherlands, Spain, Sweden, Switzerland, United Kingdom and United States.[6] Countries are represented by their central bank and also by the authority with formal responsibility for the prudential supervision of banking business where this is not the central bank.

The Committee does not possess any formal supranational supervisory authority, and its conclusions do not, and were never intended to, have legal force. Instead, it formulates broad supervisory standards and guidelines and recommends statements of best practice in the expectation that individual authorities will take steps to implement them through detailed arrangements – statutory or otherwise – which are best suited to their own national systems. In this way, the Committee encourages convergence towards common approaches and common standards without attempting detailed harmonisation of member countries' supervisory techniques. Although still nominally informal, the Committee operates in a carefully organised and structured manner. This operational formality appears to have become more clearly established as the range of its activities and its influence have been extended and increased over time.[7]

The Committee reports to the central bank governors of the G10 countries and seeks the governors' endorsement for its major initiatives. In addition, however, since the Committee contains representatives from institutions that are not central banks, the decisions it takes carry the commitment of many national authorities outside the central banking fraternity. These decisions cover a very wide range of financial issues. One important objective of the Committee's work has been to close gaps in international supervisory coverage in pursuit of two basic principles: that no foreign banking establishment should escape supervision; and that supervision should be adequate.[8] To achieve this, the Committee has issued a number of documents since 1975.[9]

The initial document issued by the Committee in 1975 spells out a division of responsibilities between parent and host supervisory authorities in the supervision of globally operating banks.[10] This 'Concordat', in which the origins of home country control can be traced, states that banks should be supervised by the authorities in the country of their incorporation while certain areas of responsibilities constitute tasks for the recipient authorities. This seeks to ensure that no activities escape supervision. In 1983, the principle of consolidated supervision was included.[11] A bank's subsidiaries were also to be supervised by the parent institution's authorities. The Concordat was further revised in 1990, 1992 and 1996 to include recommendations on cross-border information flows and international banking.[12]

In 1988, the Committee decided to introduce a capital measurement system commonly referred to as the Basel Capital Accord.[13] This system provided for the implementation of a credit risk measurement framework with a minimum capital standard of 8 per cent by the end of1992. Since 1988, this framework has been progressively introduced not only in member countries but also in virtually all other countries with active international banks. In June 1999, the Committee issued a proposal for a New Capital Adequacy Framework to replace the 1988 Accord. The proposed capital framework consists of three pillars: minimum capital requirements, which seek to refine the standardised rules set forth in the 1988 Accord, supervisory review of an institution's internal assessment process and capital adequacy, and effective use of disclosure to strengthen market discipline as a complement to supervisory efforts. Following extensive interaction with banks and industry groups, a second consultative document, taking into account comments and incorporating further work performed by the Committee, was issued in January 2001, with a view to introducing the new framework in 2005.[14] In December 2001 the Basel Committee announced a revised approach to finalising the New Basel Capital Accord and the establishment of an Accord Implementation Group.

Over the past few years, the Committee has moved more aggressively to promote sound supervisory standards worldwide. In close collaboration with many non-G10 supervisory authorities, the Committee in 1997 developed a set of 'Core Principles for Effective Banking Supervision', which provides a comprehensive blueprint for an effective supervisory system. To facilitate implementation and assessment, the Committee in October 1999 developed the 'Core Principles Methodology'.

In order to enable a wider group of countries to be associated with the work being pursued in Basel, the Committee has always encouraged contacts and cooperation between its members and other banking supervisory authorities. It circulates to supervisors throughout the world published and unpublished papers. In many cases, supervisory authorities in non-G10 countries have seen fit publicly to associate themselves with the Committee's initiatives. Contacts have been further strengthened by an International Conference of Banking Supervisors, which takes place every two years, most recently in Basel.

The Committee's Secretariat is provided by the Bank for International Settlements (BIS) in Basel. The twelve-person Secretariat is mainly staffed by professional supervisors on temporary secondment from member institutions. In addition to undertaking the secretarial work for the Committee and its many expert subcommittees, it stands ready to give advice to supervisory authorities in all countries.

3. The International Association of Insurance Supervisors (IAIS)

Established in 1994, IAIS represents insurance supervisory authorities of some 100 jurisdictions. It was formed to promote cooperation among insurance regulators, set international standards for insurance supervision, provide training to members, and coordinate work with regulators in the other financial sectors and international financial institutions.

Since 1999, the IAIS has welcomed insurance professionals as observer members. Currently there are more than 60 observers representing industry associations, professional associations, insurance and reinsurance companies, consultants and international financial institutions.

The IAIS issues global insurance principles, standards and guidance papers, provides training and support on issues related to insurance supervision, and organises meetings and seminars for insurance supervisors. The IAIS works closely with other financial sector standard setting bodies and international organisations working to promote financial stability. It holds an annual conference where supervisors, industry representatives and other professionals discuss developments in the insurance sector and topics affecting insurance regulation.

An Executive Committee, whose members represent different geographical regions, heads the IAIS. It is supported by three main committees: the Technical Committee, the Emerging Markets Committee and the Budget Committee. These committees organise subcommittees, subgroups, working groups and task forces, as needed, to accomplish their objectives.

The Insurance Concordat is one of the most important sets of principles issued by IAIS.[15] First approved in September 1997, these principles have been amended in December 1999 to extend the scope of this paper to insurance business that is conducted on a services basis without any foreign establishment. Their aim is to improve the supervision of internationally active insurance companies, stating that all insurance establishments should be subject to effective supervision, that authorisation involving cross-border activities should be subject to consultation between the relevant supervisors, and that provision should be made for external audits and for information sharing with other supervisors.

Following the Concordat, IAIS issued the 'Insurance Core Principles' in October 2000. Intended to serve as a basic reference for insurance supervisors in all jurisdictions, these principles set out the framework for insurance supervision, identify subject areas that should be addressed in legislation or regulation in each jurisdiction and provide a framework for the IAIS to develop more detailed international standards. The Insurance Core Principles were revised to include essential regulatory and supervisory principles on 'Organisation of Insurance Supervisory Authorities', 'Market Conduct' and 'Cross-Border Business Operations' and replace the Insurance Supervisory Principles issued in September 1997.

The 'Principles on Capital Adequacy and Solvency' came in January 2002 to form an essential building block in the development of more detailed standards relating to capital adequacy and solvency. This paper elaborates 14 principles for evaluating the solvency of life and non-life insurance undertakings. It is also relevant to reinsurers, depending on the degree of regulation of the reinsurance industry in their jurisdictions.

4. The International Organisation of Securities Commissions (IOSCO)

IOSCO is the most important international group in the field of investment services and securities markets. It constitutes a private organisation that developed out of the Inter-American Association of Securities Commissions and similar agencies. In contrast to the Basel Committee, which has limited its memberships to the major developed countries, IOSCO follows a more liberal policy seeking to attract any interested party, even non-governmental organisations. In 2001, its membership included 101 securities regulators, seven associate members, consisting of other financial supervisors and sixty-five affiliate members, including stock exchanges, ISMA and the European Commission.

As it is not a formal international organisation, IOSCO was not formed by treaty or interstate agreement. Rather, IOSCO gathers world's securities regulators to promote high standards of regulation and to adopt common standards. In particular, its members have resolved to cooperate with each other and promote high standards of regulation, to exchange information on their respective experiences, to unite their efforts to establish standards and an effective surveillance of international securities transactions and to provide mutual assistance to promote the integrity of the markets by a rigorous application of the standards and by effective enforcement against offences.

Regarding its organisation, IOSCO has four major components: (a) the Presidents' Committee; (b) the Executive Committee; (c) the General Secretariat; and (d) four Regional Committees. The Presidents' Committee, which meets once a year, has all the powers necessary or convenient to achieve the purpose of the Organisation. The Executive Committee, which consists of nineteen members and meets several times during the year, takes all decisions and undertakes all actions necessary to achieve the objectives of the Organisation. The Regional Committees meet to discuss specific regional problems of the members of the Organisation that constitute them.[16] Finally, IOSCO has a small dedicated secretariat, so that much of the work is done by the members and their staff.

To facilitate the work of the Organisation, the Executive Committee has established two specialised working Committees. The first, the Technical Committee, is made up of sixteen agencies that regulate some of the world's larger, more developed and internationalised markets. Its objective is to review major regulatory issues related to international securities and future transactions and to coordinate practical responses to these concerns.[17] The second specialised Committee, the Emerging Markets Committee, endeavours to promote the development and improvement of efficiency of emerging securities and futures markets by establishing principles and minimum standards, preparing training programs for the staff of members and facilitating exchange of information and transfer of technology and expertise.[18]

IOSCO's website[19] and its Annual Reports show the extent of work done in recent years on setting standards, both for supervisors and supervised institutions. These standards relate to principles of supervision, rules of disclosure and accounting standards, minimum capital requirements and risk management. But progress towards an effective international standard with meaningful specific standards that apply to all financial institutions has been slow.[20] *A fortiori*, by focusing on the preparation of reports, the very weakness of IOSCO lies in its inability to impose its rules. IOSCO has not achieved the regulatory success of the Basel Committee, for example, in implementing global standards for investment firms. Nevertheless, although its principles and rules are not legally binding, the Organisation often seeks to ensure compliance through moral persuasion applied to non-conforming regulators.[21] In this light, IOSCO monitors whether its members have adopted and implemented its standards.[22]

IOSCO must be given some credit though for one of its most significant achievements, namely the first multilateral Memorandum of Understanding (MoU) on consultation, cooperation and exchange of information, which was endorsed by its members in May 2002.[23] This MoU is the result of a process that began in October 2001. Following the events of 11 September

2001, IOSCO announced the creation of a Special Project Team, which explored actions that securities regulators could take to expand cooperation and information sharing.

IOSCO has long been at the forefront of international cooperation and information sharing. This multilateral MoU has been seen as a significant step forward for the Organisation and its more than 170 members. It builds on the many previously existing IOSCO Resolutions and Principles to establish an international benchmark for cooperation and information sharing. Prior to signing the IOSCO MoU, member regulators must establish through a fair and transparent process that they have the legal capacity to fulfil its terms and conditions. It is thus hoped that the process adopted for the implementation of the MoU will provide further incentives for members to raise their respective national standards.

5. The Joint Forum and the Financial Stability Forum (FSF)

Although the Basel Committee, IAIS and IOSCO have been developing general principles for the supervision of the international financial institutions and financial groups on a consolidated basis, they have also been concerned with the specific difficulties created by the development of financial and mix-activity conglomerates. In light of these difficulties, these groupings set up a multidisciplinary working group, made up of regulators from each of the three principal supervisory areas involved, to examine the feasibility of developing general principles for the supervision of financial conglomerates. This working group subsequently became known as the Tripartite Group of Banking, Insurance and Securities Regulators and in February 1996 was formally reconstituted as the Joint Forum.

The Tripartite Group met for the first time in February 1993 and produced a progress report in 1994.[24] A technical subgroup was also set up to examine in further detail issues related to the overall assessment of capital adequacy in financial conglomerates although the results were not made publicly available. As a result of the further work undertaken by the Group, a final Report came out in 1995.[25] Nevertheless, the Report was only issued as a discussion document given the informal nature of the Tripartite Group. A more formal Joint Forum was subsequently established by the Basel Committee, IOSCO and IAIS to develop practical working arrangements between the different supervisors involved.[26] The Joint Forum published a Progress Report on its work in April 1997 in advance of the Denver G7 Summit.[27] It subsequently issued a series of consultation documents on the supervision of financial conglomerates in February 1998. This work was later drawn together in the Joint Forum's final set of recommendations in 1999.[28] Since then, significant work has been conducted by the Forum. In carrying out its new dimension of its original mandate, the Joint Forum has lately performed sectoral comparisons on issues of common interest to the three parent committees. These included the Core Principles issued by the banking, securities and insurance sector and risk management systems and approaches to capital in the three sectors. Reports on these issues were published in 2001. Following the tragic event of September 2001 in the United States, the Joint Forum is about to finalise a cross-sectoral comparison of corporate governance and the use of audit and actuarial functions for supervisory purposes.

The work of the Joint Forum notwithstanding and following the crises experienced during the late 1990s in Asia and elsewhere, a number of immediate and then more considered responses have been developed. Although this work has always been G7 or G10-led, much of this has involved coordinating the efforts of all the existing separate actors concerned. The most important single statement of interest was possibly the 1999 Teitmeyer Report, which was presented to the G7 Bonn Financial Ministers and Central Bank Governors Summit.[29] The specific mandate of the G7 was to consider the arrangement for cooperation and coordination between the various international financial regulatory and supervisory bodies and international financial institutions. In considering appropriate proposals for improved cooperation, it was accepted that fundamental institutional changes were not required. However, a new FSF was necessary to meet regularly and assess issues and vulnerabilities affecting the global financial system and to oversee actions needed to address the problems identified. The FSF was thus formally established in Bonn on 20 February 1999.[30] While many of the key aspects of its composition, mandate and working structure had been set out in the Tietmeyer Report, some more specific operational issues were left to be dealt with at its first meetings.[31] Its core objective was to create a new contact vehicle through which all of the separate bodies represented could meet and exchange views on systemically important issues. In terms of the underlying incentive, however, it could be argued that the FSF was simply set up to allow finance ministers to follow and exercise more substantial control over developments in the financial market area.[32] It is too soon to draw any conclusions. As in the case of the EU, one of the core omissions that exist in terms of international financial market supervision is the absence of any central or overall policy development and central management function. The FSF could represent a significant achievement if it could close these fundamental control gaps, by assuming coordination and a leadership role in this area.

6. Observations on the development and work of international *fora*

Global financial innovation and internationalisation has resulted in the emergence of a substantially unified international banking, insurance and securities system with significant new types of risks that have had to be managed actively at all times. Against this background, financial authorities have attempted to develop an appropriate new national and international control framework. Although the response has initially been limited and essentially *ad hoc*, more comprehensive programmes have subsequently been established in response to particular areas of concern.

While a significant number of problems remains in the creation of effective programmes in the area of financial services, a number of important supervisory and regulatory themes or principles can be identified that are capable of further revision and development. Traditionally, interest has been focused on information exchange and cooperation between national authorities, consolidated supervision and control adjustments, especially through capital adequacy standards. Only recently has attention been shifted to the fundamental objectives of financial supervision, namely the identification and measurement of financial risk and its proper and effective management and control. To the extent that risk often generates from the individual financial institutions, supervision must precisely focus on the quality of the entity's internal risk management systems and on the clear allocation of supervisory responsibilities between the authorities involved. Although little action was, for a long time, taken with regard to internal control, some important work has recently been undertaken in this area.[33] To what extent this will be sufficient remains to be seen. With respect to responsibilities allocation, more work needs to be done in order to take into consideration new challenges that arise in modern international financial markets, such as conglomeration and cross-border provision of financial services.

In the EU context, the European Commission has often incorporated international groupings' standards in its legislative proposals, although in hardly a straightforward and consistent manner. One cannot but agree that international regulatory and supervisory initiatives increasingly exert a significant influence on domestic regulatory policy.[34] Nevertheless, the policy-making role of international groupings and organisations in supervisory arrangements within the single financial market is merely limited if not non-existent. Especially in the investment services field, IOSCO shares similarities with the Committee of European Securities Regulators, as it constitutes another network of supervisors that endeavour to cooperate on issues that do not affect their sovereign supervisory powers. In a financial supervisory environment, which is not yet fully harmonised, national regulators ought to pay more attention to the problems stemming from supervisory arrangements. As the next chapters will show, this constitutes the greatest impediment to the free provision of cross-border investment services within the EU today.

C. The EU policy-making on securities regulation and supervision

Within the EU context, regulation and supervision moves in parallel and is greatly influenced by international initiatives. However, the procedure, by which EU policy-making in general is agreed and supplied, is more formal and complex. It may involve prelegislative consultation, lobbying, delegated legislation and its associated comitology procedure, democratic involvement through legislative hearings and co-decision. Legislation is based on a framework of legally binding, harmonisation directives or regulations, which are founded upon the principles of mutual recognition of national regulators. This combination creates a 'single market', in which financial institutions are supervised by national 'home country' supervisory authorities. The relevant legislative tools are adapted to the rapidly changing financial environment on the basis of proposals developed by the Commission in cooperation with the newly established ESC and the CESR. In this process, the EU ministers of finance, represented in the ECOFIN Council, are jointly responsible with the Parliament for approving the directives, while they are individually responsible for keeping European legislation and national regulation in line with each other.[35]

Interestingly, after stage three of EMU and since Denmark, Sweden and the United Kingdom have decided not to opt for the single currency, a new body has emerged regarding economic and financial policies: the so-called Eurogroup, which consists of the Ministers of Finance of the twelve EMU Member States.[36] The Eurogroup was designed to enable Finance and Economy Ministers of the eurozone to discuss issues relating to their specific responsibilities in the single currency field. Despite its *de facto* informal character, the Group tends to privilege pragmatic formulas for the coordination of EU economic and financial policy.[37] The question, therefore, to be asked is: has the Group emerged as an important body for open heart debates on the orientation of the policies to be conducted by the Member States or is it only a 'talking shop'?[38] Some do not hesitate to regard the Eurogroup Council as an 'embryonic economic government for Europe and a heavy political counterparty to the ECB'.[39] *A fortiori*, the European Council officially recognised the role of the Eurogroup as a forum for economic policy coordination in its December 2000 Nice Summit.[40] Although Euro-12's 'milk teeth' may lack legal sharpness, this does not mean that they will not bite.

Giving, however, the Group visibility and a voice is one thing. Elevating its status beyond that of an informal club is quite another, requiring a Treaty amendment and hence the consent of all EU members. Coordination of economic policies is a vital requirement. Nevertheless, Member States tend to subscribe to commitments that are closer to soft law than to hard Community law.[41] In a recent Communication, the Commission observes that this coordination 'within the Euro-area is based on consensus. It does not aim to impose a decision on a particular Member State but to convince it to apply the policy deemed to be desirable'.[42]

Transferring some responsibilities from the EU to the eurozone level would risk complication and confusion across the board. *A fortiori*, it could also have implications for other EU bodies, such as the important but low profile Economic and Financial Committee (EFC), which prepares the ECOFIN and Euro-12 agenda, the newly established ESC, or even a future European Securities Regulator. Disturbing the smooth functioning of such bodies could affect the EU's entire sense of balance and the effectiveness of EU financial market regulation and supervision.

The currently radical change now affecting European securities regulation is associated with the aforementioned problem as well as with political tensions that need to be offset legally. An important theme within this context is the relations between national and European regulation. It is clear that these relations are yet far from reaching any sort of stable equilibrium, although national and EU legal systems are 'in many ways related with each other, intertwined with each other and open to mutual influencing'.[43] A trend towards greater centralisation in some areas coexists with signs of an evolution towards patterns of coordinated networks in others.[44] Nevertheless, one ought to pay more attention to old and new protagonists that are about to become more and more involved in the process of EU investment services regulation and supervision. These are considered below.

1. The European Commission

The European Commission is the guardian of the Treaty. It has a wide range of general duties imposed on it by the Treaty, many of which are relevant for its regulatory role with regard to investment services. The main source of the Commission's power is its monopoly right to initiate legislation within the first pillar. Because of this right, the Commission plays the most important role on the supply side. Another important function is to ensure that the provisions of the Treaty are implemented and it also monitors the observance of secondary legislation promulgated by all EU institutions, particularly Regulations, Directives and Decisions. With respect to securities regulation, the Commission has been the driving force behind the 1992 'new approach' development and the introduction of home country control. However, the Commission may have extended independent – including regulatory – powers within circumscribed policy areas, such as the CAP, external trade and (especially) competition policy.[45] In all other areas of importance, legislation is adopted jointly by the Council and the Parliament (Article 251 EC Treaty) with the Commission remaining the only institution present throughout the legislative process.

The Prodi Commission, which took office in 1999, flagged the need to reform and move towards 'a single economy and single politics'. In a recent Communication,[46] after referring to a continuing process of European governance, in which national policy coordination and Community policies complement and reinforce each other, the Commission states that it must remain the driving force within that process both through its vision and its action. It will thus 'focus more on its core functions of policy conception, political initiative, enforcing Community law, monitoring socials and economic developments, stimulation, negotiation and where necessary legislating'.[47] How this is done is elaborated in the White Paper on 'Reforming the Commission', which, however, is mainly concerned with its internal organisation, management and working methods.[48]

Nonetheless, the power of the Commission may well extend the political initiative and monitoring role to engage in acts of purely legislative nature. This power is usually delegated by the Council through the comitology procedure, which is employed consciously as a legislative and control mechanism by Member States.[49] The questions that logically arise are why and under what conditions a group of Member State principals might delegate powers to a supranational agent, such as the European Commission. Moreover, what if such an agent behaves in ways that diverge from the preferences of the principals?[50]

It seems that the Commission's most important role is that of a 'manager of policy' decided by other institutions, which themselves have more explicit and less challenging sources of power.[51] This role is encapsulated in its 'European' mandate. In a cross-border context, where all EU countries share the responsibility for achieving the objective of a single market, national authorities and governments may not always be the natural promoters of further integration, since their perspective is mainly domestic. Only the Commission and other EU bodies can play the significant role of bringing an area-wide perspective into the picture. Within this policy management capacity, however, and notwithstanding its significant role in financial regulation, the Commission lacks any supervisory competence over market participants and investment services. Yet the home country control principle, as developed by EU secondary legislation, leaves no doubt. Supervision of individual financial institutions remains in the hands of Member States.

2. Member States' securities commissions

The supervision of securities intermediaries and investment services is ceded to the securities commissions of EU Member States. Of course, when one refers to 'securities commissions' one does not necessarily mean the public authorities that are only responsible for the regulation and supervision of the securities sector. In many countries, securities supervision is conducted by the central bank or by integrated authorities, which are responsible for the banking or the insurance industry as well.

Financial supervision at national level evolved largely in response to events or to EU legislation. Most authorities are of recent origin.[52] The activity of the EU in securities regulation during the last decade has been an important stimulus in the creation of national securities supervisors, which were non-existent before. Their core tasks are quite comparable across border, especially after the creation of FESCO, which allowed a certain degree of convergence in regulatory and supervisory practices. However, the institutional structure of national regulators, as well as their power to develop and implement binding rules, differs substantially from country to country. Different jurisdictions have adopted manifold regulatory and supervisory regimes. In some Member States, all regulation and supervision of markets, clearing-houses and market participants is conducted by one body. In others, different elements of supervision are allocated to different bodies. More particularly, in seven EU countries, securities supervision is carried out by a separate institution (securities commission) and in three, it is integrated with banking supervision;[53] in Denmark, Sweden, the United Kingdom and recently, in Austria, it constitutes part of a single financial regulator.[54] In Ireland, it is the responsibility of the central bank.[55] Current research shows that, in employment terms, around 4000 people work in the different national securities regulators in the EU. Staff numbers, however, vary substantially from Member State to Member State.[56]

Logically, such a complex and fragmented institutional picture of securities supervision does not facilitate cooperation and coordination in supervisory issues. Progress may have been made with the establishment of bilateral and multilateral networks, such as the CESR, but more work needs to be done. National regulators have first to coordinate with the various sectoral authorities within their own national boarders, and then try to establish pan-European groupings. A second impediment relates to the competence of these authorities to adopt or, at least, to influence the adoption of the rules and standards that they agree at EU level. Finally, excessive legalism and mistrust often results in poor or non-compliance with agreed rules as well as in non-convergence of supervisory practices. All these problems, however, are discussed later in Chapter 5.

3. The Lamfalussy Committees and the Forum of European Securities Commissions

3.1. The European Securities Committee (ESC)

The ESC, which was established by the Commission Decision of 6 June 2001,[57] has succeeded the High Level Securities Supervisors Committee (HLSSC).[58] It was initially proposed by the Final Wise Men Report, which was adopted by the Stockholm Council on 23 March 2001 and by the Parliament on 5 February 2002.

Initially, the ESC Decision established the ESC as an advisory body. Later, it was called upon to act in a regulatory capacity, within the framework of the Comitology Decision of 1999.[59] The ESC constitutes the starring actor of the four-level regulatory approach adopted by the Wise Men Reports to speed up the regulatory process of securities regulation and make it more flexible and efficient. The whole process takes full account of the conceptual framework of overarching principles set out in the Reports. Accordingly, Level 1 refers to EU framework legislation and essential measures, which will be adopted by the standard co-decision procedure by the Council and the Parliament. These two bodies will also agree on the nature and extent of the implementing measures to be decided at Level 2 on the basis of Commission proposals. Level 2 refers to EU implementation and the non-essential measures, which will be defined, proposed and adopted, in application of the Comitology Decision, by the Commission and the ESC, while the CESR will act in an advisory capacity. Level 3 refers to strengthened cooperation between regulators to improve implementation, which will be designed to improve consistency of day-to-day transposition and implementation of Levels 1 and 2 legislation. This stage involves the Member States and the CESR. Finally, Level 4 refers to enforcement and involves the Commission and the Member States.

Although the new legislative structure is believed to respond to the need for speed, efficiency and flexibility in securities regulation,[60] it may actually create more problems than it was meant to solve. Mutual suspicion among national and European institutions has complicated the enactment of financial legislation in the EU. Criticism of the framework has come particularly from the EP, which voted in favour of an appeals or 'call back' procedure that would enable the EP to review and halt legislation proposed at Level 2 beyond the scope of the Wise Men Reports. Moving a step further, the Parliament adopted the so-called sunset clause, which will bring to an end the ESC four years after the entry into force of the relevant directives, unless its powers are redefined by a new Commission proposal adopted by the Parliament and the Council.[61]

It comes as no surprise that the EP concerns appear to be shared by market participants, the securities industry and the academia, which foresee a lack of transparency in the adopting of Level 2 implementing measures. The industry requires observatory, at least, participation in any structure of European securities legislation in view of the acceleration pace of change and innovations.[62] Moreover, the European Shadow Financial Regulatory Committee regards the regulatory approach as cumbersome and complicated, for it proposes to create two new committees, rather than simplifying the process.[63]

Another striking drawback and the decisive question of efficiency of the new approach is how one can distinguish between these two levels of legislative measures. How are the essential measures of Level 1 being differentiated with the implementing measures of Level 2? What is to be decided by the normal co-decision procedure of the Council and the Parliament and what should be delegated to the Commission and the ESC? The Wise Men Committee has failed to give sufficient guidance on this issue, but it is clear that the success of the new regime will heavily depend on the clear definition and distinction between essential and non-essential measures.[64]

3.2. The Forum of European Securities Commissions (FESCO)

FESCO was founded in December 1997 by the statutory securities commissions of the EEA area transforming the pre-existing Informal Group of Chairmen into an international organisation. In September 2001, it was replaced by the CESR, as the group of the European securities supervisory authorities. However, a few characteristics of FESCO deserve mention, while some credit should be given to it for creating a forum in its four years of existence, where different supervisors could come together, discuss and agree on hot issues affecting the European securities industry.

FESCO work has concentrated on developing common regulatory standards and enhancing cooperation between members on enforcement and market surveillance. It has been carried out through different structures, such as regular meetings, secretariat general and experts groups. Regular meetings of FESCO, attended by the chairmen of each authority, have been deciding on policy issues, mandates of new work and approval of final reports and standards prepared by the experts groups. These groups were discussing and drafting papers according to the mandate agreed by the chairmen, which were made public after appropriate consultation and approval by FESCO members. The latter were committing themselves to implement the standards approved in their home jurisdiction, where possible, or to press for their implementation.

The problem with FESCO was that it only promoted cooperation and convergence of regulatory and supervisory standards between its members. It did not have a legally binding mandate. A second drawback, which has been inherited by the CESR, was that FESCO (and now CESR) members have different levels of delegated power. This means that negotiations of changes in practice are not easy and implementation powers differ substantially. Even if convergence and adoption of common standards is achieved, their benefits will be undermined or even annulled if one or more national supervisors do not have the necessary power to implement them. The present structure of multiple supervisory authorities reveals that there is no perfect way of demarcating responsibilities between regulatory agencies.[65]

3.3. *The Committee of European Securities Regulators (CESR)*

Following the suggestions of the Wise Men Reports, FESCO has been replaced by CESR ('Caesar' in Brussels vernacular), which was also established by the Commission on 6 June 2001.[66] Like FESCO, the CESR comprises the securities commissions of the EEA countries. Its role is to act as an independent advisory group to assist the Commission, in particular in its preparation of Level 2 draft implementing measures. At this level, as in its Level 3 role, the CESR consults extensively in an open and transparent manner, fully involving market participants, consumers and end-users. The aim is to achieve a balance between effective consultation and efficient use of the limited resources devoted by all interested parties in the regulatory issues in the securities field. It also attempts to balance effective consultation with the fact that, at Level 2, the Committee will be constrained by the scope and timetable of the mandates given to it by the European Commission. All those involved in the consultation process will need to 'play a co-operative game', in other words, to work in a manner that promotes the success of the process.[67]

The CESR organises its own operational arrangements.[68] The costs relating to the administration of the CESR is borne entirely by the national supervisory authorities comprising the membership of the committee. Interestingly, as with the ESC, the Commission plays a key role in the CESR procedures, giving the CESR mandates to discharge within defined time limits. It informs the CESR of ongoing political priorities and contributes to discussions of emerging ideas. The Commission is represented at all meetings of the CESR and is entitled to participate in its debates.

Beyond its consultation role, other tasks of the CESR include:

(a) the fostering and review of common and uniform day-to-day implementation and application of Community legislation (in Level 3);
(b) the issuing of guidelines, recommendations and standards that the members will introduce in their regulatory practices on a voluntary basis;
(c) the development of effective operational network mechanisms to enhance day-to-day consistent supervision and enforcement of the Single Market for financial services; and
(d) the assessment of the evolution of financial markets and the global tendencies in securities regulation and their impact on the regulation of the Single Market for financial services.[69]

As far as transparency and accountability issues are concerned, both the ESC and the CESR have to submit an annual report to the Commission, the Council and the Parliament. The chairmen of the Committees will periodically report to the EU institutions, while maintaining close links between them.[70] It is doubtful, however, whether both the ESC and the CESR documents are subject to a public access obligation. Perhaps the inter-institutional committee, foreseen in Article 15 of Regulation 1049/2001 of 30 May 2001 regarding public access to Parliament, Council and Commission documents,[71] could also discuss future developments in the framework of the comitology procedure in order to develop good administrative practices in the institutions.

Finally, as the last piece in the Lamfalussy jigsaw, an Inter-institutional Monitoring Group was formed and met for the first time on 7 October 2002.[72] It has a mandate to assess the progress made on implementing the 'Lamfalussy process' to secure a more effective regulatory system for securities markets and to identify any possible emerging bottlenecks in this process. In particular, the experts will initially deal with the processes related to the forthcoming Directives on market abuse and on prospectuses, as well as the future proposals for the revision of the Investment Services Directive and for a Directive on transparency of security issuers. The Monitoring Group is expected to report results twice a year, with its first report in spring 2003.

D. Constitutional concerns about the institutional design

Whether regulating and supervising at European or international level, the issues and concerns arising for regulators and policy-makers are similar.

Generally speaking, whether the coordinated partnership involving national, Community and global regulators will operate effectively, depends on two conditions in addition to political independence: first, each participating body must be able to perform the tasks assigned to it and, second, there must be sufficient trust among the partners to keep the costs of transacting within acceptable limits.[73] Especially in the EU, we shall see that both conditions are problematic.[74]

What is evident today is that activities of EU political institutions during the last decade have become less concerned with the management and application of the strategies, structures and instruments associated with the Single Market and more preoccupied with rulemaking through legislation. This evolution raises key normative issues concerning the balance of power between the institutions and, perhaps more importantly, the role of law in structuring and regulating participation in governance networks beyond the formal institutions and procedures.[75] These issues, in turn, raise particular concerns about the relationship between EU legislation and the competitiveness of European financial business.[76] After the introduction of the principle of subsidiarity by the Maastricht Treaty in the early 1990s, as an impulsive response to the fear about the extension of EU-level competence, and the concern that European financial markets acquire potential disadvantages in the global market arena, the European Commission has found itself trapped in the framework it has created. The effectiveness of existing and proposed legislation at that time was brought into question.

Regretfully, the result of these concerns has not been a single and coherent regulatory reform agenda. In March 2001, the Lisbon European Council urged the Commission, the Council and the Member States to develop during 2001 a coordinated strategy to simplify the regulatory environment. Traditionally, legislative review has been conducted by the introduction of the annual 'Better Lawmaking' Reports,[77] the launch of the Simpler Legislation for the Internal Market (SLIM) initiative[78] and, lately, by the establishment of comitology committees. In its interim report to the Stockholm European Council,[79] the Commission contemplated the possibility of making greater use of delegation of the implementing powers vested in it by virtue of Article 202 EC, whereas its 2001 White Paper on Governance proposes re-examining the conditions under which the Commission adopts implementing measures.[80]

This reform, however, was not welcomed smoothly. The Wise Men proposals and the newly established committees have repeatedly faced a campaign, orchestrated by certain circles against the regime they introduced. Robert Goebbels, PES Group Vice President, has condemned the campaigns, which say that the European Parliament is about to 'kill' the proposals of the Wise Men Committee.[81] The main reason for these reactions is that, following the entry into force of the Amsterdam Treaty, the comitology system does not square with the equality between the Council and the Parliament, which underlies the co-decision procedure, since it reinforces one legislative role (the Council) to the detriment of the other (the Parliament).[82] In order to accommodate the European Parliament's concerns and the need for transparency and participation of the industry, the European Parliament has been given reassurance by the CESR with respect to the involvement of all interested parties by creating different layers of consultation, the result of which will be made public. Regretfully, no comparable working relationship has been established with the SEC. Unless this unbalanced situation is resolved and unless a hierarchy of rules and clear distinction between essential and implementing measures is achieved, the efficiency of the new legislative regime and the newly established securities committees will remain under doubt.

At this point, attention needs to turn to the establishment of common strategies, structures and standard procedures for the review of legislative proposals in pursuit for the goal of delivering quality and on-time regulation. Additionally, a further step has to be taken; even if the production of these strategies and standards is accomplished, the question arises, who is going to enforce them and against whom? Are inter-institutional responses well suited to solve the puzzle? These are questions that will be addressed in Chapter 6.

E. Concluding remarks

This chapter has considered the institutional structure of global financial and EU investment services regulation and supervision, which has recently become an issue of public policy debate. A key issue in that debate is whether the current supervisory structure of home country control has an impact on the overall effectiveness and efficiency of regulation and supervision, since this should be the ultimate criterion when making judgements between alternative formats.

The Wise Men proposals came to address and resolve the everlasting problems of legislative delay and ineffectiveness. However, it is more likely that the new four-level approach will create more confusion than it was intended to eliminate, bringing new impediments to the ultimate goal of a single financial market and truly free provision of investment services. The protagonists of the EU securities policymaking face difficulties in defining the limits of their responsibilities and in cooperating within these limits. International non-EU actors, on the other hand, have even less to say in this process. Even if the operation of the new Securities Committee proves successful, institutional and democratic concerns regarding the horizontal delegation of legislative powers limit the Committee's scope and existence. The von Wogau Report merely gives the ESC a very short life, as an ultimate effort to provide the Parliament with leverage over the Commission and the Council to ensure that a 'call-back' mechanism is introduced in the next IGC.

In order to understand the policy process of EU investment services in its institutional context, it is necessary to look at it as a concentrated point of intersection, interaction and filtering between national, supranational and international bodies. Nonetheless, this is not always the case. It is obvious that the attention of the Commission and international bodies often focuses merely on standard-setting and decision-making arrangements, that is the adoption of rules. But the quality of rules also depends on the process of policy-making – including the preparation before and implementation and enforcement after their adoption. Ultimately, the impact of 'first-class' EU decision-making depends on the willingness and capacity of Member States authorities to ensure that rules are transposed and enforced effectively, fully and on time. The latter, however, is hardly guaranteed by the present institutional structure of EU investment services regulation. The following chapter specifically focuses on the advantages and, more importantly, on the drawbacks of the current institutional supervisory regime of home country control.

5
Assessing Home Country Control and Mutual Recognition

A. Introduction

This chapter assesses and critically analyses the principles of home country control and mutual recognition, their position in the context of EU legislation and their effectiveness, efficiency and contribution in the provision and supervision of investment services. Does home Member State supervision of investment firms and mutual recognition of services have negative consequences for the efficient and truly free provision of financial services, as envisaged in the EC Treaty? The answer to this question will assist this book in defining the need for alternative solutions and institutional reforms. Indeed, the first criterion, by way of which the Commission justifies action at EU level, is that the absence of that action might have negative consequences for the effectiveness of instruments envisaged by the Member States and/or be contrary to the requirements of the Treaty.[1]

The 1992 Single Market Programme has brought a new dynamic impetus to the morphology of European financial market regulation and supervision. As analysed in Chapter 2, the centrepieces of the 'new approach' have been the home country control and mutual recognition principles, which have replaced previous full harmonisation strategies. Liberalisation has for long been the desire of financial industries, regulators and consumers. However, it is often alleged that the effects of the new regime on EU financial markets could not have been straightforward. Almost ten years after their imposition, home country control and mutual recognition have not produced the results needed for a real single market. Besides a few brief reports of the European Commission on the progress of the free provision of financial services, as yet there appears to be no overall assessment of the role of home country control. On the contrary, a number of initiatives proposed by the Commission to improve the application of mutual recognition date as long ago as 1980.[2] But, what has been the impact of the current supervisory regime on the flow of capital and the provision of financial services within the Community? Have mutual recognition and home country supervision been proved to be the tools for cross-border liberalisation of financial services, or is it time for EU leaders and regulators to consider other more efficient structural approaches?

In areas where competence is not exclusively held by the EU, the test of 'comparative efficiency' should be applied. EU action should always be proportional to the dimension of the issue at hand. In case the disadvantages and costs of a regulatory and supervisory regime outweigh its benefits, the issues of regulatory approaches and institutional structures should be readdressed. Especially in an area, such as financial services, where market developments move at extremely high speeds, regulatory responses should be prompt and efficient.

As discussed in Chapter 3, the current EU investment services supervisory regime constitutes a division of powers between the home and the host Member State and supports a predominant power of the former although the latter preserves important tasks especially in the area of conduct of business rules (CBR). The new regime has provided financial firms with the European passport, which has made it possible for them to move freely across their home country's borders. At the same time, however, it has failed to overcome certain hurdles to the free provision of investment services, or has even created new grey areas of uncertainty, which hinder intra-Community trade.

This chapter is set out in a simple way. The second section explains the importance of home country control and mutual recognition and the benefits that the new regime has brought to the operation of the Single Market in investment services. On the antipode, the third section analyses the structural faults and the problems of substance, which are responsible for the ineffective functioning of the approach. Finally, the last section draws the main conclusions of this chapter.

B. Advantages and the importance of the principles

The analysis of this chapter begins with the advantages of the 1992 approach. The principles of home country control and mutual recognition play a central role in the operation of the Single Market. The current supervisory structure is characterised as a successful implementation of the 1992 Programme, as it allows free movement of financial services without the need for harmonisation of national legislation at Community level. For the first time, credit institutions and investment undertakings were permitted to operate throughout the EU under the same rules and conditions as in their home Member State, that is under one single set of regulations. Under this regime, the host Member State may oppose the lawful provision of a service by a provider established in another country only under extremely restrictive conditions that involve reasons of public interest, such as consumer protection. It is often argued that home country control has allowed the respect of national sovereignty according to the principle of subsidiarity, has promoted regulatory competition between States and has given way to more flexibility and experimentation in the imposition of supervisory rules. The following paragraphs examine closely these beneficial parameters and assess their validity.

1. Subsidiarity

The application of the home country control and mutual recognition principles is consonant with the idea of a dynamic approach to the application of subsidiarity.[3] The greater the conflict of rules between Member States, the greater the scope for subsidiarity in the sense of the responsibility for decisions being left at the national authorities level. With the avoidance of the drafting of detailed harmonised rules at EU level, this approach ensures more careful observance of local, regional and national needs and traditions, providing thus 'a pragmatic and powerful tool for economic integration'.[4]

In light of the commitments undertaken by the European Commission's Action Plan of 1999 to legislate less but to legislate better,[5] mutual recognition and home country control are considered essential for the operation of the Single Market. Subsidiarity is supposed to be a criterion for choosing what should be done at EU level and what should be left for Member States to regulate. Its dynamism lies in its dual function: on the one hand, it allows Community action to be restricted or discontinued where it is no longer desirable and, on the other, it allows it to be expanded within the limits of its powers.[6] The political will to leave the investment services supervisory power to the home Member State serves the main thesis of subsidiarity that functions discharged satisfactorily by Member States should not be handed over to the centralised EU decision-making bodies.[7] This is the so-called negative version of subsidiarity, according to which the competences of a large organisation should be kept to the minimum in relation to the smaller entities.[8]

Nevertheless, some argue that the subsidiarity principle can only be applied if, in a clear constitutional agreement, the basic allocations are defined, separating in quite a detailed way the competences of the Community level from those of the national and regional levels.[9] Such an arrangement has to include clear specifications as to what and to the extent that responsibilities will have to be shared between different levels and according to which rules. If one accepts the aforementioned argument, it is vital to know, in the home country control context, what is regulated at EU level and most importantly what are the responsibilities of the home and the host Member State with regard to the supervision of financial undertakings. This institutional allocation seems to provide more transparency and precision as well as lower risk and uncertainty than a regime with more blurred functions. Regretfully, as revealed in the following analysis, such an allocation of responsibilities in financial services is not without problems. EU financial supervision reality is characterised by complexities and overlap rather than by the clear division of functions and their clearly delineable effects. In such an environment, the strategic behaviour of Member States' supervisors in the process of negotiating and bargaining may produce non-stable rather than equilibrium solutions suggested by the subsidiarity principle.

2. Regulatory competition

Competition among rules or decentralisation has been seen as the best alternative to the (failed) policies of complete harmonisation that were followed by the Community during the 1960s and 1970s. Its benefits have been heavily debated.[10] First, the advocates of regulatory competition borrow their arguments from the economics of federalism, which deals with the allocation of functions and responsibilities between different levels of government. Firms and consumers can benefit from a wide choice of national regulations revealed thereby and 'vote with their feet'.[11]

Second, those in favour of regulatory competition advocate the need to cope with asymmetric information, between competent authorities and regulated firms or even consumers.[12] According to this view, supervisory authorities (either national or supranational) may have an information disadvantage *vis-à-vis* the undertakings they want to control. Therefore, it may be argued that it is more difficult for firms to hide or to provide false information to decentralised authorities than to a more remote pan-European agency.[13]

Third, the fact that the home country control and mutual recognition principles allow diversities between Member States' rules permits better regulatory competition among them.[14] This can be better realised in the context of CBR. Changes are more easily implemented by the competent authorities because of the freedom to mix strict and liberal rules and to adopt regulation and self-regulation principles. As a result, Member States' supervisors are keen to adopt the most efficient regulatory solutions, which would serve the traditional concerns especially for the health of the financial system and the protection of the small consumer. In addition, regulatory competition, as opposed to centralisation, not only guarantees that the rules in force in a Member State democratically correspond to the preferences of the majority of its subjects, but also enables the minority to seek a more suitable regulatory environment.[15] To the extent that such competition has ever functioned in the area of investment services in the EU, the European passport and the home country control principle have been major facilitating factors.

The authorisation and supervision, for instance, of investment firms by their home Member State allows in theory investment firms from fourteen different regulatory backgrounds to commence business in the financial market of the same host country. This leads to the most interesting consequence that different regulatory regimes would operate side by side within one EU country depending on the origin of the relevant institution within the EU and 'shows the dynamics of the internationalisation even in regulated areas'.[16] Such a multiregulatory environment could make domestic supervisors observe closely the regulations and standards of foreign supervisors through their investment firms and could ultimately force them to alter their own standards and adopt the best practice. Consequently, national supervisors may seek to adopt efficient regulatory solutions as early as possible since this may drive domestic financial institutions to abandon potential moving decisions.[17] On the other hand, foreign supervisory authorities can also be benefited from the level playing field and the exchange of information and expertise between them and regulators from other Member States. Finally, other advantages, such as the reduction of the danger of regulatory failure or the limitation of the loss of national sovereignty, have not benefited from wide acceptance.[18]

Competition, however, in this domain is a double-edged sword. It either has the potential to raise standards and improve the efficiency of regulation and supervision in place or, alternatively, it can promote a general lowering of standards, especially in the consumer protection area. The new supervisory approach in investment services introduced by the White Paper accepting the idea of one licence on the basis of home country control has led to the interesting consequence that different regulatory regimes could operate side by side within the EU. *Prima facie*, it could be alleged that this is the essence of regulatory competition, which might force Member States' regulators to amend their own standards so as to create a level playing field between their own and foreign supervised financial institutions within their territory.[19] Reality, however, does not always mirror theory. It is doubtful whether in the European practice the new approach benefits from the advantages of regulatory competition and whether the conditions for Tiebout-competition apply.[20] Competition between regulatory regimes runs the risk of reducing rather than improving quality and it may better serve the interests of the supervised than of the public. Additionally, regulatory competition presupposes a set of conditions, which have to be met in order for its benefits to apply. As we shall see, these conditions are not being met in the European home country control context, mainly because of two reasons.

First, regulatory competition presupposes economic movement. According to Tiebout's theory, the 'buyers' of legislation (i.e. companies) select among the competing 'sellers' by moving to the place where the legal rules are better. The question arises then, whether financial firms are able to move and whether they actually move. In the field of financial services this movement can take the form of a branch establishment or the provision of cross-border services. However, mobility in the case of a branch requires mobility of capital, goods and workers.[21] While capital can be easily transferred with the new means of telecommunications, for workers the decision to migrate may be more complex. Citizens depend heavily on ties with families and social environment. *A fortiori*, especially in Europe, many movements and cross-border activities are still hindered by linguistic and cultural differences, differences in laws and the blurred division of responsibilities between the home and the host supervisory authorities, which can have a much more significant effect on such decisions than one can consider. Consequently, one should be cautious of advocating competition between rules, since mobility of firms remains modest.[22] While home country control and differences in national regulations set the stage for regulatory competition, 'such competition will not actually occur unless economic agents react to these differences'.[23]

Secondly, for regulatory competition to function, a response from the political market or 'regulatory emulation' is required. Even if one accepts that a reaction does occur within the EU economic market, the response from national supervisors can only have a limited size. The scope or 'margin' for regulatory response is a function of the degree to which national regulations diverge. Home country control and mutual recognition are static notions; the host Member State has to 'accept' as equivalent the regulatory regime of the home State, under which the financial service is produced and marketed. Moreover, the financial services directives have established a certain level of harmonised rules and standards, which limit the possibility for differences between national regimes and, thus, the possibility for defensive regulatory changes.[24] No or slight regulatory adjustments may, thus, be applied. Regulatory competition, on the other hand, is dynamic and presupposes a more diverge regulatory environment.[25] This has hardly been the case in Europe after the 1992 liberalisation programme. On the contrary, EU regulatory and supervisory policies tend to be so bundled together and interdependent, that it is difficult, if not impossible, to identify the impact of differences in regulation in one specific area.[26]

What is evident today in Europe is not a competition between Member States' rules. Member States hardly strive to alter their regulations in a way that it would attract foreign financial entities. Instead, it becomes apparent that they endeavour to retain as many supervisory responsibilities as possible, in order to control domestic and foreign undertakings. This conflict could be described as 'supervisory competition'. The result of conflict and supervisory competition between Member States is that there are weaknesses in the EU's rules for the Single Market in investment services. First, there is considerable doubt whether the minimum harmonisation set out in the directives provides an adequate basis for supervision. Second, the EU still relies much on territorial concepts, which are no longer appropriate to modern financial markets. This reliance leaves too much scope for individual action by Member States, which could interfere with the free intra-Community financial trade and the development of the Single Market.

3. Simplification and experimentation

In addition to subsidiarity, home country control and regulatory competition enables experimentation, innovation and an advantageous flexibility not only to the rules themselves but also to their enforcement.[27] The home country control and mutual recognition principles obviate the need for a certain degree of *ex ante* minimum harmonisation. Certain aspects, such as capital adequacy requirements and prudential supervision, are regulated at EU level, which simplifies the work of national regulators and politicians. Perhaps more importantly, the allocation of responsibilities between Member States offers them the flexible opportunity to find the solution, which best accommodates the needs of the financial industry and consumers. At the same time, national authorities endeavour to identify, in a dynamic way, channels of cooperation with each other.

As such, advantages from home country supervision and competition among rules may follow from a dynamic approach. Both formulation of rules and enforcement are learning processes originating from different regulatory experiences. As stated by Hayek, competition is the most effective discovery procedure, which leads to the finding of better ways for the pursuit of human aims.[28] New legal arrangements may lead to the production of 'voluntary' or 'natural' harmonisation of rules, the scope of which may be superior to the degree of uniformity brought about by an imposed set of harmonised rules.

The EU's implementation of mutual recognition and home country control has hardly reached perfection. The European Commission admits that 'mutual recognition is not always a miracle solution for ensuring the free movement in the single market'.[29] Gerard Hertig characterises the current regime as 'imperfect mutual recognition' but supports its superiority to 'pure' mutual recognition, that is the system where essential requirements have been completely agreed upon in all sensitive areas between the Member States.[30] As it has been proved in financial services' practice, host Member States are more open to accept home country's rules *per se*, especially when they are allowed to retain part of their sovereign supervisory power to pursue non-prudential goals.[31] At the beginning of the twenty-first century, regulatory and supervisory policy must not lag behind the dramatic changes in technology, markets and financial institutions, but it must remain flexible and adjustable to market developments. Where home Member States retain control, they are able to offer more dynamism in regulation and supervision than a single set of harmonised standards.

C. Disadvantages and problems of application: the antilog

After an exploration of the advantages, this section focuses on the drawbacks of the home country supervision and mutual recognition approach.

As the European Commission acknowledges in its latest 'Internal Market Scoreboard', according to results of a business survey presented in November 2001, up to 71 per cent of the European companies asked are still dissatisfied with the way home country control and mutual recognition have eliminated regulatory barriers to trade within the EU.[32] The underlying problems behind the statistics are various and complex. In order to assist this analysis, we shall divide them as structural faults and problems of substance.

1. Structural faults

In light of the institutional structure examined in Chapter 4, three structural faults of the current supervisory system are identified: protectionism and regulatory arbitrage, differences in legal systems and cultures and complexity and competence of national supervisors. Some of these weaknesses may have preceded the home country control and mutual recognition regime. It's imposition, however, has made them more visible and acute.

1.1. Protectionism and regulatory arbitrage

As described in Chapter 2, the philosophy underlined in the EC Treaty and the Single Market Programme is that of economic liberalisation; Member States' supervisors are obliged to accept unduly provision of financial services within their territory originated from undertakings authorised by their home country. Nevertheless, despite their agreements in drafting investment services directives and by taking advantage of the Achilles' heel of the present regime of home country control, national supervisors may still attempt to protect their national financial markets, given their inherent strategic importance. The most problematic issue in this context is that EU law, which was primarily designed to promote competition, may be misused by a Member State to justify a protective national policy as a priority, which can have a negative effect on foreign financial firms.

It has been suggested that the EU regulatory and supervisory framework suffers from regulatory arbitrage,[33] which is not considered by the Community to be inherently desirable. Hence, the investment services directives lay down only minimum standards, which means that Member States can, if they choose, impose stricter or additional conditions of authorisation to those set out in the directives. Yet, the picture is not the same in fields that the EU harmonisation programme has left untouched. One such field is CBR. The trend towards consolidation of European stock exchanges may leave a bulk of EU peripheral countries out of the race. Hence, it would not be irrational to assume that these countries may endeavour to find other ways of attracting trading volume, without necessarily being interested in raising consumer protection standards. Consequently, the hypothesis that some investment entities might be interested in the possibility of regulatory forum shopping and of becoming incorporated in the Member State, where conditions in general are perceived to be more favourable to them, becomes more realistic.

The same conclusion would be drawn if recent market developments were viewed from an economic and political analysis point of view. The theory of 'public choice'[34] or the 'economic theory of regulation' use economic analyses to explain the outcome of collective or non-market decision-making.[35] Since man is *homo economicus*, he behaves as utility maximiser seeking to satisfy his self-interest, which is defined narrowly as net wealth.[36] Hence, financial firms demand regulation to advance their private interests. They value regulation according to their interest and choose the one, from which they gain the highest utility. To this end, it is likely that these financial groups lobby Member States' governments and solicit their intervention in order to achieve maximum benefit. Accordingly, politicians and regulators, who are also utility maximisers according to the aforementioned theories, might provide rules that serve particular financial institutions in order to further their own interest.[37] Although European countries are increasingly becoming more interlocked as a result of financial market integration, it is not always the case that they are interested in resolving their differences.[38] Consequently, it would not be immoderate to allege that the ability of host country's regulators to negotiate with market intermediaries and to enact rules under their responsibility is seriously prejudiced by the increased influence of financial institutions over national regulator's rule-making, and not by the public good.

Where arbitrage opportunities are provided through the free movement of services, the targets are the companies, which are involved in the provision of these services. These undertakings will seek to respond in either of two directions. They will either endeavour to directly relocate and migrate to another Member State, the regulatory framework of which better serves their economic objectives, or they will try to reform their corporate structure, in order to compete – at least to a certain extent – with other financial firms operating in countries with lighter regulatory burden.[39] Both responses could have a negative effect on the provision of investment services within the Internal Market. The former could be characterised as a direct expression of approval of the Member State's move to lower its regulatory standards and thus undermine the protection of its consumers. On the other hand, the latter could have a direct effect on the quality of services provided by the firms concerned or even on the macroeconomic situation of the country, where it is incorporated.[40]

Regulatory arbitrage comes into direct conflict with the philosophy that each Member State's authorisation procedure should broadly reflect the same standards. To this end, the directives have set up some defence mechanisms against this eventuality. In the Preamble to the ISD, for instance, it is envisaged that Member States' competent authorities should hinder the authorisation of a financial firm, when it is clearly indicated that it

> has opted for the legal system of one Member State for the purpose of
> evading the stricter standards in force in another Member State within

the territory of which it intends to carry on or does carry on the greater part of its activities.[41]

Accordingly, the ECJ has acknowledged that a Member State is entitled to take steps to prevent a service provider whose activity is entirely or mainly directed towards its territory, but which has become established in another Member State in order to circumvent the rules that would apply to it if established in the State where it commences business, from exercising the freedom to provide services.[42] Nevertheless, tantalising questions come inevitably to one's mind: in what way is a supervisory authority capable of identifying the true intentions of an investment firm in order to refuse granting authorisation? Do factors, as the content of programme of operations, the geographical distribution or the activities actually carried on, suffice to underline such intentions?

In the recent decision *SIB v Scandex*,[43] the Civil Division of the Court of Appeal revealed the danger of regulatory arbitrage. The case involved a British citizen, who established a Danish investment firm and tried to take advantage of the less sophisticated rules of Danish law[44] in order to obtain authorisation and use the passport to commence investment business within the United Kingdom. Scandex has never applied for authorisation under the Financial Services Act of 1986. Instead it only secured interim authorisation by the Danish authority, which was not enough to satisfy the UK requirement under the FSA. The evidence shows that Scandex began trading in the United Kingdom before the implementation of the ISD by Denmark. Consequently, it was not regarded as a European investment firm to take advantage of the European passport. The result could have been different if the Danish authority had granted full authorisation, which would have insulted the intention of the Preamble to the ISD and would have supported allegations of regulatory arbitrage. However, the Preamble expresses no more than a pious hope, for the operative provisions of the ISD do nothing to force the competent authorities of the Member States to turn away investment undertakings applying for authorisation. This hope will not avert a potential race to the bottom in the Single Market, so it would be desirable for the EU to act to prevent regulatory arbitrage as soon as possible.[45] However, since home country control and mutual recognition presuppose a certain degree of harmonisation, the scope of arbitrage is correspondingly lower than if free provision of services had been recognised without any prior harmonisation. It could be alleged, therefore, that the scope of arbitrage is reversibly analogous to the degree of harmonisation.

1.2. *Differences in legal systems and cultures and complexity*

Differences between Member States' legal orders and cultures have always been one of the main obstacles to European integration. One could begin with the fundamental distinction between common law and civil law countries. Based on Roman Law, codification started in Europe in the second half of the eighteenth century, but it really expanded in the nineteenth.[46] However, a number of European Anglo-Saxon countries have pursued a different legal route,[47] while others were less influenced by Roman Law.[48]

Europe is far from homogeneous in economic models too. From the Scandinavian social model through the Dutch 'polder model'; from dirigisme in France, public/private partnerships in the United Kingdom to the 'family capitalism' in Greece and Italy. These diversities are evident in the securities sector. The national legal systems relating to the nature of and dealings in securities have evolved to reflect the specific socio-economic culture of each Member State. As a consequence, there is substantial diversity in the legal treatment of securities across the EU. While the law may be well understood by participants in any one national market, the scope for complexity and uncertainty in the legal treatment of securities where more than one jurisdiction is involved leads to an inevitable lack of clarity for all. Problems of legal complexity and uncertainty are set to intensify as securities transactions increasingly involve more than one jurisdiction.

Variations between investment services and cultural differences between Member States may be illustrated by a number of paradigms. Characteristic is the one of investment services marketing. Member States, where cold-calling[49] is a useful technique, are likely to regulate such activities in more detail than Member States where the phenomenon is unknown. Here, an example, which makes the European passport completely useless, deserves mention. It involves a significant hurdle that non-French investment firms have to face when intending to provide cross-border services in France; French law has a provision relevant to '*démarchage*' (door-to-door selling) since 1972,[50] which is still in force. According to that provision, foreign investment firms are obliged to obtain a '*carte d'emploi*' from a French public authority, before commencing any business in France.[51] If they fail to do so, they may have to face civil and penal sanctions in accordance with Article 1384 of the French Civil Code and Article 405 of the French Penal Code respectively.[52]

It was a matter of time that a case with reference to cold-calling would reach the European Court. In *Alpine Investments*,[53] the Court has recognised the right to prohibit this marketing practice in financial services after examining a provision of Dutch law, which was designed to protect the reputation and reliability of the financial market in the Netherlands. Nevertheless, pending harmonisation in this area,[54] we shall avoid trying to establish any general rules for the compatibility of cold-calling. Each case should be assessed individually.[55]

Another field where different cultures and lack of consensus have prevented the emergence of a Single Market is pension funds. Many Member States still impose portfolio restrictions that limit foreign investments. Consequently, pension funds have little incentive to commence cross-border financial business.[56] The liberalisation of this field would surely give a great boost to cross-border financial services trade.

Divergences do remain between Member States' private laws, as the EU legislature does not have general competence to create harmonised or uniform private law. The multiplication of legal orders and variations in the level and methods of protection in the regulation of the same transaction leads to increased costs of compliance and raises the possibility of conflicts of rules.[57] Here, one can recall the paradigm of the German Stock Exchange Act, which protects investors against the risk of futures contract.[58] This provision has initiated the *Koestler* case, which involved a conflict between German and French rules.[59]

In addition, many Member States' cultural barriers are playing a significant role in slowing market integration. Two types of cultural barriers can be identified. First, those that can be dealt with by public policy, such as different approaches to corporate governance, market consultation, and, more importantly, to practical implementation of EU directives on the mutual recognition of prospectuses and listings.[60] Second, others that hopefully will converge as markets integrate, such as different entrepreneurial cultures, which in many cases are slowing the supply of new high-growth companies for the equity markets.[61]

Finally, differences may occur in interpreting certain conditions and provisions in the field of investment services. In electronic trading, for example, reaching consensus on a pan-European approach to the question of when a web site communication will be considered to be an offer of financial services taking place within a particular jurisdiction is unlikely, because that determination must be based on the particular circumstances and the laws of each jurisdiction.[62]

All these paradigms remind us that divergences in minimum standards and supervisory practices have not yet disappeared entirely with the Single Market Programme. Integration has been incremental, rather than dramatic. Many of these gaps and deficiencies are being tackled by new legislation. But results will take far too long at the present rate of progress. Secondary legislation presupposes a complex and time-consuming process, which may cause disparities between national laws and their implementation.

Despite the improving coordination role of the European Commission, it often finds itself ill equipped to monitor implementation and enforcement of Community measures. It is true that European regulators tend to pay more attention to rulemaking than to the effective enforcement of the rules they produce. Thus, by limiting the role of the Commission in the implementation process, Member States have encouraged a tendency to focus on the transposition of EU directives rather than on effective compliance, convergence of supervisory practices and actual results.[63] This problem was highlighted in the Report of a high-level group appointed by the Commission,[64] which pointed out that by abandoning the imposition of uniformity, the 1992 approach had created intricate arrangements lacking transparency and requiring improved coordination.[65] The blurred supervisory responsibilities between the home and the host Member State in the field of investment services justify that approach.

The outcome is that over-complex or ill-conceived legislation imposes additional costs and burdens on business, *inter alia* reducing competitiveness. The Commission has already made some effort to simplify legislation and to facilitate free movement within the Internal Market[66] including the implementation of the SLIM initiative and the Business Test Panel scheme. The SLIM project, however, has not yet blessed the field of investment services. The results in terms of impact on existing or planned legislation continue to fall short of the expectations of financial intermediaries, issuers and consumers. Alternatively, truly free intra-Community trade of investment services and a level playing field for financial operators require increased market integration and a different regulatory response by EU institutions and Member States' supervisory authorities.

1.3. Competence of competent authorities

The success of home country control within the Single Market Programme in investment services depends to a great extent on an assumption by each Member State that the supervisory authorities of the other Member States will be competent[67] to ensure that the financial firms, which they authorise and prudentially supervise, abide by the minimum standards prescribed in the relevant directives and the soft law. Yet, there is no legal act or established body at EU level that specifies and ensures such a competence. Instead, Member States' competent authorities rely on their mutual trust and mutual agreements as well as on established Community law and harmonised minimum standards.

Naturally one may wonder: who ensures the propriety of the national supervisory houses and how competent are the 'competent authorities'? Because of institutional, historical, legal and other factors, and notwithstanding certain harmonisation in specific rules, different supervisory authorities tend to practice their supervision by different methods, and consequently there is no single methodology that can be used as a 'standard' within the EU. The problem may acquire a more serious dimension, when their tasks comprise the consolidated supervision of multinational financial groupings.

One of the most significant institutional impediments national supervisors face today is the divergence in the range of powers available to them. Some have wide discretion to issue rules – which can be used to implement directives – whereas in other Member States directives have to be implemented through legislation.[68] This can lead to some Member States being less able than others to implement directives quickly. They will also find it more difficult to act on agreements of standards reached in bodies such as the CESR. Quite importantly, the question arises whether some Member States have failed to implement Article 22(3) of the ISD, which provides that 'the authorities must have all the powers necessary for the performance of their functions'.

Although there is no mechanism to ensure the incompetence of a national supervisor, certain examples of behaviour may imply its lack of propriety. First, one could mention the extent and quality of the prudential reports, which the home country supervisor receives. Do these adequately measure capital adequacy, market risks, asset quality and provisioning requirements? Second, the methods employed by or available to the competent authority to verify the accuracy of prudential reports. Third, the willingness and capability of home Member States' supervisors to visit and examine entities in other countries, as well as the willingness of the host authorities to provide the requested information. It is essential that both authorities establish information links in order to overcome legal impediments, as bank secrecy rules. Fourth, the track record of the home supervisor in taking remedial action and enforcing rules, when problems arise in the operation of financial firms. Last, but not least, the misunderstanding and misuse of certain concepts and principles. A characteristic and hardly theoretic paradigm is the misuse of the 'general good' concept. There is evidence in the area of financial services of the inappropriate use of the concepts of 'general interest' or 'general good' to justify exemptions from the application of home country control and mutual recognition and to prevent the marketing of financial products, which are validly sold in the home Member State. The European Commission has found that the misuse of 'general good' stems from differences in interpretation and application by national authorities.[69] According to the analysis carried out by the Commission, there is a need to improve and reinforce the knowledge of the competent authorities of the Member States regarding the principles of home country control and mutual recognition.

Nevertheless, the most convincing and visible way of assessing the incompetence of a Member State supervisor is when one of the investment firms, which lie under its supervision, fails to meet the minimum standards when commencing business beyond its national borders. In this way, the incompetence of the home supervisor will become evident and may cause anomalies not only in the home market, but also in the host market, where the firm provides cross-border services. Consequently, the host supervisors may become reluctant to welcome investment firms authorised by the supervisory authority in question, without first checking its competence, and thus an unpleasant situation would be created, which could undermine the free provision of services and the function of the European passport itself. Of course the task of monitoring the behaviour of any institution, which conducts its investment business on a cross-border basis, is not the simplest task. A potential violation of its behaviour may test the competence of the host regulatory authority as well, since a request made directly to the investment firm may not be sufficient and the assistance of the host supervisor may be vital.

Competence of the competent authorities is vital, for the credibility of the home country control approach requires mutual trust between the national supervisors. Mutual trust and loyal cooperation among the Member States were mentioned as the first elements of home country control in the White Paper of 1985, as they were supposed to replace the (then) impossible task of harmonising vastly different national systems. Welby writes 'the law cannot and should not hope to cover every wrinkle of business practice. Poor ethics in the long term destroys business'.[70] If a national supervisory body does not trust the competent authorities of other Member States to keep the providers of investment services up to the minimum EU requirements, there will be a reluctance to recognise the services supplied from the country concerned. In such a case, pressure for the reintroduction or maintenance of national control on the host Member State basis could be increased, which could endanger a reversion to fragmented EU financial markets. At the very least, lack of mutual trust between the competent authorities would mean that the home country control and mutual recognition regime does not work, which, in turn, would undermine the function of the Single Market itself.

To conclude, structural defects of home country supervision and regulation and mutual recognition, including protectionism, legalism, non-competence and excessive complexity may be explained in part as a consequence of insufficient trust among Member States and between them and Community institutions. It is sometimes argued that such faults and complexity reflect the technical protectionism of the Commission, but this explanation lacks plausibility: the Commission is not only understaffed, but also lacks in-house research capabilities and is largely composed of generalists and not technical experts. Instead, the 'majonist' mistrust reasoning shall be accepted; doubting the commitment of other governments to implement European rules honestly, national representatives often insist on spelling out mutual obligations in the greatest possible detail.[71] Mistrust among the Member States and other structural faults of the present system contribute significantly to the exploration of alternative cooperation solutions and potential centralising trends at EU level, which national governments may deplore.

2. Problems of substance

Following the structural faults, five more drawbacks closely interlinked with the substance of the home country control and mutual recognition system deserve mention. Two of them constitute problems of definition, one relates to the overlap of responsibilities between the home and the host country, one deals with the state-of-the-art means of provision of investment services and the last considers the treatment of third non-EU countries.

2.1. What is the 'home country'?

For reasons of identifying the principal supervisor of a financial firm, it is essential to know where exactly a firm is incorporated. According to the ISD, the allocation of the home country is a simple task. It provides that 'home Member State' shall mean:

> a) where the investment firm is a natural person, the Member State in which his head office is situated and b) where the investment firm is a legal person, the Member State in which its registered office is situated or, if under its national law it has no registered office, the Member State in which its head office is situated.[72]

Unsurprisingly, the Directive does not specify the definition of the 'head office'. It would be convenient to suggest that 'head office' is the establishment of the headquarters and the management of the firm. However, this solution would hardly serve the scope of the Directive in the case where a firm had its headquarters in a Member State, but it solely commenced investment business in another.[73] Would it be rational for the first Member State to supervise a firm that is not conducting business within its borders? Apparently not for the drafters of the ISD.[74]

The interest is presumably less in the administration than where the business is done, where the records are kept, or where the contract notes are issued from.[75] The ISD provides that not only has a firm to actually carry on its business be granted authorisation by its home State, but also it has to deal at least with the 'core' investment services, specified in Section A of the Annex.[76] Nowadays, of course, the inquiry of where securities business actually takes place is not one without complexities. But, it would be appropriate to assume that the 'head office' is the location of the central administration and decision-making management of the firm *and* where the main or principal investment business is established.[77]

The aforementioned solution is valid whenever the competent authorities have to deal with a financial institution, which is dressed with a clearly domestic costume. But would it also be applicable if financial firms were to be established under European law? As financial firms consolidate and reorganise themselves on a cross-border basis, their nationality and the identification of their responsible principal supervisory authority is becoming more difficult. It is easy for financial institutions to mask their origin. This is particularly true in the European context, especially after the recent adoption of the European Company Statute. Additionally, and in an effort to face consolidation, the solution proposed by the European Commission, that is the appointment of a coordinating supervisor for large financial groups by national authorities, is not one without problematic parameters.[78] However, the European Company and associated consolidation issues will be taken up later in Chapters 6 and 8.

2.2. Grey responsibilities between the home and the host Member State

As analysed in Chapter 1, two of the primary considerations and objectives of financial services supervision are financial integrity and consumer protection. To this end, home and host competent authorities are responsible for the prudential and business activities supervision of financial firms respectively. However, the separation between prudential and transactional supervision implies two levels of rules applying, which have the same focus and objectives. From the very moment the ISD was passed, it has been criticised for its failure to achieve this separation,[79] as it has given rise to a great deal of overlapping rules and ambiguity. This problematic approach is more acute in the SBD, where neither explicit division is made between authorisation and transactions, nor is there an Article 11-style provision with regard to CBR.[80]

Although a certain harmonisation has already taken place in the areas of consumer protection and in advertising,[81] one could identify various differences from country to country. First, difficulties arise in the application of home country control and mutual recognition to investment services when host Member States take steps to protect the general good. By this means, the principal Treaty freedom of services within the Single Market can be hindered. Second, variations could occur because of different interpretations of authorisation and prudential rules on one hand and transactional rules on the other and their assignment to the supervisory power of the home or the host Member State respectively. The vague drafting of the relevant ISD provisions intensifies the grey areas of responsibility. Third, CBR between investment firms and their clients vary substantially from country to country. Consequently, a financial firm wishing to establish itself or to provide cross-border services can hardly avoid complying with more than one set of CBR, which constitutes a significant obstacle to the free provision of financial services. Fourth, problems could arise because of different priorities given to the needs of investors. Indeed, the ISD itself states that, when applying CBR between the financial institutions and their clients, Member States shall take into account the professional experience of the person to whom the service is provided. However, the Directive does not offer any further guidance regarding the shape of application of CBR and the construe of 'professional' investors. It is, therefore, very likely that Member States, in which consumerism is more developed, will devise more stringent CBR *vis-à-vis* inexperienced persons than other Member States.[82] Finally, rules relating to advertising and marketing of investment services are not clearly allocated to the home or the host Member State, which also creates a great deal of confusion. Although the letter of Article 13 ISD gives the impression that advertising rules are subject to the host State power in the interest of the general good, nothing hinders the home competent authorities from imposing their own rules on financial firms as well.

In an effort to assess the magnitude of problems in the provision of investment services one could consult the potential complaints that originate from businesses or individuals. In its Mutual Recognition Communication, the Commission states that it has received many complaints for services including business communications, construction, patent agents and security services. However, if one attempted to apply this test on investment services, one could possibly come to the conclusion that the criterion for receiving complaints is not very appropriate in that providers of investment services, for example, do not tend to submit complaints to the Commission. Instead, in most cases, such complaints should be directed to the host Member State's competent authorities, with which the financial firm is required to develop a long-term relationship.[83]

2.2.1. The general-good concept.   The main purpose of the ISD is to enable authorised financial institutions in a Member State to supply, throughout the EU, cross-border investment services either by the establishment of a branch or under the freedom to provide services. EU law has not, however, harmonised in full the content of financial activity. It is likely, therefore, that a financial firm wishing to provide services in another Member State will be confronted with different rules applicable both to the service itself and to the conditions in which it may be offered and marketed.

As described in Chapter 3, the home country control principle includes a mixture of responsibilities between the home and the host Member State. In between the struggle of the home and the host country to keep for themselves more and more regulatory and supervisory tasks interferes the general-good concept, which blurs this division even more. It is, thus, crucial in the assessment of the efficiency of home country control to examine where lies the power of the host State to impose its own rules – namely CBR and marketing rules – on foreign financial undertakings. The greater the competence of the host authorities, the greater the possibility for differences and conflicts, and the greater the disadvantage for firms, which provide intra-Community services. On the other hand, if the host country's supervisory responsibility is limited by the general-good concept, the burden on foreign firms is lighter and the European passport acquires a more pragmatic dimension.

It is well established that a measure restricting freedom to provide services may be justified on the basis of two different categories of grounds, namely: (a) by an exemption expressly provided for by the Treaty (e.g. Articles 45 and 46 EC that are applicable pursuant to Article 55), or (b) by other grounds of justification that are not provided for by the Treaty but which have been recognised by the Court and accepted by it as overriding requirements in the general interest.[84] With regard to investment services, in particular, EU secondary legislation considers that a financial firm operating in the context of home country control and mutual recognition could be forced to bring its services into line with the rules of the host country only if the measures relied on against it are in the interest of the general good, whether it is acting via a branch or under the freedom to provide services.[85] This approach is, moreover, confirmed by the ECJ. In the following analysis, the drafting of the ISD as well as the relevant case law of the European Court shall be examined.

The financial services directives do not contain any definition of the general-good concept.[86] The reason for this, according to the Commission, is that, in non-harmonised areas, the level of general good involved depends on the assessment of the Member States and can vary substantially from one country to another according to national traditions and the objectives of each Member State.[87] Similarly, the directives do not specify within what limits and under what conditions the host State may impose its general-good rules upon a European financial undertaking. It is, thus, necessary to refer to the relevant provisions, before exploring the case law of the ECJ. In investment services, a careful examination of the ISD reveals that, in general, various limitation on an *ad infinitum* applicability of the host country's CBR already flow from its provisions. Therefore:

(a) Article 28 ISD prohibits rules of discrimination;[88]
(b) Article 11(1) ISD requires that rules of conduct be 'applied in such a way as to take account of the professional nature of the person for whom the service is provided';[89]
(c) Certain CBR may fall under the provision of Article 14(2) ISD, which prevents host Member States from applying on foreign investment firms measures that have an equivalent effect to the provision of endowment capital;[90]
(d) With regard to the establishment of a branch or the provision of cross-border services, Articles 17(4) and 18(2) ISD empower the host Member State to indicate the conditions of business of the foreign investment firms in the interest of the general good;[91]
(e) In addition to the indication of conditions, Article 19(6) empowers the host Member State 'to take appropriate measures to prevent or to penalize irregularities committed within their territories which are contrary to the rules of conduct introduced pursuant to Article 11 as well as to other legal or regulatory provisions adopted in the interest of the general good'.[92]

As it becomes obvious, the wording of these provisions hardly removes the ambiguity of the broad drafting of Article 11. Especially the latter provision of Article 19(6)[93] is less clear with respect to the dilemma in issue. If CBR are considered to be part of the 'other legal or regulatory provisions adopted in the interest of the general good', then the host Member State can only impose CBR subject to the principle of general good. On the other hand, it is argued that the word 'other' comes to distinct CBR from the rules adopted in the interest of the general good.[94]

The latter view cannot be easily supported. The formulation of the aforementioned provisions as well as the general background and objective of the ISD imply a different approach. The wording 'including the rules of conduct' of Articles 17(4) and 18(2) indicates that CBR constitute a part of the conditions that lie under the scrutiny of the general-good concept. Additionally, when one observes the background of the ISD, one clearly realises that the aim is to secure freedom of establishment and freedom to provide services through the principles of mutual recognition and home country control.[95] In this light, host Member States must ensure that there are no obstacles to prevent activities that receive the European passport from being carried on in the same manner as in the home Member State, as long as they do not conflict with laws and regulations protecting the general good in force.[96] Although the ISD hardly endeavours to completely eliminate the differences between the Member States' national regulatory and supervisory regimes, the broader the power of the host State remains, the greater is the risk of dominant differences. Limiting the host State's regulatory and supervisory power to the general-good concept is better suited to the main objectives mentioned earlier. At the end of the day, the concept of general good is an exemption to the fundamental principles of the Treaty with regard to free movement and must, therefore, be interpreted in a *stricto sensu* fashion.

Given the ambiguity of the ISD outlined before, one should read and interpret the host State's power to draw up and supervise CBR in conformity with the ECJ case law. Although the Court has traditionally confirmed that only the general-good rules can restrict mutual recognition and hinder the exercise of the two fundamental freedoms, namely the freedom to provide services[97] and the freedom of establishment,[98] an uncertainty prevails at present with regard to the case law concerning the Treaty freedoms. The *Keck* judgement especially has reopened the issue and initiated a new series of discussion.

Going back to *Cassis*,[99] the ECJ tried to control the host (importing) State's power in light of Article 28 EC (former Article 30) by laying down two principles. First, it recognised a derogation from the free movement of goods in so far as the measures of the importing country are necessary to satisfy mandatory requirements.[100] Second, the Court accepted that the unilateral requirements imposed by the rules of the importing Member State are incompatible with the provisions of Article 28 of the Treaty, if the goods have been lawfully produced and marketed in the home Member State.[101]

With regard to services, the Court made clear in *Säger* that Article 49 EC Treaty (former Article 59) applies to host country's rules and requires the abolition of any restriction, even if it applies without distinction to national providers of services and to those from other Member States, when it may impede the activities of a provider of services established in another Member State. The only requirement is that host Member States may impose measures on a non-discriminatory basis justified by 'imperative requirements of public interest', if that interest is not subject to the rules of the home State, and that they are objectively necessary to attain the interest involved.[102] Applying the general-good concept and the 'no overlapping controls' and 'proportionality' tests in a number of judgements,[103] the ECJ limited the power of the host State.

Yet, the ECJ found it necessary in *Keck* to re-examine its case law and widen the scope of application of the *Cassis* doctrine arising from Article 30 EC Treaty regarding free movement of goods. The Court made a distinction between provisions relating to 'marketing, selling arrangements and methods of sales promotion' on the one hand, and rules laying down product requirements on the other.[104] The latter falls within the scope of Treaty provisions.[105] In contrast to what has previously been decided, the application to products from other Member States of the host State's former measures is not as such so as to hinder directly or indirectly intra-Community trade, as long as the rules 'apply to all relevant traders' and affect them 'in the same manner, in law and in fact'.[106]

The Court clearly departs from its earlier practice relating to goods. In assessing the consequences for services, the difficulty lies in the application of the aforementioned distinction in the provision of financial services and especially in CBR.[107] Although the ECJ hardly provides clear support for limiting the host State's power to draw up and supervise CBR, one should not immediately conclude in favour of its *in toto* authority. In addition, the case law does not attempt to remove the dubious status of the ISD and clarify the dilemma. In any case, even if one accepts that CBR are not limited by the concept of general good, the general principle of EU law still applies that national measures used to achieve a given end must not go beyond what is appropriate and necessary to achieve that end, that is the proportionality test.[108]

At least in banking, the Commission's guidance[109] does emphasise that rules, whose objective is to protect consumers, are more likely to be regarded as satisfying the general-good test, except perhaps where the client has on his own initiative chosen to use a European institution established only outside his/her own Member State. Much will depend on individual cases, where the need for protection of the consumers will be examined, as well as his level of sophistication and the nature of the service.[110] In *Commission v Germany*, the European Court held that 'there may be cases where, because of the nature of the risk insured and of the party seeking insurance, there is no need to protect the latter by the application of the mandatory rules of his national law'.[111] The scope of this ruling inevitably goes beyond the field of insurance.

The ambiguity of the extent of the host Member State power interests this analysis in that it makes difficult the assessment of the hindrance to the cross-border provision of investment services and to the operation of financial firms in general. Moreover, the efficiency of the present system of allocation of supervisory responsibilities is also doubtful. For instance, as to which grounds of justification may be invoked, the Court recently extended that power of the host State by abandoning its previous distinction between discriminatory and non-discriminatory restrictions on the provision of services.[112] By interpreting the Treaty *stricto sensu*,[113] there seems no reason to apply one category of justification to discriminatory measures and another category to non-discriminatory restrictions. Moreover, there are general-good aims not expressly provided for in the Treaty (e.g. protection of the environment, consumer protection), which may in given circumstances be no less legitimate and no less powerful than those mentioned in the Treaty. The analysis should, therefore, be based on whether the ground invoked is a legitimate aim of general interest and if so whether the restriction can properly be justified under the principle of proportionality.

Given the above and as was made clear by the ECJ in *Ambry*,[114] the extent to which the host State is empowered to take measures that impair the access to the market by a EU-based financial firm, may still give rise to interpretation problems.[115] The lesser the supervisory rules are harmonised, the greater the power of the host State to impose its rules under the general good. And, the greater the power of the host State, the bigger the disadvantage for investment firms, which wish to commence investment business out of their home country, and the less the competition and the burden on the national investment firm of the host State.

The Commission's guidance on banking and insurance hardly provides the final answer to everything. It may require radical changes to be made into domestic law, which, due to various legal and cultural differences, may be refused by Member States.[116] Consequently, ambiguity surrounding the interpretation and application of the general-good concept makes financial firms face legal uncertainty, as regards the arrangements applicable to them in the different Member States. This unsatisfactory situation may seriously undermine the workings of the machinery set up by the Single Market Programme and is thus likely to deter certain financial undertakings from exercising the freedoms created by the Treaty.

2.2.2. Authorisation. As described in Chapter 3, the responsibility to authorise investment firms lies in the hands of the competent authorities of the home Member State. It may be disputed, however, whether sole competency is vested in the home country or whether the host supervisors are allowed to carry out checks to determine if the financial firm, intending to operate in the territory of the host country under the freedom to provide services or through a branch, meets the standard conditions under which it was granted the European passport in its home State.

Such checks ought to be carried out by the home Member State alone. When the home authorities grant a licence to a financial firm to commence cross-border business, the host Member State should not be allowed to question the granting of such authorisation. Both the European Court and the Commission[117] seem to support this view. In *Commission v Belgium*,[118] a case involving broadcasting services, the Court held that the host Member State was not authorised to monitor the application of the law of the originating

Member State applying to television broadcasts and to ensure compliance with the 'Television without Frontiers' Directive.[119]

If the host Member State has reasons to believe that a financial firm, which was granted authorisation, does not comply with the standard conditions, it shall find other ways to satisfy itself. It may have recourse to Article 227 EC Treaty (former Article 170)[120] or request the Commission to take action against the home Member State for failing to meet its obligations pursuant to Article 226 EC (former Article 169). In no circumstances shall it take action by itself and monitor compliance with the minimum requirements, which may well constitute an infringement of the Treaty freedoms of establishment and provision of services.

2.2.3. *Prudential versus transactional rules.*

Articles 11 and 10 ISD contain respectively the CBR a financial firm has to comply with and some rules about prudential measures that investment firms have to introduce with respect to their organisation in order to be able to comply with the code of conduct as far as possible. The distinction between prudential-organisational and transactional rules is significant for their application to non-core investment services and for the appointment of the principal country-supervisor. Prudential rules cover the authorisation and effective supervision of financial institutions to trade in securities. They control the conditions for the initial and continuing permission to offer securities to the public or to deal in securities on behalf of the investors. On the other hand, transactional rules control the transactions between issuers, dealers and investors and impose the CBR between the financial undertakings and their clients.

Regarding the former, the following distinction and observation shall be made. Article 10 and 11 rules apply to all investment services listed in Section A of the Annex to the ISD.[121] In addition, however, CBR contained in Article 11 may also apply 'where appropriate' to the non-core services listed in Section C of the Annex.[122] Consequently, although not explicitly drafted in the Directive, it is very probable that a Member State imposes additional rules relating to underwriters, safe custody services, capital structure consulting or credit granting.

With regard to the latter, the clear distinction between prudential and transactional rules will automatically reveal the specific responsibilities of the home and the host regulators. Here, the drafters of the ISD have failed throughout. One could presumably imply that anything that is not specifically stated in the Directive as being a home country responsibility will fall to the host State and vice versa. Yet, the drafting of Articles 10 and 11 ISD hardly allows such a simple solution. Instead, it raises major questions and confusion, as the applicable rules may well cross the separation of competence for prudential and transactional supervision.

There is a considerable overlap, both conceptually and in practice, between prudential and conduct of business regulations. Both, for example, have a close and legitimate interest in the senior management of any financial undertaking subject to both these types of regulation, in particular because of the crucial roles of senior management in setting the 'compliance culture' of the firm.[123] On the other hand, the organisation and 'internal control mechanisms' of the financial firms are directly related to the nature of the transaction from the consumer protection perspective. [124] The host supervisors may be interested on behalf of the general good in having some control on matters, which fall under the home country's prudential supervision. For instance, prudential rules for personal transactions by the firm's employees may well conflict with the host country's CBR relating to conflicts of interest.[125] Illustrative in this context is the Belgian law, which clearly comes in conflict with the home country control principle, when it empowers the Belgian supervisor, the *Commission Bancaire et Financiere*, to verify in emergency cases whether the activities of the Belgian branch of a foreign investment firm are in conformity with the laws, which apply to it, and with the principles of a 'sound administrative and accounting structure' and 'adequate internal controls'.[126] In addition, the requirement that home Member States shall 'arrange for records to be kept of transactions executed' appears to imply that the host State would not have any power in that area. But isn't included in the host country's tasks the ability to control its own markets and monitor the transactions taking place within them, for the interest of market confidence and consumer protection?

Rules on record keeping are closely interrelated with CBR. If a host Member State is to be able to ensure that the participants in the markets, for which it is responsible, abide by host CBR, it will be important for that host authority to have the ability to establish an 'audit trail' of transactions that have been undertaken by a particular firm in particular securities or in a particular market within its jurisdiction. This significant tool of supervision may provide evidence of possible breaches of rules, not only those covered by the ISD, but also breaches of national rules, as for example on insider dealing. It is, therefore, more than necessary for the host supervisors to have the power to impose particular record keeping requirements, based on the nature of their markets in order to monitor their own rules of conduct.

The ISD has only taken account of the problem of conflicting rules with regard to conflicts of interest, at least in the case of a branch establishment.[127] Yet, the unhelpful drafting of the Directive's provision has not managed to overcome specific doubts. The host State may draw up a code of conduct to avoid conflicts of interest, or to ensure fair treatment, when such conflict cannot be avoided.[128] At the same time, the home country is vested with the power to require a certain structure and organisation by the financial firm, so that the client's risk of being prejudiced by conflict of interest is minimised.[129] Doubts need to be removed as to the ability of the host Member State to impose CBR relating to the management and disclosure of conflicts of interest. This is not something that can be left exclusively to the home competent authorities. Doubts need also be removed as to the magnitude of the host country's power; it might be said that a power for the host State to draw up CBR that is not limited by the general good, will make the risk of overlap even greater.[130] In any event, overlap might still occur, which could result in the host State's interference in the organisational structure of foreign investment firms.

Correspondingly, a major question arises from the last phrase of Article 10: Does it establish a hierarchy between prudential and transactional rules, that is between Article 10, fifth indent and Article 11, sixth indent?[131] The drafting design of that phrase leaves open the possibility that, at least in the case of a branch establishment, home State prudential rules may retreat in favour of the host State's CBR, when they are controversial. However, if one accepts that host country's rules prevail, this can easily lead to the unpleasant situation, where the structure of an investment firm depends on and is continuously adjusted according to the conflict-of-interest rules of every Member State, in which it provides cross-border services. It is self-evident that such a hierarchy and wider application of host country's rules cannot be accepted. In any case, it is necessary for any regulatory structure to address these issues because of the potential trade-off between CBR and prudential objectives. Likewise, the need for a clear allocation of responsibility between the home and the host Member State is intensified.

2.2.4. Conduct of business rules.   The first Community initiative in the field of rules of conduct was the 1977 Commission Recommendation for a European Code of Conduct.[132] The Recommendation provided several principles and model rules with regard to market conduct and conduct of business in EEC financial markets. However, it is not surprising that Member States never implemented these rules, since the Single Market Programme came as late as fifteen years later. Instead, the Community's main harmonisation focus has been on listing and disclosure requirements.

2.2.4.1. The risk of overlap.   CBR continue to differ significantly throughout the EU, wherever they exist of course.[133] Consequently, even if the European legislator was to achieve the clear differentiation between prudential and transactional rules and allocate the home and host country responsibilities in a functional manner, there will always be rules of conduct, which will play the role of the 'apple of discord' between jurisdictions.

The magnitude of the difficulties potentially created by the provisions of the financial services directives will be fully appreciated when it is borne in mind that a single investment firm may have to obey fifteen different CBR in order to commence cross-border investment business. The ECJ's jurisprudence regarding the scope of general-good restrictions provides guidance about the legal scope of national CBR drawn under Articles 11 ISD and 16(4) and 21(5) of the SBD.[134] Thus, the functions of Articles 11(1)[135] and 11(2) directly or indirectly confirm that the host State's rules apply in addition to those of the home State. The ISD does not prohibit a home Member State from continuing to subject financial firms authorised by it to its CBR even though the services are provided in other Member States.[136] The Dutch law, for example, considers CBR binding for investment firms constituted under Dutch law, without further specification about the activities directed abroad.[137] Luxembourg law goes even further, not only does it expressly impose CBR to foreign branches of Luxembourg firms, but also extends their application to foreign *subsidiaries* (emphasis added).[138] As a consequence, a financial firm that exercises its freedom to provide services, cannot be hindered only by CBR of its home country, which its competitors in the host State do not have to comply with,[139] but also runs the risk of being subjected to several overlapping or conflicting rules. Unharmonised CBR, therefore, constitute an inevitable – often acute – hurdle to the Single Market race of free flow of investment and free provision of financial trade.

The risk of rules overlapping may also have a direct and diversifying effect on the protection of consumers and the enforcement competence of each supervisory authority. Since each Member State has the task of regulating transactions and imposing CBR within its own territory, the scope of consumer protection and enforcement will inevitably vary between Member States. The minimum common base-line set by the directives does not necessarily reduce or soften the territorial divisions between national securities systems.[140] One may argue, however, that the scope of consumer protection extends beyond the express provisions of the financial services directives and the national securities legislation. It may include general matters of civil and commercial law, company law, competition law and consumer protection law. On the other hand, investors will be mostly concerned with the reliability of their brokers and the reliability of their investment. Thus, the core concern is the transaction itself, which is regulated by the CBR and supervised by the host country's competent authorities. When CBR are not harmonised across the EU, then diversities between investor protection standards can hardly be avoided.[141]

It is acknowledged by the Commission itself that there may ultimately be a need to reconsider the extent to which host country application of CBR is in keeping with the needs of an integrated market.[142] Verifiability under a justification and proportionality test not only appears desirable with regard to CBR, which increases cost for foreign investment institutions, but also when impediments to market access originate from overlapping or conflicting national CBR. Only time will reveal whether the ISD II will eliminate the smoke of ambiguity and will achieve the so-desirable uniformity of CBR across Europe. Yet, even if the problem of responsibility for devising and applying CBR is resolved, attention has to be given to an additional issue: which supervisor is best placed to monitor compliance with those rules and to enforce compliance?

2.2.4.2. The wholesale market: who is the 'professional investor'?   Whether or not investment firms choose to obey one set of CBR depends mainly on the relative size of the wholesale and retail markets. Article 11(1) requires that Member States shall apply rules of conduct 'in such a way as to take account of the professional nature of the person for whom the service is provided'.[143] Nevertheless, it may be possible for Member States to draw up CBR in violation either of the standards codified by the ISD Article 11(1) or of primary EU law.[144] While other investors will require a level of protection that reflects their lesser expertise, professional investors need fewer externally imposed intervention and protection.[145] It is in their own and in their clients' best interest to assess the risks related to investment services and build a risk-efficient portfolio.

Given the perception that wholesale investors need less protection than retail individuals, host supervisors will logically be less concerned to offer them excessive protection with the imposition of their own CBR. They will be more willing to waive such detailed requirements in order to win their trust and give incentives to large investment houses to do business within their country.[146] In this way, they will achieve the opening-up of their borders and markets to foreign capital flows and cross-border services, without placing under risk their primary objectives of consumer protection and financial integrity.[147] For these reasons, the Commission considers that home conduct of business regimes 'can be deemed to offer adequate and equivalent protection to professional investors'.[148] However, a number of key issues need to be addressed in this context: how should 'professional' market users be defined and with which criteria should market participants be differentiated according to their relative expertise? How should requirements for inter-professional business be structured in a manner consistent with regulatory and supervisory objectives?

The ISD is mute regarding the criteria and standards that distinguish between wholesale and retail markets and constitutes a 'professional' or 'sophisticated' investor. To fill the gap, the members of FESCO have issued a paper,[149] in which they adopt a set of criteria for defining professional investors and they bind themselves to implement these standards in their regulatory objectives and, when possible, in their respective rules. This work has already been followed by the Commission in its assessment of the ISD revision.[150] FESCO stresses in its paper that the conduct of business regime for professionals is an exceptional regime, that is it should be considered as an exemption to the application of the standard CBR, which aim to ensure adequate protection for less sophisticated investors. In this context, FESCO seems to have chosen a three-way classification as more appropriate than a two-way split.[151]

Even though Member States have agreed on the content of the FESCO paper and have accepted the three-tier classification of investors, the constitutional and legal status of that agreement becomes critical. Yet, the paper remains a consultative document, without any legal binding effect. It still needs be implemented by Member States' legislation or be incorporated into EU secondary law. In either case, the intervention of the Commission is required in relation to its binding statement in its 1999 FSAP. However, even if implemented, the FESCO paper will reveal its weakness. Regretfully it fails to address the crucial issue of which rules will apply in cross-border trades. Will it be those of the home Member State or those of the host? Will we have an enhanced home country control principle, or will the host country increase its supervisory power? According to the paper, only investors of the first category would automatically benefit from a home country professional conduct of business regime. In addition to this group of 'automatic professional', national authorities will decide whether to apply or waive the application of local regime to investors, which do not automatically qualify as 'professional'. And this regime only applies to the cross-border provision of services. Regretfully, the Commission's intention is to leave the treatment of branch establishment untouched. Branch-based investment business will still justify, in accordance with the Treaty, the application of the host country conduct of business regime to all of the client-related functions of the branch. This will be valid for both professional and retail investors.[152] Even if the FESCO paper exerts the influence it deserves, the problems of the application of CBR and the categorisation of investors will remain unresolved.

2.2.5. Marketing rules.　As discussed previously, CBR govern in general the transaction of financial products and their delivery from the financial firm to its client. In this context they are closely related to rules controlling the marketing of these products and especially their advertising.[153] Whereas authorisation and prudential supervision are requirements relating to the responsibility of the home Member State, Article 13 ISD implies that marketing and advertising rules are a matter of the host State.

This division of competences is similar to the one established by the ECJ with respect to the free movement of products. In *Alpine Investments*, the Court distinguished between marketing and product rules.[154] To avoid a double burden, the Court's case law has divided regulatory capacities between Member States. In particular, the home country controls the product rules while the host country deals with selling arrangements.[155] However, if the home Member State endeavours to apply its own rules to selling arrangements, a double burden cannot be avoided. The justification for the measures has to be examined.[156]

One certain conclusion that can be drawn from the *Alpine Investments* decision is that national standards regarding the marketing of investment services vary significantly between Member States.[157] Furthermore, the same case reveals the major difficulties that national regulators are facing to act against these egregious practices.[158] Indeed, even compared to CBR, marketing rules are lagging behind as far as their harmonisation process is concerned.[159] Without any particular explanation, the European legislator has chosen to provide investment firms with one more hurdle, when entering into cross-border financial business. Investment firms wishing to establish pan-European practices have to obey fragmented national marketing rules.

As with CBR, the adoption by Member States of conflicting or different investment services marketing rules impedes the functioning of competition between firms and of common consumer protection standards within the Community.[160] To this end, a major step towards the completion of the Single Market will be achieved with the adoption of the proposed Directive on distance marketing. Because of their intangible nature, financial services are particularly suited to distance selling. It is, thus, in the interest of consumers to have access without discrimination to the widest possible range of financial services available in the EU. This can only be safeguarded with the adoption of common marketing rules, which can accordingly ensure a high degree of consumer protection and confidence, especially in the use of new techniques such as electronic commerce.

However, even if the difficulties encountered by regulators were overcome and marketing rules were harmonised to a minimum extent, there would still be doubts and ambiguities with regard to the country, which constitutes the *fons et origo* of remaining non-harmonised marketing rules. Similarly for the free movement of goods, Article 13 ISD does not establish that cross-border transactions falling within the ambit of the ISD are regulated exclusively under the host Member State marketing or advertising rules.[161] The feeling arousing from the wording of this provision is that it is the rules of the host State that have to be adopted and examined in the interest of the general good. Again, the principle of general good will define the exact form and content of the rules to be applied and supervised by the host competent, without leaving it completely free to impose its own financial services marketing laws. This blurred division of responsibilities cannot be cleared out even with the final adoption of the Directive, which will harmonise minimum standards of marketing rules, but will also leave more specific responsibilities that have to be divided between the home and the host Member State. Certainly, as in the case of prudential and transactional rules, this dichotomy will not be without problems and bilateral conflicts.

2.3. What is the 'host country'?

2.3.1. The host Member State in cross-border provision of services.   According to the ISD, the European passport is only available when investment services are provided 'within' the host Member State, either through the establishment of a branch or through the provision cross-border services.[162] Sometimes issues are raised relating to the definition of a branch, or to the Member State where the cross-border services take place. If the recipient of financial services comes to the home country of the provider, a case can be made that no cross-border services are being rendered at all.[163] It is, thus, vital that the place of supply of financial services of a financial undertaking is 'located' in order to determine whether prior notification is required.[164] Moreover, the question whether at the present stage we should return to the subject of the CBR and explore the possibility of harmonising them, so that the home Member State approach could cover cross-border investment business, draws heavily on the correct interpretation of the definition of the host Member State.

The difficulty in locating the source and destination of financial services lies in the fact that, unlike other services (legal, medical, construction and so on), they are almost impossible to pin down and be connected to a specific location. They also differ significantly from one another and are increasingly provided in intangible form. The growth of distance services and the use of electronic means of telecommunication make them even more untraceable.

Occasionally, questions may be raised with respect to the definition of a branch. In an attempt to provide solutions, the ECJ has made fairly clear that a permanent establishment, from which financial services are provided, will constitute a branch and will be covered by the Treaty provisions on the right of establishment. In *Gebhard*,[165] the Court held that:

> a national of a Member State who pursues activity on a stable and continuous basis in another Member State where he holds himself out from an established professional base to, amongst others, nationals of that State comes under the chapter relating to the right of establishment and not the chapter relating to services.

However, the permanent establishment can be extended beyond the form of a branch. In *Commission v Germany*,[166] a case relating to insurance services, the Court held that:

> (...) an undertaking of another Member State which maintains a permanent presence in the Member State in question comes within the scope of the provisions of the Treaty on the right of establishment, even if that presence does not take the form of a branch or agency, but consists merely of an office managed by the undertaking's own staff or by a person who is independent but authorised to act on a permanent basis for the undertaking, as will be the case with an agency.

The issue of provision of services can be more problematic, especially where financial undertakings have to follow the notification procedure before they commence cross-border financial business. This is detailed in the following.

2.3.2. Prior notification.   In an attempt to clear out and interpret the definition of the place of supply of financial services, the European Commission
has examined certain possibilities for locating the service – for example,
origin of the initiative, customer's place of residence (*lex dominilii*), supplier's
place of establishment (*lex sedis*), place where contracts are signed (*lex con-
tractus*), and so on – and has considered that none could satisfactorily apply
to all the activities listed in the Annexes of the ISD and the SBD. Instead,
its guidance provides that the determinant is the place of 'characteristic
performance' of the service with a few implications, that is the essential
supply for which payment is due must be determined.[167]

In our view, the notion of 'characteristic performance' leaves unanswered
questions and also needs to be construed.[168] It deserves mention that not
all EEA Member States subscribe to the Commission interpretation.[169] The
solution to the case of legal uncertainty of the notification procedure could
be for financial institutions to make use of it even if it appears that notification may not be necessary. It seems that such a possibility is open.
Nonetheless, it is doubtful whether blanket notification (i.e. notifying all
activities in respect of all EEA Member States) regardless of any genuine
intention to carry out the activity is encouraged. The reasons could be
practical and financial.

The major problem seems to be the provision of distance financial services
via the Internet. In the Commission's view – as indicated in the 1997
Banking Communication – the provision of services through the Internet
does not require prior notification, since the supplier cannot be deemed to
be pursuing its activities in the customer's territory.[170] Moreover, the
Commission leaves it open for the financial institutions to choose, 'for reasons of legal certainty' to make use of the notification procedures provided
even if, according to the criteria proposed above, notification may not be
necessary.[171] But with such freedom given to undertakings, where does legal
certainty originate? If a financial firm chooses not to notify its intentions,
how shall the host competent authorities be informed of the nature of the
financial firm, its programme of operation and the financial services that
intends to provide?

Another question to be asked is: how shall the financial firm be informed
of the host State's rules of conduct and the general-good rules, with which
it has to comply, if no notification has taken place? This approach highlights
the link between the notification procedure and the application of conduct
of business and general-good rules. A financial firm that moves 'out of its
home' and provides services 'within' another Member State needs to notify
its intentions, so that the host State's CBR apply. This is a delegate matter
for the host Member State, which involves sovereignty and its power to
protect its own consumers and investors.

Furthermore, uncertainty may also originate from the obligation incum-
bent on the host supervisors. In its 1997 Banking Communication, the

Commission argues that the wording of Article 19(4) of the SBD does not justify the inference that the host country has an obligation to notify a credit institution wishing to set up a branch in its territory of its general-good rules. Moreover, any unnotified rules would still be binding on it.[172] We shall conclude that a similar argument could be applied to investment services, given the wording of Article 18(2) ISD. Nonetheless, the Commission's stance could create competitive distortions between financial services providers operating in the same territory. Uncertainty as to whether the information supplied is complete may well handicap foreign companies, which may feel obliged to undertake their own research in order to avoid the risk of their transactions being invalidated.[173]

The complication of the issue of notification and the 'incapability' of the Commission to deal with it also become evident in the 1999 Communication regarding the insurance sector. Here, the Commission makes a 180-degree turn[174] and takes the view that insurance activities carried on via electronic commerce (e.g. the Internet) and covering a risk located in a Member State other than that in which the insurer covering the risk is established, are subject to the provisions of the Insurance Directives relating to the freedom to provide services.[175] In plain English, insurance firms wishing to conclude via the Internet insurance policies covering risks or commitments situated in other Member States, should therefore follow the notification procedure.

Although the two Communications hardly constitute binding legal documents for national authorities to follow, they do create inevitable confusion to supervisors, financial firms and consumers. It may be alleged that regardless of whether notification procedure is required or not, the financial activities under question remain the subject of the principles of mutual recognition and home country control. Although the Commission considers the notification procedure necessary for insurance companies, it points out that it hardly constitutes a consumer protection measure. Rather, the measure pursues a simple objective of exchange of information between supervisory authorities.[176] Therefore, and in accordance with the third phase of the SLIM project, the Commission has welcomed a recommendation to make adjustments and ease the burden for European insurers, without however evading the notification procedure.[177]

In our view, the above Communications reveal an artificial dealing of the issue, as they treat notification as a procedural issue of residual scope, without really considering its importance for the consumer protection sensitivities of the host country supervisory authorities. In addition, they reveal the weakness of the present home country control and mutual recognition system and the lack of programme at Community level regarding the future of the procedure. On the one hand, in 1997 the Commission was envisaging the abolition of this disproportionate restriction in the context of the freedom to provide services in order to bring it in line with the Treaty.[178] Two years later it was proposing the adjustment of the procedure, without abolishing it completely. As the Commission has not yet issued a similar guidance regarding the provision of investment services, any speculations as to the interpretation of the term 'within' in Article 14 of the ISD are dangerous to be made.

As it was observed before, the criteria applied by the ECJ in its attempt to clarify whether national restrictions are compatible with Article 49 EC resemble those applied in the Court's case law under the free movement of goods.[179] Accordingly, unless the restriction, which a notification procedure is regarded to be, serves a particular purpose, which is worthy of protection by the host Member State, it is contrary to Article 49 of the Treaty.

As noticed before, the Commission's 1997 Banking Communication emphasised that rules, whose objective is to protect consumers, are more likely to be regarded as satisfying the general-good test.[180] Moreover, the ECJ explicitly accepts host country restrictions founded on the interests of consumers.[181] The protection of consumers, therefore, might justify the need for notification. Nevertheless, the notification procedure seems to serve no particular purpose and it is clearly not adopted with a view to secure that financial firms receive information about the host country measures adopted in the interest of the general good. *A fortiori*, the Commission admits in the 1999 Insurance Communication that it hardly constitutes a consumer protection measure and it should therefore seek ways to ease this host Member State restriction.

Whatever the future of the notification procedure may be, it will threaten the prosperity of the mutual recognition and home country control regime. Even if abolished, the host supervisory authorities would still need a way to check compliance with the interest of the general good and with consumer protection rules.[182] Even if adjusted, the notification procedure would still remain an administrative formality, a restriction to intra-Community provision of financial services. In any event, the existence of the current uncertainty could easily lead to the imposition of more than one set of CBR, if more than one Member State considers the service to have been provided in its jurisdiction. The burden on financial firms will be retained and the Single Market Programme will be devalued.

2.4. Electronic trading

This section focuses on issues arising from the supervision of electronic investment services and their provision by innovative trading platforms. What are the latest trends in Europe and what associated challenges do regulators have to face in relation to the principles of home country control and mutual recognition?

2.4.1. Trends. Trends such as globalisation, technological innovation and consolidation of financial services have an impact on how market services are being provided as well as on market structure. Technology is perhaps the most powerful force. It has allowed intra-day trading, online provision of investment services, electronic broking, elimination of trading floors, online IPOs, dematerialisation of securities and creation of virtual exchanges. In Europe alone, over twenty-five ATS[183] are having a considerable impact on wholesale investment services. The number of online European trading accounts is expected to increase by ten times or more in the next four years.[184]

Securities exchanges are not just places where securities are traded; in fact, securities exchanges are hardly 'places' at all nowadays. Trading, clearance and settlement are in most of the world screen-based and electronic. It is, thus, not surprising that the emergence of new electronic trading systems raises new challenges not only for financial undertakings and investors, but also for supervisors.

The move towards electronic trading has brought many benefits to brokers and investors, but also has raised new issues of concern for supervisory authorities. The benefits can be easily figured out and will be outlined briefly. The first is information. Technology has the ability to produce huge quantities of information, which can be easily accessed by anyone, even the simplest retail investor. As a result, every investor can theoretically control his own order instructions. The second is remote access. A physical trading floor is no longer necessary. Electronic markets can offer participation to far more people – and potentially a much wider range of people – than you could ever squeeze into a pit or on to a floor.[185] The final benefit is speed, automation and cost. Electronic markets have the capacity to perform these functions at mind-numbing cost-efficient speeds. The boundaries of automation of trading are extended by the electronic nature of the system, without human intervention. Old market process has given way to accuracy, efficiency and low cost, which has opened up new business opportunities.

2.4.2. Risks and challenges.   It is common belief that the unique cross-border characteristics that have emerged in financial markets due to the 'information universe'[186] pose new risks and constitute a regulatory and supervisory challenge for supervisors. Within the EU investment business arena, electronic networks not only challenge the systems of home country control and mutual recognition, but also question their ability to follow market structures and even threaten their existence. Emblematic is the approach of the European Commission, which discerns the obstacles to cross-border sales of retail financial products as the new technologies bring retail financial services to the reach of any Internet user.[187]

The first obstacle is one of substance. The offer of investment services through electronic networks from an institution's home State, which can be used by Community investors based in different Member States, seems to fall outside the ambit of the financial services directives' European passport.[188] Article 14 of the ISD and Article 20 of the SBD require that financial services be offered 'within' the host Member State. The two contradicting

Communications introduced by the European Commission hardly clear the confusion.[189] If the *locus* of the provision of services cannot be identified, then financial firms conducting electronic trading do not have to comply with the prudential and CBR of the directives. Instead, primary Community law will apply and more specifically Article 49 EC Treaty (former Article 59). Hence, such activities face the realistic danger of being subject to the CBR of not only the home country, but also of all the host Member States that constitute the destination of services and that can uphold their rules on the basis of the general-good principle.

To solve the supervisory problem, the 2000 E-commerce Directive has adopted a similar – yet, different – to 'home country' approach for information society services. Its cornerstone is the 'internal market clause',[190] which enables online providers to supply services throughout the EU on the rules of the Member State where they are established (country of origin). Although, however, the Directive was designed to ensure that online services can be freely provided throughout the Community, there are at least two issues that undermine such an optimistic proposition. The first is that the Directive itself provides for a number of significant derogations from the internal market clause by means of 'host' country measures that may hamper or, at least, make less attractive the provision of electronic investment services from other Member States and, thus, hinder intra-Community trade.[191] This, in turn, creates a distinct regime in respect of electronic cross-border trade from that using other distance selling modes. Where investment services are provided partly offline and partly online, different legal regimes will be applied to each part, since offline activities are not within the Directive's scope even if connected with an online service. The second problem is one of definition. Differences in the competence and power of national supervisors still hinder the consistent application of EU legislation. The undefined country of 'establishment' or 'origin' in the E-commerce Directive might not be the same Member State as the 'home country' within the meaning of the ISD. This may easily lead to confusion with regard to the country responsible for the prudential supervision of the information society or investment firm.

The 2000 Commission Communication on the Application of Conduct of Business Rules[192] and the consultative documents on the revision of the ISD suggest that the Commission is pushing away from host country control at least in the CBR wholesale field. However, what is far from clear is where exactly conduct control will end up. The E-Commerce Directive will subject online provision of investment services to the supervision of the State where the branch of the financial firm is established. On the contrary, the 2001 E-Commerce and Financial Services Communication strongly support greater convergence of CBR and a 'smooth transition to a home country approach'.[193] It is without doubt that this field involves significant complexities and difficulties, which may result in the creation of a great deal of legal uncertainty. More clarity is, therefore, urgently needed.

A similar problem seems to exist in the case of ATS. It is a fact that the ISD does not contain any explicit reference to ATS.[194] ATS hardly constitutes regulated markets with the meaning of Article 1(13) of the ISD. Most of them are authorised as broker/dealers and have differences with regulated markets in the area of access, transparency and market abuse. Here lies the difficulty with their surveillance.[195] In the case of regulated exchanges, the regulatory focus is on the supervision of the market, on its fair and efficient operation. In the case of brokers, supervision does not concern the market *per se* but the firm's conduct of business in relation to its customers and their protection. Given the above, the question arises whether ATS should comply with the prudential and CBR of the ISD. Should they be treated as markets or as investment firms? Will ATS cause the potential ending of broker intermediation as gatekeepers to the market?[196] The current home country supervisory regime fails to address the issue of the dichotomy of supervisory responsibilities between the home and the host competent authorities, where electronic trading platforms conduct intra-Community trading.

In connection to the above, an issue faced by EU regulators may be that of risks inherent in the asymmetry of supervision of ATS across Europe. Today, most EU jurisdictions regulate ATS as investment firms rather than as regulated markets. Although ATS usually fulfil at least some of the core functions of regulated markets, the question arises whether the current regulatory and supervisory approach to them is adequate to address the risks that their operations might pose to meeting the regulatory objectives. According to CESR, a number of risks can be identified that ATS might pose for consumer protection: access to trading, best execution, and conflicts of interest. On the other hand, these risks are closely linked to those potentially created by ATS in relation to financial stability: fragmentation, transparency, monitoring, enforcement and operation risk.[197] Consequently, regulating an ATS as an investment undertaking may not address the risks related with regulated markets and *vice versa*. In addition, the current Commission ISD II proposals subject ATS to a case-by-case assessment of core functionality, which means that such entities could be subjected to customised application of supervisory arrangements.[198] The confusion created by a regime that fails to treat these systems in a pan-European uniform way is more than obvious.

Especially the issue of monitoring and enforcement of ATS with cross-border elements can constitute an extremely problematic issue. Electronic remote access, besides beneficial, can also prove a nightmare for supervisory authorities. How does an exchange with remote cross-border members enforce its rules, when each member-financial firm is subject to the regulators of its home country? Above all, how does a market, a supervisor or a criminal prosecution authority enforce provisions against market abuse and fraud at a cross-border level?[199] Is the mixture of cooperation, exchange of information and the division of responsibilities between the home and the host State enough to address these issues? The present communication network facilities can be widely used in such a way that a criminal plan can be devised and put in practice so rapidly that the authorities are hampered in reacting promptly to it or in taking *ex ante* measures.[200] Besides, the 'de-localised' and 'non-territorial' character of electronic criminal activities makes it impossible to identify in proper time which regulator is responsible for taking *ex ante* or *ex post* action.[201]

On the other side of the Atlantic, US securities regulators are leading the way. The SEC and the self-regulated National Association of Securities Dealers (NASD) have already taken countermeasures against electronic trading fraud.[202] At the international level, IOSCO has discovered the sign of times and has established the Internet Task Force (ITF) to meet the challenges of electronic trading.[203] However, it is doubtful whether IOSCO's proposal for greater cooperation and coordination among regulators in different jurisdictions is feasible.[204] In any Internet investigation, huge amounts of information may need to be obtained from different countries, while illicit activity may implicate the securities laws of several jurisdictions. It becomes obvious in this context, that even an enhanced supervisory agreement as the 'traditional' EU home country control and mutual recognition system will be ill-equipped to meet the new demands. New principles reconciled in a more liberal attitude need, therefore, to be taken into consideration.

A final fundamental issue is whether advertising and subsequent provision of financial services in an electronic network platform, such as on the Internet, fall within the scope of the financial services directives. Are electronic financial services being provided at a cross-border basis, where a client is resident in a Member State different than that of the provider? Speaking in a 'virtual' context, some may allege that there is no cross-border activity since the client visits the web site of the service provider and thereafter purchases the financial product in such a way, that the client 'virtually' visited the home State of the provider.[205] This is especially significant for the notification procedure. Logically the financial firm will argue that there was no requirement for notification, since the client has taken the initiative and has 'visited' the firm in its own home State. In any event, a link between advertising and notification would be artificial, for it is not the prior offer of a service but merely the intention to carry on activities within the territory of another Member State that the financial services directives make conditional on notification.[206]

Conversely, others may argue that the fact that financial services are advertised and provided in electronic form does not mean that they should be legally treated in a way different than traditional media, such as mail, telephone, fax or personal contact. Consequently, financial firms should follow the notification procedure before commencing electronic financial activities with clients of other Member States. In such a case, financial undertakings will be, practically, obliged to provide registration formalities, in order to identify the personal details of their potential clients, as well as disclaimers warning them that their services may not be available in specific jurisdictions, where the notification procedure has not been followed. Moreover, the blanket notification should be avoided for the reasons mentioned before.[207] However, the unduly legalistic and impractical character of such a solution should be examined. How could the accuracy of the registration procedure be monitored by supervisors?[208] And which country's regulators should pursue such an *ex ante* investigation, since at that early stage the nationality of the potential client of the financial undertaking cannot be known? These are enquiries that the principles of home country control and mutual recognition leave unanswered.

2.5. The status of third non-EU countries

Overlaps or conflicts cannot arise only between the rules of the home Member State and the country where the service is provided within the meaning of Article 11(1) ISD, but also between these rules and the rules of the Member State where the service is actually carried out, if this occurs in a third Member State. One could give the paradigm of a French branch of a British investment firm that carries out orders for its French clients on the Athens Derivatives Exchange (ADEX). By virtue of the ISD, the branch will be obliged to comply with the rules of the regulated market in question.[209] However, the case would be different if the aforementioned branch was commencing transactions on the Belgian futures and options market of Euronext,[210] where the rules of French and Belgian markets tend to be fully harmonised. In addition, does the ISD (or the SBD) allow a EU financial institution to provide cross-border services from a branch outside the EU or even the EEA? The Commission's 1997 Banking Communication hardly addresses this difficult question. As Article 49 EC (former Article 59), on which the European passport is based, refers to a Single Market 'within' the Community, this is perhaps unlikely.

The EU should not be considered as an international agreement with relevance for only its signatories. This fundamental characteristic is enshrined in the introductory Article 3(s) of the Treaty.[211] With regard to investment services, Article 5 ISD provides that 'in the case of branches of investment firms that have registered offices outside the Community and are commencing or carrying on business, the Member States shall not apply provisions that result in treatment more favourable than that accorded to branches of investment firms that have registered offices in Member States'. Although the word 'reciprocity' is not employed in the provision, it follows from its reading that it obliges competent authorities to arrange their practices after a rigid principle of reciprocity.[212] This, however, is of very limited value given that foreign financial firms very rarely establish branches within the EU. The most favoured method to obtain presence in a Member State is by means of subsidiaries.[213]

There is no sign that access to EU financial markets has been made easier for non-EU financial firms with the home country control and mutual recognition regime.[214] Today, there is clearly a market difference in the treatment of financial firms whose home country is outside the EU, by each Member State acting as host State.[215] This is particularly obvious in the field of capital flows and payments. The Treaty itself still makes a distinction between the relationship between Member States on the one hand and their relationship with third countries on the other, despite the seemingly clear wording of Article 56 EC (former Article 73b).[216] Articles 57, 59 and 60 EC (former Articles 73c, 73f and 73g respectively) allow the continued application of restrictions that exist under national or EU law with respect to the movement of capital to or from third countries involving direct investment, provision of financial services or the admission of securities to capital markets. In most cases, the imposition of further restrictions to third countries becomes a matter of the Community and especially the Council. Nevertheless, the wording of Article 58(1)b (former Article 73d) may become problematic. This provision entitles even Member States to take unilateral measures against third countries, particularly, *inter alia*, in the field of the prudential supervision of financial services, as long as they constitute infringements of their national law. Yet, despite the prohibiting wording of Article 58(3), it may be difficult to distinguish between measures taken on the grounds of public policy or public security and measures that constitute arbitrary discrimination or disguised restrictions.

It becomes obvious that, with respect to relationships to third countries, EU law is not only ill-equipped to abolish existing restrictions, but also tries to freeze these restrictions or even impose new ones. If the aim of the Treaty, the ISD and the other financial services directives is not to close Community's financial markets, but rather to keep them liberal and open to the rest of the world,[217] an alignment of conditions for establishment and cross-border provision of services by investment firms of third countries should be promoted, at least in relation to countries that meet the requirement of reciprocity of treatment. It is clear that such an agreement becomes almost impossible for non-EU financial firms that wish to commence financial business throughout the Community, but have to face the rules of fifteen supervisory authorities.[218] On the other hand, the potential benefits of EU economic and regulatory reform will be considerably greater if they take place in a global environment of market opening and supervisory reform.

D. Concluding remarks

The conclusion derived from this chapter is that home country control and mutual recognition do not work. This is evident through a bulk of substantive and structural problems in the current EU regulatory and supervisory regime of investment services. More than ten years after their imposition, the Commission admits in its Second Biennial Report that these principles cannot be a miracle solution for ensuring free movement in the Single

Market. Indeed, the pan-European provision of investment services remains limited to specific areas and it is difficult to evaluate those areas where it does take place. In any case, it does not seem to owe much to the home country control regime and the European passport. On the contrary, the new regime has been the source for the creation of more hurdles and grey areas of uncertainty, which freeze the development of intra-Community investment services trade.

The European Commission often argues in favour of the twin principles of home country control and mutual recognition, which gives the impression that the Commission favours this instrument over harmonisation and centralisation.[219] Indeed, this approach has brought many advantages by giving expression to the principle of subsidiarity and by promoting innovation and competition among different regulatory jurisdictions. However, the case for home country control and mutual recognition is argued too strongly here.[220] Even if the initial idea was suitable for the time it was adopted, its implementation by the Commission and Member States has failed due to lack of political will, enforcement compliance and administrative capacity.

Whilst part of the problem concerns the incomplete regulatory coverage at EU level, the greater part of the responsibility lies in the way in which EU legislation has been decided (or left undecided) and implemented (or not implemented) and in which financial institutions and services have been supervised (or not supervised). The problem is the *system itself*. In areas where home country control could have made a difference, the failure to omit obstacles and adopt EU minimum standards has prevented the emergence of a truly single financial market. Notions, like the 'general good' or the 'characteristic performance' hardly provide the European lawyer, financial provider or consumer the legal certainty that is required when dealing with such a vague but dynamically changing business environment, as the financial services. Instead, they create a legal risk, which naturally hinders the free flow of cross-border capital and the free provision of cross-border financial services. Furthermore, the increasing dominance of ATS as a means of state-of-the-art conduct of electronic trading and provision of investment services and the asymmetry in their supervision in Europe jeopardise the competitive equilibrium, the stability of the financial system and the protection of individual consumers. Efficient markets require a predictable and transparent legal environment, as well as clear allocation of supervisory responsibilities.

Supervisory responses stop short of expectations and seem unable to deal with powerful technological and market developments. Proposed and adopted solutions take us back to the basics and back to the same things that have failed for the past ten years. EU regulators are focusing on breaking through in terms of bringing innovative solutions and they are broadly ignoring the effect of new developments, such as electronic trading. It is suggested that we should enhance the EU philosophy of mutual recognition of home regulation and supervisory control. But, where is 'home' in the state-of-the-art methods of cross-border provision of investment services? That concept does not fit comfortably in a unified European financial market.

To tackle the problem, the EU decision-making bodies should respond with a more integrated framework for financial services supervision supplemented by a removal of remaining barriers to cross-border provision of financial services, in order to ensure consumer choice while maintaining consumer confidence and protection. This response admits two solutions. The first would be the preservation of the present supervisory *status quo*, with the addition of significant changes in key issues, which are necessary to enhance the provision of cross-border investment services within the EU and to facilitate their supervision by the Member States competent authorities. This route has being followed by the Commission, the Council and the Wise Men Committee. The second position would argue that the aforementioned problems of the current regime are so significant and hinder the evolution and development of intra-Community investment services in such a way that they urge a major institutional and regulatory reform.

Generally speaking, the first approach suggests an updated home country control and mutual recognition principle with a 'fast-track' regulatory procedure and consolidated supervisory jurisdiction, while the second argues for further harmonisation of existing rules and the potential development of a centralised investment services supervisory regime. The question today concerns how EU rules and institutional structures will evolve. The balance of harmonisation and competition among rules and the clear benefits of alternative institutional solutions will have an important influence on the whole shape of EU financial services regulation and supervision in the near future. The following chapter will deal with these parameters and will concentrate on the rationale and costs and benefits of a potential pan-European Securities Regulator.

Part III
Moving Ahead

6

The Case for a European Securities Regulator

A. Introduction

This chapter considers the case for an alternative supervisory approach within the field of EU investment services, namely the establishment of a European Securities Regulator (ESR). According to the Prologue, the second criterion that justifies action at EU level is the production of clear benefits by reason of its scale or effects compared with action at the level of the Member States. Where Union action is required, the combination of different policy tools should be considered.[1] Does Europe need a pan-European securities regulator? If yes, is the creation of such a body feasible within the legal, political and economic context of Europe? These questions have recently gone beyond the purely academic domain to form the subject of specific political debate between regulators, practitioners and market participants. Although the results of these debates usually end up giving a negative dimension to such a suggestion,[2] the very fact that this question is raised in this particular period of time reveals that something is wrong with the present regulatory and supervisory financial architecture.

It is argued that, in order to prevent institutional structure from being a purely arbitrary and *ad hoc* process, several key issues need to be considered, such as the clarity of regulatory agencies' remit, the costs of a particular institutional structure, the accountability of regulatory agencies, questions relating to the efficiency of the regulatory process, the merits of a degree of competition in regulation and issues relating to the concentration of power.[3] In addition to these, the following paragraphs suggest the need for examining three more issues: issues relating to administrative efficiency, externalities and enforcement.[4] At the end of the day, the solid rationale of a single ESR stands on whether the supervisory objectives analysed in Chapter 1 will significantly be better served under the proposed centralised regime.

For the purposes of this discussion and because law on its own may not provide sufficiently accurate and reliable standards for evaluating the effects of legal rules and institutional structures, economic theory will also be incorporated into the legal analysis. In this light, by stressing the need to take the effects of the proposed action into account, the EC Treaty itself also rejects a pure legal formalistic approach.[5]

Naturally, as in any great reform, bringing investment services supervision to the centre of Europe may involve the imposition of legal hurdles or practical drawbacks. Some scholars do not find centralisation particularly attractive, since such a move could open the way to excessive federalism and over-regulation, resulting from the lack of regulatory competition, and the disregard of the special characteristics of national markets.[6] However, vertical centralisation of investment services supervision responds to the need for an authority free not only from all national leanings but also from other EU institutions. Therefore, regulatory and supervisory centralisation could also be seen as decentralisation at horizontal level, as far as certain Community competences are moved to a specialised pan-European authority.

In addressing the effect of different supervision policies, it is an important part of any policy assessment to weigh the costs and benefits of alternative proposals. Although a number of factors cause significant difficulty for such an approach, it is still worth considering the cost and benefit analysis of the choice of the relevant supervisor within a structured framework. When the regulatory and supervisory divergence of home country control and mutual recognition fails to deliver in the EU, centralisation appears to be the best solution for free and efficient movement of investment services. Many commentators maintain that the present arrangement of supervisory tasks at national level cannot be sustained in a monetary union.[7] The following paragraphs will argue that economies of scale and great power over individual regulated entities should make a EU securities supervisor more effective than national competent authorities. In turn, the reduction in the latter's responsibilities would permit more resources to be devoted to the more local areas that remain within their supervisory power, increasing their effectiveness. Centralisation in supervision and more flexible regulation will be the only answer to the hurdles of inconsistencies and loopholes, systemic inflexibility, high transaction cost, problematic cooperation and coordination and the Union's failure to 'speak with one voice' at international negotiations.

The previous chapter has answered the question, whether there are any major problems with the existing legal and supervisory basis governing the financial and particularly the investment services in the EU. This chapter will signal the ways – if any – in which the EU institutional structure might be changed in order to remedy such problems. To this end, this chapter will provide a cost–benefit analysis for centralisation and the potential establishment of a pan-European Securities Regulator by explaining its legal base with or without a Treaty amendment, its rationale and its legal, political and economic position within the Single Financial Market. More specifically, the second part will discuss the legal base of a European Supervisor with or without a Treaty amendment. The third section will analyse the rationale for establishing a central regulatory body, by focusing on issues regarding trans-action costs, independence and accountability, legislative delay, consolidation and alliances of securities markets, the impact of the euro, crisis management, imperfect information and deficient cooperation of national authorities and the relationship with third countries. Finally, the question will be raised, whether at the end of the day the reasons for 'sabotaging' the establishment of the single regulator do not relate with its 'drawbacks' but with the political unwillingness of national regulators to lose their sovereignty. The final section of this chapter will draw its main conclusions.

B. The legal basis for a single supervisor

1. The extent of legal authority

Before any discussion is commenced on the rationale for a pan-European Securities Regulator, this section seeks a stable basis in law. Generally, the legal problems of establishing European bodies are considerable. EU law does not have any powers to set up autonomous institutions not provided for in the Treaty. It is, thus, clear that the Community may not create a European securities authority unless it has the necessary power, competence and legal authority to do so. The extent of that legal authority is considered below.

The first paragraph of Article 5 of the EC Treaty (former Article 3b) states that:

> The Community shall act within the limits of the powers conferred upon it by this Treaty and of the objectives assigned to it therein.

The Article establishes what is better known as the principle of 'conferred powers', under which the EU only enjoys the powers expressly conferred on it by the Treaty.[8] It may be construed, however, that this position is more complicated, because, by referring also to 'objectives', the definition admits the possibility of additional, less certain, 'implied powers'.[9]

Member State competence is the rule, EU competence is the exception. The EU must accordingly first establish its Treaty-based individual competence and then check whether the Community objective cannot be adequately realised by the Member State and can therefore be achieved better at the EU level.[10] The Union is, therefore, empowered and mandated to act in certain areas by the Treaty as interpreted by ECJ case law. The Community's power to take actions is constrained by a number of general concepts including:

- subsidiarity
- proportionality, and
- non-discrimination

1.1. Subsidiarity

As indicated in Chapter 5, the EU may only create an ESR if the necessary powers for the intended action have been transferred by Member States to the Community. The latter may either have exclusive competence or concurrent competence to act with Member States. In the latter case, the Community can only exercise its powers if the subsidiarity test is satisfied.[11]

However, one may wonder whether this form of attribution of powers still corresponds with the present legal form of the EU and its state of development.[12] The subsidiarity hurdle should not be difficult to be legally overcome, since it is principally a political concept; the ECJ has never decided that an act was illegal for lack of EU competence (as opposed to institutional competence or wrong legal basis).[13]

The problem set out above has obtained a new dimension as a consequence of a ruling of the ECJ. In *Commission v Council*,[14] the Court held that the concept of the Internal Market referred to in Articles 95 (former 100a) and 175 (former 130s) EC Treaty has to be interpreted very widely. Consequently, the scope of the Community's power to harmonise national legislation has become so vast that one may allege that this provision can no longer be seen as the attribution of a specific power.[15] Instead, it amounts to a general authorisation for the Community to legislate in nearly all areas, which directly or indirectly concern the Internal Market.[16] More specifically, the European Court has recently decided that when the scope of a proposed measure 'has immediate effects on intra-Community trade, it is clear that, given the scale and effects of the proposed action, the objective in question can be better achieved by the Community'.[17]

It is important in this respect to take account of the interdependence of Member States in the outcome of a specific policy, such as investment services regulation and supervision. McDonald suggests that sound reasons for supranational policies in a particular area exist only if national policies have significant spillovers to other countries.[18] In some cases, potential cross-border spillovers can be addressed by coordination efforts and not necessarily by a common centralised response. However, if the costs of coordination are greater than the benefits of taking into account spillover effects, it is not efficient to coordinate policies.[19] It is, thus, suggested that solid reasons for centralisation and Community action may arise when the costs of reaching coordination agreements or preventing spillovers is high. Section B of this chapter reveals these costs in relation to the supervisory system of home country control and the coordination of multiple agencies.

On the whole, the importance of subsidiarity should be acknowledged. Nevertheless, the principle may be less relevant in areas, such as financial services, where businesses, including SMEs, as well as consumers are better off with single pan-European standards and common regulatory and supervisory practices.[20] Article 5 of the Treaty clearly gives priority to the general objectives of the EU concerning transnational action. Where the intention is to have an impact throughout the EU, 'Community-level action is undoubtedly the best way of ensuring homogeneous treatment within national systems'.[21] Consequently, any decision of the European Council allocating specific prudential tasks to a supranational body, should be accompanied by a justification that centralised supervision would present manifest advantages in comparison with action at Member State level. *A fortiori*, given the comparative advantage of regulatory and supervisory centralisation, both the Community and the Member States should have legitimate interest to intervene. Since such a transfer of responsibility would require unanimity and a potential Treaty amendment, the unanimous consent of all Member States would render the question of subsidiarity purely academic.[22] This view is further reinforced by the Treaty itself. Article 105(6) already enables the Council to confer upon the ECB specific tasks concerning prudential supervision policies of credit and other financial institutions. Therefore, Community institutions can clearly arrange the delegation of Member States' responsibilities to other European bodies. In this light, they could also provide the institutional framework to determine such solutions for the Member States.

1.2. Proportionality

Even when the home country control and mutual recognition principles incorporated in the investment services directives may be argued to fulfil the legal and substantive criterion of subsidiarity, they must also be shown to be proportionate with their expressed aims. The principle of proportionality of Article 5 EC reflects the well-established jurisprudence of the European Court of Justice.[23] Pertinent questions for the Commission to ask before framing its proposal for the establishment of a European Supervisory Authority may be: is it necessary to establish a European Regulator to achieve the objectives of the EC Treaty in the investment services area? Could the objectives be achieved by other means? Will the detriment to those adversely affected be disproportionate to the benefit to financial institutions and investors?

In the case of a Securities Supervisor, if a balanced approach is adopted and if the arguments in favour are sufficient to rise above the subsidiarity threshold, they are also likely to satisfy the proportionality test. Chapter 5 has shown that, for the objectives of the Treaty to be achieved (i.e. freedom of establishment and freedom to provide services), a reform of the current institutional structure of financial services supervision is necessary. This chapter will show that the benefits of the establishment of a European Regulator outweigh any costs, which constitutes it as the only feasible solution.

1.3. Non-discrimination

A further principle governing EU institutions is that of non-discrimination or equality. When one refers to discrimination, the European Court clearly states that the Treaty not only prohibits overt, but also all forms of covert or disguised discrimination, which, although based on criteria that appear neutral, do lead in practice to the same result.[24]

In practice, the establishment of an ESR should not offend against the principle of non-discrimination, but rather promote it. Its *de facto* and *de iure* independence will ensure that it will refrain from discriminatory measures.[25] Care, however, will be needed when formulating its procedures and competences.

Given the posture that the general concepts of subsidiarity, proportionality and non-discrimination do not constrain the centralisation of securities regulation and supervision, a further question arises as to whether the legal and institutional framework is provided in order to meet this objective. Is a Treaty amendment necessary in order to establish a pan-European regulator? This is considered in the following paragraphs.

2. Is a Treaty amendment required?

It has been well documented that for an ESR to be created, an amendment of the EC Treaty is required.[26] This, however, may not always be the case. This section shall examine the extent, to which the creation of an ESR would require an amendment to the Treaty. ECJ case law dictates that the ESR would require an amendment, if it were given very wide power and discretion in its activities. If, however, it is created on the basis of a more specific and narrowly defined set of tasks, then it is possible to create such a body without the need to amend the Treaty.

In *Meroni v High Authority*,[27] the ECJ held that delegation of powers to a Community agency is permissible, but only when

> it involves clearly defined executive powers, the exercise of which can, therefore, be subject to strict review in the light of objective criteria determined by the delegating authority.

The Court justified its reasoning by referring to the 'balance of powers which is characteristic of the institutional structure of the Community'.

On the other hand, the ECJ found that a delegation of authority which involves a discretionary power and implies 'a wide margin of discretion which may, according to the use which is made of it, make possible the execution of actual economic policy' may not be authorised as 'it replaces the choices of the delegator by the choices of the delegate, bring[ing] about an actual transfer of responsibility'.[28] In the following paragraphs we shall examine the legal basis (and its limits) of a new Community body without and with amendment of the Treaty.

2.1. Establishment of a European Securities Regulator without a Treaty amendment

According to ECJ case law, the several Treaty provisions, which confer legislative powers on the EU, may form a sufficient legal basis for establishing an agency at the EU level. Defined tasks may be delegated to that agency, but only within the limitations set by *Meroni* and only when its establishment contributes to the pursuit of the objectives, for which the legislative power in question has been granted. These limitations have been restricted even further by the Court in *Romano*. It held in that decision that the body under question 'may not be empowered by the Council to adopt acts having the force of law'.[29] The reasoning was mainly due to the fact that, under the judicial system of the Treaty, acts of such an agency could not be subjected to review by the Court. Therefore, the ECJ decided that the delegation of decision-making powers to an agency, even subject to the restrictions laid down in *Meroni*, is not possible if such an agency adopted acts having the force of law.

Applying the principles of *Meroni* and *Romano* to a potential ESR, it appears that its potential enabling legislation would need to dictate specific executive functions for an ESR to perform, while leaving high-level decisions affecting economic policy in the hands of the Commission. Furthermore, the establishment of a Securities Regulator will require a choice of legal basis on the present Treaty.

2.1.1. *Choice of legal basis.*

On numerous occasions, the European Court has confirmed that the choice of legal basis for EU measures is a matter of law rather than a matter of discretion. The choice must be based on objective factors, which may be amendable to judicial review.[30] These factors, which form the standing doctrine of the Council of 'principal objective' or 'centre of gravity',[31] include the aim and content of the measure concerned.[32] The significance of the issue has been consistently acknowledged by the ECJ.[33] As long as a conflict between EU institutions[34] about the choice of legal basis takes place and the Court has not pronounced its opinion, the risk remains that the choice of a particular legal basis will turn out to be wrong. In turn, if the wrong legal basis is actually chosen, the Court will not merely declare that the decision is vitiated by a purely formal defect, but that there has been a breach of an essential procedural requirement invalidating the measure. Finally, the selection of the legal basis may also have a decisive influence on the content of the measure, that is, when it requires unanimous act from the Council or when it requires simple consultation or co-decision procedure.[35]

For the purposes of this analysis, the principal candidates for forming the legal basis for the creation of an ESR are examined as follows:

- Article 86 (former Article 90)
- Article 95 (former Article 100a)
- Article 308 (former Article 235)

2.1.1.1. Article 86 EC (former Article 90).   Article 86 permits the Commission to impose, by the adoption of Directives or Decisions, general obligations, with which public undertakings must comply under the Treaty.

In theory, this Article could constitute a legal basis for further Community action in the investment services area. However, there are reasons to believe that a sufficient basis cannot be established for the creation of a Securities Regulator:

First, Article 86 is designed to deal with actions of Member States and not actions of undertakings, the proper legal basis for which would be Article 81 or 82 (former Articles 85 and 86).[36] Therefore, while Article 86 could be an appropriate legal base for regulating the relationship between national supervisors and investment firms, it would not appear to allow regulation and supervision of investment services providers by the ESR.

The second reason is that Article 86 may be used to remedy breaches of the Treaty rules, flowing, *inter alia*, from the existence of special and exclusive rights. The establishment of an ESR would be creating an administrative framework rather than remedying breaches of the Treaty or effects inherent in monopoly situations.

2.1.1.2. Article 95 EC (former Article 100a).   Article 95 EC, stemmed from the radical Article 100a,[37] prescribes the 'long and winding' cooperation procedure as set out in Article 251 EC (former Article 189b).[38] Here lies one of its major differences with Article 86, under which the Commission is the only institution involved in the adoption of a measure. Article 95 requires the Council to harmonise all national legislation, which, because of disparities between national laws, may exercise an effect on cross-border trade. It may well, thus, be alleged that the scope of this provision may be characterised as extremely wide, which could provide the Community with an almost free choice to legislate.[39]

Nevertheless, the case law indicates that this provision will only be the appropriate legal basis where the measure intended has a harmonising effect.[40] The 'object' of this provision must 'necessarily and specifically be the establishment and functioning of the internal market'.[41] Article 95 cannot oust other valid legal bases, as the expression 'save where otherwise provided in this Treaty' establishes.[42] On the other hand, systematic misuse of this provision will weaken its effect and lead to confusion.[43]

Whilst the establishment of an ESR will doubtless further the single internal market and harmonisation of Member States' regulations, it is far from clear whether Article 95 is a sufficient legal basis in itself. In *Spain v Council*, the European Court justified recourse to Article 95 when harmonising measures are necessary to deal with disparities between the laws of the Member States in areas where such disparities are liable to create or maintain distorted conditions of competition [or] in so far as such disparities are liable to hinder the free movement of goods within the Community.[44] The Court has recently refined the aforementioned principles: resource to Article 95 as legal basis is possible if 'the aim is to prevent the emergence of future obstacles to trade resulting from multifarious development of national laws provided that the emergence of such obstacles is likely and the measure in question is designed to prevent them'.[45] Nevertheless, it is doubtful in this context whether EU measures of a mere institutional character may constitute harmonisation measures in the sense of Article 95. In light of this suggestion, it is, thus, not easy to hold that the conditions laid down by the case law of the ECJ for the application of Article 95 will be fulfilled in the creation of an ESR in the future.

2.1.1.3. Article 308 EC (former Article 235).   Article 308 fully embraces the concept of implied powers.[46] It becomes evident from its wording that its use as a legal basis for a measure is justified only when no other Treaty Articles give the EU institutions the necessary power to adopt this measure.[47] Although the Article is silent on the formation of a body, as the proposed ESR, it should not lead us to the conclusion that this will prevent its establishment altogether.[48] As Weiler puts it, this provision has been interpreted in such a wide and radical manner that 'it would become virtually impossible to find an activity which could not be brought within the objectives of the Treaty'.[49]

Nevertheless, one shall not argue that Article 308 is limitless. Opinion 2/94 of the ECJ stated that this provision 'cannot serve as a basis for widening the scope of Community powers beyond the general framework created by the provisions of the Treaty as a whole and, in particular, by those that define the tasks and the activities of the Community'.[50] However, Thieffry is right to contend that these limitations are not relevant to the proposed creation of an ESR. Instead, he proposes to focus more on what, in practice, Article 308 has been used to achieve, namely the objectives of the Treaty.[51] To this end, by filling the gap where it did not possess more specific legislative authority, this Article has been a useful residual legislative power for the EU.

Another argument in favour of using Article 308 as a legal base can be found in the ECJ's *Massey-Ferguson* ruling.[52] It was argued in that case that the necessary power to adopt a regulation was granted already by other provisions of the Treaty, provided that these were given a sufficiently broad interpretation. It was thus maintained that Article 308 could not be used as the appropriate legal base. However, the Court held that even if, given a broad interpretation, other Articles did grant the necessary powers, this interpretation was subject to doubt and, therefore, recourse to Article 308 was legitimate.[53]

The Commission, on the other hand, has changed its view on Article 308 since the introduction of the SEA. It used to invoke this provision quite frequently as a way of avoiding squabbles about legal bases and EU competence, since nearly everything could go under Article 308.[54] Now, the Commission seems more anxious to shift the legal basis of EU legislation away from Article 308 and towards other Treaty provisions that require qualified majority, particularly Article 95.[55] Article 95 has been used, for example, for the newly established European Food Safety Authority (EFSA). Nonetheless, as we have seen, the European Court does not seem to share the same views with the Commission.

Even under the burden of unanimity, Article 308 appears to be the most appropriate and logical basis for establishing a Securities Regulator. This conclusion is supported by the fact that it has been used as the basis for creation of several new legal entities in the past, such as the European Economic Interest Groupings (EEIGs), the Office for Harmonisation and the European Medicines Evaluation Agency. To be beyond challenge by current EU institutions, legislation for the creation of the ESR must attain the objectives of the Treaty.[56] The objectives are included in Articles 2 and 3 of the Treaty and the ECJ is not likely to reject their use, since these provisions exactly 'define the tasks and activities of the EC'. Yet, the difficulty remains in conferring upon such a body the power to exercise mere political discretion without further control by the EU institutions interacting in accordance with the applicable Treaty provisions. The decisional content of regulatory and supervisory powers delegated to the Securities Regulator will be limited, for the *Meroni* constitutional requirement that the 'balance of powers' be preserved remains in force. In this light, the following paragraphs examine the possibility of creating a Securities Regulator by amending the EC Treaty.

2.2. Establishment of a European Securities Regulator with a Treaty amendment

Amendment of the Treaty will be required if it is considered that an ESR should have more than an executive function, including the power to undertake policy decisions with certainty and in complete, unfettered independence. However, the distinction between constrained discretion and policy-making powers is sometimes difficult to draw, particularly in the absence of more or clearer guidance from the ECJ. In this light, it would be useful to look for guidance by examining the degree of power granted to existing EU agencies in the financial services sector. A brief review of some of these agencies, their powers of decision-making and the nature of their decisions demonstrates the various levels of authority the Commission has conferred, which may be instructive when considering the establishment of a Securities Authority.

2.2.1. The European Investment Bank (EIB) and the European Central Bank (ECB)

Paradigms of bodies created through amendment of the Treaty include the EIB and the ECB. Both are autonomous legal entities, which have policy-making functions within the EU institutional framework. The EIB was created in 1958 as an autonomous body set up to finance capital investment furthering European integration by promoting EU economic policies,[57] while the main function of the ECB is to define and implement the monetary policy of the Community.[58] Moreover, the latter has the capacity of producing regulations on monetary policy that are binding and directly applicable to all Member States. However, the policy-making operation of these bodies should not be construed as being without restraints. They both have to comply with their founding agreements and the provisions of the Treaty and are subject to judicial review by the ECJ. In addition, the Council and the Commission also have some input into the decisions made by the policy and executive arms of these entities as they may designate who serves on the representative boards. Nevertheless, we shall revisit the ECB paradigm as a model for the ESR later in Chapter 7.

2.2.2. A time-consuming process?   Critics of supervisory centralisation may allege that a Treaty amendment would require long time-consuming negotiations between Member States, which could eliminate the scope and purpose for the establishment of an ESC. However, 'where there is a will there is a way'. The passage of the SEA, for instance, which made major changes to the Treaty, demonstrates that even this apparently cumbersome process can be completed with surprising rapidity when sufficient political clout exists.[59]

Ideally, the potential future ESR would have specific policy responsibilities adhered to the supervision of European financial firms and securities markets. However, if such a solution fails or finds itself unable to overcome in practice political conflicts between Member States, EU regulators and Member States' leaders should consider – and they have already done so, but without first even considering the best solution[60] – the second-best solution, the establishment of a Securities Committee without Treaty amendment, but also with less or no regulatory and supervisory tasks. For the reasons analysed in this chapter, it seems inconceivable to compromise the stability and further development of European financial markets because of national controversies. It is ironic that while the international financial community is studying the possibility of setting up a 'world financial regulator', petty national jealousies appear to be preventing this from happening at the European level.[61]

3. The need for a 'hard' Regulator

The Treaty provisions, which allow for law approximation to the extent necessary for the establishment and the functioning of the internal market, continue to be applicable. The existence of different national legal systems and Member State supervision is not contrary to the Treaty. The previous chapters have identified the weaknesses of the present supervisory structure in investment services to create a real Single Financial Market within the EU. This section has answered the question whether it is legally feasible to reform the existing supervisory architecture with or without a Treaty amendment. However, the specific legal base of a new federal securities body will draw heavily on the justification of EU action in the investment services field.

By establishing a Securities Regulator on the basis of provisions of the present Treaty, its weaknesses will soon be revealed. It is far from clear whether the practical consequence of ECJ case law permits the delegation of decision-making powers to outside bodies. The several Treaty provisions granting legislative powers to the Community may form a sufficient legal basis to establish an 'internal body' having a distinct legal personality and to entrust it with tasks, which do not involve the autonomous exercise of mere political discretion, provided that the establishment of such a body contributes to the pursuit of the objectives for which the legislative and supervisory power in question has been granted to the Community.[62] The Commission, which already suffers from insufficient personnel resources, will face therefore difficulties in reducing the pressure by delegating powers to external bodies, and the design and implementation of basic acts will remain mainly within its competencies. This directly strengthens the comitology system, since the Council, by delegating implementing powers to the Commission, can fully supervise it via committees.[63] Given, however, the importance of the need of a 'hard' Regulator, a comitology committee such as the ESC does not suffice as a solution.[64]

To the extent that it appeared appropriate to create a Community body outside the traditional EU institutional structure laid down in Article 7 EC Treaty (former Article 4), to take the necessary political decisions in complete independence, it would be for the constitution itself to create such a body. An amendment of the Treaty will be required if national governments and EU institutions wish to provide the ESR with the power it needs. The inclusion of clearly defined objectives and regulations of the Regulator in the Treaty, which constitutes primary law and has direct effect on and within Member States, would furnish the ESR with stronger law-based competence to achieve its goals. Since the Treaty can only be amended if all Member States agree on and ratify changes, the ESR will have a very high legal, *de facto* constitutional status. Does the creation of a single securities supervisor constitute the 'centre of gravity', which will demand EU action? Is the ESR necessary to foster greater economic cohesion? In light of these questions, the following section will endeavour to critically respond to the call for a pan-European Securities Regulator, by establishing its rationale and examining its contribution to the creation of a Single Market for EU investment services.

C. The rationale for a single regulator

After drawing the legal umbrella, under which the central European body could be established, we now come to the question: why do we need a central ESR and why action at the EU level would clearly produce benefits by reason of its scale or effects to the free provision of investment services? A question that can be easily posed *vis-à-vis* the assessment that the current EU financial supervisory structure is ineffective.

In an effort to explain the rationale for a single European securities market regulator, this analysis may borrow inspiration and arguments from the theory of neo-functionalism. Neo-functionalism originated as an optimistic analysis of the benefits of informal cooperation. The theory developed from the English political scientist David Mitrany's functional approach to world unification. However, its interpretation has evolved over time. Ernst Haas reformulated Mitrany's idealistic functionalism and applied it to European integration.[65] Haas questioned 'how and why nation-states cease to be wholly sovereign, [and] how and why they voluntarily mingle, merge, and mix with their neighbours so as to lose the factual attributes of sovereignty while acquiring new techniques for resolving conflicts between themselves'.[66]

Whatever the drawbacks and the criticisms levelled at neo-functionalism,[67] it is argued herein that the theory has a role to play in explaining the emergence of the need for centralisation in the investment services field. Minimum harmonisation should be seen today as a transitory stage on the way towards European legal unity.[68] Even if they were initially designed to keep open competition between national legal orders, the principles of minimum harmonisation and home country control have failed their mission. On the other hand, competition among rules cannot be seen as an end in itself, but must be critically assessed against a range of possibilities, such as the desirability of transferring power to EU institutions. To this end, centralisation is important to avoid a reversion to regressive national tendencies.[69] The introduction of a EU supervisory authority with responsibilities in the investment services sphere would assist in ensuring that rules would be applied in the same way in all Member States.

Neo-functionalists were undoubtedly correct in assuming that the functional needs of an integrated European market would necessitate a considerable transfer of policy-making powers to EU level.[70] With a single currency and a single market base, the lack of a single regulator is a dangerous absurdity.[71] Indeed, an important reason for delegating powers to a politically independent regulator is to enhance the credibility of the Union's long-term policy commitment to create a single financial market. Furthermore, certain drawbacks, such as the cost of the investment services industry originating from the blurred home and host supervisory powers, slow and inefficient legislation, imperfect information exchange and deficient cooperation between Member States supervisors, doubtful credibility and independence and lack of efficient crisis management in emergency situations, will support this analysis. Given this general posture, it is necessary to analyse the particular reasons that are relevant to the arguments for the establishment of a single regulator.

1. Transaction costs

The initial simple reason why we need centralisation of investment services supervisory responsibilities is to exploit regulatory economies of scale and scope, especially for financial intermediaries, which already provide cross-border services in more than one Member States, and to consumers.[72] If scale economies are important, central rulemaking may be required.[73] As it would make little sense for water pollution standards to vary mile by mile along a river, so it would make no sense for regulatory and supervisory standards to vary from country to country. Multinationals and other export-oriented investment firms tend to prefer European to national supervision not only to avoid the costs of meeting different and often inconsistent national standards, but also to avoid the risk of facing progressively more stringent regulations in some of the Member States.[74] This section will make an effort to identify and discern the significant bearing of current supervisory structure on the costs of regulation and the benefits that may derive from a more centralised approach.

For the purposes of this discussion, it would be useful to examine all kinds of transaction costs after we endeavour to define them. In Coase's definition, transaction costs occur in order

> to discover who it is that one wishes to deal with, to inform people that one wishes to deal and on what terms, to conduct negotiations leading up to a bargain, to draw up the contract, to undertake the inspection needed to make sure that the terms of the contract are being observed, and so on.[75]

By adapting this definition and by moving a little further one could divide transaction cost into three categories: *institutional* or *direct* cost, *compliance* cost and *indirect* cost.[76]

1.1. Institutional or direct cost

First, *institutional* or *direct* cost is the cost of operation of the regulatory and supervisory agencies themselves. The smaller the number of regulators, the lower the institutional cost should be. Although the institutional cost of supervisors may be comparatively smaller than other kinds of cost, it may have a significant chain-effect on compliance and indirect cost. An ineffective institutional structure may raise overall cost on investment firms if it leads to inappropriate regulation and supervision.

Here is where the establishment of a single Securities Regulator would require particularly careful considerations and delicate actions. For instance, to the extent that multiple regulators have overlapping competencies – as is the case with the home country control regime – each regulator may impose costs on others. This lays the basis for what Scharpf has called the 'joint decision trap'.[77] The solution to avoid the overlapping 'trap' would be to provide a regime of clear allocation of responsibilities or to combine them in one body. In addition, given that the single regulator would be responsible for a wider range of functions than national authorities, it would be more able to take advantage of economies of scale in their provision by allocating its resources in a more efficient way.[78]

Naturally, the process of establishing a central European regulator means, by definition that most Member States and financial firms will have to alter their practices. Change costs time, money and effort. Of course creating a central body should not be entered into lightly. Nevertheless, the cost of centralisation should be balanced against the need for centralisation along the lines of the materiality and the benefits it will deliver for the entire Single Market.

1.2. Compliance cost and legal certainty

Second, *compliance* cost is the cost imposed on financial firms and consumers. It seems to be the most significant drawback created by the present home country control and mutual recognition regime. A recent survey suggests that companies could save an average of 15 per cent if current regulation were to be better designed.[79] Compliance cost refers to the incremental cost of compliance caused by regulation, but not to the total cost of activities that happen to contribute to regulatory compliance.[80] Although institutional structures may have an effect on compliance cost, the opposite (i.e. increase of the cost of the competent authority due to a specific regulatory measure) is unlikely to happen. Compliance cost may include information and research cost, legal cost and lobbying cost.

One of the main aims of financial services supervision should be the correction of information asymmetries between regulators and the regulated. Today, European citizens and companies are confronted with a system of regulation and supervision that is difficult to comprehend. Given that keener competition in financial services could tempt some institutions to expose themselves to higher risks, the problem of asymmetric information becomes especially acute. Investors would not easily be able to identify a heightening of such a risk situation.

Under uniform pan-European regulation and supervision, national supervisors, financial firms and consumers need not expend resources on information and research costs.[81] They do not have to inform themselves of the differences in the substantive law of Member States and the way, in which these rules are enforced. Nonetheless, the reduction of information and research cost constitutes only one part of any economic analysis; another part is the gains from legal certainty as an incentive for more efficient conduct.

Legal certainty is a very significant issue for lobby groups representing large industries. Large financial firms want to be informed as soon as possible about the legal validity of their cross-border transactions and the applicability of their supervision. Smaller firms, on the other hand, which would traditionally provide services only at national level, would also welcome cuts in research and legal cost as an incentive to expand their business and enter intra-Community trade.[82] To this end, supervisory fees of financial undertakings should decrease, insofar as they no longer need to comply with prudential rules or rules of conduct of both home and host Member States, and their overall lobbying costs may be reduced as they will have to deal with a single supervisory body. The assumed preference is for the minimisation of legal cost, consistent with ensuring the outcomes desired by those involved in the transaction.[83] A single Securities Supervisor could then operate a single database for the authorisation of financial firms, avoid unnecessary duplication or overlap across home and host country authorities and adopt a more effective and focused approach to areas of common interest to most regulated financial activities. This regime would enhance the production of more stable and predictable jurisprudence,[84] while it would also guarantee the legitimacy of the actions of the independent regulator.[85]

1.3. Indirect cost

Finally, *indirect* costs are those that are least obvious from a cash perspective. Although they are hard to gauge, they are not of minor importance. Indirect costs include those stemming from regulatory capture, regulatory escalation and moral hazard, reduced competition and public choice.

The issues of regulatory capture, regulatory escalation and public choice will be discussed later in Section 2.1. As far as moral hazard and competition is concerned, we shall make the following observations. The process of regulation and supervision is not simply one where the regulators command and the regulated obey. It involves a far more complex web of bureaucracy and bargaining, where regulated firms bargain for the rules that will be applied to them. Obviously, such a practice is encouraged by supervisors, who are reluctant, for political reasons, to impose excessive cost on industry.

Investors, particularly non-professionals, always feel closer to their national regulator. They tend to have a feeling of protection originating from the authority that monitors their national market and the financial firms that operate within that market. Research reveals that seatbelts encourage drivers to drive more aggressively. Similarly, that feeling of protection may more easily lead investors to take risky decisions, which will increase moral hazard. However, a radical change in the regulatory structure of European investment services market supervision would alter investors' psychological behaviour. A single Securities Regulator may deliver benefits in the reduction of moral hazard, especially among retail investors. Indeed, Goodhart asks whether under a single regulator 'a potential moral hazard would result from a public perception that the risk spectrum among financial institutions had disappeared or become blurred'.[86] In practice, the public's understanding of the new regulatory system is – regrettably – likely to be so low that this type of moral hazard should not arise.[87] On the other hand, for those consumers, who commence cross-border investment business, a single regulator would be a one-stop-shop for complaints handling, compensation schemes and information. This could facilitate the regulator's ability to enhance public awareness of the risks, costs and benefits of different investment services and to clarify the limitations of what regulation can deliver, thus reducing the potential moral hazard.

Finally, the cost from reduced or eliminated competition may have a severe impact on the free provision of investment services and on consumer protection. In a uniform market, different national regulators may have the effect of distorting competition, either because they interpret uniform regulations differently or because they react differently, or at different speeds, to new developments.[88] Domestic interests and protectionism also play a major role. When national authorities regulate and supervise in parallel in the Single Market, the principle of competitive neutrality[89] is at risk. Imagine, for instance, a situation, where a financial firm wished to provide cross-border services in a host country and offered a financial product or service that was innovating for the domestic market and was not provided by domestic firms. In order to protect their institutions, host authorities could easily impede or prohibit the provision of that product or service on the grounds of the general good, so that domestic firms do not acquire an inherent disadvantage. It would take years for the foreign firm to bring the case to the ECJ, which would give enough time to domestic institutions to prepare and provide similar products or services. The home country control regime could give rise to several other similar impediments to competition, which could burden financial firms with additional and unjustified costs. Moreover, in contrast to the rhetoric associated with the launch of home country control,[90] consumers are not benefited either. Consumer choice is inhibited because consumers are not able to buy or, in some cases, even be informed about what may be available from foreign suppliers.

In a perfect Europe without borders and a financial environment with transaction costs equal to zero, there would be no reason for national authorities to transfer power to a federal pan-European body. Instead, investment firms and markets could be managed by intergovernmental agreements or even by means of non-cooperative mechanisms. However, this is not the case we currently witness in Europe. Costs involved in financial supervision are frequently quite easy to measure with some accuracy. The same, however, cannot be said for the benefits. More or less, the economic benefits of supervision lie in the prevention of disaster and in the constitutional free provision of investment services. As we shall see, there can be little doubt that a pan-European Securities Supervisor offers scope for significant efficiencies. At least in theory, a single supervisor ought to be able to generate a number of efficiency gains. Equally, however, it may be difficult to deliver these in practice, especially at the beginning of its function.

2. Independence and accountability

The potential delegation of prudential responsibilities to the ESR raises significant questions of public control, independence and accountability, which justify the switch to centralisation. This section endeavours to address these questions.

2.1. Public choice theory and independence

Any existence of multiple supervisory agencies and different regulatory regimes entails the possibility that powerful interest groups may impede any national or cooperative supranational developments. Public choice theory, which lies at the heart of the concern about regulatory failure, depicts the struggle over regulatory and supervisory action as a kind of competition between discrete groups and the general welfare, with information serving as the principal weapon. Financial firms, exchanges, issuers and investors have incentives to endeavour to influence the scope, content and enforcement of financial regulation in order to promote their private interests.[91] Furthermore, political actors and interest groups are well aware that institutional choices have significant consequences for the context and direction of policy. This, of course, might seriously undermine the independence of various Member States' supervisory authorities or of the ESR. Accordingly, the elimination of political control and influences in this area is justified on the basis that it ensures an institutional environment conducive to the attainment of the supervisory objectives of financial stability, consumer protection and competition promotion.

Regretfully, data regarding the role of interest groups in influencing regulation is not sufficient enough to comparatively assess the influence at the national and EU level and thus to drive us to specific conclusions. Nevertheless, it may be possible to make certain speculations with regard to specific interest groups. Interest groups may be strong enough to influence supervisory authorities. Firms, for example, established in jurisdictions with more costly legal structures and which have already invested resources in complying with such regimes will not wish to lose the competitive advantage, which they thereby acquire over newcomers.[92] On the contrary, small and medium financial firms, which yet face difficulties in penetrating markets beyond their home country, will have a more growing interest in centralisation. Traditionally, these financial firms, which are increasingly lobbying for centralisation and additional harmonisation to further diminish existing barriers in intra-Community trade, have limited power and take slower steps.

Securities exchanges, for their part, have repeatedly lobbied for regulation at EU level to better incorporate tools allowing Member States to limit competition between them.[93] Although pan-European trading platforms's consolidation plans have not been very successful in the past – with notable exceptions such as Euronext and Euro.NM – there is growing evidence that true pan-European exchanges will soon become common, chiefly owing to technological progress.[94] In this perspective, it is in the interest of major regulated markets to lobby to further diminish cross-border trading barriers and even campaign for a single ESR.[95]

Finally, issuers and investors are initially unlikely to show much direct interest in the institutional supervisory structure, and, thus, have relatively less influencing power. They should be keener in harmonisation of Member States' laws with regard to accounting standards, disclosure, company law and consumer protection issues. It comes as no surprise that, for the very reason that these interest groups have limited powers in lobbying at the EU level, harmonisation efforts of these issues have been blocked for decades. However, being in favour of a European passport and in order to reduce transaction costs and increase liquidity, they may become more supportive of centralisation and consolidation of regulated markets as well as of real freedom of cross-border trading. In this respect, a centralised body could be seen as the only means of making the single financial market a reality.

In short, heterogeneous interest groups have different powers in influencing the content, the scope and enforcement of financial regulation and supervision. Since the power of issuers, investors and smaller financial undertakings is limited to their home competent authority, it is more likely that a single Securities Regulator will be under less pressure. Diverse interest group pressure means diverse financial regulatory and supervisory standards. A centralised body should tackle this problem by establishing a level-playing field as far as supervision is concerned and by keeping itself far from regulatory capture efforts. However, this issue is examined below.

2.2. The problem of regulatory capture

A response to the issue whether regulatory and supervisory decisions should be taken at the national or EU level requires a comparison of the possibilities of decentralisation and centralisation to cope with the problem of regulatory capture.[96] Keeping national supervisors' knowledge up to date may require structured training in cooperation with industry or a system of inward and outward secondments between supervisors and the supervised. These steps would bring supervisors closer to the market, but carry the potential risk or perception of regulatory capture and conflict of interest.

Ogus suggests that large areas of law are 'interventionist' in that they protect defined interests and/or supersede voluntary transactions.[97] Such 'interventionist' law creates winners (the beneficiaries of protection) and losers (the subject of legal obligation), who, in a decentralised regime, will both attempt to exert pressure on lawmakers for more favourable law. National regulators, on the other hand, may also benefit from their close relationship with the market. They could, thus, allege that the closer a regulator physically is to the firm and the market that it regulates, the better and more efficient its supervision is. Nevertheless, any close relationship entails the risk of regulatory capture. But again one may ask: don't we always face the risk that market participants will try to capture their regulator in order to promote their own interests, irrespective of their distance with it? It should be argued that the possibilities of regulatory capture have their limits in the design of institutional structure. Although appropriate institutional architecture, such as a centralised supervisory body, will not prevent regulatory capture altogether, it may limit its scope. We elaborate below.

A centralised supervisory body should redress the imbalance. The risk of capture of a national regulator is higher compared to a supranational supervisor, which keeps itself at a safe distance from the financial institution it regulates. This may be depicted by the recent experience in many East Asian countries.[98] Also in Europe, incidents such as Crédit Lyonnais and Banco di Napoli suggest that domestic supervisors have sometimes been too close to the institutions they regulate, thus risking being captured, particularly when those institutions are state owned and supported by powerful political lobbies.[99] Because of their independence from electoral considerations and party political influences, supranational regulators are less likely to be captured by special interests than a national authority.[100] Hence, the natural distance, the pan-European Securities Regulator should keep, appears as a healthier solution.

Furthermore, the supervisory objectives, analysed in Chapter 1, can be used to control and to ensure the ESR's political independence. A central regulatory and supervisory body ought to observe supervisory objectives that underline its specific policy initiatives. The fact that a supervisor has been appointed with the responsibility of observing more than one supervisory objectives means that it has been granted goal independence.[101] Such independence is actually superior to simply having one ambiguous policy objective, for it guarantees the existence of democratic check and balances. Sticking, thus, to its objectives and policies and being less sensitive to external influence, a single regulator should respond with two different, but complementary characteristics: transparency and accountability.

2.3. *Transparency and accountability*

Under the current home country control regime, every regulator is and should be independent and accountable at an appropriate national level and subject to full judicial review of its implementing rules. It is certain that all Member States' legal systems contain rules, which try to promote and improve political accountability. Nonetheless, the often unclear distinction between national authorities' responsibilities may undermine such efforts. It is, thus, logical to assume that there is a great deal of accessibility asymmetry between market players that are close to the national regulator and other market participants – possibly from other Member States – that lack these advantageous contacts. Lack of clarity in the objectives of multiple regulators equals to lack of accountability, not only across themselves, but also across the institutions and markets they regulate. In addition, practical hurdles, such as language and distance foster the problem.[102] As a result, Member States' supervisors are far away from producing an open, transparent and accountable regime.

On the other hand, if a single regulator is given a clear set of responsibilities, then it ought to be possible to increase transparency and accountability,[103] at least in terms of its performance against its statutory objectives, the regulatory regime, the cost of regulation, its disciplinary policies and the supervisory failures.[104] When the pan-European supervisory framework is clear, then it has the advantage of pinning appropriate accountability on the different actors in the system. In contrast to the home country control system, there is clearly no doubt who is responsible in the event of supervisory failure. Consequently, an open pan-European Regulator will be better accepted by individuals and undertakings. Edwards argues that Europeans need to have more than a minimum knowledge of the European institutions, procedures, norms and values in order to accept them.[105] This is the definition of legitimacy.[106] Transparency, thus, is an integral factor in the process of legitimisation and the single regulator, as every other EU institution, must be seen as more efficient, democratic and effective, both in terms of policy-making and policy implementation. Sometimes, however, as a result of transfer of certain powers to a new organ some of the legitimacy may be lost. Legitimacy, for instance, may not automatically follow delegation of powers from the Commission or the Council to the ESR. According to a different view, it is also possible that transparency and legitimacy are enhanced. This is likely to be the case when powers are transferred from the less powerful national supervisory authorities to a central body. It is, thus, vital in this context that the new Securities Regulator creates and establishes its own legitimacy, which, as the establishment of the ECB has shown, may take a significant amount of time.[107]

We must acknowledge that the creation of a pan-European Securities Regulator will result in a significant increase in concentration of supervisory powers to a single body. There is always a concern that a single regulator 'could potentially become an overmighty bully, a bureaucratic leviathan divorced from the industry it regulates'.[108] It is therefore vital that this body establishes a robust transparency and accountability framework, explicitly laid down in Article 1 EC Treaty, so that firms, individuals and markets approve and accept its competence. Right from the beginning, this major institutional reform ought to be based on the broadest possible debate, participation and consensus as the declaration appended to the Nice Treaty has called.

Transparency is further improved whenever the influence of considerations is made visible.[109] Of particular importance herein is the right of access of documents. It should be noted, however, that the new right of access, as introduced by Article 255 EC (former Article 191a), is limited to the documents of the three main institutions,[110] and hence does not seem to cover other bodies. Nonetheless, encouraged by recommendations of the European Ombudsman that agencies, too, should adopt rules on access to documents,[111] most institutions have adopted relevant decisions.[112] Regardless of the responsibilities undertaken, the single regulator should be obliged to undertake consultation on all rules and guidance that it adopts; it should publicise all responses received and explain the reasons that led to specific policy decisions; in making its proposals, it should include cost–benefit analyses of potential measures adopted; also, it should submit reports to the European Parliament and the ECOFIN Council on its work and publicise the records of its meetings;[113] finally, all measures adopted should be subject to judicial review.[114] At the same time, the accountability and legitimacy of regulation of the Securities Supervisor can be fostered by its relationship with the network of Member States' authorities. The better the relationship and interaction with existing national regulators, the more open and accountable its decision-making process will be.

To conclude, it is obvious that an open and easily accessible single regulator is more likely to reduce the information asymmetries for market participants by facilitating public access to financial market information and, thus, by coping with unequal costs of gathering information. On the other hand, it has by definition a significant advantage compared to a more fragmented supervisory structure: as soon as it keeps a clear distance with the industry it regulates, it will dramatically lessen the possibilities of being captured or pressured by private interest groupings. As long as it manages to incorporate an independent administrative structure and culture of open communication and clear lines of accountability, it will enhance decision-making and will maintain confidence in the European financial system.

3. Legislative delay and inflexibility: the Wise Men proposals and the harmonisation prerequisite

Another reason that justifies centralisation of EU securities supervision and regulation is the regulatory inflexibility of the current regime. It is argued herein that a single Securities Regulator will be in a better position to legislate fast and better, while complete harmonisation of European financial laws should not serve as a prerequisite for the establishment of the ESR.

3.1. Regulating after Lamfalussy

Until recently, there has been no structure in the European securities industry parallel to the legislative committees existing in the banking and insurance field.[115] Any technical adaptation of the core directives needed to take the form of a formal amendment, with the problems and delays this can imply. Has the recently established ESC, proposed by the Lamfalussy Group, been able to change the scenery? Whereas the goal of the Wise Men Report was to speed up EU securities regulation, it appears that Level 2 with its five-step procedure may actually delay it. Besides the problem of multi-institutional involvement, the very distinction of essential Level 1 and non-essential Level 2 measures raises significant theoretical and practical hurdles.[116] Almost one-and-a-half year after its creation, the ESC has failed to commence operation, let alone to deliver. Mutual suspicion between national and EU institutions has complicated the enactment of investment services legislation. Criticism of the framework has come mostly from the European Parliament, which voted in favour of an appeals procedure or 'call-back' that would enable it to review and halt legislation proposed at Level 2 beyond the scope of the Wise Men Report.[117] The same concerns are shared by a number of market participants and academics.[118] Moving a step further, the von Wogau Report has already limited the life of the ESC to four years, as an ultimate effort to provide the Parliament with leverage over the Commission and the Council to ensure that a 'call-back' mechanism is introduced in the next ICG.[119] It becomes, thus, obvious that new institutional arrangements need to be addressed and adopted before that time lapses.

Beyond the constitutional concerns, the current regulatory and supervisory regime has practical implications on how legislation is passed. Here, one should pay special attention to the lock-in problem that the home country control regime delivers. As admitted by the Commission and the Lamfalussy Group, the present functioning of the European legislative system cannot meet the challenge of regulating modern financial markets.[120] It is beyond evidence that every attempt to regulate at the EU level and to implement at Member State level is doomed to be lost in the vortex of severe delay and bureaucracy.[121] The problem unfolds beyond the financial services sector and has, thus, been one of the main concerns of the 2001 White Paper on European Governance and the 2001 Laeken Council. It takes time and effort to construct a pan-European regulatory regime, as each Member State negotiates both with its counterparts and with domestic lawmakers and interest groups. The current process for promulgating and amending Directives is inadequate to deal with fast-moving financial markets so that 'even new provisions for setting standards, by the time they are enacted, may very well be out of date'.[122] Directives end up being rather inflexible and almost impossible to alter once adopted. It seems, thus, likely that EU regulation runs the risk of becoming outmoded and anachronistic.[123] *A fortiori*, it also runs the greater risk of being less qualitative and efficient, since it will constitute the product of controversies and compromises.

The Wise Men fast-track agreement solution to speed up the legislative process does not seem likely to change the scenery. Although this procedure consists of only one reading for Commission proposals, the whole legislative process will not be actually shortened for the following reasons. First, the Lamfalussy approach is very much dependent on the political will of the Parliament and Council. It is up to these institutions to clearly define what is 'essential legislation' and what are 'technical issues' to be left to comitology.[124] Second, experience has proved very difficult for the Parliament and the Council to agree in the first reading, due to the technical nature of the legislative proposals in the financial sector.[125] Finally, it is likely that 'technical measures' will be more and more regarded as political issues and thus become part of the Level 1 'framework legislation'. Hence, this procedure could become a 'legal battlefield' and struggle between EU institutions and national regulators.

A further issue is that, even if adopted, EU laws – mostly in the form of Directives – are delegated to Member States to be implemented. The average delay in implementation of a Directive, once the deadline has passed, is thirteen months.[126] Moreover, since national securities markets regulation is often differently organised at Member States' level and national supervisors merely share the same powers,[127] it is inevitable that the principles of EU law will be turned into workable day to day rules in a way that they could be characterised as anything but uniform.[128] For example, the freedom left to Member States as to the choice of means and methods to attain the objectives prescribed by Article 11 of the ISD is reflected in the relative diversity of implementing rules with respect to both the substance of the rules and the legal instruments used.[129]

It has, thus, been suggested that the Council should adopt EU investment services rules using 'fast-track' procedures, namely in the form of Regulations, in order to improve transparency, speed and accuracy of transposition and implementation.[130] In our view, however, it is debateable whether Regulations will achieve the so-desirable efficiency and uniformity. Since they do not need Member State transposition,[131] Regulations often constitute a mixture of controversial trends and require greater efforts and compromises by national governments to reach agreement; and like most compromises, they are likely to be unsatisfactory – from the outset, slow to draft and simultaneously difficult to amend in the light of changing circumstances. Normally 'every "t" must be crossed and every "i" must be dotted since Member States are not to tamper with them'.[132] In such a complex and technical area of law as financial services regulation, it is almost impossible to devise Regulations, which have the requisite specificity and are also suited to immediate impact into all of the Member States. For this reason, they are by nature often less detailed and more vague than Directives, which explains their rare usage by the Community legislator.

Here lies the weakness of Regulations. Vagueness may easily upset the advantage of direct effect. According to Craig and de Burca, if a provision is vague, if it sets out only a very general aim which needs further implementing measures to be made concrete and clear, then it is difficult to accord direct effect to that provision and to allow its direct application by a national court.[133] Indeed, despite its general disapproval to Member States' transposition, the ECJ did accept in *Amsterdam Bulb* that Member States could provide in national legislation for appropriate sanctions, which were not provided for in the Regulation, to assist in its enforcement.[134] This opens the way for domestic legislation to continue to regulate various related matters, which – given its less detailed and inflexible structure – were not specifically covered in the Regulation.

The lock-in problem of inflexibility of the present regulatory system admits of two solutions. First, Member States may delegate substantial lawmaking and implementation power to a pan-European body to permit flexible responses to changes in the regulatory environment of investment services. Second, Member States could explore alternatives to regulatory cooperation at the EU level. With regard to the latter, however, it shall be shown below[135] that current coordination efforts between national supervisors have not been proved efficient enough. Nothing indicates that this situation is about to change in the near future.

At this stage, it is thus vital that investment services lawmaking and implementation is delegated to a single Securities Regulator. Presumably, reversing an assignment of regulatory power through Member States' negotiations would be as difficult and cumbersome a process as extending the authority in the first place. The very belief, however, that this will strongly contribute to the increase of the speed and efficiency of future legislation makes any such suggestion a minor issue. Flexibility is a structural attribute. Arguably, if the regulator is empowered to promulgate, repeal, amend and interpret regulation, then the system should be able to provide the right dose of flexibility. National authorities have to realise its significance on the one hand and to abandon the principle that the current allocation of responsibilities between them is sacrosanct on the other. Bearing in mind that, even with a fair wind, a new Directive scarcely ever takes less than three years between inception and delivery, decisions originating from the pan-European Regulator would speed up the legislative process in Europe. More, however, with respect to the ESR's competencies will be discussed in Chapter 7.

3.2. Is there a need for further harmonisation before the creation of the ESR?

It is argued by many critics of centralisation that a further harmonisation of investment services rules is needed before a single ESR can be established.[136] Should there be no harmonisation, a potential ESR would be ill equipped to function efficiently,[137] for it would have to operate across different legal and cultural structures. The Joint Forum Report on the role of coordination[138] stressed the importance of taking account of these factors in defining the role and responsibilities of a coordinator. These include the different legal frameworks of the countries where a financial firm operates, the different statutory responsibilities and powers of the individual supervisors concerned, the divergences of enforcement methods and the varying abilities of these regulators to share information across sectors and across borders. Hence, the deep differences in the legal tradition of the Member States will result in even more regulation, leading to even greater differences between national rules. The following paragraphs endeavour to analyse the scope of such an allegation and defend the view that *ex ante* full harmonisation cannot constitute a precondition for operational effectiveness of a pan-European regulator. Instead, the latter can better perform as the effective means of harmonisation of securities regulation within the EU. In any event, European market integration has, in fact, proceeded further than is commonly perceived so that Member States should be able to accept a supranational solution of this kind.[139]

Opponents of a pan-European Regulator argue that private market incentives will find and maintain an optimal level of investor protection.[140] None the less, the real question for the near future is whether the fragmented Member States supervisory authorities will be willing and able to establish a harmonised regulatory structure or whether a pan-European Securities Regulator would be better able to do the job. To rephrase the main thesis of subsidiarity, 'the functions handed over to the Union [should be] those which the Member States, at the various levels of decision-making, can no longer discharge satisfactorily'.[141] At the heart of its relation with subsidiarity, the home country control principle does not amount to maximising the number of tasks and responsibilities, which can be taken on at a Member State level, but to achieving an optimum distribution of such tasks and responsibilities.

In any harmonisation process, what is often examined is whether rules that result from harmonisation are better than those emerging from competition among national rules.[142] When the latter is the case, then many scholars contend that regulatory responses should follow market developments and not lead them.[143] This argument is not convincing for two reasons: first, regulation should keep pace with market developments and not lag behind, at least for the better achievement of the financial supervisory objectives analysed in Chapter 1. Second, the regulatory environment and the institutional structure of financial supervision is actually one key factor affecting harmonisation and market integration. As demonstrated before, the present regime of home country control is responsible for serious obstacles to achieving a truly integrated European market and free flow of cross-border investment services. Breuer rightly observes that this is not a 'chicken and egg' problem, so we should not waste time debating who should move first.[144]

Hence, harmonisation should not serve as a prerequisite for the establishment of a federal regulator. Complete harmonisation may be neither necessary nor wholly realistic at this point. Instead, a pan-European Securities Supervisor should serve as means of further harmonisation of EU financial services law. Just as the euro required the establishment of a European Central Bank, a pan-European securities market will require an ESR. Given the difficulties in legislating at EU level and implementing at Member State level, we clearly need a uniform way of creating EU rules and an easy, efficient and unconditional way of transforming it to national legal systems. As the following section will show, rivalries between the London, Frankfurt, Euronext and other markets are too strong and there hardly exists a sufficient European tradition of investor protection to overcome the hurdles of cross-border investment services provision.

Solving the problem of harmonisation through implementation of Directives or Regulations formulated by Member States' regulators seems both time-consuming and impractical. Securities markets are far more creative and dynamic. This is the reason why self-regulation has functioned well for the investment services industry, despite its inherent limitations.[145] Transferring supervision of the self-regulatory process to fifteen different national authorities will hardly result in a pan-European market. It would rather compound the problems of a fragmented system for the trading and regulation of securities. A central, flexible regulator that could deal directly with markets and financial operators could provide more appropriate and better oversight.

What is important is that, despite major delays, market integration and harmonisation in securities and other financial services legislature has proceeded further than is commonly perceived to support a federal institutional structure and a level-playing field for market participants and consumers. Although there remains a concern about the pace to deliver the FSAP in line with the agreed timeframe and political statements, there has been a certain degree of progress. The political agreement on the Distance Marketing Directive and the final adoption of the anti-Money Laundering Directive, the Statute for a European Company Regulation and the UCITS Directives have been considered as further steps towards integrating European financial markets. A final adoption of the Regulation on IAS and the proposed Directives on Distance Marketing, Insurance Intermediaries and Collateral were within reach before the end of the Spanish Presidency (June 2002). Moreover, political agreement has been reached on 7 May 2002 on the proposed Directives on Market Abuse and Financial Conglomerates, with the aim of adopting them as soon as possible in early 2003. Political agreement in the Council was also expected by the summer of 2002 on the proposed Directives on Prospectuses and Supplementary Pension Funds, with final adoption by December 2002 for Pension Funds and in 2003 for Prospectuses.[146] However, the most important updates of CAD and ISD are still under preparation. The FSAP mid-term review of 19 February 2002 urges the need for renewed efforts, but remains optimistic that the priorities and measures of the Action Plan will be in place by the next IGC.

4. Securities exchanges consolidation and alliances

A further reason that demands centralisation of securities regulation and supervision is the consolidation and alliances between securities exchanges and trading platforms. Despite growing consolidation efforts between financial markets, a strong home bias persists in primary and secondary market activity in the EU. Partly, this situation reflects inertia in investment patterns. However, it is also the case that cross-border issuance, trading and settlement are beset by 'numerous outstanding legal and technical obstacles'.[147] On the other hand, it becomes now evident in Europe that the investment horizons of funds and private investors are slowly becoming more European. Exchanges, traditionally organised and managed as national monopolies, are now competing for order flows between themselves and with new competitors that offer trading services, such as ATS. As a consequence, many of them are seeking European reach through organic growth, while others are looking to far-reaching alliances or fully fledged mergers. It will be argued herein that this situation raises new consideration and challenges that are unlikely to be met by the existing financial institutional structure. Therefore, truly pan-European markets will soon require a real pan-European Regulator.

4.1. Exchanges

The higher cost of transacting cross-border deals in Europe compared to the United States, means securities exchanges consolidation is necessary and inevitable. Once the traditional fragmentation of European markets has been resolved, the pan-European market will be able to respond in terms of cost, technological development, capacity to adapt and strategic vision. In the short to medium term, market developments' effects on the regulatory mechanisms for securities markets will gain substantial gravity.[148] But there is more. All this is happening at a time of unprecedented volatility in stock market indexes, driven in part by the behaviour of the 'new economy' and in part by the weak single currency and world financial situation.

New types of markets create new types of investors and new types of risks, which in turn require new types of solutions. Whatever the outcome of the market consolidation initiatives across Europe, there will be tough questions posed for national regulators. What will the role be for national regulators of undertakings operating as remote central exchanges? How can we ensure an adequate degree of harmonisation to allow an exchange to operate in a number of different Member States? Regulators will face a difficult task. A complex one: the challenge of progress. A challenge, which will imply overcoming the internal inefficiencies that stem directly from the desire to continue with local *status quo*.

The boom of telecommunications and EMU make securities markets more attractive. Twelve EU national markets have gone through a major structural change and have received a strong impetus to integrate into a single euro area market. This means that divergences purely related to the *locus* of market participants within the euro area become less and less relevant over time. In particular, the reduction in government debt securities owing to fiscal consolidation under the EMU, low inflation rates, elimination of exchange risk and the commitment of national governments towards improving the sustainability of public finances is expected to boost markets for securities issued by private entities.[149] This is also likely to be supported by the enhanced liquidity and less transactions cost of the private stock and bond markets resulting from the increase in the number of investors and issuers operating in the same currency.[150] A research conducted by Hardouvelis,

Malliaropoulos and Priestley has shown that the average cumulative saving in the cost of capital from integration of stock exchanges over the period 1992–98 is estimated at around 2 per cent for the EU-12 countries.[151] It is also likely that a larger currency area, the eurozone, will attract new foreign investors and issuers to the European securities markets. In this context, the efforts already undertaken to set up alliances and mergers between stock exchanges will be facilitated.

Nevertheless, while joint ventures and mergers among exchanges are yet in the planning process, there are numerous obstacles to their successful fruition. European markets still compete with each other with regard to liquidity, transparency and cost.[152] Within euro, they also compete for listings and new products. Stock exchanges have already been privatised and now are demutualising. Some have and others may become listed companies, while their corporate structure differs. Take, for example, the collapse of the iX project, the once promising alliance plans between London and Frankfurt exchanges: what disclosure and accounting standards would apply to their listed companies? Which regulator should monitor trading and enforce insider dealing and similar laws? These problems were partly set out in a report issued by Merrill Lynch, advisers to the London exchange: 'UK regulators believe that Anglo-German attempts to harmonise share trading rules will be a "nightmare" if the London Stock Exchange and the Deutsche Börse merge to create iX. The report says that senior staff at the FSA have said privately that it will be difficult to achieve "any practical level of harmonisation" of UK and German stock market regulations'.[153] Similar problems still torture the, otherwise successful, project of Euronext markets alliance.[154]

Vis-à-vis this evolving environment, regulators cannot remain still. Since present and future markets will soon have very little in common with the 'regulated markets' envisaged in the ISD, it becomes blurred as to who will regulate and supervise them. Under the ISD, for instance, home supervisors oblige 'regulated markets' to deal only in formally 'listed' stocks. As a result, it is completely unclear under the current regime whether a trading system operator designated as a 'regulated market' in one Member State will not be denied single passport rights in another jurisdiction on the basis that the particular operator does not itself 'list' the securities that it trades.[155] On the other hand, let us assume that an ATS, established in a home Member State, wishes to enter the market of another (host) Member State by use of its screen-based capacity. The ISD states that Article 15 'shall not affect the Member State's right to authorise or prohibit the creation of new markets within their territories'.[156] It seems that the intent of this provision was to furnish the host State with another escape clause from the European passport for screen-based electronic trading systems. By declaring a foreign trading system to be a 'new market', any host Member State could deny it European passport rights. The potential for abuse is now considerable. And the question arises: will national supervisory authorities be more capable than a pan-European regulator to deliver the job and offer solutions? A centralised supervisory regime will offer solutions at least in three fields, namely single passport for markets, competition and transmission effects.

First, under a centralised supervisory regime, any physical or electronic market, wishing to offer cross-border listing or trading services, would not need to face any EU authority's denial of its single passport rights on the grounds that it is seeking to create a 'new market' in its territory. After a single authorisation for operation and with a fully operational single passport, markets will be free to place screen trading facilities in partner Member States, so as to serve 'remote members' in other Member States. This will tackle the problem of fragmentation and will boost the potential for competition.[157]

Second, closer integration of securities markets increases the possibility that regulatory or supervisory differences influence competition between exchanges for trading volume. All aforementioned developments involve conflicts of interest between the commercial interests and regulatory responsibilities of exchanges that stand in the way of an integrated European regulatory system for a pan-European securities market. These conflicts could be best addressed and eliminated by an independent central authority, which would have no such commercial interests and would guarantee efficiency and stability in the function of European markets. On the other hand, a single authority will be needed in the near future to independently scrutinise the various inter-exchange cooperation agreements for their effects on competition between exchanges. To the extent that cooperation leads to substituting a single trading platform to competition for trading in specific securities, agreements may be considered to produce anti-competitive effects in the relevant market and may run contrary to Article 81 EC (former Article 85).[158] Although current securities markets' agreements are framed in a context of 'coopetition', in which inter-exchange competition and cooperation are said to coexist, the issue will remain crucial for future European financial market supervision structures.

Finally, developments in one regulated market may well have immediate and potentially major repercussions on the trading environment in other Member States. A central body would serve as a rapid response to transmission effects by upholding market integrity, confidence and stability. Regulatory or supervisory arrangements governing a large scale of European markets cannot be permitted to evolve on an *ad hoc* basis in response to the technical challenges presented by a particular merger or alliance. As it will be subsequently analysed,[159] building a mechanism of concentrated regulatory and supervisory power would offer legal certainty, stability and efficiency in a fast-evolving and so volatile European market.

4.2. Clearing and settlement

Relevant to the challenge of the ESR to ensure the proper function of the market is the need to eliminate undue and unnecessary risks and costs of inefficient and inadequate clearing and settlement systems within Europe.[160] According to the initial report of the Giovannini Group, which describes the current European clearing and settlement landscape, the existing arrangements within the EU are largely efficient in respect of domestic securities transactions.[161] These arrangements, however, are national-based and do not combine to provide respective post-trade processing for cross-border transactions. It has been calculated that as much as €1 billion a year of operating cost savings would be secured if cross-border equity settlement were conducted as efficiently as that in the United States. As part of this saving, economies of scale could be created and the larger part of the cross-border clearing and settlement in Europe could be eliminated, greatly reducing risk, if a single European central counterparty (EuroCCP) were introduced in displacement of the present fragmented netting arrangements that operate mainly on Member State basis.[162] This would have the advantage of allowing netting of all national and cross-border transactions concluded on the same day and, ideally, compress all transactions of a trading participant into a single cash flow or obligation.[163]

Although further restructure of clearing and settlement systems seems necessary in the EU, Dalhuisen is right to assume that the unproblematic history of these systems does not call for their regulation *per se*.[164] Rightly, the securities industry and the Final Wise Men Report accept that market forces should determine the contours of clearing and settlement in Europe.[165] This does not mean, however, that there are and there will be no public policy issues that have to be addresses and coped with by a central public body. Although the establishment of a EuroCCP seems an early target for the short-to-medium term, the benefits that this achievement would deliver, such as risk reduction at a member and systemic level, cost savings, reliability, scalability and integrity of services, call for a move towards this direction in the long term.[166]

In a recent Communication, the European Commission has identified two main policy objectives for the creation of an integrated clearing and settlement environment.[167] The first is to remove barriers to the finalisation of individual cross-border transactions in the form of Member States' differences in technical requirements/market practice, tax procedures and laws applying to securities. Although it is acknowledged that the removal of technical barriers will be primarily in the hands of the private sector, the remaining barriers will require public intervention, as in the case of defining the legal system that is applicable to securities transactions and holdings in the EU.[168] The second objective is to remove competitive distortions or unequal treatment of entities performing similar clearing and settlement activities. A fully integrated EU system requires that rights of access to systems be comprehensive, transparent, objective and, above all, effective.

These policy objectives go hand in hand with the general objectives of financial regulation and supervision analysed in Chapter 1: the maintenance of financial stability and consumer protection, the extension of consumer choice and the fostering of competition. Consolidation of exchanges and clearing systems in Europe will lead to an acute political question, for which the ESR will provide the only answer and solution. Even if the EuroCCP were to be governed and regulated by private market forces, there will ultimately be a need for oversight by the ESR with regard to prudential and competition implications in order to avoid duplication of compliance and shield its members from systemic risk.[169] Also, there are concerns about the actions of national regulators, who would have the right to object on grounds of adverse implications for the smooth operation of the market. In the absence of agreed standards for the authorisation, oversight and supervision of SSS, national authorities may have concerns about the use of systems in other jurisdictions for the finalisation of transactions on their markets, or involving their institutions and investors. Central supervision, common standards and high-level principles should thus be sought given the pan-European character of an integrated financial market.[170] However, it is possible that common industry and/or regulatory standards may not be sufficient to provide a fair, efficient and stable framework for cross-border use of clearing and settlement systems. They may leave room for continued constraint on the exercise of rights of access and choice and on the stability of the system. In that case, a European regulator will have the most proper resources to carry out its oversight functions, such as authorisation, risk management techniques, gathering information on the participants' systems, assessing the operation and design of the systems and taking action to promote the systems' observance of European standards.

5. The euro as a catalyst

The introduction of a single currency within the eurozone calls for a single supervisory regime for EU investment services. One of the most significant economic effects of the EMU will be the achievement of an internal financial market as envisioned in Article 14(2) EC. The motto of the Maastricht Treaty has been 'one market, one currency'. The introduction of the euro in twelve EU Member States constitutes a 'quantum jump' which gives a new dimension to the internal financial market, brings economic agents closer together and has the effect of increasing and intensifying legal relationships across the euro area.[171]

5.1. The EMU and supervisory concerns

It is true that European financial markets have not been automatically unified by the introduction of the euro. Nor has financial supervision. Local habits, regulations and vested interests will keep market segmented for some time.[172] Yet, it is also certain that competitive pressures will become irresistible in the medium to the long run. The EMU has discerned the inadequacies of the Community internal market legislation as it exists at the start of the third stage.[173] Moreover, the geographical domain of monetary policy and prudential supervision do not coincide anymore; monetary policy is now conducted at the euro area level, whereas supervision of markets and individual financial institutions has remained the responsibility of national authorities. By the same token, the Monetary Union is triggering a broad debate on the adequacy of the supervisory framework for financial institutions and markets.

This debate involves three concerns: first, the strong interpenetration of financial markets and the enlarged scope of systemic risk as a result of which the EMU poses a challenge to the limited integration and cooperation in the supervision of financial markets. Second, the trend towards conglomeration and competition in the financial services sector, partly caused by the single currency, raises the question of whether the current institutional structure for the supervision of financial intermediaries is adequate for the task. Finally, the transfer of monetary policy to the ECB raises the question of what role it will play in the area of prudential supervision and financial stability, which yet remain Member State responsibilities. This section addresses the second issue, namely the consequences of the introduction of the single currency in the supervision of financial firms.[174] Its conclusions may be summarised in the motto 'one market, one currency, one regulator'.

5.2. Impact on financial institutions

5.2.1. Consolidation and competition

The impact of the euro on financial intermediaries providing financial services is not as direct as that on financial markets. Over the past few years, a favourable climate has prevailed across the entire European capital market, both in bonds and equities. Buoyant securities markets have stimulated new issues and helped to finance a wave of mergers and acquisitions (M&A). Of course, M&A historically preceded the EMU. However, an ongoing wave of mergers is occurring within the EU banking and investment systems after the EMU, which is expected to keep momentum at least in the short to the medium term.[175] Although most M&A at the EU level take place in the domestic area, two basic strategies are to be observed with reference to cross-border M&A: first, expansion into market niche abroad and, second, entering into foreign retail markets. The latter involves a need for access to an adequate distribution network, which is easier to achieve via strategic alliances or mergers. The introduction of the single currency and developments in electronic remote provision of investment services facilitate the cross-border conduct of financial services. This is likely to outweigh traditional hurdles of cross-border M&A, such as legal, fiscal and cultural differences with regard to management style and strategic goals.

The single currency will also have a significant effect on the risk faced by financial firms when conducting cross-border business, which may give

them an incentive for increasing their intra-Community trade and competition. European financial intermediaries already face increased competition
after the introduction of the euro, as it has facilitated the comparison of the
commissions charged and has led to cost reductions. Overall, credit, market,
liquidity and market liquidity risks are generally expected to decrease,
whereas legal and operational risks are likely to increase at least in the short
term.[176] The positive macroeconomic effects of the EMU are expected to
mitigate credit risk in European financial markets. In addition, market and
liquidity risks will be positively affected by deeper and more liquid markets.
On the other hand, while legal and operational risks are expected to increase
in the short term owing to the major changes to the overall legal environment, they are likely to decrease in the long term.

The creation of mega pan-European financial institutions and holding
companies of financial groups in the EMU brings the question of the division of responsibilities for such businesses into sharp focus. The post-BCCI
Directive provides for a measure of financial firms holding supervision by
the home competent authority. A new Commission proposal purports to
introduce specific prudential legislation for financial conglomerates and
coordination arrangements between supervisors.[177] In these circumstances,
the responsibility of home authorities in conducting efficient consolidated
supervision will increase considerably.[178] On the other hand, host supervisors could find that they have insufficient information either to monitor the
health of the financial system to anticipate a crisis or to be able to react to
it rapidly and effectively.[179] In any event, the task of appointing one or two
lead supervisors is not one without significant operational difficulties. These
may include: (a) acceptance of the leading role by the supervisor concerned
and by all other authorities, (b) ensuring that the supervisor concerned has
all the necessary human and financial resources, (c) securing full agreement
on the precise conferred powers and responsibilities, ensuring comprehensive information collection, and (d) agreement on the scope of supervision
conducted and removal of any relevant jurisdictional difficulties.[180] The
pan-European Securities Regulator or even a Single Financial Regulator[181]
may take an interest in the application of this Directive and study whether
there is a need for further Community legislation to enable pan-European
holding companies to be established and supervised on a European basis.
Indeed, the emergence of large banking and investment groups requires an
adequate legislative and supervisory response, which, in view of the size and
the spread of the entities concerned, should come about at the EU level,
instead of being confined to national competent authorities.[182]

5.2.2. The European Company (Societas Europeae – SE) Project

In the same line comes the resuscitation of the 30-years old project for
the European company, the last legislative effort for which was made
in 1991. When the bulk of the business of the financial undertakings is

conducted domestically, the home authority has the least difficulty in carrying out consolidated supervision. But, will the solution of home country consolidated supervision apply to the case, where financial firms are established under European law? In October 2001, the Council of Ministers reached its final agreement on the Regulation to establish a European Company Statute.[183] The European Company will become a reality some 30 years after it was first proposed. As a result, financial firms and their subsidiaries will have the option of being established as a single company under Community and home country law and so able to operate throughout the Union with one set of rules and a unified management and reporting system. Indeed, consolidation of financial market participants, such as pan-European stock exchanges, banks and investment firms, multinational SSSs and EuroCCP for repo clearing houses, would benefit from a legal construction that is single and valid throughout the EU.

A further significant benefit of the SE is that it can easily transfer its registered and principal office to another Member State, which is generally not possible at present, as such a transfer is treated as a liquidation under applicable company and/or tax law.[184] This may substantially facilitate regulatory arbitrage, while it makes it obvious that placing European financial companies under the home country supervision system is extremely difficult, if not impossible. The European Company framework, when it will result in institutions having a substantial share or even the majority of their operations in other than their establishment countries, is bound to loosen the ties with their home supervisors.[185] Although European companies will still have to be registered in the Member State where they have their registered office, it is doubtful whether their supervisors will be able to efficiently keep under surveillance their whole pan-European business. Therefore, the supervisory concerns highlighted in Chapter 5 would be greatest.[186]

When this project becomes reality, it will radically change the concept of home country control, as we perceive it today. Just as national companies need national supervisors, European financial companies will need the supervision of a European Regulator. As European companies' activities will not be limited by Member States' borders and as the currency will be common in the whole eurozone, so should a central European Authority have surveillance powers beyond them.

On the whole, EU Member States have decided to abandon their national currencies and join a common money area in an attempt to integrate their financial markets. However, the main problem that financial services are not yet enjoying full free movement lies with national regulators themselves. Yet, governments remain answerable to their national electorates. Monetary union notwithstanding, Member States still defend their economic policies on the grounds of protection of the people within their jurisdiction. The road towards financial market integration is of an evolutionary nature, where each legal action is determined on a case-by-case basis.[187] In order for investment services and markets to take full advantage of the introduction of the euro, we need an institutional convergence to complete the legal convergence and enhance the operational convergence. 'One regulator' should be added to the 'one currency' in order to deliver the 'one market' that will contribute to the smooth and efficient functioning of financial services.

6. Externalities and crisis management

Externalities constitute one of the most significant reasons that require the involvement of a federal pan-European body as the only means of ensuring financial stability. International securities swindles have undermined the global financial system from the time of the 1929 stock market crash to the 1998 collapse of the Russian and East Asian economies.[188] There is no need to assess the cost of such financial crises.[189] Although each crisis has a set of local explanatory factors, they all share common elements. The chaos theory teaches us that all results have a cause. In addition, the spillover impact of such crises cannot be 'local'. The purpose of this section is to explore the possibilities of effective crisis management by the current home country supervision regime and to examine whether a more centralised structure would execute a more successful pre-crisis assessment or rescue programme in the case of an emergency. In this regard, it is useful to consider the circumstances surrounding the bankruptcy of the BCCI, once the fastest growing bank in the world, in 1991.

6.1. The BCCI

The collapse of the BCCI was the result of a massive fraud. It posed particular supervisory problems because the two companies, through which it carried out its international banking business, were registered in Luxembourg and the Cayman Island, its principal shareholders were latterly based in Abu Dhabi and the group was largely managed from London.

The Bank of England had been aware of some of the problems facing the BCCI, but had judged that, on the information then available to it and in light of a commitment from its principal shareholders to re-capitalise the bank and to oversee changes to its management, systems and groups structure, the interests of depositors would be best served by dealing with the weakness within the on-going business.[190] The formal enquiry, conducted by Lord Justice Bingham after the BCCI failure,[191] criticised the Bank of England's supervisory approach, although it did not call for any radical changes to the basic system.[192] *Per contra*, in the *Three Rivers* case, the House of Lords did not accept that the Bank of England failed to provide continuous and effective supervision according to the provisions of Community law and, thus, it refused to recognise enforceable rights for depositors on the basis of the FBD.[193]

From a EU international standpoint, the most important legacy of the Bingham Report was the attention which it drew to the prevailing shortcomings in the supervision of internationally operating financial groups.[194] This has led to a tightening of international standards, as established by the Basel Committee, which have since given legislative backing in the EU. The post-BCCI Directive constitutes an emblematic paradigm. Nonetheless, the Bingham Report stopped short of posing any major questions to national or international regulators with regard to the supervision of the BCCI – and generally of pan-European or international financial firms. Was the Bank of England or the *Institut Monetaire Luxembourgeois* (IML) the principal supervisor of the BCCI?

The fragmentation and the tensions in reconciling domestic and international policies encourage the regulatory process to be primarily state-centred. In the case of the BCCI, its trading activities had considerable impact on the United Kingdom; accordingly, the United Kingdom should be obliged to accept major responsibility for regulating the BCCI empire and to cooperate with other regulators in a cross-border context. Here, an intersection of domestic and global interest was extremely significant. However, 'each regulator tended to focus on its own domestic concerns rather than accepting full collegiate responsibility'.[195] The Bank of England, for instance, could have closed the BCCI at any time since its arrival in the United Kingdom, especially as it lacked a LLR and an effective supervisor, or as it was involved in money laundering activities. But, in its interest to encourage foreign investment in the United Kingdom, the Bank permitted the BCCI to trade.

Certainly Luxembourg had a problem, because the BCCI was registered and licensed there and the IML was the lead supervisor under the Basel Concordat. But it was also the Bank of England's problem because BCCI's effective base was in the United Kingdom, it was widely perceived as a British bank and UK depositors stood to lose much more than those of Luxembourg had things gone wrong.[196] Both Member States, however, refused to undertake the burden of consolidated supervision. Consequently, BCCI continued worldwide operation without being monitored on a concrete and consolidated basis.

Both the Bingham Report and the *Three Rivers* case raise questions about the adequacy of the decentralised framework based on minimum harmonised prudential standards and suggest a review of the effectiveness of the current EU supervisory arrangements. Especially the House of Lords case shows exactly what the FBD was meant to prevent: that regulators can claim non-responsibility because of the involvement of other Member States' regulators.[197]

Obviously, had a centralised pan-European supervisor existed at that time, it would have taken the aforementioned responsibility. The Treasury and Civil Service Committee, in its Report on the BCCI,[198] noted that a number of parties involved considered the College[199] a second best solution when compared to a single supervisory authority. The Bingham Report suggests that if a single supervisor could have been designated, it might have been able at least to clarify responsibilities and to avoid the lack or deficient supervision of any of the BCCI's operating arms. Although it would not be safe to make assumptions of the likely course of events in that case, it is without doubt that a pan-European supervisor would be the best means of requiring a much more detailed independent examination of the group's worldwide business. What it might have discovered is speculative. But again, both the Bank of England and the IML failed to measure up the task.

6.2. *Crisis management and pre-crisis analysis*

The BCCI collapse represents without doubt a conflict between the domestic and international interest of supervisors. Both the United Kingdom and Luxembourg, Member States of a Union that was supposed to guarantee close avenues of collaborative work, were reluctant to undertake their responsibilities. This leads us to four factors, which determine the appropriate structure and size of the supervisory domain and reveal the need for a single supervisory authority to protect consumers and retain financial stability.

The first factor, which has attracted a great deal of debate, is the timing for intervention in the event of a crisis. EU regulators agree that the objective of regulation is 'not to pre-judge where all market developments are heading to, but to ensure that, in the face of massive change, investors do not lose the protection that they can rightly expect to receive from the regulatory system'.[200] We do not share this proposition. Of course, prevention and cure are related, since the way in which each crisis is managed sends out powerful signals for the future. Nonetheless, incidents of the past clearly indicate that modern supervision must be forward looking. The lesson derived from failures of the past is that 'more important than crisis management is pre-crisis risk analysis and loss prevention'.[201] Almost all crises of the past – especially the latest Asian crisis, besides their weakness in the fundamentals, shared the element of panic. And panic cannot be an effective consultant is such circumstances. What was needed then was a stronger surveillance, which would be more focused on preventing policies that enabled a panic in financial markets. Similarly, European regulators must always be looking for trouble ahead instead of waiting for a crisis to occur. Prolepsis is the key in efficient crisis management and the European supervisor can be the key-holder.

The second factor is speed. When the principals of the hundred-billion-dollar hedge fund Long-Term Capital Management called the New York Fed in September 1998 and declared their inability to meet margin calls on the huge positions accumulated in several markets, they knew they were contacting an institution with unmatched clout. As a supervisor, the Fed had detailed information on the financial situation and relationship to LTCM of most major players on the worldwide financial scene. In a very short time, the Fed was able to congregate all the large creditors of LTCM and twist their arms into allotting US$3.6 billion in the recapitalisation of the failing hedge fund, thus reinstating its ability to meet outstanding obligations and pre-serving the financial stability of the US market.

On the morning of 24 September, the Fed in New York took a few hours to guarantee LTCM positions. Would such a swift and effective response be possible within the EMU if a similar situation were to arise? A similar intervention by the ESCB or the CESR would require agreement with each national authority. Every central bank would have an interest in not declar-ing the exposure of its own banks, hoping to limit its exposure to a rescue operation. The same applies to the investment services field. In a major emergency situation, there may be time to make some phone calls or call a meeting, but not to get involved in complex bureaucratic procedures. It is certain that the less the supervisory bodies involved in an emergency crisis, the faster and the more focused response they could achieve. In this respect, the existence of a single supervisor appears ideal. Only a single body would be able to guarantee prompt and efficient crisis management without hav-ing to take into consideration micro-political issues of purely domestic Member State interest.

The third factor-query that arises is what kind of information supervisors will likely want to obtain during the course of an emergency situation and how feasible it is to obtain such information. In contrast to basic finan-cial and operational information generally available to home authorities, the information that a supervisor will likely want to obtain from a supervised entity during an emergency would not necessarily be available to the super-visor prior to the emergency situation.[202] It would be the particulars of the emergency – the nature and scope of the problem – that would indicate what information would be required by supervisors. Moreover, it is the very scope and nature of the crisis that will usually point out to supervisors, which finan-cial firms would likely be affected by the spillover of the emergency. The euro-peanisation of investment business makes it extremely hard for the home supervisor to keep track of risk exposures of individual financial firms con-tinuously. Centralisation of supervision, on the other hand, could enhance supervision practice by putting some emphasis on public disclosure and inter-nal control mechanisms. This issue, however, will be discussed later.[203]

The fourth factor has to do with incentives and conflicts of interest. Under the home country control regime, home and host countries do merely share the same incentives for effective supervision. While home countries would be more interested for protecting financial institutions established within their territory, host supervisors' incentives to monitor foreign firms and deliver their input to the supervisory process may be blunted by the fact that they do not have the ultimate responsibility of overseeing the safety and soundness of these firms.[204] The early stages of the BCCI incident demon-strate that supervisors trying to protect their own investors, depositors and creditors can actually work against each other rather than cooperatively, when the appropriate crisis management mechanisms do not exist.[205]

Whilst the UK, Luxembourg and other College authorities ultimately cooperated to close down the BCCI in July 1991, they also remained sensitive to 'local' interests.[206] The differences between market sizes within the EU also play a role in incentives issues. It would be logical to assume that the provision of investment services by small financial firms in large financial centres may not receive so much attention from the host authorities.

Per contra, a supranational supervisor will not have any particular reason for not being equally interested in the effective monitoring of all EU firms and markets that will fall under its competency, irrespective of where they operate. The European Regulator could then be required to lay down a specific set of procedures, which it would follow in emergency circumstances, in advance so that its actions are predictable. It would also be easier for it to cooperate with other non-EU supervisors involved and avoid this 'tragedy of errors, misunderstandings and failures of communication',[207] which is often unavoidable in any network that tries to coordinate.

In light of these factors, coordination among fifteen or more supervisors runs two additional risks: first, it is unlikely that a rescue operation could be carried out without market participants being aware that such an operation is in progress. Second, national supervisory authorities have private information concerning the exposure of individual financial firms in their jurisdiction and they might be reluctant to reveal such information due to their interest to protect them. Coming to a decision for immediate action could thus involve a complex game: among the supervisors first and then between the supervisors and the financial firms. This may severely cause delays in the information exchange, which could undermine any rescue operation itself.

All these require the immediate action that only a pan-European centralised body could offer. The recurrence of financial failures calls for a combined preventive and remedial response.[208] Naturally, not only is it impossible to prevent all crises, but also crisis prevention comes at a cost.[209] It may involve gathering and updating of information from more than one financial undertaking and group in more than one jurisdiction in order to expedite the assessment of the emergency's impact. A supervisory authority, therefore, has to strike a balance between the costs of holding back the financial system and the costs of crises. Furthermore, the sheer existence of mechanisms to handle crises effectively may make their occurrence more likely – the well-known problem of moral hazard. Taking these drawbacks into consideration, a pan-European Securities Regulator will be compelled to act immediately when the signals of threat become traceable. Moreover, the host country's incentives problem could be overcome by placing the weight of the systemic and cross-border issues at the EU fora, where host supervisors could base their contribution on their expertise of local market conditions. *Per contra* it is unlikely that a network of fragmented supervisors – irrespective of how well organised and communicative it is – will be able to deliver the job. This issue is discussed in the following section.

7. Imperfect information and deficient cooperation

It is widely accepted that the key issues of regulation and supervision of financial institutions are exchange of information between supervisors and coordination of effectives mechanisms for their supervision and intervention when problems arise.[210] However, problems of coordination will emerge in any structure of multiple agencies.[211] Beyond the doubtful competent and sufficient trust between national competent authorities, other factors, such as lack of loyal cooperation and imperfect flow of information, may undermine the efficiency of cooperation between multiple players. This section supports the idea that, albeit the improvement of current coordination structures at the EU and international level, there are still not enough to prevent future crises and guarantee financial stability and consumer protection within the Single Market. This has clearly been the outcome of an assessment conducted by the Lamfalussy Group.[212] To assist our argument, this section shall make use of the results and considerations that followed the collapse of Barings, the United Kingdom's oldest merchant bank, in February 1995.

7.1. Barings

Although the Barings incident exceeds the geographical borders of the European Union, the assessment of its causes may assist this discussion in assessing the weakness of national supervisory networks to supervise transnational investment business.

A general problem in financial supervision is that the jurisdiction of national regulators is smaller than the geographical business area of regulated financial institutions. In contrast to the BCCI case, the Barings collapse was brought about by the trading activities of a member of its Singapore Futures branch combined with a failure of oversight and compliance at every level of organisation.[213] Responsible for the consolidated supervision of the Barings Group was the Bank of England, which acted as the 'lead supervisor'.[214] The Bank received and considered data on Barings' consolidated capital ratios and consolidated large exposures, but was not responsible for the individual supervision of its subsidiary, Barings Futures Singapore (BFS). The Bank of England Report found that the Bank did not review Barings' overseas subsidiaries. Instead, it relied on the auditors and reporting accountants' statements regarding the existence of the connected lending limits of Barings' exposure to the overseas securities subsidiaries. Moreover, the Bank of England also relied on the supervision of BFS by the relevant overseas regulators.[215] The Bank Report clearly criticised the ineffective way the Bank of England was cooperating with overseas supervisors and recommended that it should clearly define its relationship with other regulators and effectively coordinate with them.[216] Moving a step forward, the Singapore Report surpassed the Bank of England Report in criticising the Singapore Monetary Exchange (SIMEX) for having concerns about BFS' activities, not following up on them with urgency and not informing the central bank of Singapore and the Bank of England of these concerns.[217] In addition, the Report observed that the Singapore supervisors should diligently initiate enforcement actions against BFS rather than rely on the parent institution's reputation or on foreign authorities supervising the activities of the head office of such an institution.[218]

7.2. Is cooperation adequate?

The Barings collapse clearly represents a textbook example of the failure of respected national supervisory authorities to carry out their mission and to coordinate and exchange information on a cross-border basis to prevent the failure of a well-respected financial group.[219] Both Reports made clear that, just as in the BCCI incident, international coordination and cooperation were ineffective until true damage was complete.

As with transaction costs, given complete information between Member States' supervisors, there would be no need for sovereign states to delegate power to supranational bodies. Nevertheless, this is hardly the case in real life. The problem with national supervisors is that they are working in the context of national laws and regulations, whereas the core institutions of the EU financial system are now mainly pan-European in coverage. Coordination, for instance, of reporting standards is no small difficulty. As new issues arise, each supervisor will adopt its own reporting requirements to deal with them.[220]

A second problematic issue, especially acute within the EU context, is the institutional structure of financial services supervision. While some countries, such as the United Kingdom, Luxembourg and Denmark, have adopted the idea of a single regulator for their financial sector, different structures are in place elsewhere in Europe, some within finance ministries, some outside. These differences should have a practical impact on collaboration at cross-border level. Given the consolidation of financial services and their regulatory approaches, channels of cooperation may well require feedback from more than one supervisory institution in each Member State, which can easily jeopardise the reliability of communication.

A major issue in this debate is compliance, not in the sense of firms complying with the supervisors' standards, but in the sense of supervisors complying with their international and EU agreements and standards. 'Setting standards is the first step: maintaining them is the hard part', was an apt lecture title by Charles Goodhart.[221] The IOSCO, for instance has issued a Report, which is hoped to serve as guidance on information sharing between national regulators during periods of crisis.[222] Nonetheless, even in the unlikely case that all these recommendations are followed to the letter, certain problems may be impossible to overcome. First, authorities may be sensitive on giving information with an inherent significance for their domestic financial markets.[223] Second, the requested information may be in the possession of more than one authority, which may complicate the cooperative mechanisms. Thirdly, there may be legal or practical reasons, which prevent the exchange of information in some jurisdictions,[224] confidentiality laws that accommodate access to and sharing of information or legal conditions that have first to be met.[225] Serious delays, therefore, are almost inevitable to occur.

In the EU context, FESCO (now CESR) members have agreed on a Multilateral Memorandum of Understanding,[226] which establishes a general framework for cooperation and consultation between supervisory authorities. Nevertheless, it is debatable whether the response to a potential emergency crisis will be facilitated by the time-consuming procedure described in this informal Memorandum (in as much as it is not legally binding) with regard to information exchange, investigations, compliance and enforcement assistance.[227] Although more information is available on MoUs between securities supervisors and regulated markets, cooperation through MoUs raises the questions of effective coordination of supervision, supervisory methods[228] and the content of information exchange. According to Mayes, MoUs do merely provide for regular transfer of routine information among supervisors, but only in the case where possible supervisory problems arise, including suspected misconduct.[229]

The BCCI and Barings crises taken together mandate that cross-border coordination and cooperation in the supervision of financial groups are equally as important as national supervisory efforts.[230] Cooperation mechanisms are indeed useful for specific objectives like discussion and issuing of recommendations and consultative documents to be implemented either by economic agents or by the various regulators. Nevertheless, their mandate is not equally powerful. The rather informal character and weak powers of these mechanisms, the lack of public report and accountability prevent them from being effective administrative instruments.[231] In any given network, from IOSCO to Basel and CESR, all members-supervisors seek to operate by consensus. None has formal powers to censure let alone impose sanctions on members. No national supervisor has the power to intervene in a resolute manner in the event of cross-border financial problems or to undertake drastic actions to prevent distress becoming a major or system-wide crisis. After all, all these groups are composed of national representatives, who – unlike, for example, members of the European Commission or the ECB's Governing Council – do not have an explicit mandate to discard their national perspective in favour of a supranational or pan-European one.[232]

While these networks are mostly concerned with firms' ongoing business, it is doubtful whether their contacts and mutual trust built up are helpful if crises occur and information is sought at very short notice. The principles of home country control and mutual recognition are very demanding in terms of mutual trust, for trust is a basic social mechanism for coping with system complexity and for sustaining long-term cooperation.[233] If national authorities withhold information from each other and treat feedback as unwarranted criticism, conciliation to resolve conflicts is unlikely to be perceived as legitimate. Given that 'constituent organisations lack the capacities and incentives to overcome the obstacles to collective action posed by joint decision traps',[234] it may come as no surprise that networks, such as CESR, are often undermanaged. Since reliance on hierarchical authority is ruled out, capacity development depends on multilateral negotiations to define the terms of reliable regulatory and supervisory cooperation. Networks also entail a final risk: they may turn out to be a degeneration of the hub model, with the hub being not a multilateral institution, but one or two national authorities, dealing bilaterally with each peripheral supervisors. In the economists' jargon, it would be a hegemonic outcome, the hegemony being possibly assigned by the choice of location of an integrated securities market.

A European supervisory kingdom with fifteen kings and queens who frequently meet but do not elect an emperor, may in due course be difficult, if not impossible, to administer. Even an enhanced multilateral code of cooperation among EU securities supervisors should not work in practice. An alternative centralised institutional solution has to be sought and developed.[235] A centralised institution should not simply be a body that develops and imposes regulatory procedures. It should also be a forum, within which the objectives and rules of European financial cooperation are developed and implemented. Many of the goals of an efficient EU financial policy can be achieved by effective coordination of the activities of national authorities. The problem is that the means of achieving that coordination are, at the moment, quite limited. The European supervisor will fill that gap. Such a model should not preclude the establishment of an arrangement to assist or add value to the existing role of Member States' competent authorities and CESR. In particular, the European supervisor could play a constructive role in making CESR a viable and effective organisation for harmonising regulation and ensuring enforcement cooperation.

Of course, it is not argued herein that a perfect institutional structure is attainable. Also within a single regulator structure, there will always be potential problems of communication, information sharing and persistency. But, it is difficult to see how these problems could be more acute within a single regulator with a unified management structure and an effective internal decision-making process than across multiple authorities, each with its own individual and largely independent culture and decision-making structure.[236] What will the case be after the impending enlargement of the Union to CEEC, Cyprus and Malta? No matter how developed and enhanced cooperation is achieved, as a growing body of opinion now demands,[237] it will never substitute the timely access to information and the facilitation of coordination of a single regulator. Yet, outside observers are sceptical about how well such informal arrangements might work and tend to press for explicit pan-EEA arrangements.[238]

Speed is the 'A' and the 'Z' in responding to any fraudulent activity or default, especially when conducted within an electronic network.[239] A central regulatory system should seek out opportunities to leverage national supervisors' efforts to investigate transactions that they view as questionable. Acting as a neutral and independent coordinator, the single regulator will much easily achieve better flow of information, exchange of supervisory mechanisms and equivalence of regulatory capacities between national bodies. This is required, if not demanded, when problems involved are EU area-wide – because of the institutions and markets involved – or there are concerns of systemic problems spreading across borders. Moreover, centralisation enhances the quality of supervision by examining common trends in the financial system that may not be revealed from the national perspective only.

To conclude, despite existing enhanced cooperative efforts within the European supervisory regime, it is important that these be underpinned by a clear EU-wide coordinating authority, which will eliminate and substitute misunderstandings, institutional rivalry and excessive forbearance by national regulators. Managerial time is limited in the period before, and even more after a crisis, where response needs to be prompt and efficient. The gradually consolidating European markets simply cannot afford a crisis to emerge in order to realise that current regulatory and supervisory arrangements are ill-adapted to deliver the job.

8. Relationship with third countries

A final reason that asks for central regulatory and supervisory arrangements is the enhancement of the relationship between the EU and non-EU financial markets. In this critical period of time, where the Community moves towards its objective of a fully integrated financial services market, it is essential that our trade concerns emerge beyond the EU internal market as well. EU is not an island in financial markets. Financial transactions between EU markets and the rest of the world are as important as those within the Union. It is, therefore, equally important that both European financial institutions have unconditional access to the markets of the EU's competitors and foreign organisations have access to the Member States' markets.

Barriers, however, do remain in connection with many markets, including the large market of the United States. Many paradigms can be recalled here regarding investment services. Foreign financial firms do not 'benefit' from the European passport. The home country control and mutual recognition principles do not entitle non-EU financial firms to establish branches or offer services throughout the Community on the basis of one authorisation given by a Member State, and therefore arguably they are at a competitive disadvantage. On the other hand, EU securities markets cannot establish trading screen in countries such as the US, even though the core principles protecting investors and market integrity are similar in both jurisdictions. Although the US derivatives regulator has allowed Liffe and Eurex to install screens in America, Europe's equities exchanges find it harder to persuade regulators to let them in too. Furthermore, US stock exchanges cannot list companies that do not follow the US Generally Accepted Accounting Principles (GAAP). So, even if EU and US exchanges were to establish links, most listings brought in by the European side could not be traded in the United States. Finally, even though US investment funds can be freely marketed in the EU, EU funds are required to establish 'mirror funds' in the United States before they can market their products.[240]

With respect to supervision, there are at least fifteen governmental voices, besides the Commission, speaking today on regulatory and supervisory issues on behalf of Europe. Yet, the Union is not fully represented in international financial institutions or UN agencies. Even a regime for supervisory cooperation in external relations requires, at a minimum, that the Union 'speaks with one voice' and ensures that divergences of view among Member States are dealt with. Even this modest level of coordination will not work unless consultation and communication networks between the relevant national and EU actors are reliable. The problem will become more acute with the forthcoming enlargement of the EU. A Union of 25-plus countries will be more diverse, with a greater variety of economic and geo-political interests. It is certain that in core areas of the Single Market it will become difficult to establish consensus in an enlarged EU. The most pessimist scenario envisages a 'Europe in Shambles', which does not preclude the danger of institutional deadlock and political chaos.[241] The process of integration may become deadlocked if current institutional arrangements and financial frameworks are not sufficiently changed. This is the nightmare of every thinking EU citizen.

This situation does not give Europe the effectiveness with respect to international issues that it would have if a single negotiator, a pan-European supervisor existed. This could be better understood in bilateral relations with powerful counterparties. The need, for instance, to harmonise US and European securities regulation[242] could be accomplished more easily by a single European regulator working with the SEC than by fifteen or later twenty-seven different negotiators. At the moment, the SEC remains the dominant regulator in Europe, as its rules are applied worldwide. This is a very compelling reason why the Union should bring into existence a regulator that can act as a counterweight to the SEC to represent Europe's interests in multilateral organisations. The size and power of an integrated pan-European market would make the single regulator an effective and reliable negotiator on issues of policy and law enforcement. Moreover, the ESR would be the perfect authority to maintain and foster these issues on the WTO/GATS agenda.

Given the fact that supervisory policies become increasingly important elements in international financial trade, developments in this field will become more rather than less important for international trade relation.[243] It has to be ensured that 'European markets are attractive to capital from outside the Union and that our regime is market-friendly'.[244] The establishment of a single supervisory authority in Europe constitutes an urgent need not only within the EU market, but also in the international context. With growing international economic interdependence, existing WTO principles of national treatment are reaching the limits of their effectiveness. Markets remain more integrated than their regulation and supervision. A pan-European authority, which could multiply existing integration efforts, could more easily export its work to the international multilateral system. Instead of importing standards and implementing them to fifteen different systems, the pan-European body could have the power and the impetus to find wider acceptance abroad. European financial governance will, therefore, have to be placed in a wider context.[245] Given the worldwide visibility of the euro and enlargement, the necessity has become obligation for the Union to reinforce its voice in the world.

D. The political conundrum: real drawbacks or political unwillingness?

Given the aforementioned rationale and the necessity and feasibility of transfer of certain regulatory and supervisory tasks from regional to centralised level, one may logically but also naively wonder: why is there still such an opposition to a pan-European Securities Regulator? It may be alleged that the logic of functional effectiveness is unable to fully explain current Community competences. This is encapsulated in the words of Majone,

> even in the case of economic regulation, where functional logic is most compelling, the timing and quality of many developments cannot be understood without taking into consideration other factors such as the policy entrepreneurship of the Commission or the activism of powerful actors who cannot wait for incremental task expansion to produce the policy outputs they want.[246]

After assessing the pros and cons of the single Securities Regulator idea, the issue boils down to the political question, whether Member States would be ready and willing to give up their powers over the biggest, most sophisticated flagship. Therefore, one cannot really expect national supervisors to show a lot of enthusiasm for the prospect of being relegated to a local league and the role of junior partner to some remote super-body. This becomes evident when Professor Lamfalussy, the chairman of the Wise Men Committee, which concluded that a pan-European regulator is not yet feasible, explicitly admitted that he was given instructions by the Council to propose a solution only within the restrictions of the present Treaty.[247]

The principle of home country control has brought a negative effect on how Member States perceive 'home country' supervision. Member States today, do hardly look beyond their national markets and have less interest in how supervision is done in other countries. This is best illustrated by the Chairman of the FSA himself: 'While we have no formal responsibility for the prudential supervision of Deutsche Bank, it would be curious if we did not take an interest in what it got up to in the London market, where its presence is very considerable and even profitable on occasion'.[248] The notion of the phrase 'take an interest' is debatable.

Traditionally, the reluctance of European countries to entrust regulation and supervision to 'specialised, single-purpose commissions or administrative agencies' is reflected by the high degree of nationalisation of public-utility industries.[249] Indeed, major national regulatory authorities have their own domestic reasons for advocating against the establishment of a centralised supervisory body. Up to now, the British have not believed it was in their national interest to have a European Securities regulator created.[250] The DG Internal Market of the Commission is British-dominated and London has the biggest capital market in Europe. In addition, members of the FSA play a major role in the decision-making process of CESR. Hence it is logical that the present institutional structure is more than satisfactory to them. On the other hand, the FSA considers the argument for a single EU supervisor as misplaced and counter to their philosophy of supervision. At a time, when the forces of consolidation are bringing together supervisors of all financial services in the United Kingdom, it would be odd to recreate at EU level a structure, which would divide securities supervision from other types of financial services regulation.[251] Also, Austria, Denmark, Germany, Finland and Sweden, which have already moved or are moving towards the consolidation of their financial services supervisory bodies, may have similar perceptions.

Conversely, although regulators acknowledge the deficiencies of the existing regime, they consider them relatively unimportant because they may not affect financial stability at the moment. A piece of the Brouwer Report deserves to be quoted in length:[252]

> The regulatory framework in Europe leaves some discretion to national authorities for interpretation and translation into national legislation. This could potentially result in regulatory arbitrage and an unlevel playing field. (...) However, this does not necessarily mean that the stability of the European financial system is negatively affected by remaining differences in national financial regulation.

Although many believe that a single regulator in investment services is a necessity, steps cannot be implemented towards this end until the political patrons of the national authorities are persuaded that it is the right direction to take. A strong political will is needed, as it was the case with EMU. The Franco-German relationship, for instance, with its constant attempts to reconcile the very different interests of the two governments, drove monetary integration from 1969 onwards. It is striking that governments were willing then to pool their sovereignty as far as monetary policy was concerned – which after all is one of the most powerful instruments of national economic policy – but now shy away from taking the logical steps that follow.[253] It is as if 'Member States are suddenly afraid of their own daring'.[254] Now is the time. European financial market integration cannot be jeopardised by unnecessary national disputes and misunderstandings, while the international community is moving towards a single body to monitor the global financial architecture.[255]

E. Concluding remarks

This chapter has presented the case for a European Securities Regulator and has raised the question: is what is being done or proposed enough? The answer lies far from an unequivocal yes. To date, the availability of the European passport and home country control has not produced the so desirable freedom of pan-European provision of investment services. Home country control and decentralisation have their limits. As a result, both major financial undertakings and investors have an interest in further supervisory centralisation supplemented or not by further harmonisation.

Although the proposals of the Wise Men Committee to speed up the legislative process may actually slow it down, they may be welcome for the time being as means of setting the stage for the creation of the ESR. Europe, however, cannot stop here. A strong trend towards a 'hard' single European Regulator is perceived. Although, as a first step, a pan-European Securities Supervisor could be solidly built on the current provisions of the Treaty, a more powerful body with decision-making and supervisory powers will need to become part of a new Intergovernmental Conference. Placing all central rules regulating the Regulator in the Treaty, will give the ESR a strong law-based status and will further strengthen its independence.

Rephrasing the theory of neo-functionalism, the functional needs of a single market in investment services would necessitate a considerable transfer of policy-making powers to the EU level. Regulatory economies of scale and scope for financial undertakings and securities markets call for efficiency gains that only a central regulator can deliver. The potential integration of financial markets and the europeanisation of investment and other financial services, which will be boomed as the introduction of the euro breaks down the barriers in Europe, will pose serious problems to the current fragmented multiplayer regulatory and supervisory structure.

The current supervisory regime has implications on the slow legislative process witnessed in Europe. Nobody argues against that but also nobody moves against it. Today comes the proposed regime by the Commission and the Wise Men, which, nevertheless, is doubtful whether it will speed up securities markets and investment services integration. In any event, supervision remains untouched, while developments cannot wait. Home supervisors will find their task more difficult to extend their supervisory power to financial business conducted abroad. Host supervisors, on the other hand, are likely to become less informed about the firms and the market as a whole, which means that their ability to take *ex ante* action and resolve a crisis situation is limited.

Thoroughgoing 'enhanced cooperation' between members of CESR may ease the problem of information exchange but this is not adequate. National authorities tend to consider the financial industry as a sector that is entrusted with a 'national mission'. The need to act promptly, decisively and away from national political and socio-economic interests in emergencies supports a wider role for a pan-European supervisor with clear crisis management tasks. More important than crisis management, however, is pre-crisis risk analysis and loss prevention. One of the important lessons derived from crises of the past was that, although a number of indicators of potential exposure or collapse arose, they were not properly assessed on a coordinated basis. What has to be done in the event of cross-border crises within the EU? Who has to be informed? Where can regulators meet? The ECB is in charge of monetary stability, but not of financial stability, which remains a Member State responsibility, together with prudential supervision. The institution that could provide a *point d'appui* is lacking. More importantly, the nightmare of institutional deadlock or political chaos in decision-making may become inevitable.

A single regulator can be more flexible. Lawmaking in its hands will never follow market developments, while its flexibility will smooth national conflicts and provide an adequate forum for exchange of expertise and information, as a better shield to prevent or even repulse emergencies. Establishing a central authority will improve the way rules are decided, applied and enforced across the Union. Its advantages will include its ability to draw on highly technical, sectoral know-how, its increased visibility for the securities sector and the cost-savings it will offer to business. In addition, the pan-European Regulator will constitute the powerful counterparty that will negotiate and foster the European interests in the global financial arena and the WTO.

In light of its functions, it is important that the European Regulator remains immune to political pressure and regulatory capture. Its tasks and operation should be designed in such a clear way as to promote transparency and accountability. In turn, transparency will reduce information asymmetries within European markets and accountability will foster confidence, democracy and legitimacy. The establishing Treaty rules should set out the limits of its activities and powers, its responsibilities and requirements for openness. Moreover, such a major institutional reform ought to be based on the broadest possible consensus right from the beginning, as the declaration appended to the Nice Treaty called. The ESR will need a clear yardstick for the evaluation of its performance in the achievements of its objectives.

Although regulators acknowledge the deficiencies of the present regulatory and supervisory system, shortsighted perspectives and partial success of the past make them reluctant to move towards its radical reform. Complete harmonisation should not stand as a prerequisite to centralisation, as the necessary common European financial laws are already in place to justify and demand such a radical institutional shift. From what has been said, a need for action can be identified in a number of areas, including the removal of overlapping of jurisdictions to boost supervisory efficiency, the adoption of a more flexible response to innovations and the assumption of a united external stance. In the near future, the issue of a single EU regulator cannot be avoided by the markets and their participants. Acting in a single currency and unified securities market environment, the new regime would have the advantage of the *status quo* of a bigger body of common regulations, lower costs and greater flexibility. On the other hand, the lack of a single supervisor can impede competition and innovation beneficial to financial firms, issues and consumers. Europe has a responsibility to pursue financial institutional reform; not only for its own benefit, but also for the good of its neighbours – helping drive global economic growth, and promoting international cooperation beyond its own borders to ensure that globalisation works for the benefit of all.

At the end of the day, the rationale and the success of the ESR will heavily draw on its capacity to better serve and further promote the supervisory objectives of financial stability, competition and consumer protection. As put by Demarigny, the problem of European investment services regulation and supervision today is basically a lack of a 'bridge' between the upper level, the EU black-letter law written in stone, and the lower level, the day-to-day practical implementation, supervision and enforcement.[256] The pan-European Securities Regulator could be seen as the constructor of the bridge, as soon as micro-political interests and national conflicts are left aside. The following chapter will endeavour to identify the structure, the competencies and the role that the proposed constructor would need to play.

7
Structure and Operation of the European Securities Regulator

A. Introduction

This chapter makes suggestions with regard to the principal objectives of the ESR, its competence and its tasks that might constitute its legitimate regulatory, executive, supervisory and judicial functions and its relationship with Member States supervisory authorities and EU institutions. In the same context, arguments for potential problematic parameters will be identified and analysed.

There is much talk today about 'hard law' and 'soft law'. The same distinction could be made concerning regulators. If the regulatory and supervisory regime at the EU level moves towards greater reliance on existing methods of legislating, such as Directives and/or Regulations, it may be appropriate in the context of the existing home country control regime for there to be considered a role for EU regulatory involvement with a lesser role and powers than that of a 'hard' regulator. On the other hand, a 'hard' regulator would require a far more Member States' political willingness for a Treaty amendment to incorporate policy, regulatory and supervisory responsibilities.

The constitutional, legal, operational and political problems analysed in previous chapters and associated with clarifying the role, responsibility and power of the EU regulator go in particular to the establishment of a 'hard' regulator. As discussed in Chapter 6, major issues relating to subsidiarity and proportionality will be raised. Vertical centralisation or horizontal decentralisation involves the delegation of some tasks to central authorities. Should supervisory areas be removed from national competent authorities and if so, which ones? Should regulatory powers be conferred from the Commission and the Council? How should these powers be exercised? What guarantees need to be provided and what will be the consequences for national authorities and relatively recently enacted financial services laws?

In order to address these questions, this chapter is set out as follows. The next section draws some arguments and lessons from the institutional structure and substantial powers of other federal institutions, namely the

European System of Central Banks and the US Securities and Exchange Commission. The third section makes reference to the structure and powers the new regulator will need to achieve its objectives, namely its competence, resources allocation, executive, regulatory, implementing, supervisory, judicial and enforcement powers, while potential drawbacks of the proposed system are criticised. The main conclusions of this chapter are summarised in the final section.

B. Lessons from the ESCB and the SEC

1. Lessons from the European System of Central Banks (ESCB)

The institutional structure of the ESCB could constitute a plausible functional model for the ESR. Although the ESR would differ in terms of regulatory and supervisory functions and objectives, an analysis of the institutional structure of the ESCB will provide some clues as to how the proposed ESR could effectively operate within the complex Community structure.

The Treaty and the Statute of the ESCB established the ESCB. The ESCB is composed of the ECB and the national central banks (NCBs) of all fifteen EU Member States.[1] The 'Eurosystem' is the term used to refer to the ECB and the NCBs of the Member States, which have adopted the euro.[2] The NCBs of the Member States, which do not participate in the euro area, however, are members of the ESCB with a special status. While they are allowed to conduct their respective national monetary policies, they do not take part in the decision-making with regard to the single monetary policy for the euro area and the implementation of such decisions.

1.1. Decision-making bodies of the ECB

The process of decision-making in the Eurosystem is centralised through the decision-making bodies of the ECB, namely the Governing Council and the Executive Board.[3] As long as there are Member States, which have not yet adopted the euro, a third decision-making body, the General Council, also exists.

The Governing Council comprises all the members of the Executive Board and the governors of the NCBs of the Member States, which have adopted the euro.[4] The main responsibilities of the Governing Council are:

(a) to adopt the guidelines and take the decisions necessary to ensure the performance of the tasks entrusted to the Eurosystem;
(b) to formulate the monetary policy of the euro area, including, as appropriate, decisions relating to intermediate monetary objectives, key interest rates and the supply of reserves in the Eurosystem, and
(c) to establish the necessary guidelines for their implementation.

The Executive Board comprises the President, the Vice President and four other members, all chosen from among persons of recognised standing and professional experience in monetary or banking matters. They are appointed by common accord of the governments of the Member States at the level of the Heads of State or Government, on a recommendation from the EU Council after it has consulted the European Parliament and the Governing Council of the ECB.[5] The main responsibilities of the Executive Board are:

(a) to implement monetary policy in accordance with the guidelines and decisions laid down by the Governing Council of the ECB and, in doing so, to give the necessary instructions to the NCBs; and
(b) to execute those powers which have been delegated to it by the Governing Council of the ECB.

1.2. Legal status, regulatory and enforcement power

The ECB has legal personality under public international law.[6] In each Member State it enjoys the most extensive legal capacity accorded to legal persons under the respective national law. Thus, it is in position to conclude agreements under international law and it may be party to legal proceedings.[7] Placing all central rules regulating the ECB in the Treaty and the Statute, which constitute primary law with direct effect on Member States, gives the system a very high legal, *de facto* constitutional status and strengthens its independence even further.[8] Such a strong basis on law is extremely important for a legitimate 'hard' ESR as well.

The Treaty assigns to the ECB not only the power to conclude agreements, but also the regulatory powers to adopt any legal acts necessary to fulfil the tasks assigned to the Eurosystem. As such, the ECB has the power to adopt Regulations, take Decisions, make Recommendations and deliver Opinions to the extent necessary to carry on its responsibilities, which are limited by its Treaty clearly stated competence.[9] ECB Regulations have general application, are binding in their entirety and directly applicable in all Member States.[10] Decisions are merely binding upon those to whom they are addressed. On the other hand, Recommendations and Opinions do not have binding force.[11]

Geographically, the ECB has general law-making powers as it can adopt legal acts that have direct effect in the whole euro area. Regarding substance, however, the ECB has not any general law-making powers, as its competence is limited to a specific area, namely monetary policy.[12] The ESR would definitely have broader regulatory powers, both with regard to geography and substance. Its competence will be valid within all Member States that adopt the centralised regime and not only within the countries of the euro area. Moreover, its supervisory competences could be extended to cover a broad range of objectives, such as the stability of the financial system and the protection of consumers.

The ECB's role as a regulator is further strengthened by its responsibility to initiate infringement procedure and to impose sanctions on undertakings for failure to comply with obligations under its regulations and decisions.[13] The prerogative is subject to the principle that sanctions need to be precisely specified (*nulla poena sine lege*).[14] Within this context, the exchange of information within the ESCB relating to infringement detection and the competence of the ECB to request NCBs to enforce its sanctions, are crucial.

1.3. Judicial control

The freedom of action of each and every EU institution is restricted. According to Article 8 EC Treaty (former Article 4a) the ECB shall act within the limits of the powers conferred upon it by the Treaty. Like all EU institutions, the acts and omissions of the ECB are open to review or interpretation by the European Court of Justice.[15] The Court has also unlimited jurisdiction over the review of final decisions of the ECB whereby a sanction is imposed and competence to give preliminary rulings concerning the acts of the ECB.[16] Its jurisdiction with regard to the control of the fulfilment by NCBs of their obligations reflects the special character of the ESCB and the power of the ECB, which is parallel to that of the European Commission (Article 226). If the ECB considers that a NCB has failed to fulfil an obligation under the Treaty, it may deliver a reasoned opinion and, if that fails, it may bring the matter before the Court.[17]

1.4. Independence and accountability

One might conclude from that brief analysis that within the realm of its powers, 'the ECB constitutes an independent regulatory agency with real supranational status'.[18] The financial and institutional autonomy of the ECB with regard to both national governments and EU institutions is constitutionally guaranteed.[19] Since the ratification of the Maastricht Treaty, however, the independence of the ECB has been a much-debated and criticised subject.[20]

In a democratic context, it is vital for a central bank not only to be independent, but also open and transparent about the reasons for its actions and accountable for its performance.[21] In some observers' opinion, however, there is a fundamental trade-off between central bank independence and accountability, in that pure independence rules out accountability and substantial accountability rules out independence.[22]

The ECB preserves its accountability mainly through transparency. It publishes a weekly consolidated financial statement of the Eurosystem, it draws up and publishes reports on the activities of the ESCB every quarter, it makes statements on the economic situation and price developments, which are supplemented by a Monthly Bulletin and it addresses an Annual Report on the activities of the ESCB and on monetary policy to the Parliament, the Council and the Commission. Moreover, the President of the Council and a member of the Commission may participate in the meetings of the Governing Council without having the right to vote.

Nevertheless, restrictive exceptions do apply to the general principle of transparency. According to the European Ombudsman, public access to documents should be the core rule and all exceptions should be implemented restrictively.[23] Yet, since the EMI era, the Ombudsman recommendations only concerned administrative documents of the ECB predecessor.[24] All documents connected with monetary policy could remain confidential unless the Council decided otherwise.[25] The ECB has confirmed that the same limitation is applicable to its archives.[26] The Parliament, for its part, has been trying, since the very beginning of the third phase of the EMU, to balance independence and accountability, in order to invent a state of 'accountable independence'.[27] It is not, however, within the scope of this book to assess whether restrictions on transparency contradict the idea of democracy, or whether the democratic legitimacy of the monetary policy within EMU can be realised on the basis of traditional methods.[28] It is important, though, to assess whether similar controversies and limitations will be applicable to the proposed Securities Regulator.

1.5. *Final comment: ESCB as a model?*

Given the reasons that led to the creation and the institutional structure of the ESCB, one may wonder what contribution it could make to the drafting of the rules, procedures and the institutional design of the proposed ESR and its place within the EU system. It would have been inconceivable for one particular NCB, say the *Bundesbank*, to be merely in charge of the single currency of eleven other sovereign nations. Equally, it is an illusion believing to see a national financial authority, like the FSA or BAWe, in charge of the central elements of a modern European economy. Whereas, however, a single currency can be argued to be beneficial in an integrated market setting,[29] politics, not economic logic, seems to be the overwhelming factor shaping the geography of money and institutional structures within the Union. The political benefits of a supranational monetary institution revolve around its potential to serve as an engine of political integration and as a tool of policy management.[30] Indeed, the ECB's decisions profoundly affect not only the monetary policy of the EU, but also they may be transforming its politics, since critical decision-making is transferred to the European level. The same political and economic integration and policy management arguments could also be used for the creation of a single Securities Regulator.

With respect to its institutional structure, the ECB constitutes an independent body entrusted with EU-wide monetary policy. Equally, the appointment of more than one policy objectives and the introduction of a regime of democratic check, balance and judicial review should provide the ESR with goal independence.[31] Furthermore, the ECB and the ESCB illustrate an example of how far the logic of an agency mechanism can go in terms of autonomy with regard to the normal European institutional system of political decision-making. This example, however, is not and should not be limited.

Indeed, Article 105(6) of the Treaty leaves open the possibility for transfer of prudential supervisory responsibilities – over credit and 'other financial institutions' – from the national to the ECB level.

Accordingly, although there may be no direct comparison between a central bank and a supervisory authority, the creators of the ESR will have much to learn from the institutional structure and the operation of the ESCB.[32] Even though prudential supervisory tasks are not attached to the ECB, the structure of the ESCB provides a regime for better supervisory coordination. The establishment of the ESCB has 'improved the ability to cooperate, as national central banks that are part of this system are either formally responsible for, or closely involved in, banking supervision'.[33] The supervisory coordination within the CESR will be even more enhanced, since all national authorities are responsible for investment services supervision in their country. In addition, the great regulatory and enforcement powers of the ECB may also lend great credence to the ESR as a pan-European regulator.

Finally, the emerging relationship between the ECB and the EP foreshadows a new model of democratic organisation, which could be expanded to other independent organs in the EU. Nevertheless, restrictions on transparency and accountability that apply to the ECB because of its nature and objective may not apply to the ESR as well. Given the delicate objective of monetary policy and in order not to lead the market in an unprecedented way, the ECB has gone through a combination of different supervisory and accountability arrangements, which, of course, create legitimacy. The Securities Regulator, however, could follow more traditional democratic methods to secure its legitimacy. As mentioned before,[34] if a single regulator is given a clear set of responsibilities, then it ought to be possible to increase transparency and accountability. If the single regulator is endowed with a strong legally ordained bias and a clear allocation and prioritisation of objectives, then it will preserve its independence and legal transparency.

2. Lessons from the Securities and Exchange Commission (SEC)

Unfolding the history and examining the main tasks and powers of the US federal securities watchdog, the Securities and Exchange Commission, will demonstrate the relevance of the parallelism with the European model and how much it could assist this chapter in shaping the European Securities Regulator.

2.1. The history of a new agency

US securities regulation began with the supervision of trading in public utilities around 1900. The SEC's foundation was laid in an era that was ripe for reform. Before the Great Crash of 1929, there was little support for federal regulation of the securities markets.[35] This was particularly true during the post-World War I surge of securities activity. Proposals that the federal government require financial disclosure and prevent the fraudulent sale of stock were never seriously pursued. [36]

The SEC was created at the conclusion of the Senate Banking and Currency Committee's 1932–34 investigation of stock exchange practices, usually called the Pecora Hearings, in recognition of the decisive role played by the committee's counsel, Ferdinand Pecora.[37] The public response to the Pecora Hearings was directly responsible for the passage of the Banking Act of 1933 (Glass–Steagall Act).[38] However, the most enthusiastic appreciation of Pecora's work came from the Executive Branch. On 27 May 1933, President Roosevelt signed into law the Securities Act of 1933, the most important consequence to that date of the stock exchange hearings.[39]

Each of Roosevelt's principal 1932 presidential campaign advisers favoured the creation of a very different type of federal agency to direct the flow of new investment in private industry and to enforce the 1933 Act.[40] Early in 1933, however, President Roosevelt asked his old friend Felix Frankfurter for assistance in drafting the new federal securities regulation, and Frankfurter summoned James Landis, a young Harvard Law professor, who designed and later administrated the SEC.[41]

Landis arrived in Washington in April 1933. Already, the early drafts of the 1933 Securities Act had run into problems, and Landis thought his role was going to be like that of a theatre 'doctor'. Roosevelt, however, had set many others to work on the same problem, which caused a significant amount of confusion about people and responsibilities.[42] Landis, for example, came to Washington on a Friday train from Cambridge, expecting to be released after a weekend of work. He ended up staying four years.[43]

Drafting the new securities bills was hardly a simple and easy task.[44] The institutional and administrative framework of the new regime would receive special attention. According to the initial plan of Landis, the Federal Reserve Board would have power to raise and lower margin requirements, while the Federal Trade Commission (FTC) would administer the rest of the act. The plan, however, did hardly receive a warm welcome in the Senate. Senator Carter Glass led the opposition to the draft 1933 Act, aiming to protect his own creation, the Federal Reserve, from being 'mixed up with stock exchange market gambling'. In two close committee votes he won amendments to eliminate fixed margin provisions and to establish a Securities and Exchange Commission to administer the entire act. Hence, Glass became the 'father' of the SEC.[45]

At first, Landis vigorously opposed the creation of a new agency. Later he would acknowledge that he had been wrong to oppose the creation of a separate commission, since an agency with a narrow jurisdiction, like the SEC, had advantages in providing administrative expertise that an agency with a broader jurisdiction, like the former FTC lacked. But as we noted, the SEC had not been sought by the New Deal. Its birth, in a sense, was an accident.[46]

2.2. Tasks of the SEC

As shown above, the key period of US securities legislation was the early 1930s, when the SEC was established by the Securities and Exchange Act of 1934.[47] This Act created the SEC as a unique regulator supervising investment services and the various autonomous stock exchanges in the United States. Since then, the SEC has focused on ensuring adequate disclosure by issuers of securities and combating fraudulent and manipulating practices, but it still relies heavily on the monitoring capacity of Self-Regulatory Organisations (SROs).[48] The principal responsibility for securities regulation and supervision is borne by the federal SEC, but State 'blue sky' regulators also have a significant role.

From its earliest days, the SEC was expected to play a strong normative role. Today, the SEC describes its mission as 'to administer and enforce the federal securities laws in order to protect investors, and to maintain fair, honest, and efficient markets'.[49] Enjoying a significant level of independence, the SEC does not answer directly to the Congress or a specific department of the government. Moreover, it is free from monetary reliance on the industry it regulates and has clearly delineated regulatory responsibilities.

The SEC's structure comprises many divisions. However, of particular interest is the Division of Investment Management, which oversees investment companies and investment advisers, including the mutual fund industry.[50] The starting point for investment firms' (brokers-dealers in the US terminology)[51] regulation and supervision is the basic requirement of Section 15(a) of the 1934 Act: no person may act as a broker or a dealer in securities unless registered with the SEC or expressly exempted from the registration requirements.[52] These market participants are subject to statutory prohibitions and procedures intended to protect consumers, by requiring disclosure, record keeping, consumer approval of certain transactions and the avoidance of situations that give rise to conflicts of interest.[53] Provisions of the Investment Company Act of 1940[54] require investment firms to submit management contracts to their shareholders for approval and to obtain the SEC's approval before entering into any transactions with their officers, directors and affiliates.

The SEC and the SROs share responsibility for supervising the conduct of investment firms.[55] As to authorisation, the SEC is given the authority pursuant to Section 15(b)(1) to deny a registration based upon evidence of misconduct or false statement.[56] With respect to more traditional activities, Section 15(a) provides that brokers-dealers who do business wholly on an intrastate basis and do not make use of any facility of a national securities exchange need not register with the SEC.[57] The Uniform Securities Act requires the annual registration of brokers-dealers doing business in a particular State and provides for both supervisory and disciplinary authority of the blue-sky State regulators. Hence, US securities regulation follows a hybrid system, according to which investment firms engaged in interstate business are supervised by the SEC and SROs and firms solely engaged in intrastate business are supervised by the State regulator. Recently, however, the National Securities Markets Improvements Act of 1996 (NSMIA)[58] imposed restrictions on State supervision, especially where the effect could be to create conflicting or duplicate substantive requirements. Importantly, Section 19 of the Securities Act of 1933[59] engenders the SEC to cooperate, coordinate and share information with State regulators for the purposes of carrying out its policies and projects, including maximum effectiveness of regulation, maximum uniformity in federal and State regulatory standards and a substantial reduction in costs and paperwork to diminish the burdens of raising investment capital (particularly by small business) and to diminish the costs of the administration of the government programs involved.

Finally, crucial to the SEC's effectiveness is its Enforcement Division. Each year the SEC brings between 400–500 civil enforcement actions against individuals and companies that break the securities laws. Typical infractions include insider trading, accounting fraud and the provision of false or misleading information about securities and the companies that issue them. Section 15(b)(4) of the 1934 Act empowers the SEC to hold hearings and impose disciplinary sanctions ranging from censure to revocation of the registration of investment firms.[60] This authority is either exclusive or primary. The SEC's powers were increased in 1990 when the Congress passed the Securities Enforcement Remedies Act,[61] which granted the Commission the authority to impose monetary sanctions and to handle many cases before an administrative judge, rather than to try the cases in the federal courts. Under Sections 6 and 15A of the 1934 Act, the SROs are also given both the power and the responsibility to discipline firms and individuals.[62] However, with respect to all SRO enforcement activity, the SEC has the responsibility under Sections 19(d) and (e) of reviewing the imposition of sanctions, typically on a *de novo* basis. It may modify or overturn a sanction, but may not increase it. In turn, SEC reviews may be reviewed by a federal court of appeals.

2.3. *Final comment: SEC as a model?*

By all accounts, the SEC has been a success. It has managed to create the most efficient and liquid market in the world, which enjoys today a high level of investor confidence. As an agency, the SEC has been repeatedly praised throughout its almost seventy year history as a 'model agency'.[63]

The United States, however, is not the EU. When it was established, the SEC enjoyed the full backup of a federal government. The United States was already a unified country with a single language, a single currency, a strong political and economic ideology and, more importantly, with an integrated financial market. Today, the EU of the fifteen Member States is struggling to achieve the benefits of a single market as a basis for the European Securities

Regulator. As discussed in Chapter 5, national sovereignty and protectionism are particularly evident in Europe. Nevertheless, if one recalls the past debate about the establishment of the SEC, one can detect that the arguments striving to anchor financial activity to a specific territory were very powerful even in a country that is much more structured than the EU. Indeed, the historical developments that led to the introduction of the SEC are similar to those that are evident in Europe today.[64]

Arguably, the United States has managed to create a federal regime of securities regulation and supervision, some elements of which could serve as an ideal example for its European counterpart. These could comprise the authorisation, supervision and enforcement power on firms that conduct business on a cross-border basis and the coordination efforts with State regulator. For the purposes of the latter, it deserves mention that Section 19(a) of the 1933 Act requires the SEC to hold an annual meeting to promote a number of goals: to maximise uniformity and effectiveness of federal and state securities regulation and supervision, to reduce costs and paperwork for issuers and to minimise interference with capital formation. At this annual meeting, SEC and State regulators' representatives gather to address matters of common interest, to outline federal and state regulatory efforts and initiatives, to identify areas where joint cooperation would be beneficial and to discuss ideas and plans for more effective coordination and communication.

To conclude, it is certainly more than feasible to imagine the creation of the ESR developing common rules and establishing common standards, which would then be implemented by national regulators under its supervision. The institutional structure of the ESCB and the regulatory structure of the SEC could usefully provide lessons for a new ESR. In addition, the delegation of monetary policy sovereignty by Member States suggests that this political issue is not entirely insurmountable, even within the complex Community policy-making process. The following paragraphs provide specific recommendations with respect to the institutional formation of the ESR.

C. Structure and tasks of the ESR

1. Structure of the ESR

1.1. Achieving the objectives

In order to achieve the so desirable free provision of investment services in the Single Market without the drawbacks of excessive federalism and bureaucracy, the ESR must have a clear-cut structure and objective and an independent power of action. 'The central authority will serve as a pan-European structure for monitoring systemic risk and for protecting consumers': this could be set out in direct and simple terms in the Treaty amendment setting up the new ESR structure. The first Article of the Treaty was where the very constitutional value of the ECB was based on. A clear objective is extremely important, as people are more likely to do what you want them to do, if you tell them clearly what they are supposed to do in advance. The inefficiency of the opposite is best illustrated by the current home country supervision regime, where home and host supervisors find themselves ill equipped to allocate responsibilities between them.

Having set out the objectives in the Treaty, we must then provide an institutional structure, which ensures that we can indeed achieve it. As the Delors Committee proposed for the establishment of the ESCB, 'a new Treaty would establish not only the objective but also the stages by which it is to be achieved and the procedures and institutions required to move forward at each stage along the way'.[65] In the case of the ECB, the terminology has played a major role and has reflected the analogy to the US Federal Reserve System and the wish to avoid excessive federalism.[66] Equally, in order to be effective, the decisions on European securities regulation and supervision policy cannot be the result of intergovernmental haggling of political compromise. They must be the informed judgement of a separate institution with its own independent structure.

Finally, one of the key features of the successful introduction of a Securities Regulator should be extensive and open consultation between the interested parties. Only consultation will ensure that the proposal will not be born and developed under undue pressure stemming from individual governments, market participants or political groups. Especially when new methods of supervision are being proposed,[67] it is appropriate to try to ensure that the rationale, the benefits and the drawbacks of innovating ideas are properly understood by the parties when drawing up the new regime.

Together with clear objectives and operational independence embodied in a satisfactorily decision-making structure goes the need for democratic accountability and credibility. The ESR should have a constant role of education and information about what it is doing in order to maintain its legitimacy in the Member States. Here lies one of the weaknesses of the newly established Securities Committee. As any committee created through the comitology process, the creation of the ESC has not been accompanied by enough guarantees to ensure that the Committee does not exceed its powers of execution or does not in effect 'legislate'.[68] Following the Amsterdam Treaty, the comitology system does hardly square with the equality between the Council and the Parliament since, as far as implementation is concerned, it reinforces the one legislative role (the Council) to the detriment of the other (the Parliament).[69] Unless, therefore, a Treaty amendment is foreseen the credibility of the ESC is well undermined.

1.2. Potential drawback: bureaucracy and delay?

Given the independent power of action of a pan-European Regulator, the sceptics of centralisation of investment services regulation and supervision may argue that the downside of the establishment of a European regulator would be an extra layer of bureaucracy and delay in the harmonisation process of EU investment services regulation.[70] They may envisage a long period of political debate and haggling prior to such a movement. This would indeed be undesirable, but not even the most fervent advocate of a single authority would seriously envisage anything like that for the reasons explained before.[71]

1.3. A federal structure

It is true that the establishment of a 'hard' regulator would demand a consensus of approach at a political and operator level. However, the single regulator would not constitute a bureaucratic monstrosity. Instead, it would need to have a federal structure very much like the ESCB.[72] This comes in line with the suggestion of two financial experts that the growing integration of markets 'could lead to the creation of a European system of national regulation in the same vein as the ECB, with decisions taken centrally but applied nationally'.[73]

The optimal structure would comprise a European System of Securities Regulators (ESSR), which would include the national regulators (CESR) with a European Securities Authority at the centre of the system. Within this regime, the central Authority would harmonise (as necessary) and coordinate (as appropriate) securities regulation across Member States, design common standards and principles and make sure that rules are implemented by Member States in a consistent manner. The council of national regulators, on the other hand, would be responsible for the implementation of the rules designed by the central Authority. Beyond that, national regulators could also participate in defining these rules through their membership in the governing council of the ESSR. Working for common objectives, the ESSR could be compared with a horizontal group of companies, where the CESR and its controlled subsidiary ESR would form a regulatory and supervisory unity. This structure would allow market participation and communication between the regulator and the regulated industry and consumers, which would help the system avoid the problem of excessive bureaucracy.

Such a federal structure would have two main advantages. First, a central coordinator for financial stability would be appointed and secondly, the active participation and, thus, the interest of the national regulators in the regulation and supervision of their local markets would be preserved. Whereas EU-wide principles and standards would replace national interests, specific characteristics of the Member States' markets would be also taken into consideration. The following paragraphs describe more analytically the operation and functions of the proposed system.

2. Competence and resources allocation

Building an integrated European securities market in the tight timeframe that European policy-makers have defined and creating a single regulator to support it, is partly a matter of competence and resources. Today, it is acknowledged by the securities industry that competencies and powers of national supervisory authorities differ greatly. Structures vary as well as their legal foundations and the powers of information gathering and of enforcement attributed to them.[74] All in all, there are about forty public bodies in the EU dealing with securities markets regulation and supervision. Competences are mixed. Responsibilities are different. The result is fragmentation and confusion.

All public bodies involved in the regulation and supervision of investment services, from the Commission and the Parliament to the newly created national supervisory authorities, lack the sufficient staff, which is not logical given their inherent economic importance for the EU.[75] There are about one hundred people working on financial services at the Commission. Perhaps one or two dozens are sufficiently qualified for the job.[76] They are all overburdened with drafting, consultation, negotiation and enforcement. Moving a step further, the progressive loss of prestige and influence by the Commission – a loss of status symbolised by the resignation of President Santer and the entire college of Commissioners in 1999 – may lead many of the Commission's official to having second thoughts about horizontally delegating some of its powers.

Understaffing constitutes also a problem for many national finance ministries and regulators. Whatever the fascination with quasi-objective risk models, the core of the supervisory process will always be primarily concerned with human qualities. The problem is that the role of the supervisor is not glamorous, either in commercial firms or among the regulators. In contrast to the 'star' trader or investment banker, the national supervisor is usually paid for less and does hardly receive the treatment and recognition he/she would deserve. Poor macro or microeconomic performance brings unhappiness and uneasiness. When the 'star' trader or banker misbehaves, the supervisor is likely to be sacked for allowing misconduct.

Divergences in regulatory and supervisory structures need be 'absorbed' by a single centralised agency. In order, however, to achieve that, the central Regulator will need the necessary human and financial resources as well as an efficient allocation mechanism, which would ensure the perfect matching between problems and solutions. Issues to be resolved herein include the number of staff needed and the specific technical expertise required. Some of the issues that might be relevant to this body, such as the detailed specification of the regulatory framework and the prudential supervision of financial firms, would require a considerable number of highly skilled people.

A federal supervisory body is more likely to appear attractive to high-quality personnel. Its power and role within the EU financial market context would provide the right incentive. And, because the job of the supervisor is not the most pleasant in the world, supervisor's salaries must be set at a proper market rate, equivalent to those of the administrative and scientific staff of the other EU institutions. On the other hand, in order to ensure competence, the ESR should be involved in training. Only a central pan-European body could, along with the private sector, introduce the competent mechanism to lead a new EU-wide training drive, to improve the deployment of best practice and common understanding among national regulators and market participants. Ultimately, the quality of the operation of the ESR will be a function of the people it is able to attract and retain.

In this context, a single regulator should also be able to secure a more efficient and effective allocation of supervisory resources. Theoretically, communication within one body should be more effective and reliable than among a number of distant and independent authorities spread all over Europe. Moreover, as previous chapters have shown, central rulemaking and monitoring ensures that the overlapping or contradictory provisions, often found in the home country control regime, will be avoided. Consequently, resort to the ESR could relieve the Commissions' overloaded working programme from specific legislative, implementation and enforcement tasks, leaving it greater room to concentrate more on its general policy management direction. National supervisors, on the other hand, would withdraw their interest from responsibilities that expand beyond their borders and focus their resources more on local areas that remain under their supervisory power, reducing thus cost and enhancing their effectiveness.

3. Regulatory and executive power

At the European level, policy development is primarily the responsibility of the Commission, while policy decision is the responsibility of the Council and the EP through the co-decision procedure, as introduced by the Maastricht and Amsterdam Treaties.[77] Since, however, both the Commission and the Council lack the necessary staff or expertise to develop and implement legislative proposals, they use comitology and expert committees to assist them in drafting and developing proposals. The interference of comitology committees in tandem with negotiations between Member States within the Council makes Community decision-making an even harder and more time-consuming process. In such a complex field as financial services, policy proposals require scientific and technical output. This, however, does not guarantee that scientific and/or interest group advice in drafting a proposal will secure the majority in the Council and the EP. Strong national interests may block each other and lead to a further delay or even to a deadlock of the legislative process.

Had an ESR been established, the regulatory process in investment services would be a much less complex task. An *ex ante* role for a European Regulator could involve formalising existing policies and developing new ones. This would at least render the system more vigorous and facilitate harmonisation or integration especially in the fields not covered by the present directives.

For example, the centralised body could undertake the role of the Contact Committee, established by Directive 2001/34/EC,[78] or the Accounting Regulatory Committee, introduced by the proposed Regulation on the application of IAS.[79] In the latter case, its function would be to assess IAS in order to confirm that they represent a suitable basis for financial reporting by listed EU companies. It could monitor smooth implementation by listed companies throughout the EU and adopt amendments to previously adopted IAS and Community accounting Directives.

As with the case of the ECB, the ESR should be able to adopt directly applicable legal acts. This would enhance efficiency and facilitate integration. These acts should be published, which would increase transparency. Unlike the Council,[80] the Securities Regulator would use its powers independently from other EU organs, national governments and parliaments. Again, transparency should be undisputable. Finally, ESR decision-making at the highest level will have a practical impact. New standards created and developed at the EU level could be exported and endorsed at a global level. It is beyond doubt that the ESR's powerful single voice will enhance the general position of the Union in the international financial arena.

Involvement in investment services policy, however, might raise a number of issues: first, the level of policy role granted to the Regulator would determine the need for amending the Treaty.[81] Granting a high-level policy responsibility to the ESR will make it a powerful 'hard' regulator that will need a strong legal basis in the Treaty. Second, the Community has already taken measures, principally through the use of Directives, to liberalise and harmonise securities regulation, whilst the Commission and CESR are increasingly developing guidelines to stimulate best practice amongst national supervisors and to modernise existing legislation. The European Regulator should not stand as a hurdle to this process, but it should act as the connecting link that will coordinate Member States and eliminate legislation implementation disparities between them. A final particular concern might be the danger for too much harmonisation in some areas. A potential enhanced harmonisation process established by the European Regulator could result in regulation replacing a market-driven approach, which could distort competition. Its oversight intervention, on the other hand, would complement efficient self-regulatory processes to ensure market integrity and investor protection. Clearance and settlement could serve as an emblematic paradigm.[82]

Finally, the balance between efficient regulation and flexibility is best maintained when the regulatory structure permits or requires the regulator to provide written guidance and interpretations. One of the most important functions of the Securities Regulator could be to respond to requests for informal advice concerning the application of EU investment services rules and adopt a regime of guidance and advice similar to the 'no-action letter' system operated in the United States by the SEC.[83] Even though this practice would not be binding for the ESR, it could facilitate good faith compliance with the law. Indeed, since 1970, when the SEC's no-action letters became available to the public for reference, practitioners, market participants and consumers have found them to be valuable indicators of the regulatory intentions of the SEC and its staff, a practice which has been heralded as a glittering example of 'excellent practice in administrative procedure'.

4. Implementation monitoring power

Traditionally, policy implementation is the responsibility of the Commission. It is an original responsibility on the one hand (Article 211 EC Treaty), but it is also delegated from the Council responsibility (Article 201 EC Treaty). In practice, however, the Commission shares the implementation responsibility in a complex and often inconsistent manner with the Member States.[84]

In this connection, two questions arise: precisely what should the monitoring process mechanism look like and who should the monitors be? Assuming that a regulatory structure under the ESR is endorsed, there is a need for a strong system to monitor implementation and to report on the functioning of the regulatory process. The ESR would monitor both compliance with rules and the effectiveness of supervision throughout the Community. This system should identify the loopholes and the responsibilities behind them.[85] Given its recent birth, it should also report whether there is a substantive progress towards an integrated European financial market. Monitoring the implementation of its own Recommendations and Decisions should be the responsibility of the European Regulator. Moreover, overall policy implementation could be adhered to an external body, such as the Commission or the Parliament. Whereas the Commission, the Council, the EP and national supervisors have equivalent stake in this process, the need for an objective, prompt and transparent implementation monitoring procedure is essential. In this light, the ESR should cooperate with and advice the enforcement section of the Commission DG Internal Market, as well as be responsible for publishing its Implementation Reports and delivering them to the EP for examination.

5. Supervisory power

Chapter 5 has underlined that the blurred allocation of supervisory responsibilities between the home and the host country confuses both financial intermediaries and consumers and has a negative impact on the free provision of cross-border investment services. It is extremely important in this context that EU-wide supervision of financial firms involved in investment business is conceded to a centralised system. A significant degree of equilibrium between a regulatory system and an administrative system of control must be in place. On the other hand, it is equally conceived as important that before centralisation of supervision takes place, certain Member States' securities laws, such as conduct of business rules, need to be harmonised. However, as analysed before,[86] this should not constitute a precondition for the establishment of the ESR *per se*. As in the case of the creation of the ESCB, a 'progressive realisation' procedure can be adopted as a basic principle of functional integration.[87]

The significant question that arises herein is what tasks the ESR's supervisory functions should entail. In general terms, these functions could be grouped into two classes: micro-prudential and macro-prudential supervision. Micro-prudential supervision will include all on and off-site surveillance of the safety and soundness of individual financial institutions, aiming in particular at the protection of consumers and competition promotion. Macro-prudential supervision, on the other hand, will encompass all activities aimed at monitoring the exposure to system risk and at identifying potential threats to stability arising from macroeconomic or financial market developments and infrastructures. Given their inherent importance as directly aiming at the objectives of financial supervision analysed in Chapter 1, the single regulator should focus on both classes of supervision. A macro-prudential approach would explicitly seek to limit the costs to the economy as a whole from financial distress, while its micro-prudential counterpart would focus on the likelihood of failure of individual firms.

Nonetheless, the question arises whether micro-prudential control should include authorisation control as well, at least on financial institutions that operate in more than one Member States. Since the broad policy and a certain harmonisation process have been set in place, the assessment for the grant of authorisation of firms, wishing to be established as European or national companies and operate on a cross-border basis, can be seen as a supervisory task of the pan-European Regulator. Without exercising authorisation control, it is difficult to have a proactive approach to supervision in order to ensure that investment activities are conducted by institutions that have capable management, incentives to prudence and adequate internal controls in place and in operation.[88] Authorisation and licensing powers are also needed to ensure that company structures and operations remain transparent to markets and supervisors.

Hence, the ESR should be responsible for specifying the criteria for risk management systems and their ongoing quality management, enforcing sanctions in the event of non-compliance and establishing an efficient system of handling financial problems. For these purposes, it should be concerned – probably in cooperation with the ECB – in harmonising statistical data gathering across the Union for the purposes of prudential control.[89] But beyond this, as we shall see below, the major innovation of the ESR could be to gather private market forces and take advantage of their expertise in conducting its supervisory tasks. Eventually, however, it is argued in the following paragraphs that a major impediment will inevitably hamper efficient control of European financial institutions: the distance between the regulator and the regulated.

5.1. *Potential drawback: distance from markets and participants. A hybrid model?*

Opponents of investment services supervisory centralisation condemn that a pan-European body would not be able to cope with the requirements of the present financial market structures.[90] National authorities are rather more intimately acquainted with the economic and legal framework, in which their own financial systems operate. Even with a federal solution, they would have to continue to perform their present duties in order to prevent efficiency losses in the regulatory process. A potential problem stemming from the operation of a central regulator at the EU level is that it would be very distant – in terms of geography and in terms of its approach – from most of the markets and the financial firms it supervises. Hence one might ask: how should the centre exert pressure on the periphery?

Distance does not always constitute a disadvantage. The problem of regulatory capture and rent-seeking by professional groups should be seriously considered. A supervisor, which (co)operates too close to the financial industry may be ultimately influenced by its interests, which may or may not conflict with that of other market participants. Although the scope of regulatory capture will depend upon the relative strength of the industry in the various Member States, compared to their impact on centralised rulemaking, it would be rational to assume that distance in this context has a positive and protective effect.[91] However, the proposed federal structure of the ESSR would keep national supervisors close to those that they supervise and would enable them to take into account specific characteristics of national financial markets, as is the case of the ESCB.

The probability of creating a central supervisory body at EU level and the potential problem of distance have raised considerations of developing a hybrid supervisory model, equivalent to that established by the SEC. The supporters of this proposition[92] suggest central monitoring only for the big corporations operating Europe-wide, or at least in two Member States,[93] leaving the others subject to local supervision. This is similar to the US two-tier system, where the SEC and the SROs are responsible for federal supervision of investment firms and State regulators keep their tasks within their State borders.[94] Such a regime could find plausible response. However, potential difficulties may not be avoided. The hybrid model would give rise to the usual problems of definition and potential unfairness. How can one distinguish between institutions that operate in a pan-European fashion and firms that commence business locally? How many Member States does 'pan-European' include and where exactly does 'local' stop? An alternative solution could advocate for central supervision of financial firms that exceed a specific amount of capital reserves.

It is our belief, herein, that, given the urgent need for action, Europe should not hold up discussion for long with an unproductive debate on which model is theoretically superior. The solution for effective centralised supervision lies mainly in the market forces and the financial institutions themselves, in what we would like to call 'new supervision'.

5.2. 'New supervision': self-regulation and market discipline

5.2.1. Public and private sector interaction.

European and global financial markets require a supervisory framework, which national regulators alone are no longer capable of providing. It is, however, in the common interest of both the private and the public sector to secure financial market stability and competition equilibrium through adequate supervisory structures. Today, the trend is towards domestic and cross-border mergers and consolidation of major European financial firms as well as acquisition of smaller ones. This M&A stream, eventually, may not include small peripheral companies, which may be away from the supervisory power of the single European regulator. This calls for a new supervisory concept that should be engaged by the ESR and acquire a more liberal character. Emphasis should be adhered to public disclosure and forces of market discipline and self-regulation in order to strengthen the overall supervisory regime[95] – whilst, of course, acknowledging their limits. This 'new supervision' would move responsibility to the periphery, as surveillance will not just be conducted by authorities but also by the financial firms, their clients and shareholders.

The reasons that will urge the pan-European Supervisor to adopt the 'new supervision' approach are threefold. First, constant and rapid market change means that regulators always lag behind market developments and the financial firms' actual risk position. Efficient supervision can no longer be based on traditional *ex ante* risk analysis and crisis management. Second, standards and regulations developed by EU national supervisors are always two steps behind market standards, due to the long negotiation and implementation period that cross-border and cross-sector cooperation requires. And third, technical errors could be avoided if regulators were to take more, and timelier, resource to private-sector expertise when drafting new regulation. In this light, pure consultation is not adequate. The private sector should be assigned a more active role in the actual supervision process.

5.2.2. The limits of market discipline in the post-Enron and WorldCom era.

Placing emphasis on market discipline measures should not be seen as washing one's hands of supervision of financial firms, but instead as an attempt to enhance prudential supervision by offering the firms the necessary incentives to use their own methodologies for assessing their own risk. The recent collapses of Enron, once the seventh largest US company, and WorldCom, representing the largest bankruptcy in US history, revealed the limits of deregulation in the highly liberal US economy.[96] Albeit the brighter economic outlook of the United States in 2002, a series of revelations of corporate malpractice and the subsequent substantial decrease in securities markets has led consumers to lose not only patience with corporate America's greed, but also their confidence in financial regulators.[97] Although it may be too soon to measure the fallout of Enron, its bankruptcy has already changed the regulatory environment.[98]

In the European tradition, however, the political goal of creating a European single market has required a substantial degree of regulatory and supervisory activity. In this view, markets are not self-constituting and self-stabilising, but require constant regulation and supervision in order to maintain and constitute them efficient.[99] This is no accident. Rather, it is rooted in the institutional structure of the EU. A quasi-unified economy endeavours to coexist with a fragmented political system, in which each Member State has an incentive to defect from European legislation in order to maintain benefits for its own market. In this situation, an institution insulated from political and market pressures, such as a pan-European Securities Regulator, will be particularly well suited to implement credible commitments for market preservation, to draw the line between regulation and self-regulation and to balance the trade-off between setting the appropriate supervisory incentives under a rule-based system and addressing agency problems under a managerial-based incentive system.[100]

5.2.3. Advantages and concerns.   Within this context, market discipline will deliver at least three advantages. First, the safety and soundness of financial firms will be promoted, which in turn will have benefits for consumers, for financial stability in general and for the effective and efficient operation of capital markets.[101] Second, the threat of regulatory arbitrage will be reduced. Placing the firms themselves under 'looser' regulatory jurisdictions would have little impact on prudent behaviour and quality of service. Finally, the workload of the ESR would be decreased, while its efficiency would be increased, which could serve in the better allocation of supervision and enforcement to more fragile institutions that need special attention.

The argument in favour of a market discipline approach by the single supervisor may raise the question, whether similar action could be taken by the current arrangement of multiple supervisors (CESR). Indeed, the Second ISD II Consultation proposes that certain investment firms be prepared to implement appropriate monitoring and surveillance controls to detect and curtail any manipulative practices, as defined in the Market Abuse Directive.[102] Nevertheless, the rationale and argument for attributing supervisory powers to a federal authority is strengthened by the need to have binding supervisory and market discipline standards with clear remedial actions in the case for non-compliance. Today, there are major differences between the national supervisors in their legal authority to set standards across countries. While a number of supervisors have the power to directly implement standards through binding regulations, others may only be able to use 'soft' approaches, such as recommendations. Moreover, the major concerns in the present circumstances are not from the point of view of systemic risk that may occur within a country with 'lower' supervisory requirements, but from the sheer complexity of having financial institutions operating under several different regimes in the same Member State and from the problem facing the authorities in the host country, when a firm headquartered elsewhere has difficulties.[103] *Per contra*, the major advantage of the ESR will be its power to offer a single playing field for prudential supervision. Fostering market discipline, supported by an appropriate public disclosure and internal control regime, can be an effective complement to prudential supervision.

Nevertheless, two problematic issues can be identified in this context, namely tackling the inconsistency of disclosure standards and providing the incentives for a market discipline approach. With regard to the former, the relationship between disclosure and accounting requirements is critical. The Enron, Tyco and WorldCom incidents in the United States suggest that market discipline depends ultimately on the quality and enforcement of good accountancy and audit processes, while the best defence against 'infectious greed' is a healthy corporate culture.[104] The undergoing effort of the Commission to adopt IAS for all listed (and probably soon unlisted companies) surely assists the promotion of consistency across Member States disclosure frameworks.[105] Furthermore, the initial EU response to Enron has brought to light a number of significant international policy issues, including financial reporting, corporate governance and transparency in the international financial system, financial analysts' research and the role of rating agencies.[106]

Regarding the latter, it will be in the hands of the ESR to offer the necessary incentives to financial firms to adopt a public disclosure regime. Of course, the link between ethics and financial supervision can be viewed from the perspective of consumer protection and the stability of the European financial market, in which all market players should be interested. As Chapter 1 has indicated, these two aspects form the basic rationale for financial supervision. Beyond that, the ESR could offer individual incentives, such as subordinated debt or low discount rates to financial groups, which agree to communicate timely information. On the other hand, penalties should be imposed to those firms that fail to abide by the relevant standards.[107] Incentives, finally, will be produced by competition. In an integrated financial market, if a number of financial firms provide a wide range of information that permits all market participants to assess their quality, other firms that remain 'silent' on the subject will find it difficult to demonstrate their soundness and promote themselves.

Market discipline is not panacea. It can work only under certain conditions and is not, therefore, suitable for all types of risk. While the pace of change calls for the involvement of the private sector, the ESR would still have genuine comparative advantages. With a better allocation of its supervisory powers, the ESR could concentrate more on functions, where it will have clear advantages. These would include the development of disclosure recommendations and requirements that allow market participants to assess key pieces of information, the assessment of financial firms' management quality and transparency of their structures, the identification of potential problems, which relate to the individual firm or the financial market as a whole, the prompting of early corrective action or resolution of financial problems, and the assurance that all crisis management capabilities are in good shape and companies comply with the relevant disclosure requirements.

6. Judicial review, judicial power and enforcement

As every EU institution, the single Securities Regulator should not enjoy legal independence. The legality of the acts of the Securities Regulator as well as its failure to act shall be reviewed by the ECJ.[108] Moreover, given that all decisions adopted by the ESR will have a direct effect in all Member States, it will be possible for legal and natural persons, who consider themselves to have suffered from a measure infringing on their rights, to claim damages before a national court. The ECJ can be expected to make a relatively moderate review of the acts of the ESR, in the same way, as it has been careful to state that other organs have acted beyond their competence.[109] However, the situation could be different if a company or an individual proved to be directly affected by any particular ESR measure.[110]

In order to be legitimate, the future ESR should be designed in a way that ensures the respect of the rule of law providing for an adequate system of legal protection through the European Court of Justice. Indeed, the Court explained in *Les Verts* that the Community is based on the rule of law and no decisional act should escape judicial review.[111] The classic methods under Community law should be available against illegal action or damages created by the ESR. All binding regulations and decisions, therefore, invoked by the European Regulator have to be covered by the status of EU legislation.

As an alternative, or possibly in combination with an *ex ante* role, the question has to be raised, whether the ESR could and should be assigned a role in dispute resolution (a) between market participants and national supervisory authorities, (b) between national authorities or (c) between market participants, where a cross-border dimension is involved. This could have an informal character, where parties would submit voluntarily, or it could constitute part of a conventional legal process.

It is obvious that the European Regulator could not serve as a formal appellate tribunal with the power to make binding decisions without an amendment of the Treaty. However, a more limited role by means of conciliation or an arbitration procedure, where complainants renounce their rights to further actions, would be possible under the terms of the current Treaty.

With regard to dispute resolution in financial services, a new initiative deserves our attention. As promised in its Action Plan, the Commission has recommended the development of a EU-wide financial services complaints network, the FIN-NET.[112] FIN-NET is based on cooperation between national dispute settlement bodies and is the first fully functioning cross-border alternative dispute resolution (ADR) network in the European Union. As such, it plays a key role in the Commission's drive to develop a true Single Market in financial services.

Nonetheless, two weaknesses characterise this MoU. Firstly, it is limited only to consumer complaints and secondly, it is not legally binding on the parties and it does not, therefore, create any legal rights or obligations to the parties or any third party. It becomes, thus, obvious that without an ESR to police and participate in the enforcement of investor grievances, it is unlikely that such a network would have sufficient credibility to promote investor and market participants' confidence for cross-border investment and provision of investment services. Within this context, the following paragraphs will examine the general position of Member State and Community law on appeals and the possible role of a European Securities Authority in relation to appeals.

6.1. *General EU position on appeals*

Disputes with regard to investment services regulation will fall to be resolved under general Member States law, the Treaty provisions and/or specific conciliation procedures established under EU financial services secondary law. Under most civil law jurisdictions, when there is a dispute between an investment firm and the competent authority, the aggrieved party has the right to request the authority to reconsider its decision. If the request fails, then the firm is likely to be able to bring the case before a national court or tribunal under national administrative law. By contrast, in the case of the British FSA, no appeal ordinarily lies against its decisions. Instead, references should be made directly to the Financial Services and Markets Tribunal.[113]

Yet, the EU legal framework may open at least two channels, through which a dispute raising an issue with a EU dimension may be challenged. First, under Article 234 EC Treaty (former Article 177), a national court may refer to the ECJ for a preliminary ruling on the interpretation of the Treaty or the validity and interpretation of acts of the institutions of the Community and the ECB, if it considers that a decision on the point is necessary to enable it to give judgement. Second, whereas national authorities are considered to be public bodies, there is a possibility for the Commission to bring an action under Article 226 EC (former Article 169)[114] if it considers that the Member State has failed an obligation under the Treaty.

6.2. *Potential judicial role of the ESR*

If the European Regulator were to act as a forum of appeals (i.e. from decision of national supervisory authorities), this would be inconsistent with the provision of Article 220 EC Treaty (former Article 164), under which challenges to decisions of Member States, arising from a breach of Treaty or Community measures, are to be referred to the ECJ. Moreover, Article 292 EC Treaty (former Article 219) provides that

> Member States undertake not to submit a dispute concerning the interpretation of this Treaty to any method of settlement other than those provided for therein.

This view is supported by the ECJ itself. In its opinion on the EEA, the Court held that a proposed court created within the EEA Contracting Parties with the power to issue binding decisions could impact the balance of powers between Member States and the Community institutions and risk infringing the ECJ's exclusive jurisdiction.[115] Under the current arrangements, therefore, it would be appropriate for the ESR to assume a conciliation or arbitration role as a remedy to avoid intervention of the ECJ.

Today, we should recognise that the regulatory fragmentation of the financial sector, especially the retail, flies in the face of the original concept of a Single Market. To this end, the European Regulator could be seen as a means of reconciling legitimate consumer protection with a Single Market. There is great merit in the creation of the FIN-NET, the network of financial services ombudsmen, where consumers in one Member State with a legitimate grievance against a financial institution in another country could get access to a relatively cheap, straightforward and friendly means of resolving the matter and getting redress when necessary. Nonetheless, its *de facto* weak legal binding force and the fragmentation of the public bodies involved undermine its effectiveness. At least with regard to investment services, a coordination or even more active role acquired by the ESR will provide a more legitimate and efficient out-of-court settlement of consumer disputes.

6.3. *Enforcement*

In an integrated EU financial market, many violations of investment services regulation are or will be transnational. It may be suggested in this context that, unless Member States laws are given extraterritorial effect, there will be inadequate law enforcement. The present home country supervision regime has allowed extraterritorial application of the home country's supervisory power over financial firms operating abroad. Yet, inadequacy in enforcement has remained, mainly due to major disparities between Member States' substantive law, conflicts between supervisors and the confusion on the part of the regulated participants as to what the applicable rules are.

Disparities are easy to be identified, as different national jurisdictions take different approaches and require different standards of proof for the breach. In the United Kingdom, for example, market abuse is only punished if it occurs (a) in the United Kingdom or (b) in relation to securities traded on a market, which is situated in the United Kingdom or is accessible electronically in the United Kingdom.[116] *Per contra*, in Germany, the territorial scope of the criminal sanctions relating to insider dealing goes beyond the German borders. Under the German Securities Trading Act, securities subject to insider dealing restrictions are considered that are (a) admitted to official trading on a German securities exchange or traded on the free market (*Freiverkehr*) or (b) admitted to trading on a regulated market in any other Member State of the EU or Contracting State of the EEA.[117] Taken in connection with the Criminal Code,[118] the Securities Trading Act would penalise insider dealing by Germans committed abroad to the detriment of foreign nationals even if no further direct contact with Germany could be established, as long as the securities involved were listed within the European Economic Area (i.e. not even an EU-listing is required).

Yet, the EU does not dispose of any substantive powers for promoting harmonisation of proceedings and sanctions in this field. The European Regulator would alleviate these problems to the extent that substantive standards were harmonised or, at least, converged at the EU level and it was given some powers of enforcement. The ESR should have direct powers to impose penalties, while the intervention by ministerial departments at national level should be abolished. Procedures will have to be foreseen in order to enable it to act either on its own initiative, or upon the request of national authorities. Even, if however, the ESR were not to become involved in enforcing the rights of undertakings or investors, it could still play an important role in articulating standards for investor protection and in coordinating enforcement activities. Only a central authority could provide information, evidence and political pressure to national authorities to ensure that they enforce commonly accepted pan-European standards.

The CESR-Pol could play a major role herein.[119] The ESR could retain its role in the surveillance of the securities markets and in the coordination of the investigation of questionable or illegal activities by national supervisors. A coordination role undertaken by the European Regulator could offer tremendous assistance to national supervisors, given that the latter do not have the long history of mutual cooperation and the coordination of investigation activities that bank regulators have long enjoyed. It should be recalled that, albeit significant efforts within the 'informal' meetings of the CESR, most national regulators' cooperation activities lie on MoUs. Moreover, the Regulator could assist regulated markets in setting up the appropriate procedures for monitoring compliance with their rulebook, their market rules and the specific exchange rules of conduct in accordance with standards No 10 and 11 of FESCO's Standards for Regulated Markets.[120] The ESR could play a constructive role in providing the CESR with the more legitimate and effective character it needs to harmonise regulation and assure enforcement cooperation. In addition, the ESR could be seen as the simplest and most effective solution to coordinate appropriate policies and enforcement activities with European NCBs and the ECB. The ESR should take the lead in the enforcement effort by enriching it with consistency and coherence.

6.4. Potential drawback: does the ESR need harmonisation of court systems and enforcement methods?

The sceptics of the establishment of a centralised securities body argue that in order to enforce its decisions within each Member State, the European Regulator would need a unified court system underpinning it.[121] However, we do not share the same view. The enforcement of Community policies and measures as against individuals has always been delegated to Member State authorities. Hence, even the current use of legislative measures, such as Directives and 'directly applicable' Regulations, may well require enforcement on the part of national authorities. Nevertheless, Member States court procedures and systems are not any more as fragmented as before. Cooperation between courts in the transmission of judicial and extra-judicial documents and in the taking of evidence has recently been improved.[122] In addition, civil and commercial judicial cooperation has been simplified and expedited by the establishment of a European Judicial Network in accordance with Articles 65 and 66 (former Articles 73m and 73n) of the Treaty.[123] These measures have achieved to a great degree a certain harmonisation of court systems and procedures and have contributed to the clarity, legal certainty and rapid transmission of document requests and taking of evidence performance. With respect to enforcement, however, it is doubtful whether complete harmonisation of court systems and enforcement measures is feasible or even desirable for 'effective' enforcement of EU measures.

Indeed, in its *Von Colson* case,[124] the ECJ addressed the issue of the character of national sanctions in the process of EU measures enforcement. Both the Court and Advocate General Rozès stressed the importance of the functional nature of enforcement measures rather than the juridical form or label.[125] In other words, the specific form of a measure or sanction is less important than its actual effectiveness.[126]

This approach was further consolidated by the ECJ's judgement in the *Yugoslav Maize* case,[127] which arose out of the failure of Greece to use appropriate measures to deal with a major fraud relating to Community funds. Again the outcome revealed that the effectiveness of EU measures does hardly depend on specific remedies or choice of penalties, but on considerations of proportionality, dissuasion and assimilation to national responses to analogous breaches.

Divergences between national rules of procedure, allocation of resources or legal presumptions should not hinder the establishment of a European Regulator. Despite their potential significance, which could be confirmed by systematic research and could preclude any prospects for a pan-European consistent system of enforcement, it is easier to articulate a policy of realistic enforcement and so interpret 'effective' in the light of what is feasible.[128] Whereas complete harmonisation of enforcement is doubtful, the European regulator should direct efforts to two other strategies, which would result in a system of enforcement '*a la carte*': The first would be the identification of problems that hinder enforcement. This would involve a wide consultation debate with national supervisory authorities and other interested parties, which could reveal what sectors (i.e. authorisation, compliance with prudential rules, compliance with conduct of business rules, market abuse) or which geographical areas face legal, financial, political or other obstacles to efficient enforcement. Such a critical assessment would reveal the size of the potential gap between 'ideal' and 'actual' enforcement and directly lead to the second strategy, which is the allocation of enforcement resources. Investigation and research would reveal which areas of law and geography require more enforcement attention and concentration of resources. It follows that, where unenforceable compliance is observed, enforcement efforts need to be smaller and be allocated to more problematic areas. There is no doubt, however, that there will always be the risk that investigation and allocation of enforcement may be influenced by external political and economic interests. Nevertheless, the coordination role of an independent pan-European regulator is guaranteed to ensure the allocation of enforcement to where it is mostly needed and surely away from political and other factors. *Per contra*, it will provide national authorities with guidance on where priorities should be given and on what criteria in order to adopt a realistic approach on the best possible distribution of enforcement '*a la carte*'.

7. The role of national authorities

As Chapter 6 has shown, economies of scale and greater centralised power over European financial institutions should make the ESR more efficient than national supervisory authorities. The latter in turn, by reducing their responsibilities, which may well have exceeded their national borders, could focus their resources more on local areas that remain within their supervisory power and, thus, increase their effectiveness.[129] Through their membership in the governing council of the ESSR, national authorities could participate in the definition of the general strategies and principles of investment services regulation and supervision. To the extent to which national authorities exercise regulatory functions, this exercise should in addition be subject to the prior approval, or at least consultation, of the ESR. This would contribute in the avoidance of 'supervisory competition'.[130] Hence, the ESR would monitor both compliance with rules and the effectiveness of supervision throughout the Community. On the other hand, such a federal system would maintain the active participation and hence the interest of national authorities in the system, as they would be responsible for the implementation in the Member States of both the rules and the supervisory duties agreed upon at the EU level.

The right balance must be struck between the enforcement powers of the European Regulator and that of the national supervisors.[131] Drawing on best practice throughout Member States, the European Regulator could assist national supervisors in an advisory role by providing technical expertise. National authorities, for instance, should be required by the European Regulator to improve control of national financial systems. The proposal for a new Basel Capital Accord[132] views supervisory review as a critical complement to minimum capital requirements and market discipline. The European Commission's work complements the Basel Committee efforts. Being advised by the European Regulator, national supervisors will draw on their knowledge of best practices across institutions and review and evaluate financial firms' internal capital adequacy assessments and strategies, as well as their ability to monitor and ensure their compliance with regulatory capital ratios. Of course, capital is no substitute for effective risk management. Although the introduction of the euro has limited foreign exchange risk, national authorities will need to be aware of new risks and advanced approaches of supervisory methods, including on-site examinations or inspections, off-site review and discussions with management. It is important, therefore, that supervisory staff have sufficient training and experience to exercise judgement in the appropriate areas. Institutions such as the ECB and the ESR can best provide this expertise. At the end of the day, of course, the relationships between national authorities and the single regulator will heavily draw on the ultimate institutional structure that the latter will acquire.

D. Concluding remarks

This chapter has made some suggestions with respect to the institutional structure and operational mode the proposed European Securities Regulator could undertake. The ESCB and the SEC provide emblematic paradigms of the way federal bodies can succeed, even within a quasi-unified European market. Moreover, the ESCB illustrates an example of how far the logic of an agency mechanism can go in terms of autonomy with regard to the standard European institutional system of political decision-making.

One should no longer be surprised if market forces in the form of cross-border alliances and mergers of exchanges and ultimately clearing and settlement systems were making national regulation and supervision obsolete. Compared with such a sweeping prospect, the idea of a supranational supervisor, at least for the super-league of European financial service providers, does not seem so radical anymore. Rivalries and national interests between London and Frankfurt, for example, indicate that, without an ESR, a pan-European market may never come into existence.

Within the scope of the legal and institutional framework this chapter has outlined, an efficient single European Securities Regulator will make the best use of the contributions and comparative advantages of national supervisors, will be conducive to the proactive adjustment of supervision, will provide adequate and relevant information to all supervisors, will establish a prompt and effective crisis management mechanism, will coordinate implementation and enforcement networks will clear out tasks and responsibilities and will provide sufficient incentives to all authorities involved. For the European Commission, the horizontal decentralisation of regulation will constitute a useful way of ensuring it focuses resources on alternative core tasks. For national authorities, the vertical centralisation of regulation and supervision will provide them with more 'space' to focus their resources within their local markets, thus reducing cost and increasing effectiveness.

Innovation, globalisation and increasing complexity of financial business make it increasingly hard for European supervisors to keep track of the risk exposures of individual institutions. A single regulator, therefore, should seek to launch and warrantee a public disclosure and market discipline regime, which in turn would be more effective in encouraging prudential behaviour in a world of increasing complexity and speed of transactions. Market discipline, transparency and information efficiency form together a built-in incentive to companies and to the economy to reach the frontier of economic efficiency.

Naturally, as in any major reform attempt, hurdles will definitely stand before the establishment of an ESR. Issues, such as excessive federalism, concentration of power, distance from national markets and lack of a harmonised platform, will be raised. Given the political will, however, these issues should not be impossible to overcome. European financial markets desperately need and are ready for a central authority to promise and deliver a level-playing field. Any other compromise should not be acceptable.

As far as its institutional structure is concerned, a pattern comparable to the one found in the Maastricht Treaty, empowering the ECB to set policy guidelines with respect to prudential supervision and to have certain powers of verification as to the implementation of its guidelines, seems the most workable approach, which more closely follows the spirit of the EU. Moreover, the Securities Regulator should be able to initiate new regulations and engage in enforcement actions in cooperation with national authorities, following the model of the federal US regulator, the SEC. A significant degree of equilibrium between a regulatory system and an administrative system of control must exist. At the end of the day, however, the specific institutional structure of a pan-European single regulator will heavily depend on further more complex factors, such as recent financial services consolidation and conglomeration trends, market forces and developments of internal financial institutions' structures. The following chapter is concentrated on the discussion of this issue.

8

Consolidating Financial Supervision

A. Introduction

Bringing investment services supervision to the centre of the EU will raise significant questions of the ultimate institutional structure and operation of the single regulator. Accordingly, a few comments shall be made in this chapter on the trend towards consolidation and conglomeration of financial services and on issues stemming from their supervision, particularly within the EU.

In recent years, both the financial services industry and markets have changed considerably as traditional product and service distinctions have blurred and as the traditional features and structures of financial markets have modernised and become objects of technological influence. Historically, the focus in financial services was not on the industry, as we perceive it today, but on individual sectors, such as banking, securities and insurance. In turn, supervision has always followed and reinforced this approach by making specific distinctions between retail commercial banks, investment banks, building societies, securities firms and insurance companies.

Today, the evolving trends of consolidation and globalisation are being fuelled by the erosion of boundaries between financial services sectors and have contributed to significant changes in the financial services industry. Many cross-sector mergers and acquisitions have taken place during the past few years, both in Europe and elsewhere, and both domestically and cross-border. Only in Europe have there been more than 1200 deals with an aggregate value of €250 billion between June 1999 and June 2000.

This increase in the number of financial conglomerates has been accompanied by a blurring of the boundaries between financial products. The securitisation of traditional forms of credit (including mortgages, credit cards, commercial loans and corporate bonds), for instance, has weakened the distinction between equity, debt and loans, and even between banking and insurance business (where, e.g., credit derivatives share many of the characteristics of an insurance product and insurance companies offer deposit-like products).

All these trends have an enormous impact on the regulation and supervision of financial services as well. Combined financial operations may create new prudential risks or exacerbate existing ones. Hence, the 'emergence of financial conglomerates has challenged traditional demarcations between regulatory agencies'.[1] Besides the problems stemming from the cross-border provision of services, analysed in previous chapters, an immediate need has arisen to develop an effective exchange of information and coordination of regulatory requirements across the authorities responsible for different parts of a financial group's business, as well as mechanisms for coordinated action when problems arise. Other trends include the combination of supervisory functions to single or at least fewer regulatory authorities in accordance with the above-mentioned consolidation dynamics.

This chapter examines the issues stemming from the consolidation of financial services and their supervision in the global system and the considerations arising from the Single Market of the European Union in particular. What are the specific schools of thought and what is the direction that European regulators and political leaders are likely to follow? Traditional integration theories and the European practice have not provided regulators and policy-makers with many choices. However, the debate on the institutional structure of European financial supervision is being intensified and developments in financial services and markets urgently push for solutions that better serve the objectives of financial supervision.

B. Putting an end to sectoral supervision?

As described in Chapter 1, the structure and operation of financial services supervision was traditionally divided between sectoral functions. Banking supervision was emphasised more than insurance because of the sector's size and the systemic risks involved. Securities market supervision was based more on self-regulation, while in many Member States competent securities regulatory and supervisory bodies hardly existed. Increasingly, however, the frontiers between the different kinds of financial activities are blurring and there is a worldwide trend in financial services towards diversification and conglomeration.[2]

1. Consolidation of financial services

Consolidation of financial services can be explained, partly by the desire of governments to foster greater competition between financial markets and, more significantly, by the desire of financial institutions to diversify risk and to secure synergies. Consolidation solves most of the profitability problems of the financial sector.[3] The logic behind this proposition is strong: the main banks, investment firms and insurance companies have each built extensive commercial networks. If their existing network could be used for the provision of services of other sectors in addition to their own, this would be very profitable, for there would be no or little additional cost of physical or technical infrastructure. Other factors that contributed to the blurring of financial services include changes to tax laws, which removed traditional protections on certain financial products, and changes in consumer culture and investor needs.

Importantly, all these trends have been bolstered by the sweeping and radical technological developments that have invaded financial markets. New state-of-the-art possibilities provide the foundation for these trends by facilitating the creation of new kinds of markets and market participants and by altering the way traditional players conduct their financial business. Some of the new entrants, for instance, that began by offering an Internet-based deposit-taking service have since moved into investment business by offering their customers access to a range of managed funds. Hence, the Internet remains the most significant development. Of course, there are also potential costs associated with conglomeration, namely safety and soundness issues, conflicts of interest and supervisory and regulatory problems. The detailed discussion of these factors, however, goes beyond the scope of this chapter. More interesting is the point that all these elements point out the need to address the most pressing issues arising in such structures with respect to supervision.

2. Consolidation of supervision

In view of the increasing cross-border and cross-sector dimension of financial conglomerates, the need to maintain level-playing fields and the need to protect the objectives of financial stability, consumer protection and competition create an additional need to address the most pressing regulatory and supervisory issues arising in such structures. This is regarded as extremely significant to enhance legal certainty and clarity for regulators, market participants and consumers and to contribute to the stability of the global financial system.

Consolidated supervision is one key ingredient of new regulatory approaches. Under this regime, the various companies within a financial conglomerate are supervised on a group-wide basis.[4] This means that capital requirements, actual capital and risk exposures are subject to group-wide supervisory assessment. In general, the need for supervision of financial conglomerates is mandated by the fact that many financial groupings include entities that are not subject to supervision. In addition, important prudential issues addressed in sectoral regulations aiming at the supervision of banking, investment and insurance groups, are not regulated at the level of financial conglomerate. Thus, the difficulty to supervise financial conglomerates is evident. To this end, in considering institutional structures for financial supervision, it is necessary to assess all problems relating to the inability to identify separate sets of supervisory objectives and to the interdependence of risk and capital resources within diversified financial groups.

The following analysis concentrates on the considerations arising from the market of the EU.

3. Considerations within the European Union

In the EU context, the developments and problems discussed before challenge some of the traditional approaches to efficient prudential supervision and require a further policy refinement. During the mid-1980s, the European Commission addressed the particular supervisory problems of financial conglomerates. Yet, the final resolutions that emerged from these discussions did not result in legislative enactments. Current financial regulation is still very much sector-based and addresses primarily homogeneous financial groups, namely those groups whose activities are limited either to banking/investment or to insurance.[5] It was only recently that the Commission resumed the debate and chose to address particular problems of heterogeneous financial conglomerates.[6] These include:

(a) the problem of complex and non-transparent group structures, which represents a supervisory obstacle with regard to all possible group-wide and cross-border risks;
(b) the particular danger of outflow of capital through unfair intra-corporate transactions as well as by intra-corporate loans;
(c) double gearing on capital;
(d) competition distortions, mostly between banks and insurance companies; and
(e) the need to improve cooperation among supervisors.

3.1. The 'lead' supervisor

The consolidation of financial services and the emergence of complex financial conglomerates make a strong case for an institution-wide overview of financial groups. Nevertheless, the dilemma arises whether it is necessary for this to be undertaken by a single regulator or by a 'lead' regulator (or 'coordinator') appointed from among the national sectoral regulators.

Following its tradition to maintain the highest standards of prudential supervision for its financial institutions under its network of multiple regulators, the EU endeavours to implement the recommendations of the G10 Joint Forum on Financial Conglomerates[7] and the recommendations of the 'Brouwer Report' on stability in the financial sector,[8] as endorsed by the Lisbon European Council of 2000. As a result, the EU proposal seeks to introduce specific prudential legislation for financial conglomerates. It takes the first necessary steps to align the directives for 'homogeneous' financial groups[9] and for 'heterogeneous' financial conglomerates[10] in order to ensure a minimum equivalency in their treatment. In particular, the EU approach provides for the appointment of a lead supervisor (or 'coordinator') chosen among the 'solo' Member States' regulators responsible for specialised aspects of financial institutions.[11] This lead supervisor will be responsible for taking a consolidated view of quantitative and qualitative factors of financial groups and for coordinating and encouraging the exchange of information between the relevant supervisory bodies, both routinely and in the event of a crisis. Therefore, cooperation between supervisors and information sharing is the most significant precondition for effective and efficient supervision. Indeed, the 1999 Joint Forum Report on the role of a 'coordinator' stressed the importance of cooperation and coordination by taking account of the factors and problems in defining the role and responsibilities of the lead supervisor, including the different legal frameworks of the countries in which the conglomerate operates, the different statutory responsibilities and powers of the individual regulators concerned, and the varying abilities of these regulators to share information across sectors and across borders.

The benefits of appointing a lead supervisor for a financial conglomerate are allegedly significant: to avoid 'underlaps' in the prudential supervision of conglomerates, to avoid duplication of supervision, which is burdensome and costly for supervisors and financial firms and to achieve simplification of procedures and supervisory efforts.[12] *Per contra*, the major weakness of this approach is that it can lead to competitive distortions, either between financial centres or between financial services providers. In addition, given the acute problems of communication, cooperation, coordination and consistency, analysed in previous chapters, the question arises whether these make a case for moving towards some form of single financial regulator on a cross-border basis. The question is therefore less one of whether lead regulation can work – it may do so in many cases – and more one of the efficiency of such an approach when market developments make the above-mentioned problems the norm rather than the exception.[13]

Indeed, when we talk about regulation and supervision today, we must admit that 'the most constant thing is change'.[14] Market developments are unpredictable and so are institutional structures. Hence, when talking in European terms, a number of further issues need to be addressed. In particular, three schools of thoughts prevail and are examined separately in the following paragraphs.

3.2. Single versus sectoral supervision

The first issue in financial supervision is the dilemma between a single supervisor and separate sector regulators. In response to recent consolidation developments in financial services discussed before, many countries in Europe not only have re-addressed the challenges presented by the new lines of business, but also have moved towards the creation of single or, at least, fewer national regulators in order to mirror the emerging structure of financial institutions and to adequately supervise groups of growing size and complexity.[15] In other European countries, the supervisory structure is known to be under official review or informal debate.[16]

The Financial Services Authority (FSA), for example, is the single regulator for the United Kingdom's financial services industry and 'the broadest financial regulator in the world, combining prudential, conduct of business and market conduct regulation across the full range of financial services'.[17] On 1 December 2001 it assumed its full powers and responsibilities under the Financial Services and Markets Act 2000 (FSMA).[18] The FSMA was passed by the Parliament in June 2001 and came into force at midnight of 30 November 2001. It provides a single modern and flexible legislative framework, which covers the entire financial services sector.[19]

The idea of centralising and consolidating financial regulation and supervision in the United Kingdom came not only as a response to recent failures, such the collapse of Barings in February 1995, but also as part of an even more fundamental proposed restructuring of financial regulation. This would involve converting the existing Securities and Investment Board (SIB), the former British securities regulator, into a new single mega regulator, which would also gather the responsibilities of up to nine other agencies, including the Bank of England.[20] As in a number of Member States, banking regulation in Britain has always been carried out by a single agency, the Bank of England.[21] However, in a surprise decision on 20 May 1997, Tony Blair's newly elected Labour government announced that it would create a unified regulatory authority for the banking, securities, and insurance industries. The details of the restructuring were expanded in a report produced by the retiring Chairman of the SIB, Sir Andrew Large, in July 1997.[22] The Large Report was prepared in response to the request by the Chancellor of the Exchequer, Gordon Brown, to bring forward the plan to implement the Government's policy.[23]

But what is the broader rationale for creating a single supervisor? The extent of activity by financial conglomerates is always highlighted as one of the key factors supporting the case for a single supervisor. Moreover, the supporters of such a model argue that a single regulator can deliver advantages for both financial institutions and consumers.[24] It offers a one-stop shop for conglomerate financial groups, which would not want to deal with the multiplicity and expense of many authorities, and for consumers, who would prefer one ombudsman scheme, one compensation scheme and one place for complaints. A single supervisor is able to make an overall assessment of those underlying factors relating to the financial situation of an institution, without jeopardising cooperation between the different functional supervisors. The existence of a supervision-coordinator would simplify the monitoring of global risks relating to domestically controlled institutions. If this rationale is correct at the national level, it should logically apply at the EU level, in the context of a single currency, a Single Market, free capital flows and an increasingly global market place.[25] A European Financial Authority can facilitate cooperation at European and international regulatory level, for it would simplify its links with other regulators and its ability to monitor global risk run by EU-based institutions.

The arguments in favour of a single financial regulator go hand in hand with the need to create a level-playing field for service providers and financial market participants. This could best be achieved by applying the same rules to identical transactions, irrespective of the legal nature of the service provider. For the time being, however, EU financial services legislation follows a sectoral approach. Different sets of rules exist for banks, investment firms and insurance companies. While this distinction has not created major problems in the past, it will be increasingly relevant in the near future, as financial services frontiers become less and less visible. Hence, same businesses will need same rules and single supervision.

The advantages of a specialist supervisor, on the other hand, are the clearer and more dedicated focus on the business under its supervision. It should offer higher proximity to the business, more specialisation and better awareness of potential problems.[26] A single regulator might not have a clear focus on the objectives of regulation and supervision and might not make the necessary distinctions between different types of financial firms. In addition, sectoral supervision gives rise to an inter-agency competition, where institutional competition between sectoral agencies working side by side can work and create incentives for more efficient performance.[27] Finally, and perhaps the most important argument against a single supervisor is the related increase of moral hazard. The perception is created that the whole financial sector lies under the protection of a powerful single supervisor, which may increase the incentives for higher-risk investment decisions made by institutions and consumers.

3.3. The potential role of the ECB

The second issue is whether EU-wide financial supervision should be assigned to the ECB or to a separate body. Banking supervision is not a necessary or exclusive function of a central bank. Instead, many European countries' central banks are not directly entrusted with this task or they have joint responsibility with another supervisory body. In half of the eurozone Member States the functions of banking and market supervision are clearly separated from the conduct of monetary policy and its implementation, whereas in the other half they are not.[28] The 'double separation' (geographical and functional) between central banking and banking supervision, and the absence of any explicit reference to who takes care of financial stability in Europe, did cast some doubts about the efficacy of current regulatory arrangements in preventing and managing financial crisis and are currently at the centre of a lively debate. But, what are the arguments for and against these two regimes? Which factors determine (if they do) that the one model functions better than the other?[29]

The fact that both models are equally represented in the EU reveals that the answer to these enquires cannot be straightforward. Goodhart and Schoenmaker claim that the major argument for divorcing the bank supervisory from the monetary authority is that the combination of functions might lead to a conflict of interests.[30] The implied concern is that, as the central banks lends to a troubled credit institution in its role as LLR, this loan will increase the net inflow of reserves to the banking system and thus undermine monetary policy. Beyond that, it would be incompatible with basic democratic principles to entrust too much power to a single institution. Finally, the observance of particular confidentiality in respect of information falling essentially within the ambit of supervision and the intrinsic difference between the microeconomic objectives of supervision and the macroeconomic aims of monetary policy have also been identified as arguments against the concentration of these functions.[31]

Per contra, the main argument against separation of functions is systemic stability and consistency between monetary policy and financial supervision.[32] Monetary policy has a direct effect on the liquidity and even the solvency of financial institutions. Certain instruments of monetary policy, such as the laying down of minimum reserves, involve the use of instruments for the exercise of powers, which may conveniently be combined with those relating to the exercise of supervision.[33] Hence, the decision-making bodies of monetary policy must have an overall and intimate understanding of the functions of the banking system, and bank supervisors must comprehend the policy environment, in which they operate.[34] A single body would be in a much better position to focus on the macro-prudential control and portfolio performance of the European financial market and to stress the endogeneity of system outcomes with respect to the collective behaviour of individual banking and investment institutions. More persuasively, arguments for the allocation of supervisory responsibilities to the ECB correspond to the need to control credit exposures that the ECB might undertake as LLR or through its involvement in the operation of payment systems in the eurozone.[35] Thus, the ECB would be best suited to be a crisis manager.

The prudential supervisory responsibilities, which have been granted to the ESCB under the Treaty and the Protocol on the Statute of the ESCB and the ECB reflect the decision at the time of the negotiations not to alter the structure of prudential supervision by the Member States.[36] Beyond that, the prudential supervision provisions make clear that the ESCB is not to act as a separate body but as a network of national competent supervisory authorities.

Prudential supervision, therefore, does not count among the basic tasks with which the ESCB is entrusted. This does not mean, however, that it lacks any supervisory responsibility. Although not among its basic tasks, at least three supervision-related tasks are assigned to the ESCB. First, a specific provision in the task-setting article concerns prudential supervision. The ESCB is required to 'contribute to the smooth conduct of policies pursued by the competent authorities relating to the prudential supervision of credit institutions and the stability of the financial system'.[37] This is elaborated in Chapter V of the Statute entitled 'Prudential Supervision'. Secondly, the ECB is called upon to give advice on draft legislation in areas, which are within its field of competence. Prudential supervision is thus made the subject of prior consultation of the ECB.[38] Taken together, these two tasks provide the ECB with a consultative and coordinating role in prudential supervision. Finally, the ECB is vested with the power to collect the necessary statistical information in order to carry out its tasks. In accordance with the principle of subsidiarity (Article 5 of the Treaty), the ECB is to be assisted by the NCBs, which shall carry out, as far as possible, the task of collecting data.[39]

Apart from the supervisory-related tasks of the ESCB, which may be performed immediately from the start of Stage Three, the ECB may perform its own supervisory functions. The seeds of delegating a supervisory role to the ECB without amending the EC Treaty may be found in Article 105(6). This provision clearly reflects the endless negotiations that preceded its adoption by providing an enabling clause, which permits the allocation of supervisory tasks to the ECB. Pursuant to Article 105(6) of the Treaty:

> The Council may, acting unanimously on a proposal from the Commission and after consulting the ECB and after receiving the assent of the European Parliament, confer upon the ECB specific tasks concerning policies relating to the supervision of credit institutions and other financial institutions with the exception of insurance undertakings.

This enabling provision makes it possible, albeit with substantial procedural and political impediments to be overcome, to provide for a form of direct EU-wide supervision of financial institutions without amending the Treaty.[40] Nevertheless, it is debatable what specific tasks may be attributed to the ECB. What is important is that the Maastricht Treaty offers opportunities for real progress in the field of prudential supervision of financial institutions. Although the context, in which the negotiations during the IGC took place and Article 105(6) was finally drafted, reveals an absence of political agreement on the need for centralising supervision, the Treaty contains provisions that can promote progress in the development of EU law. The formation of the ESCB and the enabling clause present an institutional opportunity that has to be further exploited in order to reconsider prudential control.

3.4. Supervision by objective

Finally, the third issue is whether, because of the consolidation trend, financial supervision will become more objective-driven, since the functional divisions of the business will be increasingly difficult to make.[41] According to supervision by objective, financial supervision could be carried out separately by one agency for systemic stability, a second for prudential supervision and a third for consumer protection and conduct of business rules.[42] The advantage of this regime is that it is well adapted to consolidation in the financial sector, while remaining sufficiently focused.[43] Regulatory agencies are probably most effective and efficient when they have clearly defined, and precisely delineated, objectives.[44] On the other hand, such a system would require a revolutionarily high degree of institutional reorganisation on current supervisory structures. Also, there would remain considerable overlaps and supervisory duplication.

3.4.1. 'Twin Peaks'.   A characteristic paradigm of the supervision-by-objective model is the 'Twin Peaks' structure first proposed by Michael Taylor, formerly with the Bank of England.[45] Taylor suggests that the British financial regulatory and supervisory system should be redesigned around the twin peaks of systemic protection and consumer protection. The twin peaks would be implemented by two separate but closely interlinked bodies. The first peak, the Financial Stability Commission, would ensure that there were adequate prudential measures to ensure the soundness of the system, the capital adequacy of banks and control of risk. It would be responsible for the authorisation and on-going prudential supervision of all major financial institutions (banks, building societies, securities firms and insurance companies) on both a solo and a consolidated group basis. The second, the Consumer Protection Commission, would enforce conduct of business regulation to ensure that the consumer received a fair and honest service. In time, it could also take over the administration of consumer credit and would subsume the various Ombudsman schemes.[46]

The rationale behind this proposal is that the two aims of financial regulation and supervision, namely the soundness of the financial system and consumer protection, often conflict and are not adequately separated in the regulatory system with the result that they give rise to confusion and damage. Accordingly, Taylor argues that the benefits of twin peaks are that it eliminates regulatory duplication and overlap. It creates regulatory bodies with a clear and precise remit, while at the same time it establishes mechanisms for resolving conflicts between the objectives of financial regulation. As such, it is consistent with the philosophy of 'unbundling' the functions of public sector agencies, to achieve greater transparency, efficiency and clearer lines of responsibility. However, it is doubtful whether the twin peaks system will resolve the problem of duplication and overlap. It is also inevitable that the twin objectives of public policy will come into conflict in certain cases. Moreover, Taylor's 'Twin Peaks' does not ultimately propose the establishment of two bodies, but rather makes the case for a third 'peak', a Market Surveillance Agency, as a coordinator charged with oversight of all London's financial markets, particularly from the point of view of detecting and prosecuting various forms of market abuse. As a result, the potential cost of running two or more agencies and their compensation schemes should also be of particular concern.

3.4.2. Three peaks and regulatory matrix. A second proposal comes from Di Giorgio *et al.* and focuses on the Italian situation.[47] Di Giorgio *et al.* highlight some 'anomalies' proper to the current regulatory system. Hence, they present a proposal for a new configuration for supervising the Italian financial market through the assignment of different objectives or 'finalities' to different authorities. This perspective would entrust the attainment of the three objectives of supervision on the entire financial market – stability, transparency and investor protection, competition – to three distinct authorities regardless of the subjective nature of the intermediaries, whether they be in banking, finance or insurance. One agency should thus be responsible for financial micro-stability, another for transparency and disclosure requirements, and the third for protection of competitive features in the markets. According to the authors, this scheme would innovate current arrangements by delegating to a sole authority the objective of transparency in banking and the suppression of misleading advertising of financial products. In addition, it would highlight the objective of competition (especially in banking) as a distinct finality explicitly monitored by the regulator. Moreover, for the sake of consistency, the existing rules applying to other forms of financial intermediation would be extended to include the life insurance sector.

Interestingly, Di Giorgio *et al.* make a further step. They extend their proposal for a regulatory reform in Italy to the euro area. This requires to explicitly address the problem of who takes care of financial stability in the euro area. The authors re-examine the issue of the need for a LLR and of the proper relationship of the ECB with other financial market regulators. They propose the establishment of a European System of Financial Supervisors, with three distinct independent authorities (plus the ECB) at the European level. These agencies ought to be characterised by homogeneous procedures in terms of their creation, functioning and funding. They should be responsible for the comprehensive coordination of both legislation and execution of regulation in financial markets: the first European agency should be responsible for the microeconomic stability of all intermediaries, while the second for transparency and disclosure requirements. The third objective of guaranteeing competition in financial (and non-financial) markets is already safeguarded by having the Antitrust General Direction of the European Commission plus the domestic agencies. The alleged advantage of this regime would be a higher degree of coordination in the field of financial regulation and prudential supervision, which is both desirable and needed in the EMU. Again, however, the problems of overlap and confusion may be difficult to be avoided.

Finally, an alternative system based on the objectives of regulation is proposed by Goodhart.[48] While the focus on objectives is similar to Taylor's approach, a more differentiated structure of institutions is suggested. In this construction, Goodhart proposes the creation of a systemic regulator, a separate prudential regulator for securities firms, insurance companies and other non-bank institutions, where continued insolvency is a regulatory issue, a single conduct of business regulator for retail and a separate one for wholesale business, a competition agency with a clear role in regulation and self-regulation for exchanges. The mandate of each agency is clearly defined and their structure includes the range of institutions and the nature of regulation to be covered in each agency. It becomes apparent that, under this regime, a financial institution will necessarily be subject to the jurisdiction of more than one regulator and, depending on its range of business, possibly to several agencies. In contrast to a single regulator, it is thus, doubtful whether this 'regulatory matrix', as described by Goodhart, would be easily welcomed and accepted by firms and consumers.

4. Future policy development

All the above-mentioned schools of thought, European regulators and policy-makers in financial services have already set up the necessary links with each other to move further. Within the EU, the European Roundtable on Financial Services (ERF) is ensuring coordination between the European supervisory and regulatory committees to ensure that cross-sectoral issues are coherently and effectively tackled.[49] Regretfully, some countries, like the United Kingdom, do not seem willing to export their supervisory system. Their fear is that a pan-European supervisor could do more harm than good, if such a body were overly politicised like other continental regulators.[50] A super-regulator with effective powers to set standards and enforce them across Europe would be enormously powerful. Perhaps national regulators are not ready for this. Or maybe the reasons are more practical and simple. Member States, like the United Kingdom, which already function under the single financial regulator regime, find the trend towards sectoral pan-European supervision misplaced. A European Securities Regulator, for instance, would divide securities supervision from other types of financial services supervision in Europe, which would remain on a national basis. For these countries, it would be odd to recreate at the EU level a structure of sectoral supervision, which is progressively being abandoned nationally.[51] A consolidated full financial supervisory structure would be much more appropriate.

Much will also depend on the ECB's willingness and ability to assume more substantial supervisory responsibilities. Traditionally, the ECB has always argued on the virtues of the combination of monetary and prudential tasks in a single institution.[52] When viewed from a Eurosystem perspective, the attribution of extensive supervisory responsibilities to the central bank is likely to prove more beneficial, as it would allow closer coordination within the network of supervisors and better monitoring of risks. The recent trend, however, at the national level to take prudential supervision of credit and other financial institutions away from the central bank might provide for a glimpse into the future and suggest that the establishment of an agency, separate from the ECB, is more likely. This prediction is further enforced by the exclusion of insurance undertakings from Article 105(6).

At this stage, it is less important whether the single regulator will be called European Securities Regulator, European Financial Authority or European Central Bank. The balance of the different theoretical arguments is not clear-cut and institutional choices can also be determined by practical considerations pertaining to the historical tradition and the institutional environment. Also, empirical evidence fails to provide clear support for any of these approaches.[53] As with the cooperation model currently practised by European regulators, the current supervisory structure has worked reasonably well so far. Until now, no major crises stemming from the nature of financial conglomerates and the integration of financial markets have arisen. But this argument is missing the issue. The crucial factor is not the empirical evidence from financial conglomerates, but the softening of distinctions between financial services and national borders, which does not only bring problems of competitive neutrality, but also gives rise to doubts whether the current regime of sectoral and national supervision is flexible enough to respond speedily to the melding of different financial products by defining new uniform standards. Admittedly, there is no perfect institutional model. Current trends should be our guide for future structures and institutional responses. To be sure, there are still a large number of unresolved issues, but the general direction towards centralisation is clear.

C. Concluding remarks

This chapter considered the case for cross-sectoral consolidated supervisory structures, particularly within the EU. Predicting the future shape of EU investment and financial services supervision and regulation may be nothing more than a risky academic exercise. It may also be too early to reach firm conclusions about the success of national authorities that have consolidated supervision in delivering the benefits expected from a single national financial services regulator. Besides the trend of enhancing cooperation and coordination between national supervisory bodies, the need for greater consistency and better adoption of rules at EU level will reveal the inevitability of centralisation of financial supervision. The institutional model, which seems to be emerging from recent trends at the national and international level and from the failure of measures at the EU to address and tackle the problems of inconsistency, inefficiency and ineffectiveness is a pan-European Securities or Financial Market Regulator.

Consolidation of financial supervision will heavily draw on market forces and on developments of internal financial institutions' structures. The sectoral integration of financial firms and their increase in cross-border activities generates the need for greater coordination and cooperation across both borders and sectors. This might, eventually, generate a stronger argument for fewer authorities or for a single pan-European financial regulator to have a broad scope across a wide range of financial services activities. The balance of the different theoretical arguments is not clear-cut and institutional choices can also be determined by practical historical and socio-economic considerations as well as the institutional environment of each jurisdiction. The EU model adopts the 'lead' supervisor solution, whereas some countries have chosen a supervisory structure that goes hand in hand with the objectives of financial supervision. Moving a step further, various Member States have entrenched the rationale of creating a single regulator. The latter has induced many to adopt the view that if this is correct at the national level, it should logically apply at the EU level as well, in the context of a single currency, a single market, free capital flows and an increasingly global market place.

Regretfully, the current EU policy-making deliberately keeps its distance from structures considered in this and the previous chapter. The focus remains on the traditional regulatory approach, while supervision is left out of the agenda. So, it is back to basics and it is back to the same thing that has failed for the past ten years. Given the same institutional structure, there is a logical concern that the proposed legislative process, initiated by the European Commission and developed by the Wise Men Committee and the Economic and Financial Committee, will be just as time-consuming and burdensome as the old one. According to the chairman of the Wise Men Committee, a Treaty change will be required to institute a single supervisory agency, if the new framework fails. But why should we wait for a solution to deliver, when it is doubtful whether it makes any difference to previous attempts? What has really changed? The time for national solutions is over. What we need now is a European solution that best suits the interests of financial firms, issuers and consumers.

Epilogue

The need for a significant institutional reform of investment services supervision and regulation at the European Union level has been the central theme of this book. Problems associated with the principles of home country control and mutual recognition call for a new wave of fresh thinking and dynamic response. Today, the idea and proposal of establishing and developing a central pan-European Securities Regulator not only seems less and less remote, but also necessary for the better promotion of the objectives of financial stability, consumer protection and competition between financial intermediaries. The time has come for these thoughts and ideas to be voiced.

As early as 2500 years ago, the Greek philosopher Protagoras contributed to the idea that every issue has two sides, each one of which is completely different from the other. As such, home country control and supervisory centralisation are two polar cases along a spectrum of tension, the balance of which is central to the debate and development of the EU and the single financial market. This 'balance' is represented today by the home country control and mutual recognition approach, which allows minimum harmonisation of basic rules and standards on the one hand, and space for Member States' intervention on the other. However, in light of the fundamental restructuring of European investment services and the failure of regulatory responses, the basic nature and operation of modern EU supervisory and regulatory practices must now be reconsidered.

This book has followed a simple and logical method for defining the trade-off relationship between effectiveness of supervision and its costs and for suggesting a centralised institutional design. The first step, considered in Chapter 1, was the definition of the objectives and rationale for financial supervision in the EU. Indeed, delegating powers to a central Regulator is inextricably intertwined with the need to secure and better promote the supervisory objectives of financial stability, competition and consumer protection. The second, followed in Chapters 3, 4 and 5, was the description and marginal analysis of the current home country based supervisory arrangements in connection with the aforementioned objectives. If the current structure provides overall costs charged on national markets and market participants which are higher than marginal benefits, so as to make the Internal Market and investment services unstable and unable to function and compete with other markets, the third step has to follow: the examination of alternative arrangements and the possibility of transferring policy at a more centralised EU level. The case for a European Securities Regulator (ESR) was the main focus of Chapters 6 and 7, whereas Chapter 8 examined the pros and cons of additional solutions of institutional centralisation of supervision in accordance to the recent financial services consolidation trends.

An analysis of the issue of Member State competence versus federal EU competence involves identifying the costs and benefits of each. Indeed, the principle of subsidiarity teaches us that action at Community level is justified only when it would produce clear benefits by reason of its scale of effects compared with action at Member States level. Before that, the legal analysis of home country control and mutual recognition finds unproved that the principle should be used with the intention of systematically subordinating all other methods of cross-border regulation and supervision. In addition, the cost–benefit analysis of home country control reveals that the failure to omit obstacles and adopt common supervisory standards at the EU level severely impedes the emergence of a complete single financial market. Even though the initial idea may have been the most suitable for the time it was adopted, its implementation has failed due to the lack of political will, enforcement compliance and administrative capacity of the Commission and the Member States. The following sections highlight the main issues and arguments of this book that support or impede the establishment of a single authority in the EU.

A. Free provision of services and competition promotion

This book has argued that the establishment of a central regulator will further liberalise the provision of cross-border investment services and create a truly single, open and competitive market. The diverging concepts, on the basis of which Member States continue to work in the area of regulation and supervision, and the as yet underdeveloped structure of EU decision-making with regard to supervisory policy, are calling not only for further adaptations and alignment, but also for radical reform. The current EU investment services supervisory structure is anything but a model. Home country control and mutual recognition have created a 'Babel' of supervisory voices and standards, whereas the lack of hierarchy and clear allocation of responsibilities between the home and the host country creates specific problems of regulatory and supervisory management as well as political drift. Notwithstanding the liberalisation efforts of the 1992 approach, transaction costs, legal uncertainty and anti-competitive lack of access to foreign markets hinder the free provision of cross-border investment services and seriously disrupt the competitive equilibrium.

Almost ten years after its adoption, home country control and mutual recognition have reached their limits. The increasing concentration and integration of services providers and markets at the European level have created phenomena that can neither be governed by nationally based policies nor left to the working of unregulated markets. EU investment services regulation and supervision is chaotic. Consequently, a strong trend towards a single European Regulator is perceived to be a development, which should be supported as a necessary step. This book has strongly argued that there is no point in having a common monetary policy and aiming at a single financial market, while keeping different financial regulation and supervision rules in each Member State.

Naturally, there is always the temptation to move slowly and push steadily in the direction of change rather than take large steps and implement a new system as a whole rather than in parts. Practice has shown, however, that the disadvantage of proceeding piecemeal is that a new regime may not prove effective until most or all of it has been implemented. In the meantime, existing controls are being weakened and the burdens on European financial institutions and the costs on investment services in general increase. The result? European financial markets find themselves ill-equipped to compete in the international financial arena.

Undoubtedly, there is a cost associated with making institutional changes too. Yet, by separating the process into different steps, the total cost may be increased. This, however, does not mean that trying to move rapidly in the establishment of a European Securities or Financial Regulator is without drawbacks either. Again, the cost of centralisation should be balanced against the need for it, along the lines of the benefits it could deliver for the entire Single Market. Securing the necessary political will seems to be the most acute problem. If one party can hold up the whole process, then the period before which any change occurs is lengthened. Implementing any change takes time.

Nevertheless, it seems difficult to avoid the dictum that one should 'do as much as possible as soon as possible'. Europe has a window of opportunity and it is important to introduce institutional changes when the economy is not fragile. The introduction of the euro and the increasing integration of European financial markets indicate that rapid progress would be desirable, even if some of the changes in structure or harmonisation of securities laws come later. Efficient markets require a predictable and transparent legal environment, a clear set of supervisory responsibilities and a fast-track law-making and implementation process to keep regulators in parallel with market developments.

B. Burdensome lawmaking: 'starting the ball rolling'

Delegating powers to a federal Securities or Financial Authority fluctuates in sympathy with the search for greater effectiveness in the lawmaking process of the Union. Moving from home country control and mutual recognition to centralisation and harmonisation is more than just a change of method. While both mutual recognition and regulatory cooperation can in principle be conducted in an intergovernmental style, harmonisation obviously moves further into the direction of creating supranational structures, which may be one of the reasons why some governments are so adamant about this happening.

Attempts by national, European and international institutions to develop long-term strategies for ensuring the quality and speed of regulation are hampered not only by the need for short-term political responsiveness but also by the very institutional structure, which is responsible for the complexity of securities regulation and supervision in the first place. In response to the everlasting problem of slow and ineffective legislation, the Lamfalussy Group came to propose the establishment of two new Committees and the introduction of a four-level approach to securities regulation. Nonetheless, it is more likely that the proposed regime will create more confusion than it was intended to eliminate, as the involvement of more actors and the 'fast-track' circumvention of the traditional co-decision procedure is guaranteed to open Pandora's box.

Regretfully, the recent Commission and Wise Men proposals suggest that EU policy-makers' attention often focuses merely on the decision-making arrangements, that is, the adoption of rules. But the quality of rules also depends on the process of policy-making – including the preparation before and implementation and enforcement after their adoption. Until now, the bulk of the activity to achieve the goals of the 1992 Single Market programme was focused merely on the legislative process rather than on the follow-through, on designing rather than implementing and enforcing policy rules. The long debate and criticism on the new Lamfalussy institutional arrangements is crystallised in the compromise reflected in the Von Wogau report voted by the Parliament. The deep disagreement between the Commission and the Parliament is more than obvious, as the latter – in an effort not to sabotage the new regime altogether – has limited the ESC's period of life to four years after the adoption of the relevant directives.

Any short-term solutions to the problems of home country control, mostly analysed in Chapter 5, 'should' and have been found within the confines of the present EU Treaty. A further strengthening of cooperation between national securities supervisors is sought, supplemented by the attempt to speed-up the legislative process by the establishment of the European Securities Committee (ESC) and the Committee of European Securities Regulators (CESR). However, European policy-makers should not stop here.

The principles of financial market supervision may have worked well until now. In fact, many proponents of the present system, both in the public and the private sector, claim that home country control is a splendid principle. The same people, however, complain of the difficulties financial firms and consumers are facing to conduct their business across their country. Albeit disappointing at first sight, the Wise Men proposals could also be seen as establishing the precursor to a single pan-European regulator. The establishment of the ESC may look to be the ideal precursor to the ESR (as was the EMI prior to the ECB), while the CESR may appear as the perfect forum to pave the way to the European System of Securities Regulators (ESSR).

The single Securities Regulator promises greater flexibility. Rephrasing the theory of neo-functionalism, the functional needs of a Single Market in investment services necessitates a considerable transfer of policy and law-making powers to EU level. Regulatory economies of scale and scope for financial undertakings, securities markets and consumers call for efficiency gains that only a central regulator can deliver. Previous chapters have shown that establishing a central authority will improve the way rules are decided, applied and enforced across the Union. Beyond that, the ESR will fill the gap and become the single strong European voice to negotiate and foster the European interests with its global counterparts and the WTO. Of course, far from fearing the impact of a sole bureaucratic and powerful regulator, one should realise that the ESR, following the paradigm of the ECB and the SEC, will still resort to public consultation when it proposes rules and standards. National regulators, on the other hand, will not be isolated from this process, but rather become substantive parts of it as members of the ESSR.

C. Electronic trading and the 'virtual' future of financial services

Modern financial services regulation and supervision must be forward-looking. Powerful forces of internationalisation and technological innovation do raise further regulatory and supervisory issues for the near future. The inconsistency between EU financial laws and the E-Commerce Directive poses a significant threat to the smooth operation of markets and the free provision of services. The electronic commerce country of origin principle does not coincide with the traditional financial services home country control regime. In addition, the rules applied for the localisation of investment services at EU level are different in nature and scope from those applicable in the WTO/GATS level. The development of the E-Commerce and the Distance Marketing Directives and other initiatives taken at different levels raise questions on the coherence of the European regulatory and supervisory framework for electronic commerce. Financial services providers urgently need to know whether they have to comply with the regulatory provisions in the jurisdictions in which they provide online services and what they consist of.

Similarly, the significantly increasing emergence of Alternative Trading Systems and the confusion regarding their supervisory treatment by the fragmented European regulators entails the risk of a bulk of investment business being under-supervised or even unsupervised. These electronic trading platforms are here to stay and it is certain that they will soon dominate the European and international financial services business. It is a matter of time before most or all national and cross-border financial transactions will become totally 'virtual' and untraceable. Their dominance in the European financial arena significantly undermines competitive neutrality. In addition, the supervisory asymmetry between national authorities, closely interlinked with the relevant issues of operational risk, transparency, monitoring, fragmentation and enforcement, pose acute financial stability and consumer protection risks to regulators. In the near future, which national authority will undertake the responsibility (and the risk) to supervise a virtual exchange-service provider or settlement system? Even if it assumes such responsibility, how will it be able to enforce its rules? These questions remain unanswered by the group of European regulators.

The failure to control electronic financial commerce will be one of the greatest economic tragedies of the Internet age. Hence, a single regulatory and supervisory regime at the EU level is needed to keep pace with state-of-the-art developments and avoid creating a bias in favour of paper-based systems. In this light, the ESR should be careful not to stand in the way, whether wittingly or unwittingly, of activities which bring about improvements in liquidity, and reductions in cost for consumers, allied to an increase in competition between rival service providers and trading systems. Competition, among stability and consumer protection, continue to be the objectives of financial supervision even within the electronic era.

D. Financial stability and consumer protection

This book has adopted the view that the institutional design of regulatory and supervisory responsibilities is one of the most important matters affecting the future course of EU investment services policy. It is obvious that securities supervision in the European EMU needs to march and function in parallel with evolving national and cross-border trends and financial market integration. If traditional methods of supervision seem anachronistic, supervisory structures in Member States need to respond. The stability of the European financial market and the protection of the European consumer ought to be the ultimate goal.

If parts of an integrated area, such as the European Single Market, are subject to macroeconomic shocks that have a particular high impact in one or a few of them, there is scope for the pooling of risks. Transfers, thus, within a centralised system may be more effective, as there is no market for macroeconomic insurance. Besides, no tool or responsibility mechanism to counter and/or manage the risk of financial instability has been established in Europe. The Treaty is silent on this issue.

To cope with the impact of the euro and the Single Market, regulatory and supervisory structures do not only need to be efficient and cost-effective. When the home country control principle loses its applicability, the time will have come to be supplemented by a clear allocation of powers and responsibilities in times of crisis, and a central pan-European mechanism to ensure that all financial institutions operating in Europe have an effective supervisory authority. Thoroughgoing 'enhanced' cooperation between national authorities-members of CESR may ease the information asymmetry. Nonetheless, Member States' supervisors tend to see the integration of EU financial markets as a 'national mission.' It is, thus, doubtful whether a crisis emergency with significant spill-overs will give them the incentives to act promptly, decisively and away from national, political and socio-economic interests. In this light, the fear arises that the current institutional arrangements and financial frameworks will deadlock the integration of financial markets. The latter reveals the need for a flexible, independent and accountable central supervisory authority to smooth the inevitable national conflicts and to provide the natural shield to prevent or even repulse catastrophe.

Of course, the optimal number of failures, either of consumer protection or of financial failure, is not zero. Crises, wars, depressions, securities-market booms and crashes come and go, but they always seem to arrive as surprises. Surprise is endemic above all in the world of finance. Panic, however, cannot be an effective consultant is such circumstances. The recent Enron disaster clearly indicates that the deregulation juggernaut could not be stopped until the US authorities witnessed the complete collapse of a company that aggressively stood for the proposition that deregulation was unquestionably good. Indeed, with the notable exception of Basel II, major financial reforms have been driven by crises in the course of the global financial history of the twentieth century. This, however, does not imply that Europe should wait for a reason, but rather it should act in anticipation of a critical situation and pursue a courageous and radical supervisory reform.

Looking ahead, the need for a pan-European structure for regulation, supervision and monitoring systemic risk is foreseeable, while the notion of creating new institutions at the EU level should not be abandoned. This could be cross-sectoral as well as within traditional sectors, to marry micro and macro-prudential supervision. This book has remained open-minded on the question of whether there should be institutional consolidation of supervision or concentration within the ECB of the powers of monetary policy and prudential supervision. Empirical and theoretical research at the national level reveals that all models can perform supervisory duties. Hence, this field does not pose a dramatic dilemma. What matters at this point is that the existing enhanced cooperation between national regulators must be facilitated and underpinned by greater coordination and harmonisation of standards across the Union established by a central regulator.

E. Politics into practice and the prospects for reform

There is surely a difficult trade-off between home country control and centralisation of supervision. However, as many of the costs and benefits involved in the creation of a single pan-European regulator are rather intangible in nature, it will not always be possible to come up with a complete legal, institutional or economic evaluation. Hence, the ultimate decision may be based on mere political motives. Indeed, if there is one single, burning question that is derived from this book (the debate on the future of European financial services regulation and supervision), it is the political question: given the solid rationale for centralisation of financial regulation and supervision, why is there still such resistance to the establishment of a single pan-European regulator?

Although politics has hardly been the focus of this book, policy-making is part of a wider political process and politics does pervade the way EU policies are made. The issue of independent and credible European bodies is still alive, as shown by the importance attached to it by the Commission's 2001 White Paper on European Governance. The vigorous internal debate stimulated by the preparation of this document indicates that a growing number of Commission officials have abandoned the traditional non-delegation *Meroni* doctrine and openly endorse the creation of strong regulatory agencies. This is particularly obvious in policy areas, such as food safety, energy, transport and telecommunications, where a series of food scares and other regulatory deficiencies have compromised the credibility of traditional approaches. Financial services, however, still remain out of the agenda, despite the shortcomings of the current approach, described in previous chapters. One may logically wonder whether a crisis, in the form of a financial 'mad cow disease' would make the last defenders of the *status quo* reconsider radical institutional reforms.

The European Parliament, on its part, looks less able to give a lead in the debate on institutional reform than it had been in the 1980s ahead of agreement on the SEA. As we saw in the case of the ESC, the EP generally supports independent agencies, as long as they do not undermine its position in the legislative process. Hence it is uncertain whether the Parliament will also be in favour of a 'hard' pan-European Regulator with extended legislative and supervisory powers.

The Parliament's role notwithstanding, the strongest resistance to the establishment of a single regulator stems from national governments and parts of the Commission – especially its Legal Service, which sees itself as the guardian of the balance of power among EU institutions, and the poorly staffed DG Market, which is British dominated and may be reluctant to move towards the acquisition of more financial services' experts to strengthen its human resources. Despite conspiracy theories, however, much will heavily fall on the position of national policy-makers and regulators.

Naturally, large Member States, which fuel the European economy and traditionally have a saying on its policy, remain strictly adhered to their own principles and interests. The official efforts in attaining the common goal of creating a Single Market in financial services have been transformed into an unofficial *'bras de fer'* game between the European financial centres of London, Frankfurt and Paris. Of course, there is nothing new about the EU being used for narrow and ostensibly national purposes to extend the policy resources available to Member States. Yet, the increasingly frequent institutionalisation of collective governance in ways that explicitly preserve micro-political national interests has been and will be the major impediment to a successful single European financial market.

Even though the United Kingdom has opted out of the EMU, London remains the financial centre of Europe. In this light, the British FSA is and will be unwilling to lose control of its market and delegate its sovereignty to a central independent body. However, its preoccupation with the battle with Frankfurt may allow the French to steal the prize: a pan-European Regulator based in Paris. On the other hand, it seems inconceivable to other Europeans to create a single Regulator without the British participation. French and German policy-makers were behind the rally to create a common monetary policy. With French and German elections taking place within 2002, however, the Franco-German axis does not seem capable of leading a debate, let alone an agenda, on financial institutional renewal, at least in the short to mid-term.

Time inconsistency constitutes a final threat to the establishment of the ESR. Voices are increasingly raised on the democratic deficit of the Community and the ongoing distance between EU institutions and European citizens. In the words of the White Paper on European governance 'people increasingly distrust institutions and politics or are simply not interested in them'.[1] In an era, when the EU seems unable to hold a major summit without anti-globalisation protests, the Laeken summit convened a Convention in 2001 to examine questions of European governance and decision-making. Nonetheless, only time will reveal whether the blessing of the Convention will touch the highly important issues of financial services regulation and supervision and European economic reform, which would oil the 2004 IGC engine.

What should keep us optimistic is the 2000 Lisbon summit, which marked a sea change in EU economic thinking. As decided by the EU Council, the strategic goal of the Union is 'to become by 2010 the most competitive and dynamic knowledge-based economy in the world, capable of sustainable economic growth with more and better jobs and greater social cohesion'.

This is an ambitious goal that cannot and will not be achieved unless the EU in general and the euro area in particular develop financial markets that are efficient and competitive and that reap the full benefits of the single currency. The price of any failure will be massive. Especially after the tragic terrorist incident in New York on 11 September 2001, the case for a European financial integration as a motor for growth and employment, a buffer against market volatility and a pole for economic stability and consumer protection is stronger than ever.

Many initiatives and activities are involved in the process of European financial markets integration, but this process seems to be taking too long. The Lamfalussy Report sets 2004 as the year of reviewing the progress of the current regulatory system and considering the establishment of a single regulator. In the meanwhile, the European society and especially our markets and the political system will increasingly feel the pressure of time and the future. Unfortunately, Member States' governments stop short of seeing the urgency for centralisation of supervision and subsequent harmonisation of regulation, the benefits and the well-being which can be achieved by market integration. 'I cannot deal with the future because it passes very quickly', Albert Einstein used to say with sarcastic exaggeration. The recent history of the EMU, however, and the subsequent creation of the ECB and the ECSB clearly indicate that nothing is inconceivable. In a political world, where most governments believe in the virtues of open and unduly provision of services, the Union must be seen as an essential driving force behind the freeing of international trade, for the EU remains the staunch defender of values that are easily jeopardised by free trade, such as environmental or labour protection. In this respect, the European financial market and economy in general could be seen as a plausible prototype for the global economy in the future. Taking the analogy further, the single Securities or Financial Regulator could be viewed as a model for global institutions that might one day govern a single international market.

At the end of the day, of course, whether there will be unified European institutions or networks of national supervisors depends on the power and willingness of both national and EU authorities to abandon their narrow perspective and protectionist policy to deal with developments arising from the Single Market. Member States are strong on rhetoric, weak on actions. The clock is ticking and it will be 2010 before we know it. Rather than taking the easy road and postponing difficult decisions for later, this is the time for EU policy-makers to move forward decisively. As Commissioner Bolkestein admits, 'unless there is a fundamental change in attitude on the part of Member States, the ambitious target set out in Lisbon will be impossible to achieve'.[2] If not now, when?

Annex I: Statistical Tables

Table AI.1 Gross capital raised on stock markets as per cent of GDP

	1997	1998	1999	2000
EU	1.1	1.8	2.8	4.5
US	2.6	2.2	3.0	3.6

Source: Eurostat, 2002.

Table AI.2 Rules of conduct in the EU Member States and Supervisory Authorities

	Date of Rules of Conduct	Law	Supervisory Authority	Year of establishment	Staff (end 2000)
Austria	30.12.1996	Art. 11–18 Securities Supervision Act	Finanzmarktaufsicht (ex Bundes-Wertpapieraufsicht)	2002 (1997)	N/A (30)
Belgium	6.4.1995	Art. 36 Law on Secondary Markets	Commission Bancaire et Financiere	1990	250 (all divisions)
Denmark	22.5.1996	Sec. 5–6 Securities Trading Act 376	Finanstilsynet	1981	168 (all divisions)
Finland	1989	Ch. 4 Securities Markets Act 495	Rahoitustarkastus	1993	120
France	2.7.1996	Art. 32 Law 96–597	Commission des Opération de Bourse	1967	300
Germany	26.7.1994	Sec. 31–32 Securities Trading Act	Bundesaufsichtsamt für den Wertpapierhandel	1995	140
Greece	25.4.1996	Art. 7 Law 2396	Επιτροπή Κεφαλαιαγοράς	1995	80

Ireland	1.8.1995	Sec. 37 Investment Intermediaries Act	Central Bank of Ireland	1943	700 (all divisions)
Italy	24.2.1998	Art. 21 Legislative Decree 58	Commissione Nazionale per le Societa e la Bors	1974	450
Luxembourg	5.4.1993	Art. 37 Circular 2000/15	Commission de Surveillance du Secteur Financier	1998	156 (all divisions)
Netherlands	16.11.1995	Art. 24 Act on the Supervision of the Securities Trade	Autoriteit Financiele Markten	1989	170
Portugal	10.4.1991	Art. 304–317 Law 142-A/91	Comissao do Mercado de Valores Mobiliarios	1991	147
Spain	1993	Royal Decree 629	Comision National del Mercado de Valores	1988	200
Sweden	1.8.1991	Section 7 Securities Operations Act	Finansinspektionen	1991	160
UK	1985	Financial Services Act	Financial Services Authority (ex SIB)	1985 (SIB) 1997 (FSA)	2000 (all divisions)
EU-15					4621 (approx.)

Source: Avgerinos, 2001.

Table AI.3   Securities Supervisors in EU

B	DK	DE	EL	E	F	I	IRL	L	NL	AU	P	SF	SW	UK
SC/BS	FSA	SC	SC	SC	SC	SC	CB	SC/BS	SC	FSA	SC	SC/BS	FSA	FSA

Note: SC = Securities Commission; BS = Banking Supervisor; FSA = Single Financial Services Supervisor; CB = Central Bank.

Source: Avgerinos, 2002.

Annex II: Figures

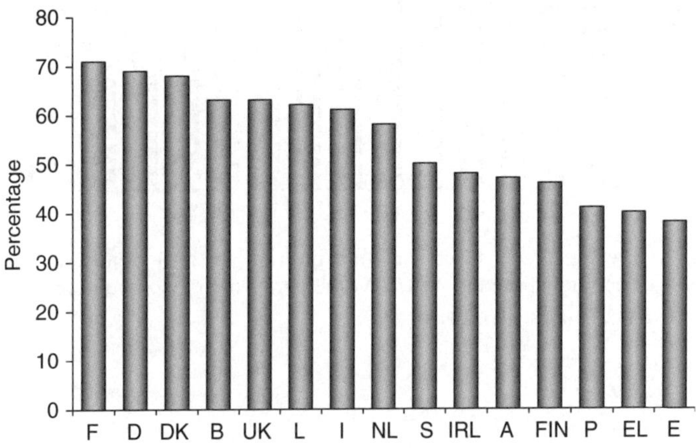

Figure AII.1   Percentage of companies who responded that the laws and regulations affecting their companies have been simplified only marginally, or not at all

Source: European Commission, 2001.

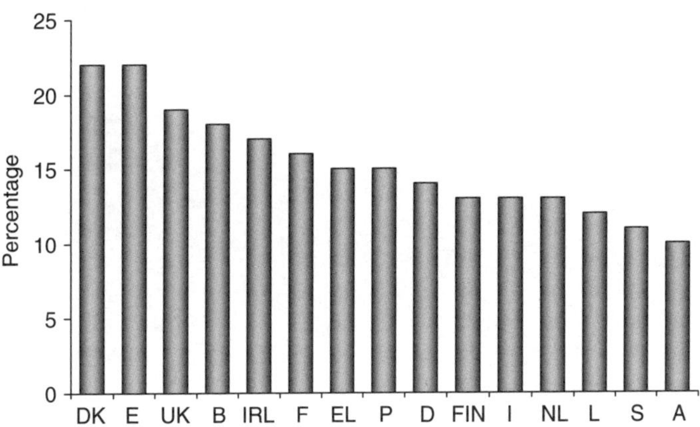

Figure AII.2   Unnecessary compliance costs as a percentage of total compliance costs

Source: European Commission, 2001.

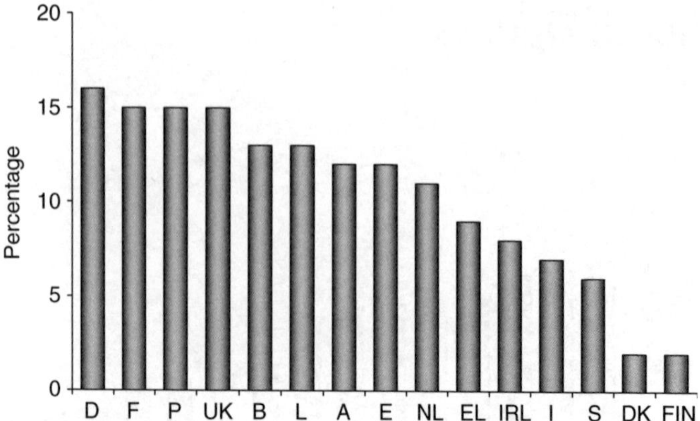

Figure AII.3   Percentage of directives' transposition in 2001. Many directives that should have been transposed in 2000 have still not been transposed nearly a year after

Source: European Commission, 2001.

Notes

Prologue

1. For the purposes of this book, unless otherwise indicated, the term 'regulation' will be used to refer to the legal rules or administrative requirements established by financial authorities or markets to limit or control the risks assumed by financial firms and to the imposition of such provisions either generally or on the activities of an individual institution. 'Supervision' shall refer to the associated or complimentary process of monitoring or reviewing the behaviour of financial firms with any specific sets of regulatory provisions imposed or with more general standards of prudent or proper behaviour. See, e.g., Gardener, E.P., *Theory and Practice in 1Banking Supervision: Some Reflections* (IES Institute of European Finance, RP 86/2) 2; Llewellyn, D., *The Regulation and Supervision of Financial Institutions* (Gilbart Lectures on Banking, 1986) 9; Goodhart, C. *et al.*, *Financial Regulation: Why, How and Where Now?* (London: Routledge, 1998) 189; Walker, G., *International Banking Regulation: Law, Policy and Practice* (London: Kluwer, 2001) 1. For a US perspective, see Breyer, S., *Regulation and Its Reform* (Cambridge: Harvard University Press, 1982); Spulber, D., *Regulation and Markets* (Cambridge: MIT Press, 1989) 21. The terms 'regulator' and 'supervisor', however, may be used in a broader sense, including all authorities that regulate, supervise or review compliance by financial institutions.

   The European Union was created under Article A of the Maastricht Treaty and is stated to be founded on the European Communities, namely the European Community, the European Coal and Steel Community and the European Atomic Energy Community. The Maastricht Treaty was subsequently consolidated under the Amsterdam Treaty (Consolidated Treaty establishing the European Community, OJ C 340/173, 10 November 1997, hereinafter 'EC Treaty').

2. EU securities markets have benefited from new trends: the total volume of international bond issues in euros is now practically equivalent to the volume of issues in US dollars and the volume of derivatives contracts traded has multiplied every quarter since mid-1998. However, indicators show substantial scope for further capital market integration in Europe. Using a survey on business services carried out by the Commission, it can be estimated that eliminating barriers to cross-border trade would increase current EU GDP by between 1.1 and 4.2%. See European Commission, *Economic Reform: Report on the Functioning of Community Product and Capital Markets* (COM(2001), 7 December 2001) 17. Another study estimates that an integrated financial sector could add between 0.5 and 0.7% to EU GDP or 43 billion euro; see Heinemann, F. and Jopp, M., *The Benefits of a Working European Retail Market for Financial Services* (Report to European Financial Services Round Table, 2002) 12. Although such figures might turn out to be exaggerated, the effects are, no doubt, big enough to deserve increasing political attention.

3. Article 2, EC Treaty.

4. European Commission, *Completing the Internal Market: White Paper to the European Council* (COM(85) 310 final, 28 June 1985).

5. Article 14(2) (former Article 7a) EC Treaty.

6　*Council Directive 93/22/EEC of 10 May 1993 on investment services in the securities field* (OJ L 141/27, 11 June 1993); *Council Directive 89/646/EEC of 15 December 1989 on the coordination of laws, regulations and administrative provisions relating to the taking up and pursuit of the business of credit institutions* (OJ L 386/1, 30 December 1989). All banking directives have recently been codified in *Council and Parliament Directive 2000/12/EC* (OJ L 126/1, 26 May 2000).

7　Even before the tragic events of September 2001 in the United States, eurozone stock market capitalisation had fallen 19% between January and August 2001; *ibid*. See also Annex I, Table 1.

8　European Commission, *Financial Services: Implementing the Framework for Financial Markets: Action Plan* (COM(99) 232, 11 May 1999).

9　White Paper, *op. cit.*, note 4. Paragraphs 102–3 provide that 'The accent is now put increasingly on the free circulation of "financial products" (...) The Commission considers that it should be possible to facilitate the exchange of such "financial products" at the Community level, using a minimal coordination of rules as the basis for mutual recognition by Member States of what each does to safeguard the interests of the public. Such harmonisation (...) should be guided by the principle of "home country control". This means attributing the primary task of supervising the financial institution to the competent authorities of its Member State of origin (...) [and] there would have to be a minimum harmonisation of surveillance standards'.

10　Regarding the ISD, see the Opinion of Advocate General Jacobs in Case C-384/93 *Alpine Investments* [1995] ECR I-1141, Paragraph 19.

11　It is characteristic that of the 36 target Internal Market actions scheduled to be achieved by June 2001, only 26 (56%) were expected to be completed on time. See European Commission, *'Working Together to Maintain Momentum': 2001 Review of the Internal Market Strategy* (COM(2001) 198 final, 11 April 2001) 4. The success rate for completing target actions fell to just over 50% for 2002; see European Commission, *2002 Review of the Internal Market Strategy: Delivering the Promise* (COM(2002) 171 final, 11 April 2002).

12　'(...) of specific tasks concerning policies relating to the prudential supervision of credit and other financial institutions with the exception of insurance undertakings' on unanimous approval by the Member States; Article 105(6), EC Treaty.

13　See IOSCO, *Supervisory Framework for Markets* (May 1999) 2.

14　See ISD, Article 19; *cf.* SBD, Article 21.

15　See e.g., Thieffry, G., 'After the "Lamfalussy" Report: The First Step towards a European Securities Commission ("ESC")?' in Andenas, M. and Avgerinos, Y., *EU Financial Market Supervision: Towards a Single Regulator?* (London: Kluwer, forthcoming 2003); Danthine, J.P. *et al.*, *The Future of European Banking* (London: CEPR, 1999) 98; Leleux, P., 'Corporation Law in the US and in the EEC' (1967–68) 5 CMLRev 133, 159.

16　See Lannoo, K., *Does Europe Need an SEC?* (Madrid: ECMI, 1999) 43; Avgouleas, E., 'The Harmonisation of Rules of Conduct in EU Financial Markets: Economic Analysis, Subsidiarity and Investor Protection' (2000) 1 ELJ 72, 84; Committee of Wise Men, *Initial Report on the Regulation of European Securities Markets* (9 November 2000) 26.

17　See European Commission, *Better Lawmaking 2000* (COM(2000) 772 final, 30 November 2000) 15.

18　See European Commission, *Enhancing Democracy in the European Union* (SEC(2000) 1547/7 final, 11 October 2000) 10.

19 Padoa-Schioppa states that 'on the whole, (...) the legislative cum regulatory reform, although rather unusual and very diversified in comparison with those of most currency jurisdictions, does not seem to present loopholes or inconsistencies that may hamper the pursuit of systemic stability'; Padoa-Schioppa, T., *EMU and Banking Supervision* (Lecture at the London School of Economics, 24 February 1999).

20 Banks, e.g., become increasingly involved in securities and insurance activities; see Chapter 8.

21 That is the case in the United Kingdom, Sweden, Denmark, Norway and, recently, in Austria.

22 Such a normative approach is worth pursuing, despite the fact that political and bureaucratic factors ultimately play an important role in the outcome of supervisory and institutional structures. Beyond that, the most persuasive general theory of regulation, popular among lawyers, economists and political scientists until the late 1950s, held that regulation grew out of a need for a regulatory programme to secure the 'public interest'; see Peacock, A., *The Regulation Game* (Oxford: Basil Blackwell, 1984) 8. In the financial services sector this interest may extend and become part of more serious risk-management and financial stability objectives.

23 See Alfon, I. and Andrews, P., *Cost–Benefit Analysis in Financial Regulation* (FSA Occasional Paper Series No. 3, September 1999) 5.

1 The Objectives of Financial Supervision

1 This chapter does not distinguish between the *objectives*, the *rationale* and the *reasons* for regulation and supervision. It is not its point to differentiate between the economic rationale as opposed to why, in practice, regulation and supervision might be imposed. For such a distinction, see Llewellyn, D., *The Economic Rationale for Financial Regulation* (FSA Occasional Paper No. 1, April 1999) 8–9.

2 See Di Cagno, D., *Regulation and Banks' Behaviour towards Risk* (Dartmouth: Aldershot, 1990).

3 Dalhuisen, J., 'Liberalisation and Re-Regulation of Cross-Border Financial Services. The Situation in the EU and WTO/GATS' (1999) 5-6 EBLR 158, 160. Dalhuisen argues that, with the exception of the ISD's Preamble, which states that investor protection is one of its objectives without defining the others, EU financial services Directives do not give an unequivocal answer to the objectives of financial regulation and supervision.

4 Mayes, D. *et al.*, *Improving Banking Supervision* (Basingstoke: Palgrave, 2001) 65.

5 Dimson, E. and Marsh, P., 'Calculating the Cost of Capital' (1982) 2 Long Range Planning 112, 113–14.

6 Cesarini, F., 'Economics of Securities Markets Regulation: Some Current Issues', in Ferrarini, G. (ed.), *European Securities Markets: The Investment Services Directive and Beyond* (London: Kluwer, 1998) 65.

7 See Austin, R., 'Commentary 2 on Report No 1', in Buxbaum, R. *et al.*, *European Economic and Business Law: Legal and Economic Analysis on Integration and Harmonisation* (New York: Walter de Gruyter, 1996) 213.

8 Dalhuisen, *op. cit.*, note 3, 159.

9 On this issue, see Chapter 5, Section C.2.4.

10 See, e.g., Dale, R., 'The Regulation of Investment Firms in the European Union (Part 1)' (1994) 10 JIBL 394; Llewellyn, *op. cit.*, note 1, 20.

11 *Ibid.*

12 See Dale, R. and Wolf, S., 'The Structure of Financial Regulation' (1998) 4 Journal of Financial Regulation and Compliance 326, 334. On the consolidation of financial services, see Chapter 8.

13 Case C-384/93 *Alpine Investments* [1995] ECR I-1141, Paragraph 42.

14 The consolidated supervision of financial conglomerates explicitly recognises the interdependence of risks and capital resources within diversified financial groups.

15 The collapse of Peregrine Investments in 1998, Asia's premier homegrown investment bank, not only sent tremors throughout the local financial community, but also had a 'domino' effect and prompted a new plunge in Asia's battered markets.

16 On the LTCM rescue, see Chapter 6, Section C.6.2.

17 Mayes *et al.*, note 4, 72.

18 See, e.g., Dale, *op. cit.*, note 10.

19 Key objectives of financial regulation have been identified in various international reviews; for banking, see OECD, *Banks under stress* (Paris, 1992); Basel Committee, *Core Principles for Effective Banking Supervision* (September 1997); for securities, see IOSCO, *Objectives and Principles of Securities Regulation* (February 2002); for insurance, see IAIS, *Insurance Core Principles* (October 2000); for cross-sectoral issues, see Joint Forum, *Core Principles: Cross-Sectoral Comparison* (November 2001).

20 Di Giorgio, G. *et al.*, *Financial Market Regulation: The Case of Italy and a Proposal for the Euro Area* in Andenas, M. and Avgerinos, Y. (eds) *Financial Market Supervision in Europe: Towards a Single Regulator?* (London: Kluwer, forthcoming 2003).

21 This approach is being followed by Advocate General Jacobs. In his *Alpine Investments* Opinion (Paragraph 75), he notes 'the need to protect investors and the need to ensure the integrity of the financial markets are related objectives'.

22 The outcome of Lamfalussy and his Wise Men Committee uses confidence as an objective, which can be used horizontally in pursuing the ultimate regulatory method. Recommending the adoption of a 'conceptual framework of overarching principles' at Level 1, on which EU securities regulation should be based, the maintenance of confidence in European securities markets constitutes one of them; see Wise Men Committee, *Final Report on the Regulation of European Securities Markets* (February 2001) 22.

23 Hawkesby, C., 'The Institutional Structure of Financial Supervision: A Cost–Benefit Approach' (2000) 3 JIBR 36.

24 Dale and Wolf, *op. cit.*, note 12, 334.

25 'Systemic risk' refers to (a) the scenario that a disruption at a firm, in a market segment, or to a settlement system could cause a 'domino' effect throughout the financial markets toppling one financial institution from another or (b) a 'crisis confidence' among investors, creating illiquid conditions in the marketplace. See IOSCO, *Risk management and Control Guidance for Securities Firms and their Supervisors* (May 1998) 7.

26 See especially European Commission, *Progress on Financial Services: 2nd Report* (COM(2000) 336, 31 May 2000) 10.

27 For the regulatory and supervisory arrangements that address such conflicts of interest, see FESCO, *Status of Implementation of the Standards for Regulated Markets* (25 September 2000) 1.

28 Chapter 5 will show that is not the case in the present supervisory regime of home country control.

29 For the division between home and host country in the international and the EU context, see Chapter 3.

30 Llewellyn, *op. cit.*, note 1, 16. See also European Commission, *Communication on Upgrading the Investment Services Directive (93/22/EEC)* (COM(2000) 729, 16 November 2000), where it is noted at 5 that 'removing regulatory obstacles to the free circulation will not be sufficient. Regulatory action is also needed to correct market failure and to facilitate the effective interaction of supply and demand for capital'.

31 Article 3(t) EC Treaty. The whole Title XIV of the Treaty (former Title XI EC) is devoted to the protection of consumers. Article 153, in particular, declares that consumer protection should be taken into consideration not only in adopting legislation to establish the internal market but also in measures adopted to define and implement other Community policies and activities.

32 See Llewellyn, *op. cit.*, note 1, 10.

33 Dale and Wolf, *op. cit.*, note 12, 327.

34 See Mayes *et al.*, *op. cit.*, note 4, 82. See also Lindsey, R., 'Efficient Regulation of the Securities Market' in McCrudden, C., *Regulation and Deregulation: Policy and Practice in the Utilities and Financial Services* (Oxford: Clarendon Press, 1999) 298.

35 According to Mayes, an additional advantage of effective disclosure is that it reduces the threat of regulatory arbitrage, as the incentives would be weakened by any implicit or explicit government guarantees to financial firms; see Mayes *et al.*, *ibid.*, 83. The issue of market discipline is analysed later in Chapter 7, Section C.5.2.

36 Llewellyn, *op. cit.*, note 1, 27.

37 Lambert, R. and Simon, A., 'An Ideal Regulatory Model for Dealing with Retail Financial Institution Runs and Failures' (2000) 4 Journal of Financial Regulation and Compliance 309, 311.

38 'By promising something which cannot, in reality, be delivered, the regulatory system undermines the inevitable fundamental responsibility which consumers must take for their own decisions. As a result, when things go wrong, investors believe they are entitled to compensation, almost irrespective of the quality of the advice received'; see Ford, C. and Kay, J., 'Why Regulate Financial Services' in Oditah, F. (ed.), *The Future for the Global Securities Markets – Legal and Regulatory Aspects* (Oxford: Clarendon Press, 1996) 145.

39 All these make straight fraud and abuse more likely; see Goodhart, C. *et al.*, *Financial Regulation: Why, How and Where Now?* (London: Routledge, 1998) 7. See also FESCO, *Market Abuse: FESCO's Response to the Call for Views from the Securities Regulators Under the EU's Action Plan for Financial Services* (29 June 2000).

40 IOSCO, *op. cit.*, note 25, 10.

41 See Cesarini, *op. cit.*, note 6, 66.

42 EC Treaty, Article 3(g). The EU rules on competition are contained in Articles 81– 6 (former Articles 85–90) of the Treaty. Dassesse *et al.* regard no coincidence that these rules are to be found at the Third Part of the Treaty, which deals with the policies of the EU; see Dassesse, M. *et al.*, *EC Banking Law* (London: Lloyd's Press, 2nd ed., 1994) 245.

43 The Internal Market Council concluded in March 2001 that 'competition should be reinforced in services sectors, supported by the removal of barriers to cross-border trade and market entry'. See European Commission, *Economic Reform: Report on the Functioning of Community Product and Capital Markets* (COM(2001) 736, 7 December 2001) 16.

44 For instance, it may be more efficient to have a single clearing, settlement or payment system; see Goodhart *et al.*, *op. cit.*, note 39, 4.

45 European Commission, *Second Report on Competition Policy* (1972) Point 50.

46 Case 172/80 *Züchner v Bayerische Vereinsbank* [1981] ECR 2021. For an excellent analysis of this case and the issues arising from it, see Dassesse *et al.*, *op. cit.*, note 42, 263–71.

47 Namely Articles 98 and 99 (former Articles 102a and 103) EC Treaty.

48 One of the first cases to deal with purely investment intermediaries was the acquisition of the German Gerresheimer Glas by Investcorp Group and Chase Capital Investments (Case No. COMP/M.2004, 27 June 2000).

49 These include the planned merger between the Swedish and Norwegian exchanges OM and OB, and the joint venture Eurex created by the Deutsche Terminbörse and the (Swiss) Softex.

50 Dale and Wolf, *op. cit.*, note 12, 327.

51 This is more evident in banking, where it is possible to use the solvency requirements to arrive at a very rough estimate of the distortion of competition caused by state aid. For this reason, the Commission has requested very substantial asset disposals in cases like *Banco di Napoli* and *Credit Lyonnais*, in order to alleviate the most important distortive effects of the aid packages; see Van Miert, K., *EU Competition Policy in the Banking Sector* (Speech delivered to the foreign bankers in the Belgian Bankers' Association, Brussels, 22 September 1998).

52 Dalhuisen, *op. cit.*, note 3, 159. Indeed, imposing excessive or irrelevant regulation and supervision into an otherwise free-market context may distort the economic outcome, possibly so much that the end result is worse than the unregulated starting point; see Goodhart *et al.*, *op. cit.*, note 39, 2. For an outline of the numerous problems associated with a highly prescriptive regulatory regime, see Llewellyn, D., 'Re-engineering the Regulator' (1996) 3 The Financial Regulator 21, 23–4.

53 Estrella, A., 'A Prolegomenon to Future Capital Requirements' (1995) 2 Federal Reserve Bank of New York Economic Policy Review 1.

54 Llewellyn, *op. cit.*, note 1, 44.

2   The Single European Market in Investment and Financial Services

1 EC Treaty, Article 2.

2 EC Treaty, Article 3(c) and (h).

3 The origins of GATT can be found in the draft treaty establishing the International Trade Organisation (ITO). The ITO was to have been one of the three Bretton Woods institutions. The original proposals for the ITO originated in interagency committees in the US administration meeting between the spring of 1943 and 1945. The ambitious ITO proposal, however, was not adopted by the US Congress. When the ITO treaty failed, only the non-discriminatory trade measures in the shape of the GATT, which had been adopted in 1947, remained. Hence, it was not until the establishment of the WTO in 1995 that an institution equivalent to the IMF and the World Bank was established for trade. The most ambitious effort at deepening and widening GATT was the Uruguay Round of international trade negotiations. It was launched at Punta del Este, Uruguay, in September 1986 by the Trade Ministers of 100 countries. By the time the negotiations were formally concluded in Marrakesh, Morocco, in April 1994 there were 125 participating countries; see Hocking, B. and McGuire, S., *Trade Politics: International, Domestic and Regional Perspectives* (London: Routledge, 1999); Odell, J.

and Eichengreen, B., 'The United States, the ITO and the WTO; Exit Options, Agent Slick, and Presidential Leadership', in Krueger, A. (ed.), *The WTO as an International Organization* (Chicago: University of Chicago Press, 1998); Trebilcock, M., and Howse, R., *The Regulation of International Trade* (London: Routledge, 1998).

4 See Kock, K., *International Trade Policy and the GATT, 1947–1967* (Stockholm: Almquist & Wicksell, 1969); Hoekman, B. and Kostecki, M., *The Political Economy of the World Trading System; from GATT to WTO* (Oxford: Oxford University Press, 1996). With regard to services, the Uruguay Round of the WTO created the General Agreement on Trade in Services (GATS), a relatively new global trade regime that, since its creation at the end of 1993, has already begun to have a liberalising effect on markets for services. The GATS establishes a basic set of rules for world trade in services, a clear set of obligations for each member country and a legal structure for ensuring that those obligations are observed. In addition to the initial provisions of the original Agreement, the last couple of years have seen the GATS enhanced with multilateral deals to open the world markets for financial services and telecommunications. The Financial Services Agreement e.g., completed on 13 December 1997, included market-opening commitments that took effect on 1 March 1999. Currently, financial services, like all services, are included in the new services negotiations, which began in January 2000; see GATS, Article XIX.

5 Both the World Bank and the IMF were conceived in July 1944 at a United Nations conference held at Bretton Woods, USA, when representatives of 45 governments agreed on a framework for economic cooperation designed to avoid repetition of the disastrous economic policies that had contributed to the Great Depression of the 1930s. The World Bank is one of the world's largest sources of development assistance. The Bank, which provided $17.3 billion in loans to its client countries in fiscal year 2001, is now working in more than 100 developing economies, bringing a mix of finance and ideas to improve living standards and eliminate the worst forms of poverty. It comprises five organisations: the International Bank for Reconstruction and Development, the International Development Association, the International Finance Corporation, the Multilateral Investment Guarantee Agency and the International Centre for Settlement of Investment Disputes.

 The IMF is an international organisation of 183 member countries, established to promote international monetary cooperation, exchange stability, and orderly exchange arrangements, to foster economic growth and high levels of employment and to provide temporary financial assistance to countries to help ease balance of payments adjustment.

6 The Organization for European Economic Cooperation (OEEC), created in 1948, was formed to administer American and Canadian aid under the Marshall Plan for reconstruction of Europe after World War II. Since it took over from and renamed the OEEC in 1961, the OECD vocation has been to build strong economies in its member countries, improve efficiency, hone market systems, expand free trade and contribute to development in industrialised as well as developing countries. Today, the OECD groups 30 member countries that share a commitment to democratic government and market economy.

7 While international organisations, such as the OECD, the WTO and the IMF, operate on the basis of 'interdependence' and do not interfere with the policy-making of their member countries, integration requires the creation of a 'supranational organisation', such as the European Coal and Steel Community (ECSC) or the EU; see Dedman, M., *The Origins and Development of the European Union 1945–95* (London: Routledge, 1996) 7.

8   See Molle, W., *The Economics of European Integration: Theory, Practice, Policy* (Aldershot: Ashgate, 2001) 43; Pollard, S., *Peaceful Conquest, the Industrialisation of Europe 1760–1970* (Oxford: Oxford University Press, 1981); Wallace, W. (ed.), *The Dynamics of European Integration* (London: Pinter Publishers, 1990) 9. On the setting of the European process in the framework of a worldwide development towards internationalisation, see Kenwood, A. and Lougheed, A., *The Growth of the International Economy 1820–2000: An Introductory Text* (London: Routledge, 4th ed., 1999).

9   Especially in circles of the Resistance the conviction was growing that nationalism was at the roots of the disaster that fascism had wrought in Europe and that, therefore, Europe should be rebuilt in a sphere of increased international integration, especially in economic terms; see Molle, *ibid.*, 59; Lipgens, W. *et al.*, *A History of European Integration, vol. 1, 1945–1947, The Formation of the European Unity Movement* (London: Clarendon and Oxford University Press, 1982). That aim was to be achieved, not through unrealistic plans for complete political union, but through a strategy of gradual integration of certain functions; see Haas, E., *The Uniting of Europe: Political, Social and Economic Forces 1950–57* (Stanford: Stanford University Press, 1958); Mitrany, D., *A Working Peace System* (Chicago: Quadrangle Books, 1966).

10 It was then perceived that economic union without monetary union is not a political equilibrium, as the liberalisation of capital movements had made intermediate exchange-rate arrangements like the pegged-but-adjustable rates of the narrow-band European Monetary System (EMS) more difficult to sustain; see Eichengreen, B., *European Monetary Unification: Theory, Practice, and Analysis* (Cambridge: MIT Press, 1997); see also Chapter 7, Section B.1.5.

11 See Weatherill, S., *Law and Integration in the European Union* (Oxford: Clarendon Press, 1995) 8.

12 Cited in Weigall, D. and Stirk, P. (eds), *The Origins and Development of the European Community* (Leicester: Leicester University Press, 1992) 58–9.

13 Duchene, F., *Jean Monnet: The First Statesman of Interdependence* (New York: Norton, 1994) Chapters 6 and 7.

14 This is a strong claim suggested by Monnet's biographer; see Duchene, *ibid.*, 392–404.

15 Monnet, J., *Memoirs* (New York: Doubleday & Company, 1978) 272–3.

16 The importance of this objective is best illustrated in the preamble to the 1952 ECSC Treaty, which was created: 'considering that world peace can be safeguarded only by creating efforts commensurate with the dangers that threaten it, considering that the contribution which an organised and vital Europe can make to civilisation is indispensable to the maintenance of peaceful relations'.

17 As one long-standing member of the European federalist movement put it: 'Federalists plan to form a small nuclei (sic) of nonconformists seeking to point out that the national states have lost their proper rights since they cannot guarantee the political and economic safety of their citizens. They also insist that European union should be brought about by the European populations, and not by diplomats, by directly electing a European constituent assembly, and by the approval through a referendum, of the constitution that this assembly would prepare'; see Spinelli, A., 'The Growth of the European Movement since the Second World War', in Hodges, M. (ed.), *European Integration* (Harmondsworth: Penguin, 1972) 68. See also Friedrich, C., *Trends in Federalism in Theory and Practice* (New York: Prager, 1968); Forsyth, M., *Unions of States: The Theory and Practice of*

Confederation (Leicester: Leicester University Press, 1981); Bosco, A., *The Federal Idea: The History of Federalism from Enlightenment to 1945, Vol. I* (London: Lothian Foundation Press, 1991); Burgess, M., *Federalism and European Union: The Building of Europe, 1950–2000* (London: Routledge, 2000).

18 At the core of the agenda of functionalists is the prioritisation of human needs or public welfare, as opposed to the sanctity of the nation-state or the celebration of any particular ideological credo; see Mitrany, *op. cit.*, note 9; Taylor, P., 'The Functionalist Approach to the Problem of International Order: A Defence' (1968) 3 Political Studies 16; Dehousse, R., *Rediscovering Functionalism* (Harvard Jean Monnet Working Paper No. 70, 2000).

19 Neo-functionalism sees integration in process terms: polity-building is seen as the result of a wide range of converging processes. See Haas, *op. cit.*, note 9; Haas, E., *Beyond the Nation State* (Stanford: Stanford University Press, 1964); Deutsch, K. *et al.*, *Political Community and the North Atlantic Area: International Organisation in the Light of Historical Experience* (Princeton: Princeton University Press, 1957); Lindberg, L., *The Political Dynamics of European Economic Integration* (Stanford: Stanford University Press, 1963).

20 Neo-liberalism is a theory of how the structural properties of anarchy provide particular sets of limitations upon possibilities for action in international politics; see Waltz, K., *Theory of International Politics* (New York: McGraw Hill, 1979); Stone, A., 'What is a Supranational Constitution? An Essay in International Relations Theory' (1994) 3 Review of Politics 56. Neo-liberal institutionalism focuses on the general problem of international cooperation, examining how the structure of the international system constrains policy-makers' ability to enter mutually beneficial agreements and how international institutions, by mitigating these systemic constraints, facilitate policy-makers' ability to achieve cooperative outcomes; see Keohane, R., 'The Demand for International Regimes' (1982) 36 International Organization 325; Keohane, R., *After Hegemony: Cooperation and Discord in the World Political Economy* (Princeton: Princeton University Press, 1984); Axelrod, R., *The Evolution of Cooperation* (New York: Basic Books, 1984); Keohane, R., *Neo-Realism and Its Critics* (New York: Columbia University Press, 1986); Oatley, T., *Monetary Politics* (Ann Arbor: University of Michigan Press, 1997).

21 Behaviouralists study the behaviour of agents – political leaders, parties, voters etc. – competing to seize power. They believe that political actors are far more interesting compared to institutions. See Sanders, D., 'Behavioural Analysis', in Marsh, D. and Stoker, G. (eds), *Theory and Methods in Political Science* (Basingstoke: Palgrave, 1995).

22 New institutionalism was a rebellion against behaviouralism. Neo-institutionalists insist that political behaviour is determined by the nature of political institutions; see Skocpol, T., 'Bringing the State Back In: Strategies of Analysis in Current Research', in Evans, P., Rieschemeyer, D. and Skocpol, T. (eds), *Bringing the State Back In* (Cambridge: Cambridge University Press, 1985); March, J. and Olsen, J., *Rediscovering Institutions* (New York: Free Press, 1989); Armstrong, K., 'The New Institutionalism', in Craig, P. and Harlow, C. (eds), *Law Making in the European Union* (London: Kluwer, 1998).

23 The point of departure for the multilevel governance approach is the existence of overlapping competencies among multiple levels of governments and the interaction of political actors across those levels. Political control is thus variable, not constant across policy areas; see Marks, G. *et al.*, *Governance in the European Union* (London: Sage, 1996) 41; Jachtenfuchs, M., 'Theoretical Perspectives on European

Governance' (1995) 1 ELJ 115; Marks, G., Hooghe, L. and Blank, K., 'European Integration since the 1980's: State-Centric versus Multi-Level Governance' (1996) 34 JCMS 341; Scott, C., 'The Governance of the European Union: The Potential for Multi-Level Control' (2002) 1 ELJ 59.

24 See Rosamond, B., *Theories of European Integration* (Basingstoke: Palgrave, 2000).

25 Monnet, *op. cit.*, note 15, 392.

26 European integration is founded on four founding Treaties. The ECSC Treaty was signed in Paris on 18 April 1951 by Belgium, France, Germany, Italy, Luxembourg and the Netherlands. It expired on 23 July 2002, 50 years after its entry into force. The Treaties establishing the EEC and the European Atomic Energy Community (Euratom), referred to as the 'Treaties of Rome', were signed by the Six (Belgium, France, Germany, Italy, Luxembourg, the Netherlands) in Rome on 25 March 1957. They entered into force on 1 January 1958. The Treaty on European Union, which was signed in Maastricht on 7 February 1992, and entered into force on 1 November 1993, created the political Union amongst the Member States and brought about considerable changes to the existing Treaties. The Treaty created the European Union, a concept comprising the European Communities (which had also been amended to the term European Community on the same occasion), as well as other forms of cooperation. The Maastricht Treaty was subsequently consolidated under the Amsterdam Treaty, signed on 2 October 1997 and entered into force on 1 May 1999 (Consolidated Treaty establishing the European Community, OJ C 340/173, 10 November 1997, hereinafter 'EC Treaty'). Finally, the Treaty of Nice, signed on 26 February 2001, will amend the existing Treaties. It will enter into force once the 15 Member States have ratified it according to their respective constitutional procedures. The ratification process has recently been completed. Until 2002, only Ireland had not ratified the Treaty of Nice. On a referendum on 7 June 2001, 53.87% of the voters voted against it, which has initiated a public debate. On 19 October 2002, however, 62.89% of Irish voters endorsed the Treaty and opened the way to EU enlargement.

27 EEC Treaty, Article 3(i).

28 EEC Treaty, Article 3(h).

29 Segré Committee, *The Development of a European Capital Market* (November 1966).

30 The Report found that 'active participation by various types of institution in the creation of a European capital market may be hampered by the rules under which they operate and the supervisory controls to which they are subject'; *ibid.*, 32. For an extensive analysis of the regulatory and supervisory obstacles faced by investment and financial intermediaries, see Moloney, N., *EC Securities Regulation* (Oxford: Oxford University Press, 2002) 308–10.

31 In October 1970, a group under the chairmanship of Pierre Werner (then prime minister of Luxembourg) produced a report that detailed how EMU could be attained in stages by 1980; see Werner, P. *et al.*, *Report to the Council and the Commission on the Realisation by Stages of Economic and Monetary Union in the Community* (Supplement to Bulletin-II 1970 of the European Communities, 1970, hereinafter 'Werner Report'). Although the objective of EMU was unanimously endorsed by the ECOFIN Council of March 1971, the Werner Report was never implemented. For an analysis of the Werner Report, see Baer, G. and Padoa-Schioppa, T., 'The Werner Report Revisited', in Collection of Papers annexed to *Report on Economic and Monetary Union (Delors Report)* (1989).

32 In spite of previous unsuccessful work on the coordination of financial services law, the first important step in the direction of genuine harmonisation was introduced in banking with the First Banking Directive (FBD); see *First Council Directive*

77/780/EEC of 12 December 1977 on the coordination of laws, regulations and administrative provisions relating to the taking up and pursuit of the business of credit institutions (OJ L 322/30, 17 December 1977). The rationale behind the Directive was the equal treatment of credit institutions, formed for the first time, and their branches. Hence, Article 4(1) of the FDB prescribed that Member States were permitted to make the commencement of banking activities, performed by branches of Community credit institutions, subject to authorisation 'according to the law and procedure applicable to credit institutions established on their territory'. Major obstacles, however, remained in force, especially with regard to national legislation on the authorisation and supervision of branches in the host State. Moreover, the definition of what amounts to a 'bank' has troubled the harmonisation efforts and has long been regarded as one of the thorniest issues in European banking regulation; see Zavvos, G., 'Towards a European Banking Act' (1988) 2 CMLRev 263.

33 European Commission, *Completing the Internal Market: White Paper to the Council* (COM(85) 310 final, 28 June 1985, hereinafter 'White Paper').
34 For example, in Copenhagen in 1982, Dublin in 1984 and Brussels in 1985.
35 In addition to the Commission, numerous universities, fifteen consultant firms and 11 000 enterprises cooperated in the exercise; see Cockfield, A., *The European Union: Creating the Single Market* (London: Chancery Law Publishing, 1994) 90.
36 Cockfield, *ibid.*, 29 *et seq.*
37 See Bulmer, S., 'Setting and Influencing the Rules', in Mayes, D. (ed.), *The Evolution of the Single European Market* (Cheltenham: Edward Elgar, 1997) 36.
38 See Fitchew, G., 'Political Choices', in Buxbaum, R. *et al.*, *European Business Law: Legal and Economic Analysis on Integration and Harmonisation* (Berlin: Walter de Gruyter, 1991) 4.
39 In banking, the Commission seems particularly concerned with the coordination of standards and principles of financial stability and management, accounting, market access and banking reorganisation in time of crises; White Paper, Paragraph 104. In the securities sector, the Commission called for the completion of the work that 'still remains to be done to ensure that securities markets operate satisfactorily and in the best interest of investors and, specifically, for the development of a "European securities market system" which would provide a Community-wide trading system for securities on international interest'; White Paper, Paragraph 107.
40 At this early stage it was perceived that 'the alternative of relying on a strategy based totally on harmonisation would be over-regulatory, would take a long time to implement, would be inflexible and could stifle innovation'; see White Paper, Paragraph 64.
41 Chalmers, D. and Szyszczak, E., *European Union Law Vol. II* (Aldershot: Ashgate, 1998) 35.
42 See Eichengreen, B., 'European Monetary Unification' (1993) 1 Journal of Economic Literature 31; Giovannini, A., 'Central Banking in a Monetary Union: Reflections on the Proposed Statute of the European Central Bank' (1993) Carnegie-Rochester Conference Series on Public Policy 38.
43 This view, however, does not appear very persuasive. Much more credible is Steil's suggestion: 'Reading the Commission's version of history in the White Paper, it is clear that the minimum harmonization principle is not seen simply as a necessary response to negative externalities deriving from free competition among rules, but rather that competition among rules is seen as a necessary but regrettable consequence of the Commission's legislative inability to achieve full

harmonization'; see Steil, B., *Competition, Integration and Regulation in EC Capital Markets* (London: Royal Institute of International Affairs, 1993) 18.

44 See Majone, G., *Regulating Europe* (London: Routledge, 1996) 269. This, however, is not always true in practice; see Chapter 5, Section B.2.

45 On the interrelationship between the two concepts of minimum harmonisation and mutual recognition, see Dehousse, R., 'Integration v. Regulation? On the Dynamics of Regulation in the European Community' (1992) 4 JCMS 383, 396; Majone, G., *Mutual Recognition in Federal Type Systems* (European University Institute WP No. 93/1, 1993) 8–9; Fitchew, G., 'Towards a completed market in financial services: The White Paper and beyond', in Castello-Branco, M. and Pelkmans, J. (eds), *The Internal Market for Financial Services* (Maastricht: European Institute of Public Administration, 1987) 132.

46 See below Chapter 5, Section C.1.3; Chapter 6, Section C.7. The European Commission predicted the problems posed for the internal market by a lack of trust at a relatively early stage. It recognised at least three situations where lack of trust might undermine mutual recognition: (a) Community legislation could not require mutual recognition if the standards designated inspection bodies had to meet were not equivalent, (b) in areas where there was no Community legislation manufacturers could not benefit from mutual recognition if the authorities in the host country did not have full confidence in the credibility of the body that carried out tests in the home State, and (c) purchasers had to have faith in the certification procedures in exporting States if they were not to insist in a product being certified twice, once in the home country and once in the host; see European Commission, *Proposal for a Council Decision concerning the modules for the various phases of the conformity assessment procedures which are intended to be used in the technical harmonization directives* (COM(89) 209 final, OJ C 231/3, 8 September 1989); European Commission, *A global approach to certification and testing quality measures for industrial products* (COM(89) 209 final, OJ C 267/3, 19 October 1989).

47 Majone, G., *Mutual Trust, Credible Commitments and the Evolution of the Rules of the Single Market* (European University Institute WP No. 95/1, 1995) 16.

48 Moloney, N., *op. cit.*, note 30, 337.

49 Steil, B., *Regional Financial Market Integration: Learning from the European Experience* (London: Royal Institute of International Affaires, 1998) 3.

50 This approach is directly linked with the principle of mutual recognition; see White Paper, Paragraph 103.

51 See Scott-Quinn, B., *European Community Regulation of Securities Markets* (mimeo) 14.

52 Article 100a EEC incorporated in Article 95 EC Treaty. On this feature of the SEA, see Moravcsik, A., 'Negotiating the Single European Act', in Keohane, R. and Hoffmann, S. (eds), *The New European Community: Decision-Making and Institutional Change* (Boulder: Westview Press, 1991) 41 *et seq.* Weiler describes Article 100a as 'the single most important provision of the SEA' for introducing majority voting in the Council; see Weiler, J., *The Constitution of Europe: 'Do the New Clothes have an Emperor?' and other Essays on European Integration* (Cambridge: Cambridge University Press, 1999) 68. For implications on financial services, see Usher, J., 'Financial Services in EEC Law' (1988) 1 ICLQ 144; see also Chapter 6, Section B.2.1.1.2.

53 Under the new procedure of cooperation inserted into Article 149 EEC, any proposal from the Commission carried much greater political force by the time it had reached the Council than in the past, as the EP together with the Commission

could eventually force the Council either to accept a submitted proposal without modification or to take no decision at all.

54 In addition to the measures designed to lead to a single market, the preamble to the Act referred specifically to monetary union as an EC goal to be 'progressively realised'. However, in a concession to both the United Kingdom and Germany, which were not strongly in favour of monetary union, this was not among the 1992 priorities laid down by the Act as legally binding.

55 Dehousse, *op. cit.*, note 18, 5.

56 See below, Chapter 5, Section B.1.

57 Dehousse, R., '1992 and Beyond: The Institutional Dimension of the Internal Market Programme' (1989) 1 Legal Issues of European Integration 109, 111.

58 See Fitchew, *op. cit.*, note 38, 3.

59 See Wallace, H. and Wallace, W., *Policy-Making in the European Union* (Oxford: Oxford University Press, 4th ed., 2000) 109.

60 See Horn, N., 'The Monetary Union and the Internal Market for Banking and Investment Services', in Norton, J.J. (ed.), *Yearbook of International Financial and Economic Law 1998* (London: Kluwer Law International, 1999) 134.

61 Since the 1970s, there has been increasing integration between international financial markets – particularly the euromarkets – and between the national financial markets, a trend that accelerated in the 1980s. The expansion of the markets for international bonds, euronotes and euro commercial paper has strongly increased the possibilities of holding both international capital assets and taking up international credit; see Banink, H., *Financial Integration in Europe* (Dordrecht: Kluwer, 1993) 9.

62 Zavvos, G., 'Banking Integration and 1992: Legal Issues and Policy Implications' (1990) Harvard International Law Journal 463, 465. While the interdependence between capital movement and financial services is easy to be identified, it may be surprising that monetary unification is connected with the liberalisation of the financial sector. Not many would dispute, however, that the free movement of capital constitutes a fundamental part of a genuine monetary union, besides being an essential corollary to financial services; see Eichengreen, *op. cit.*, note 10; Gamble, A., 'EMU and European Capital Markets: Towards a Unified Financial Market' (1991) 2 CMLRev 319, 326.

63 National differences may persist where the actual exercise of prudential control has not been harmonised. The agencies, e.g., empowered by law or regulation to supervise investment firms are considered 'competent authorities' by the investment services directives; see ISD, Article 22. Which agencies are to be considered 'competent authorities' has not been established in a harmonised way. Hence, national rules may empower one, two or multiple to exercise supervisory tasks in the area of securities regulation and supervision; see below, Chapters 4 and 5.

64 European Commission, *Progress Report on the European Monetary System and the Liberalisation of Capital Markets* (COM(1987) 650 final, 17 December 1987).

65 The Communication called for minimum harmonisation of supervisory standards, elimination of fiscal discrimination and strengthening of monetary cooperation and development of the EMS; *ibid.*, 7.

66 Article 43 provides that 'restrictions on the freedom of establishment of nationals of a Member State in the territory of another Member State shall be prohibited. Such prohibition shall also apply to restrictions on the setting-up of agencies, branches or subsidiaries by nationals of any Member State established in the territory of any Member State. Freedom of establishment shall include the

right to take up and pursue activities as self employed persons and to set up and manage undertakings, in particular companies or firms within the meaning of the second paragraph of Article 48, under the conditions laid down for its own nationals by the law of the country where such establishment is effected, subject to the provisions of the Chapter relating to capital'. Article 49 provides that 'restrictions on freedom to provide services within the Community shall be prohibited in respect of nationals of Member States who are established in a State of the Community other than that of the person for whom the services are intended'.

67   Article 48 states: 'companies or firms formed in accordance with the law of a Member State and having their registered office, central administration or principal place of business within the Community shall, for the purposes of this Chapter, be treated in the same way as natural persons who are nationals of Member States'.

68   Case C-101/94 *Commission v Italy* [1996] ECR I-2691. For an analysis of the case, see Andenas, M., 'Italian Nationality Requirement and Community Law' (1996) 17 Company Lawyer 219.

69   Case C-384/94 *Alpine Investments* [1995] ECR I-1141. On the problem of cold-calling, see Chapter 5, Section C.1.2. With regard to insurance, see Case C-118/96 *Safir* [1998] ECR I-1897, Paragraph 22.

70   As pointed out already by Advocate General Mayras in *Van Binsbergen*, the distinction is not of merely academic interest, since Articles 43 and 49 contain different legal obligations for the Member States and accordingly different rights for the persons and activities covered by them; see Case 33/74 *Van Binsbergen* [1974] ECR 1299, 1316–17. An excellent example of confusion and the clearest attempt by the Court to distinguish the two concepts is found in *Gebhard*. The ECJ held in that decision that the concept of establishment within the meaning of the Treaty is a very broad one, allowing a Community national to participate, on a stable and continuous basis, in the economic life of another Member State and to profit therefrom, so contributing to economic and social interpenetration within the Community; Case C-55/94 *Gebhard* [1995] ECR I-4165, Paragraph 25. The Court noted that the provisions on services are subordinate to those on establishment and that this concept covered all types of self-employed activity to be taken up and pursued on the territory of any other Member State, undertaking to be formed and operated, and agencies, branches, or subsidiaries to be set up; *ibid.*, Paragraphs 22–3; see also Case C-70/95 *Sodemare* [1997] ECR I-3395.

71   See Article 50 (former Article 60) EC Treaty; Case C-275/92 *Schindler* [1994] ECR I-1039; Case 196/87 *Udo Steymann* [1988] ECR 6159, Paragraph 11. On the definition of remuneration, see Case 263/86 *Humbel* [1988] ECR 5365, Paragraph 17; Opinion of Advocate General Lenz in Case 186/87 *Cowan* [1989] ECR 195, 211; Case 62/79 *Coditel* [1980] ECR 881, 890; Case 352/85 *Bond van Advesteerders* [1988] ECR 2085, Paragraph 16.

72   See Case C-55/94, *op. cit.*, note 70, Paragraph 26.

73   *Ibid.*, Paragraphs 27 and 39.

74   See Case C-221/89 *Factortame* [1991] ECR I-3905, Paragraph 20.

75   See Case 196/87, *op. cit.*, note 71, Paragraphs 16–17. The ECJ's reasoning seems to indicate that even a long-lasting presence falls under the ambit of Article 49.

76   *Council Directive 93/22/EEC of 10 May 1993 on investment services in the securities field* (OJ L 141/27, 11 June 1993).

77   *Council Directive 89/646/EEC of 15 December 1989 on the coordination of laws, regulations and administrative provisions relating to the taking up and pursuit of the*

business of credit institutions (OJ L 386/1, 30 December 1989). The SBD provides a common regulatory framework for banking together with a number of other directives: *Council Directive 73/183/EEC of 28 June 1973 on the abolition of restrictions on freedom of establishment and freedom to provide services in respect of self-employed activities of banks and other financial institutions* (OJ L 194/1, 16 July 1973), First Banking Directive, *op. cit.*, note 32, as last amended by *Directive 98/33/EC* (OJ L 204/29, 21 July 1998), *Council Directive 89/299/EEC of 17 April 1989 on the own funds of credit institutions* (OJ L 124/16, 5 May 1989) as last amended by *Directive 92/30/EEC* (OJ L 110/52, 28 April 1992), *Council Directive 89/647/EEC of 18 December 1989 on a solvency ratio for credit institutions* (OJ L 386/14, 30 December 1989) as last amended by *Directive 98/33/EC, Council Directive 92/30/EEC of 6 April 1992 on the supervision of credit institutions on a consolidated basis* (OJ L 110/52, 28 April 1992), and *Council Directive 92/121/EEC of 21 December 1992 on the monitoring and control of large exposures of credit institutions* (OJ L 29/1, 5 February 1993). All these banking directives have recently been codified in *Council and Parliament Directive 2000/12/EC relating to the taking up and pursuit of the business of credit institutions* (OJ L 126/1, 26 May 2000).

78 *Council Directive 93/6/EEC OJ L 141/1 of 15 March 1993, on the capital adequacy of investment firms and credit institutions, as amended by Council Directive 98/31/EC* (OJ L 204/13, 22 June 1998).

79 See generally, O'Neill, N., 'The Investment Services Directive', in Cranston, R. (ed.), *The Single Market and the Law of Banking* (London: Lloyd's of London Press, 2nd ed., 1991). The Preamble to the ISD describes it in Recital 1 as being 'essential to the achievement of the internal market (...) from the point of view both of the right of establishment and of the freedom to provide financial services, in the field of investment firms' and links it directly to the White Paper. The ISD explicitly refers to Article 57(2) EC (now Article 47) alone as the enabling provision of the Treaty. This is unequivocally correct as regards the enactment of the companion principles of home country control and mutual recognition on a basis of harmonised prudential regulation; see Kondgen, J., 'Rules of Conduct: Further Harmonisation?' in Ferrarini, G. (ed.), *European Securities Markets: The Investment Services Directive and Beyond* (London: Kluwer Law, 1998) 118.

80 Whereas under the SBD, banking is defined to embrace securities services, under the ISD, investment firms are defined as those that undertake broking, dealing, underwriting and investment management in respect of a wide range of financial instruments, including derivatives, as specified in Annex B of the directive; see SBD, Article 1(6); ISD, Article 1(2). Hence, the ISD also applies to banks that provide investment services. The European passport is also frequently referred to as 'Euro-passport', 'single licence' or 'single passport'; see Schneider, U., 'The Harmonisation of EC Banking Law: The Euro-Passport to Profitability and International Competitiveness of Financial Institutions' (1990) 22 Law & Policy in International Business 261, 269.

81 While the SBD has removed barriers to the cross-border provision of investment services by universal banks, it did not apply to independent non-bank investment firms. The extension of the European passport to such firms was intended with the ISD.

82 Referred to as the 'host Member State', ISD, Article 1(7). See Chapter 5, Section C.2.3.

83 See L'Heveder, C., 'The Investment Services Directive and its implications for participants in Europe's financial markets' (1996) 1 JIBFL 5.

84 See Ashall, P., 'The Investment Services Directive: What was the Conflict All About?' in Andenas, M. and Kenyon-Slade, S. (eds), *EC Financial Market Regulation and Company Law* (London: Sweet & Maxwell, 1993) 91. The main driving force behind the harmonization provisions of the ISD appears to have been the perceived need to ensure competitive equality between universal banks and non-bank investment firms; see Scott-Quinn, B., 'EC Securities Markets Regulation', in Steil, B. (ed.), *International Financial Market Regulation* (Chichester: John Wiley, 1994) 121.

85 ISD, Article 18(2); see Chapter 5, Section C.2.2.1; *cf.* SBD, Article 14(2), according to which the host Member State shares responsibility for the supervision of liquidity in corporation with the regulators of the home Member State, whereas the host country retains complete responsibility for the measures resulting from its monetary policy. The former exemption of home country control seems necessary because of the insufficient harmonisation of liquidity standards; see Gruson, M. and Feuring, W., 'European Banking Law: The Second Banking Directive and Related Directives', in Cranston, *op. cit.*, note 79, 27; Smits, R., 'Banking Regulation in a European Perspective' (1989) 1 Legal Issues of European Integration 61, 71. The latter seems less and less relevant given the centralisation of monetary policy within the European System of Central Banks (ESCB).

86 See Theil, R., 'The EC Investment Services Directive: A Critical Time for Investments Firms' (1994) 2 JIBFL 61.

87 See Lee, R., *What is an Exchange? The Automation, Management and Regulation of Financial Markets* (Oxford: Oxford University Press, 1998) 136.

88 Regulated market shall mean a market for the instruments listed in Section B of the Annex that (a) appears on the list provided for in Article 16 drawn up by the home Member State, (b) functions regularly, (c) is characterised by the fact that regulations issued or approved by the competent authorities define the conditions for the operation of the market, the conditions for access to the market and, the conditions governing admission to listing and the conditions that must be satisfied by a financial instrument before it can effectively be dealt in on the market, and (d) requires compliance with all the reporting and transparency requirements laid down pursuant to Articles 20 and 21 of the ISD.

89 ISD, Article 23(3). This provision requires national authorities to 'supply one another on request with all the information concerning the management and ownership of such investment firms that is likely to facilitate their supervision and all information likely to facilitate the monitoring of such firms'.

90 European Commission, *Upgrading the Investment Services Directive* (COM(2000) 729 final, 15 November 2000). This Communication has to be seen merely as part of a comprehensive strategy to reinforce the legislative framework for securities markets. Accordingly, the wide-ranging review based on this Communication has considered related initiatives such as the Communication on the application of conduct of business rules; see European Commission, *The Application of Conduct of Business Rules under Article 11 of the Investment Services Directive* (16 November 2000).

91 According to the Commission, a revision of the ISD should create the legal environment in which the passport can become effective immediately for inter-professional business and be progressively extended to cover provision of services to retail investors.

92 The Communication discusses whether it would be useful to apply common principles to trading systems, including new electronic trading arrangements

(Alternative Trading Systems, ATS), and if so, what these principles should be. It also seeks to stimulate collective debate on the need for common regulatory and supervisory responses to consolidation of clearing and settlement functions.

93 European Commission, *Overview of Proposed Adjustments to the Investment Services Directive* (24 July 2001). The most notable adjustments provided for: (a) a systematic review of the coverage of ISD so as to better reflect the changing nature of investment intermediation and to allow a broader range of investment services to be organised on a pan-European basis, (b) enhanced convergence of organisational and investor protection requirements with which investment firms must comply, (c) consolidation and amplification of current obligations of investment firms to respect the integrity of the market, (d) elaboration of high-level principles governing the authorisation and operation of 'regulated markets', which would allow 'regulated markets' to compete for order flow and liquidity without jeopardising the orderly and efficient operation of the European securities market system, or the interests of issuers and investors, (e) clarification of conditions under which market participants and regulated markets may seek access to clearing and settlement infrastructures in other Member States, and (f) modernisation of provisions relating to supervisory cooperation to place mechanisms for communication and cooperation between competent authorities within and between Member States on a firmer, real-time footing.

94 The Wise Men Report recommended that all new legislation in the securities field be preceded by an early, broad, and systematic consultation of all interested parties in the securities area; see Wise Men Committee, *Final Report on the Regulation of European Securities Markets* (15 February 2001) (hereinafter 'Final Wise Men Report') 25.

95 European Commission, *Revision of the Investment Services Directive: Second Consultation* (25 March 2002). Frits Bolkestein, Commissioner for Internal Market, stated after the launch of the second consultation: 'Updating the Investment Services Directive is a crucial part of the Financial Services Action Plan and part of the EU's drive towards dynamic financial markets that will stand the test of time. We are launching this final round of consultation because we are determined to get financial services legislation right. That means close and continuous consultation with everyone who will be affected by it, in line with our agreement with the European Parliament and the Council on implementing the Lamfalussy proposals'; European Commission, *Press Release* (IP/02/464, 25 March 2002). The feedback confirmed that the main regulatory issues that ISD revision needs to address are: (a) updating investor protection safeguards to help investors profit fully from a wider range of investment services, (b) enabling investment firms to provide services across borders on the basis of home country authorisation and supervision, and (c) improving the working of markets and avoiding market fragmentation by establishing a level playing field between different ways of executing investment orders through, e.g., 'regulated markets' such as stock exchanges, ATS (which enable market participants to trade at different terms than on the stock exchange) and 'in-house' order-matching by banks that execute client orders to trade securities against other client orders or their own trading positions.

96 These include: (a) fine-tuning investor protection obligations to take account of new forms of investment services, (b) broadening the scope of the ISD to include, *inter alia*, investment advice and trading of commodity derivatives, (c) simplifying the classification of order-execution systems and making it more flexible,

(d) a greater emphasis on ensuring that different trading systems performing similar functions are subject to comparable regulation, (e) clarifying requirements for the disclosure of quotes or details of transactions performed off-exchange, and (f) streamlining the high-level principles for regulated markets. Regulated markets would be able to compete for liquidity without jeopardising the orderly and efficient operation of European securities markets, or the interests of issuers and investors.

97   There was a constructive discussion amongst over 200 participants representing financial intermediaries, exchange operators and supervisory authorities. The debate focussed on creating a level playing field so that exchanges, ATSs and financial firms can compete transparently without fragmenting the market, compromising efficiency and weakening investor protection.

98   See *supra* note 77. The Solvency Ratio Directive determines how the bank's credit risk position has to be calculated. The aggregate of a bank's assets and off-balance sheet items calculated on a risk adjusted basis is set against its own funds to produce the solvency ratio. The Own Funds Directive contains the requirements for calculating a bank's capital and limits the extent to which banking capital can comprise certain elements. For example, it imposes limits on the proportion of capital that can be made up of subordinated debt; see the Codified Banking Directive 2000/12/EC, Article 38.

99   For more details see Dale, R., *Risk and Regulation in Global Securities Market* (Chichester: John Wiley & Sons, 1996) 27.

100   CAD, Article 4.

101   *Directive 98/31/EC of the European Parliament and of the Council of 22 June 1998 amending Council Directive 93/6/EEC on the capital adequacy of investment firms and credit institutions* (OJ L 204/13, 21 July 1998).

102   European Commission, *A Review of Regulatory Capital Requirements for EU Credit Institutions and Investment Firms: Consultation Document* (MARKT/1123/99, 22 November 1999).

103   European Commission, *Second Consultative Document on Review of Regulatory Capital for Credit Institutions and Investment Firms* (MARKT/1000/01, 5 February 2001).

104   See European Commission, *Commission Welcomes Significant Progress on New Basel Capital Accord: Press Release* (IP/02/1041, 11 July 2002).

105   European Commission, *Financial Services: Building a Framework for Action* (COM(98) 625 final, 28 October 1998). The Communication highlighted five imperatives for action: (a) the EU should be endowed with a legislative apparatus capable of responding to new regulatory challenges, (b) any remaining capital market fragmentation should be eliminated to reduce the cost of capital, (c) users and suppliers of financial services should be able to exploit freely the commercial opportunities offered by a single financial market, while benefiting from a high level of consumer protection, (d) closer coordination of supervisory authorities should be encouraged, and (e) an integrated EU infrastructure should be developed to underpin retail and wholesale financial transactions.

106   European Commission, *Implementing the Framework for Financial Services: Action Plan* (COM(99) 232 final, 11 May 1999, hereinafter 'FSAP'). The purpose of the FSAP was to: (a) confirm the objectives that could guide the financial services policy over the following years, (b) assign a relative order of priorities and an indicative timescale for their achievement, and (c) identify a number of mechanisms that may contribute to their realisation.

107 The most important features of the FSAP include: (a) upgrading the ISD to tackle remaining obstacles to market access for investment firms and to remote membership and to address new regulatory challenges, such as the emergence of ATS, (b) revising the disclosure regime and adopting a new market abuse regime, (c) adopting a common set of IAS, (d) addressing the systemic risk in securities settlement, (e) creating a secure and transparent environment for cross-border restructuring, (f) revising the collective investment and pension funds schemes, (g) equipping consumers with the necessary instruments and safeguards to permit their full and active participation in the single financial market, and (h) developing legal conditions in which new distribution channels and distance technologies can be put to work on a pan-European scale.

108 European Commission, *Financial Services: Sixth Report* (COM(2002) 267, 3 June 2002).

109 The Council and the European Parliament should have approved by the end of 2002 the Directives on Market Abuse, Collateral, Distance Marketing of Financial Services, Insurance Intermediaries, Prospectuses, Financial Conglomerates, Supplementary Pension Funds and the Regulation on IAS.

110 European Commission, *Risk Capital: A Key to Job Creation in the European Union* (SEC(1998) 522, April 1998).

111 European Commission, *Commission's Work Programme for 1995* (COM(95) 26 final) 7.

112 European Commission, *Action Plan for the Single Market* (CSE(97) 1 final, 4 June 1997). The rather dry Action Plan set four strategic targets: (a) making the rules more effective, (b) dealing with key market distortions, (c) removing sectoral obstacles to market integration, and (d) delivering a single market for the benefit of all citizens.

113 See Wallace and Wallace, *op. cit.*, note 59, 107.

114 European Commission, *Single Market Scoreboard No. 4* (16 June 1999).

115 European Commission, *2002 Review of the Internal Market Strategy* (COM(2002) 171 final, 11 April 2002) 5.

116 See Financial Services Sixth Report, *op. cit.*, note 108, 4. Concerns were particularly expressed for the proposed Prospectus Directive, the Distance Marketing Directive, the Supplementary Pension Funds Directive and the Take Over Bids Directive.

117 European Commission, *The State of the Internal Market for Services: Report to the Council and the European Parliament* (COM(2002) 441 final, 30 July 2002). The need for action is highlighted by the Stockholm and Barcelona Summits in 2001 and 2002, while the Internal Market, Tourism and Consumer Affaires Council, in reviewing the EU's priorities for economic reform, concluded that improving the Internal Market in services remained 'a crucial strategic challenge for the Community'; see 2412th meeting of the Council (1 March 2002).

118 See Randzio-Plath, C., *European legislation for a European Capital Market* (Speech delivered at the Sixth European Financial Markets Convention, Brussels, 29 May 2002).

119 FSAP, 13.

120 See Chapter 4, Section C.3.

121 This is further detailed in Chapter 5.

122 In addition, a second EFC report recommended arrangements in line with the Lamfalussy framework for all financial sectors and the establishment of Levels 2 and 3 separate sectoral committees; see EFC, Report on Financial Regulation, Supervision and Stability (9 October 2002); see also, Chapter 6, Section C.3.1.

3 The Home Country Control Principle

1   Articles 43 and 49 (former Articles 52 and 59) EC Treaty.
2   See Dassesse, M. *et al., EC Banking Law* (London: Lloyd's Press, 2nd ed., 1994) 68.
3   The English spelling was changed from Basle in 1999 following a decision by the City of Basel to standardise the English, French and German spelling and pronunciation.
4   See Alexander, K., 'The International Supervisory Framework for Financial Services: An Emerging Regime for Transnational Supervision' (2000) 1 JIBR 33, 35; see also Chapter 4.
5   See Bradley, C., 'Competitive Deregulation of Financial Services Activity in Europe after 1992' (1991) 11 Oxford Journal of Legal Studies 545, 549.
6   Treaty establishing the European Community (EC Treaty), Article 3(c).
7   Article 43 (former Article 52) EC Treaty.
8   Article 49 (former Article 59) EC *et seq.*
9   Article 48 (former Article 58) EC.
10   See Lomnicka, E., 'The Home Country Control Principle in the Financial Services Directives and the Case Law' (2000) 11 EBLR 324.
11   For a discussion on regulatory arbitrage, see Chapter 5, Section C.1.1.
12   For a discussion on the principle of subsidiarity, see Chapter 5, Section B.1.
13   Indeed, the full harmonisation attempt undertaken in the early 1970s failed, as the Member States found themselves unable at that point to reach agreement on the content of the relevant legislation. For a historical analysis that led to this choice, see Walker, G., *European Banking and Financial Law* (Oxford: Oxford University Press, forthcoming 2003).
14   See Bratton, W. *et al., International Regulatory Competition and Coordination* (Oxford: Clarendon Press, 1996) 31.
15   European Commission, *Completing the Internal Market: White Paper to the Council* (COM(85) 310 final, 28 June 1985, hereinafter 'White Paper') Paragraphs 102–3.
16   The Commission stated: 'harmonisation as regards the supervision of ongoing activities should be guided by the principle of home country control. This means attributing the primary task of supervision to the competent authority of its Member State of origin, to which would have to be communicated all information necessary for supervision (...) There would have to be a minimum harmonisation of surveillance standards, though the need to reach agreement on this must not be allowed further to delay the necessary and overdue decisions', White Paper, Paragraph 103.
17   With regard to credit institutions, see SBD, Article 13(1) and tenth consideration to the Preamble; for investment firms, see ISD, Article 8(3); as to insurance companies, see First Non-Life Directive, Article 13(1), as replaced by Third Non-Life Directive, Article 13, and First Life Directive, Article 15(1), as replaced by Third Life Directive, Article 8; see also Third Non-Life and Life Directives, Recital 7.
18   The role of the host Member State is already defined in the White Paper: 'The authorities of the Member State which is the destination of the service, whilst not deprived of all power, would have a complementary role', Paragraph 103. In banking, host States retain responsibility – in cooperation with the home supervisory authorities – for the supervision of the liquidity of the branches of credit institutions pending further coordination, as well as for the measures resulting from the implementation of their monetary policies; see SBD, Article 14(2). For investment services, see below, Section E.2.

19 Case 8/74 *Dassonville* [1974] ECR 837.

20 The Court held that the requirement by a Member State of a certificate of authenticity, which is less easily obtainable by importers of an authentic product that has been put into free circulation in a regular manner in another Member State than by importers of the same product coming directly from the country of origin, constitutes a measure having an effect equivalent to a quantitative restriction as prohibited by the Treaty. *Ibid.*, Paragraph 10.

21 The Court has tried to divide the regulatory capacities between Member States in Case C-384/93 *Alpine Investments* [1995] ECR I-1141; see Snell, J. and Andenas, M., 'Exploring the Outer Limits-Restrictions on the Free Movement of Goods and Services' (1999) 7–8 EBLR 252, 265.

22 The BCCI case is discussed in Chapter 6, Section C.6.1.

23 *First Council Directive 77/780/EEC of 12 December 1977 on the coordination of the laws, regulations and administrative provisions relating to the taking up and pursuit of the business of credit institutions* (OJ L 322/30, 17 December 1977) Recital 3.

24 See Basel Committee, *Report on the Supervision of Bank's Foreign Establishments (Concordat,* September 1975) 2–3. For an extensive analysis on the original principles set out in the Concordat, see Walker, G., *International Banking Regulation: Law, Policy and Practice* (London: Kluwer, 2001) 86 *et seq.*

25 The Basel Concordat, *Principles for the Supervision of Banks' Foreign Establishments* (May 1983) has replaced the 1975 Concordat. Since then, it was further supplemented in 1990 and 1992.

26 The principle of consolidated supervision has led Basel to adopt some extension of parental responsibility, to monitor risk exposure – including a perspective of concentration of risk and quality of assets – of the banks or banking groups for which they are responsible, as well as the adequacy of their capital, on the basis of the totality of their business wherever conducted.

27 See Roth, W., 'EEC Treaty Article Fifty-Nine and Its Implications for Conflicts Law in the Field of Insurance Contracts' (1992) 2 Duke Journal of Comparative and International Law 131.

28 Case 120/78 [1979] ECR 649. Although the case concentrated only on the free movement of goods under Article 30 EEC Treaty, its approach was extended, through the White Paper, to services under Article 59. However, Eeckhout notes that, if one looks at the fundamental freedoms from a personal, rights-based perspective, the potential extension of cases relating to the free movement of goods to other freedoms (such as services) should be made with great caution. See Eackhout, P., 'Recent Case-Law on Free Movement of Goods: Refining Keck and Mithouard' (1998) EBLR 271. Here, a distinction has to be made between at least three types of cross-border provision of services: (a) the service provider moves to another Member State where the service is provided, (b) the service receiver moves to another Member State in order to receive that service, and (c) neither the service provider nor the receiver move across borders. The analogy mentioned above seems more appropriate in the latter situation, where the nature of the service is such as not to involve the provider of the service in moving physically between Member States, but where instead it is transmitted by post or telecommunications. See Opinion by Advocate General in Case C-76/90 *Sager* [1991] ECR I-4221; Opinion 1/94 *Competence of the Community to conclude international agreements concerning services and the protection of intellectual property* [1994] ECR I-5267, Paragraphs 44–5. See also Kapteyn, P. and Verloren Van Themaat, P., *Introduction to the Law of the European Communities* (Deventer: Kluwer, 2nd ed., 1989) 443–52.

29 See Hertig, G., *Imperfect Mutual Recognition for EU Financial Services*, in Buxbaum, R. et al., *European Economic and Business Law: Legal and Economic Analysis on Integration and Harmonisation* (New York: Walter de Gruyter, 1996) 220.

30 Since it was set up in 1952, more than 8700 cases have been brought before the Court. There were already 200 new cases a year by 1978 and 1985 saw more than 400 cases. To cope with that influx while still dealing with cases with reasonable despatch, the Court amended its Rules of Procedures to enable it to deal with cases more rapidly and requested the Council to set up a new judicial body. In response, the Council set up the Court of First Instance in 1989.

31 Article 221 (former Article 165) EC Treaty, Paragraph 1 and Article 222 (former Article 166), Paragraph 1. The number of the Advocates General may be increased by the Council; see Article 222, Paragraphs 2 and 3.

32 The duties of the Advocates General should not be confused with those of a prosecutor or similar official. That is the role of the European Commission.

33 Article 221, Paragraph 2. The Court sits in plenary sessions when a Member State or a Community institution that is a party to the proceedings so requests, or in particularly complex or important cases. Other cases are heard by a chamber.

34 Article 224 (former Article 168) EC Treaty.

35 These include actions against a Member State for failing to fulfil an obligation under the Treaty (Article 226), actions for annulment of Community legislation and for failure to act (Article 230), actions for damages (Article 235), appeals (Article 225), and preliminary rulings invoked by national courts on the interpretation of the Treaty, the validity and interpretation of acts of any institution and interpretation of the statutes of bodies established by the Council (Article 234). The latter rulings, although not setting up a hierarchical relationship, are thought to have institutionalised fruitful cooperation between the Court of Justice and Member States' courts.

36 See Timmermans, C., 'How Can One Improve the Quality of Community Legislation?' (1997) 34 CMLRev 1239.

37 See Joined Cases C-34/95, 35/95 and 36/95 *De Agostini* [1997] ECR I-3843, Paragraph 3; Case C-233/94 *Germany v Parliament and Council* [1997] ECR I-2405, Paragraphs 12–16.

38 Case 120/78, *op. cit.*, note 28.

39 That is 'measures having an effect equivalent to quantitative restrictions on imports'; Article 28 EC Treaty. It was clear that 'the unilateral requirements imposed by the rules of a Member State of a minimum alcohol content for the purposes of the sale of alcoholic beverages constitutes an obstacle to trade which is incompatible with the provisions of Article 30 of the Treaty'; *ibid.*, Paragraph 14. The Court further established the so-called rule of reason in determining and justifying host country rules in the absence of common Community rules. It held that 'obstacles to movement within the Community resulting from disparities between the national laws relating to the marketing of the products in question must be accepted in so far as those provisions may be recognised as being necessary in order to satisfy mandatory requirements relating in particular to the effectiveness of fiscal supervision, the protection of public health, the fairness of commercial transactions and the defence of the consumer'; *ibid.*, Paragraph 8.

40 *Ibid.*, Paragraph 14.

41 Case 8/74, *op. cit.*, note 19.

42 *Ibid.*, Paragraph 9.

43 See *Commission Directive 70/32/EEC of 17 December 1969 on provision of goods to the State, to local authorities and other official bodies* (OJ L 13/1, 19 January 1970);

Commission Directive 70/50/EEC of 22 December 1969 based on the provision of Article 33(7), on the abolition of measures which have an effect equivalent to quantitative restrictions on imports and are not covered by other provisions adopted in pursuance of the EEC Treaty (OJ L 13/29, 19 January 1970).

44   Case 41/76 *Donckerwolcke* [1976] ECR 1921, Paragraph 19. See also, Case 4/75 *Rewe* [1975] ECR 843; Case 104/75 *de Peijper* [1976] ECR 613; Case 35/76 *Simmenthal* [1976] ECR 1871.

45   See Walker, *op. cit.*, note 13.

46   European Commission, *Communication concerning the consequences of the judgement given by the Court of Justice on 20 February 1979 in case 120/78* (OJ C 256/1, 3 October 1980) 2–3.

47   The Commission considered the *Cassis* decision important in confirming the scope of its earlier *Dassonville*-based definition of measures of equivalent effect in connection with technical and commercial rules; *ibid.*, Paragraphs 4 and 5. For a discussion of the Communication, see Walker, *op. cit.*, note 13.

48   The Court, e.g., held that restrictions on trade must be justified, in accordance to Article 36 EEC Treaty, on the basis of the principle of the protection of the consumer and fair competition between producers; Case 120/78, note 28, Paragraph II a.

49   Case C-262/81 *Coditel* [1982] ECR 3381.

50   Despite the absence of any equivalent of Article 30 in the field of the provision of services, the Court has invented permissible restrictions, which parallel Article 30, and possibly also the so-called mandatory requirements. See also Case 52/79 *Debauve* [1980] ECR 833, Paragraph 16 and Case C-148/91 *Veronica* [1991] ECR I-487, Paragraph 15.

51   Case C-76/90, *op. cit.*, note 28.

52   The service in question consisted of monitoring patents, advising the proprietors of the patents when renewals were due and paying such fees on behalf of the proprietors.

53   Case C-76/90, Paragraph 23.

54   Case C-205/84 *Commission v Germany* [1986] ECR 3755.

55   *Ibid.*, Paragraph 39.

56   *Ibid.*, Paragraph 47. With regard to the duplication of statutory requirements, see also the earlier Cases C-110/78 and 111/78 *Van Wesemael* [1979] ECR 35, Paragraph 28 and Case C-279/80 *Webb* [1981] ECR 3305, Paragraph 20.

57   Joined Cases C-267/91 and C-268/91 *Criminal Proceedings against Bernand Keck and Daniel Mithouard* [1993] ECR I-6097.

58   *Ibid.*, Paragraph 15.

59   *Ibid.*, Opinion by Advocate General Van Gernen, Paragraph 6; this has been settled case law since the judgement in Case 120/78, *op. cit.*, note 28, Paragraph 8.

60   See Case 177/83 *Kohl v Ringelhan* [1984] ECR 3651.

61   See Case 302/86 *Commission v Denmark* [1988] ECR 4607.

62   Case C-384/93, *op. cit.*, note 21.

63   Commodities derivatives are not included in Section B of the Annex to the ISD. The United Kingdom has managed to keep them out of the ISD passport.

64   See ISD, Articles 11 and 13.

65   Case C-384/93, Paragraph 30; See also Case C-18/93 *Corsica Ferries Italia* [1994] ECR I-1783, Paragraph 30, Case C-379/92 *Peralta* [1994] ECR I-3453, Paragraph 40 and Case C-381/93 *Commission v France* [1994] ECR I-5145, Paragraph 14.

66   Case C-384/93, Paragraphs 42–9.

67   *Ibid.*, Opinion by Advocate General Jacobs, Paragraph 19.

68 Case C-233/94, *op. cit.*, note 37.
69 Council and Parliament Directive 94/19/EC (OJ L 135/5, 30 May 1994).
70 This case is also relevant for investment services as the principles, structure, content and rationale of the DGD resemble those of the later adopted Investor Compensation Schemes Directive 97/9/EC (OJ L 84/22, 3 March 1997).
71 DGD, Recital 7.
72 Case C-233/94, opinion by Advocate General Leger, Paragraph 131.
73 See e.g., Landsmeer, A. and Empel, M., 'The Directive on Deposit-Guarantee Schemes and the Directive on Investor Compensation Schemes in View of Case C-233/94' (1998) EFSL 143, where the authors contend that Article 4(1) DGD is contrary to the principle of 'home state' as stated in the Commission's Communication of 1980, *op. cit.*, note 46.
74 Case C-233/94, Opinion by Advocate General Leger, Paragraph 126.
75 Case C-233/94, Paragraph 64. If that were the case, Community authorities would be bound 'only because of the need to respect the legitimate expectations of citizens entitled to expect the application of the principle in question'; see Opinion by Advocate General Leger, Paragraph 128.
76 The fact that home country control was introduced by the White Paper hardly implies that it has become a 'regulatory principle', as some scholars argue. For the distinction between 'judicial' and 'regulatory' principles, see Sun, J.M. and Pelkmans, J., 'Regulatory Competition in the Single Market' (1995) 1 JCMS 69.
77 Articles 3, 4 and 5 of the Treaty (former Articles 3, 3a and 3b).
78 ISD, Recital 3.
79 The role of the host Member State is already defined in the White Paper: 'The authorities of the Member State which is the destination of the service, whilst not deprived of all power, would have a complementary role', Paragraph 103.
80 For an analytical elaboration of the concepts 'home' and 'host' country, see Chapter 5, Sections C.2.1 and C.2.3.
81 ISD, Article 3(1).
82 'Host Member State' is the country in which an investment firm has a branch or provides services; ISD, Article 1(7).
83 Article 3(1) provides that each Member State is to make access to the business of investment firms subject to authorisation.
84 *European Parliament and Council Directive 95/26/EC of 29 June 1995 amending Directives 77/780/EEC and 89/646/EEC in the field of credit institutions, Directives 73/239/EEC and 92/49/EEC in the field of non-life insurance, Directives 79/267/EEC and 92/96/EEC in the field of life assurance, Directive 93/22/EEC in the field of investment firms and Directive 85/611/EEC in the field of undertakings for collective investment in transferable securities, with a view to reinforcing prudential supervision* (hereinafter 'post-BCCI Directive').
85 In light of its Second Consultation on the ISD II, however, the Commission purports to introduce new obligations for investment firms to include (a) demonstration of systematic and repeatable methodologies for obtaining best execution for clients, (b) off-exchange reporting of post-trade details and (c) general obligation to uphold market integrity; see European Commission, *Revision of ISD: Second Consultation* (25 March 2002) 23.
86 ISD, Article 3(3). Interestingly, the minimum capital level for investment firms is lower than that required for credit institutions that engage in investment services as prescribed by Article 4 of the consolidated Banking Directive.
87 *Council Directive 93/6/EEC of 15 March 1993 on the capital adequacy of investments firms and credit institutions* (OJ L 141/1, 11 June 1993). For a review of the CAD

and the issues arising from this Directive, see Moloney, N., *EC Securities Regulation* (Oxford: Oxford University Press, 2002) 486 *et seq.*

88   *Ibid.*, Article 1(2).
89   *Ibid.*, Article 3(4).
90   FESCO, *European Standards on Fitness and Propriety to Provide Investment Services* (April 1999) 5.
91   Such requirement does exist for the other authorisation criteria; See ISD, Article 8(1) for the capital requirements and the director's competence, and Article 9 for the identity and amount of holdings of shareholders.
92   FESCO, *op. cit.*, note 90, 6.
93   This is likely to cover matters such as those set out in Article 10 of the ISD, including in particular conflict of interest issues.
94   Post-BCCI Directive, Article 4.
95   *Council and Parliament Directive 2000/12/EC relating to the taking up and pursuit of the business of credit institutions* (OJ L 126/1, 26 May 2000).
96   ISD, Article 6.
97   Post-BCCI Directive, Recitals 8, 9 and 18. On the EU programme in this field, see Chapter 8.
98   ISD, Article 4.
99   *Ibid.*, Article 1(10).
100   See, e.g., ISD, Article 25. Information exchange on the fitness and propriety of individuals and on firm's operational structure is also an area covered by the MoU, signed by FESCO members in 1999; see FESCO, *Multilateral Memorandum of Understanding on the Exchange of Information and Surveillance of Securities Activities* (February 1999).
101   ISD, Article 10.
102   See IOSCO, *Objectives and Principles of Securities Regulation* (February 2002) 32.
103   Ferrarini, G., 'Introduction' in Ferrarini, G. (ed.), *Prudential Regulation of Banks and Securities Firms: European and International Aspects* (London: Kluwer, 1995) 4.
104   CAD, Articles 4, 5 and 8.
105   ISD, Article 4. The information required could include personal details, employment and work history, professional qualifications, educational background and information on any criminal record and previous civil cases.
106   *Ibid.*, Article 9(1).
107   *Ibid.*, Article 9(3).
108   *Ibid.*, Article 9(4). The thresholds mentioned in the Directive are those of 10, 20, 33 or 50% of the firm's capital. See *ibid.*, Article 9(1).
109   SBD, Articles 19 and 20. However, the notification requirements regarding investment services seem considerably simpler than those contained in Article 19 of the SBD and should involve less waiting and bureaucracy for the investment firm, which intends to set up a branch.
110   Regarding the analogous problem in banking, see Strivens, R., 'The Liberalisation of Banking Services in the Community' (1992) CMLRev 283, 291, who suggests that the most liberal interpretation of Article 20 SBD should prevail.
111   Article 17(6) states: 'In the event of a change in any of the particulars communicated (...) an investment firm shall give written notice of that change to the competent authorities of the home and host Member States at least one month before implementing the change so that the competent authorities of the home Member State may take a decision on the change (...) and the competent authorities of the host Member State may do so (...).' Article 18(3) reads: 'Should the content of the information communicated (...) be amended, the investment

firm shall give notice of the amendment in writing to the competent authorities of the home Member State and of the host Member State before implementing the change, so that the competent authorities of the host Member State may, if necessary, inform the firm of any change or addition to be made to the information communicated under paragraph 2.'

112 Since the *Van Binsbergen* judgement in 1974, it has been common ground that all requirements, that are imposed on the provider on grounds that he/she does not habitually reside in the Member State in question and that do not apply to persons established within the territory of the Member State, are in principle contrary to Article 59 EEC (now Article 49 EC); see Case 33/74 *Van Binsbergen* [1974] ECR 1299, Paragraph 10.

113 See, e.g., the *Insurance cases*: Case 220/83 *Commission v France* [1986] ECR 3663; Case 252/83 *Commission v Denmark* [1986] ECR 3713; Case 205/84 *Commission v Germany* [1986] ECR 3755; Case 206/84 *Commission v Ireland* [1986] ECR 3817.

114 See, e.g., Hartley, T., 'Recognition of Qualifications and the Right to Work', in Green, N., Hartley, T. and Usher, J. (eds), *The Legal Foundations of the Single European Market* (Oxford: Oxford University Press, 1991) 169. Hartley argues that the beneficiary of Article 49 EC might have to comply with formalities designed to inform the local professional organisation of his presence and provide evidence of qualifications. The operation of this principle is illustrated by *Gullung*, a case concerning legal services; see Case 292/85 *Gullung* [1988] ECR 111.

115 See ISD, Article 17 for branches and Article 18 for cross-border services. It is not, though, within the scope of this chapter to analyse and distinguish in detail the Treaty's basic provisions on the right of establishment and the freedom to provide services. For this purpose, see Chapter 2, Section C.3.1. Also, for such an analysis, see Nielsen, P., *Services and Establishment in European Community Banking Law* (Copenhagen: DJOF Publishing, 1994) 79 *et seq.*

116 ISD, Article 17(2).

117 *Ibid.*, Article 17(3). The same time applies for credit institutions, which, in addition, have to provide information on the amount of own funds and their Solvency Ratio. See 2BCD, Article 19(3).

118 ISD, Article 17(4–5).

119 In the case of the establishment of the branch, a further period of two months is given to the host competent authorities to prepare for its supervision; see ISD, Article 17(4). This 'preparation' period is not given for cross-border services; see *ibid.*, Article 18(2).

120 *Cf.* ISD, Articles 17(4) and 18(2).

121 ISD, Article 16.

122 OJ C 203 of 3 July 1997.

123 ISD, Article 1(13).

124 European Commission, *Report on the Operation of Certain Articles of the Investment Services Directive* (COM(1998) 780 final, 21 December 1998) 8.

125 See FESCO, *Standards for Regulated Markets under the ISD* (22 December 1999). FESCO has also taken cognisance of the principles and objectives laid down by IOSCO's, *Objectives and Principles of Securities Regulation* (September 1998), regarding consumer protection, fair, efficient and transparent markets and the reduction of systemic risk.

126 See Cruickshank, C., 'Is there a Need to Harmonise Conduct of Business Rules?' in Ferrarini, G. (ed.), *European Securities Markets: The Investment Services Directive and Beyond* (London: Kluwer, 1998) 131.

127 Hertig characterises rules of conduct as a perfect example of the imperfection of mutual recognition, as 'the freedom left to Member States is sufficient to permit the framing and enforcing of quite different rules'; see Hertig, *op. cit.*, note 29, 224.

128 Hopefully, this will be included in the forthcoming ISD II proposal; see ISD Second Consultation, *op. cit.*, note 85, 24.

129 These principles include the duty of the investment firm (a) to act honestly and fairly in conducting its business activities in the best interest of its clients and the integrity of the market; (b) to act with due skill, care and diligence; (c) to have and to employ effectively the resources and procedures that are necessary for the proper performance of its business activities; (d) to seek from its clients information regarding their financial situations, investment experience and objectives as regards the services requested; (e) to make adequate disclosure of relevant material information in its dealings with its clients; (f) to try to avoid conflicts of interests and, when they cannot be avoided, to ensure that its clients are fairly treated; and (g) to comply with all the regulatory requirements applicable to the conduct of its business activities so as to promote the best interests of its clients and the integrity of the market.

130 European Commission, *Recommendation 77/534/EEC* (OJ L 212/37, 25 July 1977).

131 It seems that the drafters of the Directive did not want to lose time and effort over the question of the content of the CBR, which would, *ipso facto*, give rise to endless discussions.

132 ISD, Article 11(2).

133 See Hertig, *op. cit.*, note 29, 222.

134 This does not mean that Member States are not allowed to preserve some power to permit them to pursue non-prudential goals. See SBD, Article 14(2) and ISD, Article 19.

135 Especially compared with banking, CBR are more specifically dealt with in the ISD. See Dalhuisen, J.H., 'Liberalisation and Re-Regulation of Cross-Border Financial Services: Part III' (1999) 9–10 EBLR 361.

136 See FESCO, *Stabilisation and Allotment: A European Supervisory Approach* (Consultative Paper, 15 September 2000) 13.

137 ISD, Article 11, Dash 7; see Horn, 'Die Aufklarungs- und Beratungspflichten der Banken' (1996) ZBB 139, 150.

138 *Cf.* ISD, Articles 17(4) and 18(2), second paragraph with Article 19(6). Also *cf.* Recitals 33 and 41 of the Preamble. The ambiguity is further increased by the formulation of Article 11(1), which speaks of 'rules of conduct which investment firms *shall observe at all times*' (emphasis added).

139 See, e.g., Wouters, J., 'Rules of Conduct, Foreign Investment Firms and the EC's Case Law on Services' (1993) 14 Company Lawyer 194; Thorkildsen, T., 'Power to Draw Up Conduct of Business Rules after the ISD' (1995) 16 Company Lawyer 102; Tison, M., 'What is "General Good" in EU Financial Services Law?' (1997) 2 Legal Issues of European Integration 1.

140 The fear that Member States might use the rules of conduct regime of the ISD as a means to enact protectionist measures has been *inter alia* expressed by Ashall, P., 'Investment Services Directive: What was the Conflict all about?' in Andenas, M. and Kenyon-Slade, S. (eds), *EC Financial Market Regulation and Company Law* (London: Sweet & Maxwell, 1993) 101.

141 See, however, Thorkildsen, *op. cit.*, note 139, 107, who argues that 'it is probably not possible in general to tell whether the conduct of business rules of the

host state may imply additional costs on a foreign investment firm'. But he admits that 'it is always a disadvantage to face other rules of conduct when operating abroad, even when they are only slightly different from those of the home state'.

142 See Wouters, *op. cit.*, note 139, 194–5. See, however, after the *Keck and Mithouard* judgement Andenas, M., 'Rules of conduct and the principle of subsidiarity' (1994) 15 Company Lawyer 61, who argues that 'the case law of the ECJ no longer provides clear support for limiting Member States authority to promulgate conduct of business rules'.

143 ISD, Recital 1.

144 ISD, Article 15(1).

145 This is the so-called remote access rule.

146 ISD, Article 15(4). The problem of electronic trading is discussed in Chapter 5, Section C.2.4.

147 Steil, B., 'Equity Trading IV: The ISD and the Regulation of European Market Structure', in Steil, B. *et al.*, *The European Equity Markets: The State of the Union and an Agenda for the Millennium* (London: Royal Institute of International Affaires, 1996) 129.

148 See European Commission, Decisions 85/563/EEC, 85/564/EEC, 85/565/EEC and 85/566/EEC (OJ L 369/25, 31 December 1985). For example, in the London Grain Futures Market Decision 87/45/EEC (OJ L 19/167, 10 December 1986) the Commission granted an exemption from Article 85 on the basis, *inter alia*, of the following statement: 'As a result of representations by the Commission, amendments have been made to the regulations concerning membership so that membership is now open and that the criteria by which applications for membership are judged are objective. The Committee is required to give reasons when it takes decisions affecting the members' rights of membership. To protect the rights of actual or potential members, an appeal has been introduced'. See Ferrarini, G., 'Exchange Governance and Regulation: An Overview', in Ferrarini, *op. cit.*, note 103, 263.

149 *Ibid.*, 264. This is extremely important in two cases. First, the openness of the market could conflict the interest of the actual firms-members to share the investment services pie with as few firms as possible. Second, as the ISD fails to take into consideration the potential function of the market as a for-profit corporation, open membership could come against the interest of the members-shareholders to retain their yield in shares of the stock exchange.

150 ISD, Article 15(2).

151 *Directive 97/9/EC on investor compensation schemes* (OJ L 84/22, 1997).

152 See ISD, Recitals 5 and 32, ICSD, Recitals 4, 14 and 19.

153 See Lomnicka, *op. cit.*, note 10.

154 ICSD, Article 7(1); *cf.* DGD, Article 4(1).

155 *Ibid.*

156 Lomnicka, *op. cit.*, note 10.

157 ICSD, Article 7(1); *cf.* DGD, Article 4(1) and 4(5).

158 ISD, Article 19(1).

159 *Ibid.*, Article 19(2). In the latter case, however, information may also be required from investment firms that operate under the freedom to provide cross-border services. The host State also retains *in toto* responsibility for the measures resulting from the implementation of their policies. See Wouters, J., 'Conflict of Laws and the Single Market for Financial Services' (1997) 2 Maastricht Journal of European and Comparative Law 161, 185.

160 ISD, Article 19(3–8).
161 This echoes the requirement in Article 26 ISD that all decisions made in pursuance of this Directive should be capable of being subject to application to the courts.
162 For example, the home State may not have the necessity for the same rule in its jurisdiction and, therefore, may not understand the reason to take the action requested by the host country.
163 Investment firms and all interested parties do still have the right to apply to the courts according to Article 26 ISD.
164 See post-BCCI Directive, Article 4.
165 *Ibid.*; ISD, Article 25.

4 The Institutional Design

1 This has become evident particularly after the release of the Lamfalussy Reports; Committee of Wise Men, *Initial Report on Regulation of European Securities Markets* (9 November 2000); *Final Report on the Regulation of European Securities Markets* (15 February 2001, hereinafter 'Final Wise Men Report').
2 See Skocpol, T., 'Bringing the State Back In: Strategies of Analysis in Current Research', in Evans, P., Rieschemeyer, D. and Skocpol, T. (eds), *Bringing the State Back In* (Cambridge: Cambridge University Press, 1985); March, J. and Olsen, J., *Rediscovering Institutions* (New York: Free Press, 1989). For behaviouralists, institutions were relatively uninteresting compared to the behaviour of political actors; see Sanders, D., 'Behavioural Analysis', in Marsh, D. and Stoker, G. (eds), *Theory and Methods in Political Science* (Basingstoke: Palgrave, 1995); see also Chapter 2, Section C.
3 See Economic and Financial Committee, *Report on Financial Stability* ('Brouwer Report', EFC/ECFIN/240/00 final, 8 April 2000) 15.
4 The G10 originally arose out of the negotiations surrounding the establishment of the General Agreement to Borrow (GAB) in 1961 and 1962. The GAB was set up as a devise for providing additional liquidity to the IMF by a decision of the Executive Board of the IMF; see IMF, *Annual Report* (1962) 234–5.
5 For the Committee's method of operation and programme construction, see Walker, G., *International Banking Regulation: Law, Policy and Practice* (London: Kluwer, 2001) 45 *et seq.*
6 The membership of the Committee has always been limited to the G10 member countries plus Luxembourg and Switzerland. Luxembourg was included with Belgium, with which it has monetary union. Although Switzerland is not an official member of G10, it has been closely associated with the GAB since the 1960s and became a full participant in 1984. Both countries are members of the OECD.
7 See Walker, *op. cit.*, note 5, 40; Blunden, G., 'Control and Supervision of the UK Banking System', in Wadsworth, J., Wilson, J. and Fournier, H. (eds), *The Development of Financial Institutions in Europe, 1956–1976* (Leyden: Sijthoff, 1977), Chapter XIII; Bank of England, 'International Conference of Banking Supervisors' (1979) Bank of England Quarterly Bulletin 298; Cooke, P., 'The Role of the Banking Supervisor' (1982) Bank of England Quarterly Bulletin 547.
8 Until the establishment of the Basel Committee, there had been no formal mechanism for the development of cross-border supervisory cooperation in connection with the activities of international banks; see Dale, R., *The Regulation of International Banking* (Cambridge: Woodhead-Faulkner, 1984); Herring, R. and

Littan, R., *Financial Regulation in the Global Economy* (Washington: Brookings Institution, 1995).

9   For comments on early activities of the Committee, see Shah, A., 'International Bank Regulation: Objectives and Outcomes – An Interview with Peter Cooke, Former Chairman of the Basel Committee, 1977–1988' (1996) 6 JIBFL 255.

10 Basel Committee, *Report on the Supervision of Bank's Foreign Establishments* (Concordat, September 1975).

11 See Basel Committee, *Principles for the Supervision of Banks' Foreign Establishments* (Concordat, May 1983). This was considered necessary following the collapse of Banco Ambrosiano in 1983 although the opportunity was also taken to develop particular aspects of some of the earlier rules. The Revised Concordat provided for the incorporation of the recommendation contained in a March 1979 paper that supervision should be conducted on the basis of the consolidated balance sheet of all international bank's constituent entities; see Basel Committee, *Consolidated Supervision of Bank's International Activities* (March 1979). It also incorporated recommendations from an interim confidential paper concerning authorisation procedures for the foreign establishments of banks and created a new mutual review or dual key mechanism for supervisory use; Basel Committee, *Authorisation Procedures for Banks' Foreign Establishments* (March 1983).

12 See Basel Committee, *Information Flows between Banking Supervisory Authorities* (April 1990); Basel Committee, *Minimum Standards for the Supervision of International Banking Groups and Their Cross-Border Establishments* (July 1992); Basel Committee, *The Supervision of Cross-Border Banking* (October 1996). The 1990 supplement contained a number of much more substantial provisions concerning the flow of supervisory information between the parent and host authorities. A number of the core principles were then restated in 1992 as a set of Minimum Standards. Following the perceived success of the 1988 Capital Accord, which introduced minimum provisions in the bank capital area, the Committee decided to reformulate its supervisory rules as absolute minimum standards to facilitate their adoption and application. The 1996 supplement reproduced a joint report prepared by a working group consisting of members of the Basel Committee and the Offshore Group of Banking Supervisors, which presented a number of proposals for overcoming the impediments experienced by banking supervisors in conducting effective supervision of the cross-border operations of international banks. The Offshore Group was established in 1980 as a forum for supervisory cooperation between the banking supervisors in offshore financial centres. Current members of the Group are: Aruba, Bahamas, Bahrain, Barbados, Bermuda, Cayman Islands, Cyprus, Gibraltar, Guernsey, Hong Kong, Isle of Man, Jersey, Lebanon, Malta, Mauritius, the Netherlands, Antilles, Panama, Singapore and Vanuatu.

13 Basel Committee, *International Convergence of Capital Measurement and Capital Standards* (July 1988).

14 Basel Committee, *The New Basel Capital Accord* (January 2001).

15 IAIS, *Principles Applicable to the Supervision of International Insurers and Insurance Groups and Their Cross-Border Business Operations* (Insurance Concordat, December 1999).

16 IOSCO has four Regional Committees: the European Committee, the Interamerican Committee, the Asia-Pacific Committee and the Africa-Middle East Committee.

17 Since 1990, the Technical Committee has been divided into five major subject areas to deal with the particular issues that arise in connection with each. Each

Working Group is instructed by way of mandates by the Technical Committee to deal with a particular issue or series of issues. The Working Groups meet several times a year to pursue the specific areas of activity set out in their mandate from the Technical Committee. Presently, there are five Groups dealing with Multi-national Disclosure and Accounting (WG1), Regulation of Secondary Markets (WG2), Regulation of Market Intermediaries (WG3), Enforcement and Exchange of Information (WG4) and Investment Management (WG5).

18 The Emerging Markets Committee was set up in 1994 to replace the earlier Development Committee. Initially, it has followed the earlier working group structure of the Development Committee, which comprised separate groups on Disclosure, Institutional Investors, Derivatives, Clearing and Settlement and Market Incentives. Now, its Working Groups reflect those of the Technical Committee. For this reason, both the Technical and the Emerging Markets Committee have agreed to exchange observers on Working Groups to facilitate practical cooperation in their activity.

19 Found at http://www.iosco.org.

20 Indeed, effective international standards could provide early warnings for the types of financial crises that occurred in the 1990s in the developed financial market of Japan and in the developing markets of Asia, Russia and Latin America; see Alexander, K., 'The Need for Efficient International Financial Regulation and the Role of a Global Supervisor', in Ferran, E. and Goodhart, C. (eds), *Regulating Financial Services and Markets in the Twenty First Century* (Oxford: Hart, 2001) 291.

21 Zaring, D., 'International Law by Other Means: The Twilight Existence of International Financial Regulatory Organizations' (1998) Texas International Law Journal 282, 295.

22 On 13 November 2001, e.g., IOSCO announced the status of IOSCO members' progress towards conclusion of an important self-assessment exercise regarding the implementation of the thirty core principles of securities regulation set forth in the *IOSCO Objectives and Principles of Securities Regulation*, adopted in September 1998.

23 IOSCO, *Multilateral Memorandum of Understanding* (May 2002).

24 Tripartite Group, *Progress Report on the Supervision of Financial Conglomerates* (April 1994). The Report was sent to the Basel Committee, IOSCO, and to the heads of insurance supervisory authorities in the G10 countries.

25 Tripartite Group, *Report on the Supervision of Financial Conglomerates* (July 1995).

26 The Joint Forum is made up of twenty-five persons representing the banking, securities and insurance sectors. An equal number of supervisors from each area attend from thirteen countries with a representative from the European Commission to coordinate with the related work carried on within the EU.

27 Joint Forum, *Progress Report on Financial Conglomerates* (9 April 1997). The Report contained a number of provisions concerning exchange of information between supervisors, the work of a specific Task Force that had been established to enhance the Forum's understanding of the operations of internationally active financial conglomerates, the possible role and responsibilities of a coordinator and the development of a number of principles of supervision for application in particular areas of supervisory activity. On the G7 (now G8) and its role, see Hodges, M. *et al.*, *The G8's Role in the New Millennium* (Aldershot: Ashgate, 1999).

28 Joint Forum, *Supervision of Financial Conglomerates* (December 1999). The Forum reviewed the various means to facilitate the exchange of information between supervisors within their own sectors and between supervisors in different sectors and investigated the legal or other barriers that could impede the exchange

of information between authorities. It also examined the means of enhancing supervisory coordination, including the advantages and disadvantages of setting out specific criteria to be used in identifying a coordinator and defining the coordinator's responsibilities.

29   Tietmeyer, H., *International Co-operation and Co-ordination in the Area of Financial Market Supervision and Surveillance* (11 February 1999).

30   The FSF was convened on 14 April 1999 in Washington. Mr Andrew Crockett, General Manager of the BIS, was appointed Chairman of the FSF in his personal capacity for a term of three years. Support for the FSF is provided by a small secretariat located at the BIS in Basel, Switzerland. The FSF is made up of representatives from the G7 countries, the Basel Committee, IOSCO, IAIS, the IMF, the World Bank, the OECD and the BIS. Its mandate is to strengthen the surveillance and supervision of the international financial system; see www.fsforum.org.

31   The FSF has created three Working Groups, one Task Force and one Study Group to deal with specific issues of global financial stability: the Working Group on Highly-Leveraged Institutions, the Working Group on Capital Flows, the Working Group on Offshore Financial Centres, the Task Force on Implementation of Standards and the Study Group on Deposit Insurance.

32   See Walker, *op. cit.*, note 5, 309.

33   This has mainly been conducted by the Basel Committee and constitutes an important part of the New Capital Accord. See Chapter 7, Section C.5.2.

34   The principles stemming from the Basel 1975 Concordat, e.g., have been adopted by European law since the First Banking Directive. Furthermore, in the wake of the collapse of the BCCI, the Basel Committee reformulated some of the principles of the Concordat in 1992. These were followed in 1995 by the EU 'post-BCCI Directive', with a view to reinforcing prudential supervision. On the cooperation between the Basel Committee and the European Commission, see Dassesse *et al.*, *EC Banking Law* (London: Lloyd's Press, 2nd ed., 1994) 73–5.

35   Changes to qualified majority voting agreed at Nice (triple majority) have made decision-making in the Council more difficult and have shifted the balance in favour of large Member States for the first time in the history of the Union.

36   The Eurogroup (first called the Euro-11) was created at the European Council Luxembourg Summit in December 1997.

37   This becomes evident by Article 111(4) (former Article 109) of the Treaty, which provides that the common position of the Community in international instances is to be decided by a qualified vote of the participating Member States.

38   See Louis, J.V., *The EMU, and After?* (Paper delivered at the Federal Trust Conference 'Consolidating EMU', London, 9 June 2000). Louis argues that the Group could play a role if two conditions were met: first, if it does not intervene too much in the exercise of internal responsibilities of national authorities, and, second, if there is a consensus on the orientations of policies to be followed.

39   The Economist, 'Dominique Strauss-Kahn, Euro-coach' (30 May 1998) 54.

40   Paragraph 33 of the Presidency Conclusions stated: 'The European Council welcomes the improvements made to the workings of the Eurogroup and its visibility. It also welcomes the intention to extend the range of mainly structural matters dealt with in this forum, while not departing from the conclusions of the Luxembourg European Council meeting. These improvements intended to enhance the coordination of economic policies will help to boost the growth potential of the euro area.'

41   On the economic coordination procedures after the emergence of the Eurogroup, see Louis, J.V., 'The Euro-Group and Economic Policy Co-ordination', in Louis,

J.V. (ed.), *The Euro in the National Context* (London: British Institute of International & Comparative Law, 2002) 352–62.

42 European Commission, *Strengthening Economic Policy Co-ordination* (COM(2001) 82 final, 7 February 2001) 2. According to the Commission, economic coordination comprises three elements: (a) common assessment of the economic situation; (b) agreement on appropriate economic policy responses; and (c) acceptance of peer pressure and, where necessary, adjustment of policies being pursued.

43 Kirchhof, P., 'The Balance of Powers between the National and European Institutions' (1999) 3 ELJ 225, 233.

44 See Majone, G., *Regulating Europe* (London: Routledge, 1996) 265.

45 On the delegation of powers to the Commission, see Majone, *ibid.*, 68 *et seq.*; Ludlow, P., 'The European Commission', in Keohane, R. and Hoffman, S. (eds), *The New European Community: Decisionmaking and Institutional Change* (Boulder: Westview Press, 1991). In respect of competition policy, Article 85 EC Treaty (former Article 89) endows the Commission with independent powers to ensure the application of the competition laws. All final decisions in competition cases are reached through a vote of the Commission; see *Council Regulation 17 implementing Articles 85 and 86 of the Treaty* ('Regulation 17', OJ P 013/204, 21 February 1962), Article 9; *Council Regulation No 4064/89 of 21 December 1989 on the control of concentrations between undertakings* ('Merger Regulation', OJ L 395, 30 December 1989), Article 8.

46 European Commission, *Communication on Strategic Objectives 2000–2005: Shaping the New Europe* (COM(2000) 154 final, 9 February 2000).

47 *Ibid.*, 6. The Commission's latter law-making competence, however, is very controversial and has been delimited by the ECJ; see Case C-57/95 *France v Commission* [1997] I-1627. For an extensive analysis of this case, see Andenas, M., 'The Financial Market and the Commission as Legislator' (1998) 4 Company Lawyer 102.

48 European Commission, *Reforming the Commission: A White Paper* (COM(2000) 200 final, 5 April 2000).

49 Article 202 (former Article 145) of the Treaty provides that the Council shall 'confer on the Commission powers for the implementation of the rules which the Council lays down'. The comitology procedure is considered later in Section 3.

50 The answer of these questions lies in the principal-agent (P-A) analysis of political scientists; see, accordingly, Tsebelis, G. and Garrett, G., 'The Institutional Foundations of Intergovernmentalism and Supranationalism in the European Union' (2001) 2 International Organization 357; Pollack, M., 'Delegation, Agency and Agenda Setting in the European Community' (1997) 1 International Organization 99.

51 Kingdon calls the Commission's role 'policy entrepreneur'; Kingdon, J., *Agendas, Alternatives and Public Policies* (Boston: Little, Brown & Company, 1984) 189–90. According to the author, successful policy entrepreneurs possess three basic qualities: (a) they must be taken seriously either as experts or as leaders of powerful interest groups, or as authoritative decision-makers, (b) they must be known for their negotiation skills, and (c) they must be persistent.

52 See Annex I, Table AI.2.

53 These countries are Belgium, Luxembourg and Finland.

54 See Chapter 8, Section B.3.2.

55 See Annex 1, Table AI.3.

56 Around half of EU employees work for the British FSA. See Annex I, Table AI.2.

57   European Commission, *Decision Establishing the European Securities Committee* (COM(2001) 1493 final, 6 June 2001, hereinafter 'ESC Decision').

58   The HLSSC was an informal group set up by the Commission in 1985 and comprised high-level representatives of Member States' securities supervisory authorities, finance ministers and central banks. Chaired by the Commission, its primary role was to assist and advice the Commission on policy issues relating to securities markets and the development of the relevant EU legislation, rather than detailed technical questions. Here lies its greatest difference with its successor, the ESC.

59   European Council, *Decision 1999/468/EC laying down the procedures for the exercise of implementing powers conferred on the Commission* (OJ L 184/23, 17 July 1999, hereinafter 'Comitology Decision') as amended by the Parliament – Commission Agreement of 2000 (OJ L 256/19 of 10 October 2000).

60   Final Wise Men Report, 24.

61   European Parliament, *Report on the Implementation of Financial Services Legislation* (A5-0011/2002 final, 23 January 2002, hereinafter 'von Wogau Report') 8, voted on 5 February 2002. The EP wishes, *inter alia*, one of its representatives to be able to attend meetings of the ESC and draws attention to its calls for the establishment of a genuine hierarchy of legal acts. It also takes the view that Article 202 of the EC Treaty has been rendered obsolete by the co-decision procedure, as the EP and the Council should have an equal role in supervising the way in which the Commission exercises its executive role, and, thus, should be amended at the next IGC.

62   See FESE, *Second Report and Recommendations on European Regulatory Structures* (January 2001) 10. FESE recommends that EU securities exchanges, under their capacity as regulators in various forms, be made members of the CESR, at least for issues that are wholly or partially within their remit. Moreover, it calls for more consideration on inviting the EP as observer in the ESC so as to optimise and strengthen the flow of information to the Parliament and increase its transparency and accountability.

63   ESFRC, *The Regulation of European Securities Markets: The Lamfalussy Report* (Statement No. 10, Madrid, 26 March 2001) 2–3. The ESFRC points out that 'keeping the legislative stage transparent through monitoring by the EP may slow down an already cumbersome process, but could also improve the quality of legislative output'.

64   For an analysis of these problems, see Avgerinos, Y., 'Essential and Non-Essential Measures: Delegation of Powers in EU Securities Regulation' (2002) 2 ELJ 269; Lenaerts, K., 'Regulating the Regulatory Process: "Delegation of Powers" in the European Community' (1993) 18 ELRev 23; Chapter 6, Section C.3.

65   Goodhart, C. *et al.*, *Financial Regulation: Why, How and Where Now?* (London: Routledge, 1998) 155.

66   European Commission, *Decision Establishing the Committee of European Securities Regulators* (COM(2001) 1501 final, 6 June 2001).

67   See CESR, *Draft Statement of Consultation Practices* (CESR/01-007b, October 2001).

68   In its first meeting on 11 September 2001, the CESR formally approved its Charter (*Charter of the Committee of European Securities Regulators*, CESR/01-002, hereinafter 'CESR Charter'). Mr Arthur Docters van Leeuwen, Chairman of the Securities Board of the Netherlands, has been elected as Chair of the Committee for a mandate of two years.

69   CESR Charter, Article 4.

70 *Ibid.*, Article 6.
71 (OJ L 145/43, 31 May 2001).
72 The group is composed of six independent experts, two nominated by each EU institution, the Parliament, the Council and the Commission.
73 Majone, *op. cit.*, note 44, 276.
74 See Chapter 5, Section C.
75 See Armstrong, K., 'Governance and the Single European Market', in Craig, P. and de Burca, G. (eds), *The Evolution of EU Law* (Oxford: Oxford University Press, 1999) 745–6.
76 This was the main reason for the adoption of the FSAP: European Commission, *Financial Services: Implementing the Framework for Financial Markets: Action Plan* (COM(1999) 232, 11 May 1999); see also Final Wise Men Report 12.
77 CSE(1995) 580; CSE(1996) 7; COM(1997) 626; COM(1998) 715; COM(1999) 562; COM(2000) 772; COM(2001) 728.
78 The SLIM project, however, has not yet blessed the securities field.
79 (COM(2001) 130 final, 7 March 2001) 9.
80 European Commission, *European Governance: A White Paper* (COM(2001) 428 final, 12 October 2001) 36.
81 See Parliamentary Group of the Party of European Socialists, *Securities Markets: European Parliament is Not Blocking the Lamfalussy Process* (Press Release, 22 November 2001).
82 See Lenaerts, K. and Verhoeven, A., 'Towards a Legal Framework for Executive Rule-Making in the EU? The Contribution of the New Comitology Decision' (2000) 3 CMLRev 645.

5 Assessing Home Country Control and Mutual Recognition

1 See Prologue, Section D.
2 In 1980, the Commission set out a number of guidelines on the application of the principle of mutual recognition resulting from the case law of the ECJ; see European Commission, *Communication concerning the consequences of the judgement given by the Court of Justice on 20 February 1979 in case 120/78 (Cassis de Dijon)* (OJ C 256/2, 3 October 1980). In its 1999 Communication to the Council and to the European Parliament, the Commission proposed many initiatives intended for economic operators and Member States and undertook to draw up an evaluation report at two-year intervals; see European Commission, *Communication on the Mutual Recognition in the context of the follow-up to the Action Plan for the Single Market* (COM(1999) 299 final, 16 June 1999). The First Biennial Report on the Application of the principle of Mutual Recognition in Product and Service Markets (SEC(1999) 1106, 13 July 1999) led to a preliminary diagnosis of how this principle operates in the Single Market. The Second Biennial Report (COM(2002) 419 final, 23 July 2002) assessed the progress made in the application of mutual recognition in the Single Market since 1999 and highlighted the fields in which the principle continues to pose problems.
3 Article 5 of the EC Treaty (former Article 3b) is the *locus classicus* of subsidiarity. It states that '(...) in areas which do not fall within its exclusive competence, the Community shall take action, in accordance with the principle of subsidiarity, only and insofar as the objectives of the proposed action cannot be sufficiently achieved by the Member States and can therefore, by reason of the scale of effects of the proposed action, be better achieved by the Community'.

4 European Commission, *Communication on the Mutual Recognition in the context of the follow-up to the Action Plan for the Single Market* (16 June 1999, hereinafter 'Mutual Recognition Communication') 4.

5 European Commission, *Financial Services: Implementing the Framework for Financial Markets: Action Plan* (COM(1999) 232, 11 May 1999, hereinafter 'FSAP') 17.

6 See European Commission, *Better Lawmaking 2000* (COM(2000) 772 final, 30 November 2000) 4.

7 See European Commission, *The Principle of Subsidiarity* (SEC(92) 1990 final, 27 October 1992) 1.

8 The positive concept of subsidiarity, on the other hand, represents the possibility or even the *obligation* of interventions from the Community, both aiming to fulfil and enhance human life; see Endo, K., 'The Principle of Subsidiarity: From Johannes Althusius to Jacques Delors' (1994) 6 Hokkaido Law Review 553.

9 See, e.g., Gretschmann, K., *The Subsidiarity Principle: Who is to do what in an Integrated Europe?* (Paper submitted to the Jacques Delors Colloquium 'Subsidiarity: The Challenge of Change', Maastricht, March 1991).

10 See, e.g., Schmidtchen, D. and Cooter, R., *Constitutional Law and Economics of the European Union* (Cheltenham: Edward Elgar, 1997). On the dilemma between centralisation and home country control, see Reich, N., 'Competition Between Legal Orders: A New Paradigm for EU Law?' (1992) 5 CMLRev 861, 865 *et seq. Per contra*, on the political feasibility of centralised regulation as well as on the possibility of dealing effectively with *sui generis* problems of international finance, see Cranston, R., *Principles of Banking Law* (Oxford: Oxford University Press, 1997) 116.

11 This idea builds upon a classic article by Tiebout (1956) on the optimal provision of local public goods, which can be specially relevant for the provision of financial services; see Bergh, R., 'The Subsidiarity Principle in European Community Law: Some Insights from Law and Economics' (1994) 1 Maastricht Journal of European and Comparative Law 337.

12 A relevant argument often advanced in legal literature is that of 'administrative efficiency'.

13 See Schmidtchen and Cooter, *op. cit.*, note 10, 151.

14 It is submitted that regulatory competition is the alteration of national regulation in response to the actual expected impact of internationally mobile goods, services, or factors on national economic activity; see Sun, J.M. and Pelkmans, J., 'Regulatory Competition in the Single Market' (1995) 1 JCMS 68.

15 Individual investors, e.g., may invest their capital in a country where the regulatory system produces a balance between risks and rewards that suits their preferences. See Snell, J. and Andenas, M., 'Exploring the Outer Limits-Restrictions on the Free Movement of Goods and Services' (1999) EBLR 252, 257–8.

16 Dalhuisen, J., 'Liberalisation and Re-Regulation of Cross-Border Financial Services: Part III' (1999) 9–10 EBLR 358.

17 See Porter, M., *The Competitive Advantage of Nations* (New York: Free Press, 1990) 648; Schmidt, H., 'Economic Analysis of the Allocation of Regulatory Competence in the European Communities', in Buxbaum, R. *et al.*, *European Business Law: Legal and Economic Analyses on Integration and Harmonisation* (Berlin: Walter de Gruyter, 1991) 55–7.

18 For a brief analysis of these advantages of regulatory competition, see Woolcock, S., 'Competition Among Rules in the Single European Market', in Bratton *et al.* (eds), *International Regulatory Competition and Coordination: Perspectives on Economic Regulation in Europe and the United States* (Oxford: Clarendon Press, 1996) 299.

19 For such a view, see Dalhuisen, *op. cit.*, note 16.
20 See note 11.
21 See Schmidtchen and Cooter, *op. cit.*, note 10, 150.
22 In the eurozone, e.g., entry into foreign markets in 1999 was still less than 10% on average in terms of banking assets. See Danthine, J. *et al.*, *The Future of European Banking* (London: Centre for Economic Policy Research, 1999) 33. For a set of paradigms, see Sun and Pelkmans, *op. cit.*, note 14, 81. We shall resist, however, from jumping to any generalised conclusion, since firms' responses inevitably vary from sector to sector and over time and can often acquire unpredictable and complex characteristics.
23 *Ibid.*, 76.
24 For a different view, see Woolcock, *op. cit.*, note 18, 294.
25 It is not implied herein, however, that for regulatory competition to function, a completely unharmonised set of national regulations is needed. This is another issue, which is beyond the scope of this analysis.
26 See Woolcock, *op. cit.*, note 18, 316. According to Woolcock, another reason that regulatory competition does not function within the Single Market is *enforcement*. Although the legislative programme set out in the White Paper has been more or less completed, Member States have only recently turned their attention to enforcement. No one can speak of a healthy competition among rules, until an effective system of enforcement of these rules is established across the EU.
27 See Hertig, G., 'Imperfect Mutual Recognition for EU Financial Services', in Buxbaum, R. *et al.*, *European Economic and Business Law: Legal and Economic Analysis on Integration and Harmonisation* (New York: Walter de Gruyter, 1996) 222. Hertig's arguments lie on the assumptions that pure mutual recognition (a) is a time-consuming process with high regulatory costs, (b) diminishes regulatory flexibility at the Member State level and (c) enhances enforcement, as Member States that are coerced into accepting too high an essential requirement may decide not to enforce the regulations.
28 Hayek, F.A., *New Studies in Philosophy, Politics, Economics and the History of Ideas* (Chicago: Chicago University Press, 1978) 188–9.
29 European Commission, *Second Biennial Report, op. cit.*, note 2, 13.
30 Hertig, *op. cit.*, note 27, 221.
31 For example, in CBR.
32 European Commission, *Internal Market Scoreboard No 9* (19 November 2001) 27–8; see also Annex II, Figure AII.1.
33 Usually the word 'arbitrage' or the 'law of one price' is used to define the non-speculative transfer of funds from one market to another to take advantage of differences in interest rates, exchange rates or commodity prices between the two markets; see *Oxford Dictionary of Business* (Oxford: Oxford University Press, 2nd ed., 1996). Here, however, 'regulatory arbitrage' shall refer to the establishment of an investment firm in the jurisdiction, which has the more favourable regulatory and supervisory standards, with the intention to commence business in another Member State with stricter rules, by use of the European passport.
34 The issue of public choice will be analysed below in Chapter 6, Section C.2.1.
35 Buchanan, J., *Liberty, Market and State: Political Economy in the 1980s* (Brighton: Wheatsheaf, 1986) 19.
36 *Ibid.*, 24–6.
37 For example, electoral campaign contributions by the regulated or avoidance of industry financed opposition; See Stigler, G., 'The Theory of Economic Regulation'

(1971) 2 Bell Journal of Economics 3, 10–13; Siebert, H. and Koop., M., 'Institutional Competition versus Centralisation: Quo Vadis Europe?' (1993) Oxford Review of Economic Policy 15, 18.

38 For a different view, see Licht, A., 'Regulatory Arbitrage for Real: International Securities Regulation in a World of Interacting Securities Markets' (1998) 38 Virginia Journal of International Law 563, 636

39 See Sun and Pelkmans, *op. cit.*, note 14, 77.

40 If companies struggle to face antagonism, they are likely to cut wages or even move towards reductions in employment. Particularly in large financial institutions, the effects would be severe.

41 ISD, Recital 4. *Cf.* SBD, Recital 8.

42 See Case 205/84 *Commission v Germany* [1986] ECR 3755, Paragraph 22; Case C-148/91 *Veronica* [1993] ECR I-487, Paragraph 12; Case C-23/93 *TV 10* [1994] ECR I-4795, Paragraph 15 and Opinion of Advocate General Lenz, Paragraphs 56 and 68; Case C-56/96 *VT 4* [1997] ECR I-3143, Paragraph 21; see also Case C-212/97 *Centros* [1999] ECR I-1459, Opinion of Advocate General La Pergola, Paragraph 18, where the Court applied its case law on circumvention developed in the context of the freedom to provide services.

43 *Securities and Investment Board v Scandex Capital Management A/S and another* [1998] 1 All ER 514, CA.

44 Prior to 1 January 1996 and the implementation of the ISD, there was no legislation in Denmark that regulated the carrying on of investment business in that country.

45 The problem may be intensified if companies choose to be established under the European company status; see Chapter 6, Section C.5.2.2.

46 Beginning with the Code Napoleon in 1804 and the Code de Commerce of 1807, the French codes applied in the codification of Belgium, Luxembourg, the Netherlands, Italy, Spain and Portugal. The Prussian and Bavarian codes of 1794 and 1756 respectively influenced codification in Austria. Finally, the German Civil Code of 1896 was almost copied by the Greek Civil Law in 1946.

47 England, Wales and Ireland did not embark upon the process of codification. They rather distanced themselves from continental Europe and pursued a common law approach.

48 The Nordic group of EU countries have framed their statutes on comparative law and, therefore, reflect the general concepts and doctrine of continental Europe, but in a more cooperative manner, which has led to highly homogenous rules.

49 'Cold-calling' refers to the provision of financial services without prior solicitation.

50 Law No 72–6 *relative au démarchage financier et a des opérations de placement et d'assurance* (3 January 1972).

51 *Ibid.*, Article 7.

52 *Ibid.*, Articles 10 and 11.

53 See Case C-384/93 *Alpine Investments* [1995] ECR I-1141. For an analysis of the case, see Andenas, M., 'Cross border cold-calling and the right to provide services' (1995) 8 Company Lawyer 249.

54 The new consultative document issued by CESR on the harmonisation of CBR has incorporated for the first time issues regarding cold-calling; see CESR, *Standards and Rules for Harmonising Core Conduct of Business Rules for Investor Protection* (CESR/01-014, 18 October 2001). Current negotiations at the Council and EP level on the Distance Marketing Directive envisage leaving the option to individual Member States to authorise cold-calling on the basis of either opt-in (prior consent by consumer) and opt-out mechanisms (express objection by consumer).

55 See European Commission, *amended Proposal for a Directive concerning the distance marketing of consumer financial services* (COM(1999) 375 final, 23 July 1999, hereinafter 'Distance Marketing Directive'). Article 10(2) provides for special arrangements concerning communications not solicited by consumers.

56 See Hertig, G., 'Regulatory Competition for EU Financial Services' (2000) 2 Journal of International Economic Law 349, 357.

57 Naturally, this analysis is interested in 'real' rather than 'superficial' differences between national legal principles. Market participants may be indifferent to divergent legal formulations provided they lead to outcomes, which match their preferences. For example, it matters not whether a tort claim for pure economic loss will be rejected because there is 'no duty of care' (English law) or because it is *'dommage indirecte'* (French law). The result is the same. See Ogus, A., 'Competition Between National Legal Systems: A Contribution of Economic Analysis to Comparative Law' (1999) 48 ICLQ 405, 409.

58 Such contracts are only binding for private investors if they have previously been informed about the risks of such transactions through a written communication accompanied by oral explanations if necessary. See Horn, N., 'The Monetary Union and the Internal Market for Banking and Investment Services', in J.J. Norton (ed.), *Yearbook of International Financial and Economic Law 1998* (London: Kluwer, 1999) 141.

59 Case 15/78 *Koestler* [1978] ECR 1971. *Koestler* concerned the application of the German Stock Exchange Act, which perceived futures contracts as wagering agreements, to a series of stock exchanges speculative agreements, entered to France by a German national. Although French law regarded futures contracts as legal investment activity, the ECJ decided that the contract was void because the German rules applied in a non-discriminatory way.

60 On these divergences see Horn, *op. cit.*, note 58.

61 See Committee of Wise Men, *Final Report on the Regulation of European Securities Markets* (15 February 2001) 11.

62 Indeed, there is no relevant provision in the Proposal for a Distance Marketing Directive.

63 See Majone, G., *Regulating Europe* (London: Routledge, 1996) 280.

64 See Sutherland, P. *et al.*, *Internal Market after 1992 – Meeting the Challenge: Report to the EEC Commission* (Brussels, 1992).

65 Although the Report accepted that in most areas enforcement must continue to be centralised, for some matters a more centralised regime has been found necessary. However, this issue will be analysed later in Chapter 7.

66 See the annual 'Better Lawmaking' report, the most recent of which is COM(2001) 728 final, 7 December 2001; also the annual Report on the functioning of Community product and capital markets, the most recent of which is COM(2001) 736 final, 7 December 2001.

67 The term 'competent' shall refer to the extent to which the relevant supervisor will be capable of undertaking adequate supervision, rather than to the question whether it has been appointed appropriate legal power to undertake such a task. See Lee, R., 'Supervising EU Capital Markets: Do we need a European SEC?' in Buxbaum *et al.*, *op. cit.*, note 27, 196.

68 See Chapter 4, Section C.2.

69 See Mutual Recognition Communication, 6. For banking services, see European Commission, Freedom to provide services and the interest of the general good in the Second Banking Directive (Interpretative Communication, SEC(97) 1193 final, 20 June 1997, hereinafter '1997 Banking Communication') 3. For insurance

services, see European Commission, *Freedom to Provide Services and the General Good in the Insurance Sector* (Interpretative Communication, C(1999)5046, 2 February 2000, hereinafter '1999 Insurance Communication') 1. The Commission has also found differences in the core concept 'fit and proper'; see European Commission, *Financial Services: Building a Framework for Action* (COM(1998) 625, 28 October 1998) 11.

70 Welby, J., 'Do Business Ethics Matter' (1992) 3 International Company and Commercial Law Review 46.

71 Majone, *op. cit.*, note 63.

72 ISD, Article 1(6).

73 See the issues arising from the *SIB v Scandex* case in Section 1.1.

74 It is stated in the Preamble that 'Member States must require that an investment firm's head office must always be situated in its home Member State and that it actually operates there'; see ISD, Recital 4.

75 This interpretation offers a solution to the Commission's worry that firms would choose to set up a head office in a Member State, which is considered to have the least stringent regulatory requirements, but would then do most of their business in another Member State, thus encouraging 'regulatory arbitrage'. The ECJ has acknowledged that a host Member State is entitled to take steps to prevent a service provider whose activity is entirely or mainly directed towards its territory from improperly exercising the freedom to provide services of Article 49 EC (formerly Article 59) in order to circumvent the rules of professional conduct, which would be applicable to him if he were established in the territory of that host State. See cases in note 42.

76 ISD, Article 3(1).

77 It is interesting to note that if the investment firm has a registered office, it must have its head office in the same Member State as its registered office; ISD, Article 3(2).

78 See European Commission, *Proposal for a Directive on the supplementary supervision of credit institutions, insurance undertakings and investment firms in a financial conglomerate and amending Council Directives 73/239/EEC, 79/267/EEC, 92/49/EEC, 92/96/EEC, 93/6/EEC, 93/22/EEC, and Directives 98/78/EC and 2000/12/EC of the Parliament and the Council* (COM(2001) 213 final, 24 April 2001).

79 See, e.g., Haines, G., 'The Investment Services Directive: Progress to Date' (1995) EFSL 30, 31; Dassesse, M. *et al.*, *EC Banking Law* (London: Lloyds, 2nd ed., 1994) 61; Abrams, C., 'The Investment Services Directive – Who Should Be the Principal Regulator of Cross-Border Services?' (1995) 2 EFSL 317.

80 See Dassesse *et al.*, *ibid.*, Paragraphs 4.6 *et seq.* and 7.5.

81 These could be described as 'indirect' rules of conduct. See, e.g., Directive 97/7/EC of 20 May 1997 *on the protection of consumers in respect of distance contracts* (OJ L 144/19, 4 June 1997) and Directive 97/55/EC of 6 October 1997 *concerning misleading advertising so as to include comparative advertising* (OJ L 290/18, 23 October 1997).

82 Hertig, *op. cit.*, note 27, 224.

83 The Hellenic Capital Market Commission, e.g., has received a number of complaints incorporated in the notification of non-Greek financial firms wishing to provide cross-border business in Greece; Interview with Eleftheria Apostolidou, Head of Division of International Relations and Monitoring of International Developments, CMC (26 June 2000).

84 Opinion delivered by Advocate General Jacobs in Case C-136/00 *Rolf Dieter Danner* [not yet reported], Paragraph 32.

85 See ISD, Recital 33. Similarly, see SBD, Recital 16, and Third Insurance Directives (92/49/EC and 92/96/EC), Recitals 19 and 20 respectively.

86 Preferring to maintain its progressive nature, the ECJ has never given a definition too.

87 See 1997 Banking Communication, 17.

88 According to the Article 'Member States shall ensure that this Directive is implemented without discrimination'.

89 This requirement constitutes an echo of the ECJ judgement C-205/84 *op. cit.*, note 42, Paragraph 27. Also *cf.* Article 11(3) ISD, 'Where an investment firm executes an order (...) the professional nature of the investor shall be assessed with respect to the investor from whom the order originates', which implies that the host State's CBR should take account of the position of wholesale investors. For the distinction between wholesale and retail investors, see also Section 2.2.4.2.

90 Pursuant to this Article, 'Member States may not make the establishment of a branch or the provision of services (...) subject to any authorisation requirement, to any requirement to provide endowment capital or to any other measure having equivalent effect'.

91 The two Articles are similarly drafted. Article 17(4), e.g., provides that 'the competent authorities of the host Member State shall (...) prepare for the supervision of the investment firm (...) and, if necessary, indicate the conditions, including the rules of conduct, under which, in the interest of the general good, that business must be carried on in the host Member State'.

92 A similar statement is provided in ISD, Recital 41. Thorkildsen contends that Article 13 ISD, which states that host Member States may take measures governing the form and content of advertising subject to the interest of the general good, should also be taken into consideration; see Thorkildsen, T., 'Power to Draw Up Conduct of Business Rules After the ISD' (1995) 15 Company Lawyer 102, 104.

93 In particular the use of the word 'other' in the provision.

94 See Wouters, J., 'Rules of Conduct, Foreign Investment Firms and the ECJ's Case Law on Services' (1993) 13 Company Lawyer 194, 195, arguing that the 'formulation of Article 19(6) seems to indicate that a host Member State can enforce any rule of conduct, as long as it has been introduced pursuant to (the very broadly formulated) art 11'.

95 See Preamble to the ISD, Recitals 1–4 and 28.

96 *Ibid.*, Recital 33. This is similar to Recital 16 of the SBD. As to the controversy regarding the latter see Wouters, J., 'Conflict of Laws and the Single Market for Financial Services (Part I)' (1997) 2 Maastricht Journal of European and Comparative Law 161, 185.

97 See Case C-76/90 *Säger* [1991] ECR I-4221, Paragraph 15. See also the analysis contained in the Commission interpretative Communication concerning the free movement of services across frontiers (OJ C 334, 9 December 1993) 3.

98 See Case 71/76 *Thieffry* [1977] ECR 765, Paragraph 12; Case C-55/94 *Gebhard* [1995] ECR I-4165, Paragraph 35.

99 Case 120/78 *Rewe-Zentral* [1979] ECR 649.

100 *Ibid.*, Paragraph 8(2). This is the so-called rule of reason.

101 *Ibid.*, Paragraph 14(3).

102 Case C-76/90, *op. cit.*, note 97, Paragraph 12.

103 See Case 279/80 *Webb* [1981] ECR 3305, Paragraph 16; Case C-205/84, *op. cit.*, note 42, Paragraph 39.

104 See Joined Cases C-267/91 and C-268/91 *Keck* [1993] ECR I-6097, Paragraphs 13–7.

105 *Ibid.*, Paragraph 15.

106 *Ibid.*, Paragraph 16.

107 Thorkildsen argues that CBR seem to be more equivalent to the former 'rules for the sale' and, therefore, fall outside the Treaty provisions. See Thorkildsen, *op. cit.*, note 92, 107.

108 *Ibid.*, 107–8.

109 1997 Banking Communication, 19. For these rules to be enforceable, however, some additional conditions may need to be met.

110 The ECJ has recognised the difference in the service by imposing a less restrictive and more 'lightweight' legal framework for provision of services than for establishment. It held in *Säger* that a Member State 'may not make the provision of services in its territory subject to compliance with all the conditions required for establishment and thereby deprive of all practical effectiveness the provisions of the Treaty whose object is, precisely, to guarantee the freedom to provide services'. See also Case C-198/89 *Commission v Greece* [1991] ECR I-727, Paragraph 16.

111 Case 205/84, *op. cit.*, note 42.

112 See Opinion delivered by Advocate General Jacobs in Case C-136/00, *op. cit.*, note 84, Paragraph 40.

113 The text of the Treaty (Article 49) does not refer to discrimination but speaks generally of 'restrictions on freedom to provide services'.

114 Case C-410/96 *Ambry* [1998] ECR I-7875, Paragraphs 25–39.

115 See Tison, M., *Unravelling the General Good Exception: The Case of Financial Services* (Financial Law Institute WP 2000-03, Gent University, 2000) 25. Tison is also concerned with the question whether the host State may impose upon the foreign firm a prior control on the compatibility of financial products with its mandatory contract law before taking up financial activity in the host State with use of the single passport.

116 The Commission's guidance is actually nothing but that; although based on ECJ case law, it constitutes only an interpretative tool and is neither a law in itself nor a Directive requiring Member States to comply with it.

117 For credit institutions, see 1997 Banking Communication, 14. For insurance undertakings, see 1999 Insurance Communication, 14. The Commission has been very sensitive with host Member States' measures derogating from the principles of home country control and mutual recognition. It has insisted, therefore, for the transparency of national measures, which would make it easier to deal quickly and at the appropriate level with problems, which may jeopardise the free movement of goods and services. See Parliament and Council, *Decision No 3052/95/EC establishing a procedure for the exchange of information on national measures derogating from the principle of the free movement of goods within the Community* (OJ L 321/1, 30 December 1995). Article 1 of the decision states that 'where a Member State takes steps to prevent the free movement or placing on the market of a particular model or type of product lawfully produced or marketed in another Member State, it shall notify the Commission accordingly (...)'.

118 Case C-11/95 *Commission v Belgium* [1996] ECR I-4115, Paragraph 34.

119 Council Directive 89/552/EEC of 3 October 1989 *on the coordination of certain provisions laid down by Law, Regulation or Administrative Action in Member States concerning the pursuit of television broadcasting activities* (OJ L 298/23, 17 October 1989).

120 Pursuant to Article 227, 'a Member State which considers that another Member State has failed to fulfil an obligation under this Treaty may bring the matter before the Court of Justice. Before a Member State brings an action against

another Member State for an alleged infringement of an obligation under this Treaty, it shall bring the matter before the Commission (...)'.

121 ISD, Articles 1(1) and 2(1).

122 *Ibid.*, Article 11(1).

123 See Briault, C., *The Rationale for a Single National Financial Services Regulator* (FSA Occasional Paper No. 2, May 1999) 24.

124 ISD, Article 10, first indent.

125 *Ibid.*, Article 11(1), sixth indent.

126 Article 12(1) Royal Decree of 20 December 1995.

127 See ISD, Article 10, fifth indent. Although this provision states that each home Member State shall draw up prudential rules to be observed 'at all times', as to the structure and organisation of the firm 'in such a way as to minimise the risk of clients' interests being prejudiced by conflicts of interest', it is added that where a branch is set up, 'the organisational arrangements may not conflict with the rules of conduct laid down by the host Member State to cover conflicts of interest'.

128 *Ibid.*, Article 11(1), sixth indent.

129 *Ibid.*, Article 10, fifth indent.

130 See Thorkildsen, *op. cit.*, note 92, 105. The author argues that there might be a lesser degree of overlap if the host State could only draw CBR when justified by the general good. Therefore, the narrower interpretation of a host State's power should prevail.

131 For such a view, see Grundman, S. and Kerber, W., *Information Intermediaries and Extending the Area of Informed Party Autonomy – Securities and Insurance Markets* (Paper submitted at the Conference 'Party Autonomy for the Internal Market', King's College London, 11–13 May 2000).

132 European Commission, *Recommendation 77/534/EEC of 25 July 1977 concerning a European code of conduct relating to transactions in transferable securities* (OJ L 212/37, 20 August 1977).

133 In many countries, CBR have been introduced with the implementation of the ISD; see Annex I, Table AI.2.

134 Lomnicka, E., 'The Single European Passport in Financial Services', in Rider, B. and Andenas, M. (eds), *Developments in European Community Law Vol. 1/1996* (London: Kluwer, 1997) 198–9.

135 It follows, *per contra*, from Article 11(1), that, unlike its regime on prudential rules, which pursuant to Article 10 have to be drawn up by each home Member State, the ISD assigns the task of drawing up rules of conduct to 'Member States' generally.

136 On the contrary, the addition that these rules must be observed by the firms 'at all times' seems to lend support to such continuing application; see ISD, Article 11(1).

137 See Act on the Supervision of the Securities Trade (*Besluit Toezicht Effectenverkeer*), Articles 34–9.

138 See Article 35(2) Law of 5 April 1993, as amended by Law of 12 March 1998.

139 See in particular Adams, G., 'The Single Market in Financial Services – An Orwellian Approach' (1996) 3 EFSL 149, who recounts the following experience of Midland bank: 'for our Swedish branch we asked the SFA if we could follow local rules and practice for [client money and customer asset rules]. SFA determined (accurately) that the Swedish requirements did not match the UK ones. So we were left with the option of exporting more onerous client money and customer asset rules to a country where our competition did not have to bear this regulatory and cost burden'.

140   Lambrecht, P. and Haljan, D., 'Investor Protection and the European Directives concerning Securities', in Houtte, H. (ed.), *The Law of Cross-Border Securities Transactions* (London: Sweet & Maxwell, 1999) 260. The authors use the paradigm of differentiated investor/consumer standards across the EU and of diverse treatment of the notions of 'investors' and 'consumers'. Indeed, not all safeguards and presumptions applying to consumers do necessarily apply to investors as well. In addition, they allege that the definition of 'consumer' for the purposes of the Brussels and Rome Conventions, having an autonomous EU interpretation, apply only for the purposes of these Conventions. There is no single EU definition of 'consumer' in the securities directives, except in the proposed Distance Marketing Directive; Article 2(d) simply defines 'consumer' as 'any natural person who, in contracts covered by this Directive, is acting for purposes which are outside his trade, business or profession'.

141   In its Second Consultation for the ISD II, the Commission proposes an extensive revisit of Article 11 so as to rectify its ambiguities and to provide an effective basis for supervision of firm–client relationships in the future; see European Commission, *Revision of the ISD: Second Consultation* (25 March 2002, hereinafter '2nd ISD II Consultation') 24.

142   See FSAP, 5. The EP strongly suggests that the ultimate goal should be the situation where all cross-border investment services are subject only to the conduct of business and advertising rules of the home State; see European Parliament, *Report on the Commission Communication on the application of conduct of business rules under article 11 of the investment services directive* (A5-0105/2001, 23 March 2001) 7.

143   See also ISD, Recital 32, which states that 'whereas one of the objectives of this Directive is to protect investors; whereas it is therefore appropriate to take account of the different requirements for protection of various categories of investors and of their level of professional expertise'.

144   In countries such as Belgium, CBR are considerably extended applying for both retail and wholesale transactions, contrary to the spirit of Article 11(1); see Wymeersch, E., 'The Implementation of the ISD and CAD in National Legal Systems', in Ferrarini, G. (ed.), *European Securities Markets: The Investment Services Directive and Beyond* (London: Kluwer, 1998) 36.

145   This does not mean that professional investors should not be subject to any CBR at all, but that there is no need in such situations for the full range of detailed rules. This can also be deducted from the wording of Article 11(1), which makes no such comprehensive exemption even with respect to the most sophisticated institutional investors. Even though the 'principles' call for differentiation, they are still mandatory law; see Kondgen, J., 'Rules of Conduct: Further Harmonisation?' in Ferrarini, *ibid.*, 128. For a different view, see Cruickshank, C., 'The Investment Services Directive', in Wymeersch, E. (ed.), *Further Perspectives in Financial Integration in Europe* (Berlin: Walter de Gruyter, 1994) 76, who alleges that 'existing wholesale business should therefore be free to operate at present without the imposition of unnecessary and administratively burdensome conduct of business rules'.

146   In contrast to investment services, the most substantial increase in cross-border banking activity and integration has taken place in wholesale activities. For example, the currency-based segmentation of the markets for unsecured interbank deposits disappeared very rapidly after the introduction of the euro; see Duisenberg, W., *The Future of Banking Supervision and the Integration of Financial*

Markets (Speech delivered at the conference 'Improving Integration of Financial Markets in Europe', Turin, 22 May 2000).

147 The broadening of the market size and increasing share of cross-border wholesale transactions has a positive impact on financial stability. If there were only a few market participants, the likelihood of a financial firm failure having stronger repercussions on the viability of other institutions would be greater. See *ibid.*

148 European Commission, *Communication on the Application of Conduct of Business Rules Under Article 11 of the Investment Services Directive (93/22EEC)* (16 November 2000) 18.

149 FESCO, *Implementation of Article 11 of the ISD: Categorisation of Investors for the Purpose of Conduct of Business Rules* (15 March 2000). FESCO has also recently fulfilled its commitment to draft standards defining the CBR regime that will apply to inter-professional relationships; See FESCO, *Standards and Rules for Harmonising Core Conduct of Business Rules for Investor Protection* (Consultative Paper, February 2001), and the follow up paper (CESR/01-014, 18 October 2001).

150 See 2nd ISD II Consultation, Annex I, 16–17.

151 Generally speaking, a three-tier classification would distinguish between *de facto* professionals, *de jure* or semi-professionals and non-professionals. This approach offers a better tailoring of requirements and minimises the cost of transitional arrangements for firms.

152 See *Communication on the Application of Conduct of Business Rules, op. cit.*, note 148, 19.

153 Advertising refers to 'the making of a representation in any form in connection with a trade, business, craft or profession in order to promote the supply of goods or services, including immovable property, rights and obligations'; see Council Directive 84/450/EEC of 10 September 1984 *relating to the approximation of the laws, regulations and administrative provisions of the Member States concerning misleading advertising* (OJ L 250/17, 19 September 1984). See also Article 2(f) of Council Directive 2000/31/EC *on certain legal aspects of information society services, in particular electronic commerce, in the Internal Market* (OJ L 178/1, 17 July 2000, hereinafter 'E-Commerce Directive'), which defines the notion of 'commercial communication'.

154 See Case C-384/93, *op. cit.*, note 53, Opinion of Advocate General Jacobs, Paragraph 55.

155 See Snell and Andenas, *op. cit.*, note 15, 265; Chalmers, D. and Szyszczak, E., *European Union Law. Volume II. Towards a European Policy?* (Ashgate: Aldershot, 1998) 304. The host country may experience difficulties in enforcing its rules as regards services moving, e.g., by telecommunications or by post. For the notion of 'selling arrangements', see Weatherill, S., 'After Keck: Some Thoughts on How to Clarify the Clarification' (1996) 33 CMLRev 885, 894.

156 Snell and Andenas, note 15.

157 Beyond marketing rules, traditionally there are different legal practices relating to them. A single financial services contract, e.g., may be subject to different legal treatment in different Member States.

158 See Kondgen, *op. cit.*, note 145, 127.

159 To date, EU marketing law covers misleading advertising with Directive 84/450/EC, *op. cit.*, note 153, and doorstep selling with Council Directive 85/577/EEC of 20 December 1985 (OJ L 372/31, 31 December 1985). The solicitation of customers at a distance by means of technology and telecommunications will be regulated by the Proposed Distance Marketing Directive.

160 *Ibid.*, Recital 8.
161 The same applies to the Proposed Distance Marketing Directive, which refers to 'Member States' in general.
162 ISD, Article 14(1). *Cf.* SBD, Article 20.
163 Dalhuisen, *op. cit.*, note 16, 365.
164 See Chapter 3, Section E.1.3.
165 Case C-55/94, *op. cit.*, note 98, Paragraph 27; see also Case C-221/89 *Factortame* [1991] ECR I-3905, Paragraph 20: 'the concept of establishment within the meaning of Article 52 [now Article 43] *et seq.* of the Treaty involves the actual pursuit of an economic activity through a fixed establishment in another Member State for an indefinite period'. See also Chapter 2, Section D.3.1.
166 Case 205/84, *op. cit.*, note 42.
167 See 1997 Banking Communication, 6. The Commission's Communication is not a ruling or soft law to be legally binding. However, it is supposed to play a persuasive role in the interpretation of the SBD. Although not directly applicable, the Communication may offer guidance for the interpretation of the ISD and the insurance Directives as well. Regarding the former, although the work of the drafters of the 1997 Communication was intended to cover only the SBD and not the ISD, it would not be unreasonable to approach the ISD using similar arguments; see Cruickshank, C., 'Is there a Need to Harmonise Conduct of Business Rules?' in Ferrarini, *op. cit.*, note 144, 132. Regarding the latter, see 1999 Insurance Communication.
168 The notion of 'characteristic performance' seems to owe its origin to Article 4(1) and (2) of the Contracts Convention of Rome (OJ L 266/1, 19 June 1980); see Wouters, *op. cit.*, note 96, 178; Dalhuisen, *op. cit.*, note 16, 355. However, its analysis is not within the scope of this paper. For this purpose, see Kondgen, *op. cit.*, note 145, 126. Eventually, the ECJ case law will have to interpret this approach and determine whether it is the right one in the context of provision of services.
169 Besides, the interpretation given by the Communication does not necessarily represent the often very divergent views put forward by the Member States and should not, in themselves, impose any new obligation on them. See 1997 Banking Communication, 3. Regarding civil-law sanctions, e.g., the Commission takes the view that the notification procedure should not affect the validity of a banking contract. Indeed, such a view can be supported only by Member States, the law of which upholds the principle that a simple agreement of the parties is sufficient to establish a contract (e.g., Greece, Germany, France).
170 *Ibid.*, 7. The Commission acknowledges that this solution will require a case-by-case analysis, which could prove difficult.
171 *Ibid.*
172 See 1997 Banking Communication, 16.
173 It may be suggested that the supply of information to service providers be compulsory for host regulators, at least with regard to references to the national legislation that applies to financial activities. However, taken that certain supervisory houses may face difficulties in compiling exhaustive lists of all the general-good-type rules and in keeping such lists up to date, it seems important that there should be a continued effort to harmonise these rules at EU level.
174 1999 Insurance Communication, 15.
175 See Council Directive 88/357/EEC, Articles 14, 16 and 17, as amended by Council Directive 92/49/EEC, Articles 34, 35 and 36 (non-life insurance), and Council Directive 90/619/EEC, Articles 11, 14 and 17, as amended by Council Directive

92/96 EEC, Articles 34, 35 and 36 (life insurance). This rests on the assumption that whenever an insurance firm agrees to sell its products to an individual, who resides in a country different from the firm's country of incorporation, there is automatically a provision of service by the insurer 'within' the Member State of residence of the client; see Dassesse, M., 'The Regulatory Implications of the Location of Financial Services Under EU Law' (2001) 10 JIBFL 473, 475.

176 1999 Insurance Communication, 17.

177 (COM(1999) 88 final of 25 February 1999).

178 1997 Banking Communication, 8.

179 In *Säger* as well as in the *Unborn Children* case, the Court was strongly urged by Advocates General to apply the *Cassis de Dijon* principle, an analogy that is most appropriate where neither the provider nor the client but the service moves physically between Member States. See Opinion of Advocate General Jacobs in Case C-76/90 *Säger* [1991] ECR I-4221, Paragraph 20; Opinion of Advocate General Van Gerven in Case C-159/90 *Unborn Children* [1991] ECR I-4685, Paragraph 20. Roth notes that the Court's ruling in *Säger* clearly employs the *Cassis de Dijon* reasoning; see Roth, W.H., 'Annotation in Case C-79/90 Manfred Säger v Dennemeyer & Co. Ltd.' (1993) 1 CMLRev 145, 152.

180 1997 Banking Communication, 19.

181 See, e.g., the German Insurance case, Case 205/84, *op. cit.*, note 42, Paragraph 30. The Court recognises that the protection of a consumer, both as a policy-holder and as an insured person, constitutes an 'imperative requirement' and could thus justify derogations from Article 49 EC. On this aspect of the German Insurance case, see Zavvos, G., 'Banking Integration and 1992: Legal Issues and Policy Implications' (1990) 2 Harvard International Law Journal 463, 485; Edward, D., 'Establishment and Services: An Analysis of the Insurance Cases' (1987) ELRev 231, 245–6; Lasok, K.P., 'Freedom to Provide Insurance Services in the Light of the Co-insurance Cases' (1988) Modern Law Review 706, 727–30.

182 Abolishment is unlikely, as the Commission, in its latest consultation for the ISD II, purports to retain the notification arrangements in respect of commencing cross-border provision of services for the first time and of branch establishment. The Commission's justification is that the notification procedure was not called into question by respondents to its consultation; see 2nd ISD II Consultation, 25.

183 Also known as proprietary trading systems (PTSs), electronic communication networks (ECNs), market services providers (MSPs) or simply electronic trading platforms, these quasi-exchanges are screen-based automated systems, run by broker-dealers as for-profit businesses, which produce in-house matching of buying and selling orders in either exchange-listed or OTC securities. See London Stock Exchange, *Competing Market Mechanisms – Their Effect on the Rules of the London Stock Exchange* (Consultative Paper, September 1995).

184 Although online securities trading is widely used in the United States (the number of households engaged jumped 30% between May 1999 and January 2000, from 2.7 to 3.5 million), online EU brokerages are only recent entrants to e-financial commerce; 65% of them started business less than two years ago and only 20% have more than two years experience; see European Commission, *Progress on Financial Services: 2nd Report* (COM(2000) 336, 31 May 2000) 6.

185 See Wisbey, G., 'The Challenge of Technology – Regulation of Electronic Financial Markets' (Speech delivered at the conference 'The Challenges facing Financial Regulation', Cambridge, 6–7 July 2000).

186 The term 'information universe' means the changing landscape of financial markets globally in the face of rapidly evolving information technology. See Tanzer, G., 'Developing Uniform Standards to Allow a Global Passport for Mutual Funds – IOSCO's Role' (2000) 5 International Business Lawyer 229, 234.

187 See 2nd Progress Report, *op. cit.*, note 184, 5.

188 Avgouleas, E., 'The Harmonisation of Rules of Conduct in EU Financial Markets: Economic Analysis, Subsidiarity and Investor Protection' (2000) 1 ELJ 72, 79.

189 See Section 2.3.2. Although it hardly clears the confusion, the banking 'characteristic performance' test leads to the assumption that the provision of banking services via the Internet does not result in the provision of services by the financial firm 'within' the Member State of residence of the client; see Dassesse, *op. cit.*, note 175, 474.

190 *European Parliament and Council Directive 2000/31/EC on certain aspects of information society services, in particular electronic commerce, in the Internal Market* (OJ L 178/1, 17 July 2000), Article 3(1).

191 These derogations fall into two categories: general and specific case-by-case derogations. See *ibid.*, Annex and Article 3(4–6) respectively. Importantly, the Directive does not apply to insurance services, the advertising of UCITS and it does not affect the party autonomy to choose the law applicable to their contract. In the latter case, the Rome Convention will determine the law.

192 European Commission, *op. cit.*, note 148.

193 European Commission, *Communication on E-Commerce and Financial Services* (9 February 2001) 12.

194 The only reference to the type of activity carried out by ATS (in-house matching) is made in Recital 13: '(...) the business of the reception and transmission of orders also includes bringing together two or more investors thereby bringing about a transaction between those investors'.

195 The differences between Member States approach to ATS are significant. In Italy, e.g., ATS are not subject to licence requirements at all. In Spain, an ATS has to be approved by the government in a procedure similar to that of an exchange. In Portugal, the legal and regulatory framework only distinguishes between regulated and non-regulated markets. Finally, if an ATS were to apply to Greece, the regulatory authorities would address the application on a tailor-made basis. See FESCO, *The Regulation of Alternative Trading Systems in Europe: A paper for the EU Commission* (September 2000) 8.

196 The ISD II is likely to include the operation of an ATS as a new core ISD activity; see 2nd ISD II Consultation, 12.

197 See FESCO, *op. cit.*, note 195, 12–14.

198 ATS will be allowed to be authorised as appropriately licensed investment firms at their discretion; see 2nd ISD II Consultation, 13.

199 Electronic criminal activity or 'cybercrime' may include activities such as money laundering, market manipulation, or price manipulation, where operations are frequently on the borderline of lawfulness.

200 See Conti, C., 'The Impact of New Technologies on the Financial Services Industry' (1997) 11 EFSL 284.

201 Especially when using the Internet, perpetrators of investment fraud can easily move both the *sites* location and the *target* location of their operations from one jurisdiction to another, or send the same message to multiple jurisdictions simultaneously.

202 These include, *inter alia*, the Stock Market Fraud 'Survivor' checklist, tips to avoid Internet investment scams, and consumer alerts on cyberfraud. The SEC and the

NASD actively investigate allegations of Internet investment fraud and, in many cases, have taken quick action to stop scams in cooperation with federal and state criminal authorities.

203 See IOSCO, *Report on Enforcement Issues Raised by the increasing Use of Electronic Networks in the Securities and Futures Field* (September 1997); IOSCO, *Report on Securities Activity on the Internet II* (June 2001).

204 *Ibid.* See also IOSCO, *Securities Activity on the Internet* (September 1998) Part IV.

205 See, e.g., Woolfson, P., 'Electronic Commerce and the Single Market in Financial Services in Europe: What Changes for Success?' (1997) 4 Journal of Financial Regulation and Compliance 306, 312.

206 That is the view of the European Commission. See 1997 Banking Communication, 7, and 1999 Insurance Communication, 18. The Commission believes that such a link could lead to the anomalous situation where a bank or insurance firm could find itself invited to notify the authorities of all the Member States, in which its advertising could in theory be received, although the undertaking may not be planning to pursue its activities in these Member States.

207 See Section 2.3.2.

208 A potential client of a financial firm may easily declare false identification, residence or nationality on an Internet web site, since, in most cases, this is the only prerequisite for registration. In this way, the client could prevent the potential refusal of the undertaking to provide its services, in case he resides in a Member State with which the undertaking has not established a notification link.

209 Either as a member thereof or as a financial firm, which has been given access to this market; see ISD, Article 15(2) and 15(4).

210 Euronext is the new pan-European exchange created by the merger of Paris Bourse SA, Amsterdam Exchanges, Brussels Exchanges and Lisbon Exchanges.

211 According to Article 3(s), one of the activities of the Community is 'the association of the overseas countries and territories in order to increase trade and promote jointly economic and social development'. The Treaty contains two instruments for the regulation of the EU's external relations. First, agreements with third countries in the field of commercial policy (Article 133), and second, association agreements (Article 310). In the current context, the questions of the Community's obligations under international agreements is very much tied in with the progress – or lack of progress – in the WTO/GATS negotiations. Since January 2000, over 140 WTO member governments have been engaged in negotiations aimed at further liberalisation of the global services market.

212 Although 'reciprocity' does not have an undisputable legal meaning, the essence of this concept is arguably equal trade opportunities; see Curzon, G. and Curzon, V., 'Non-discrimination and the Rise of Material Reciprocity' (1989) World Economy 481, 488; Stuyck, J., *Financial and Monetary Integration in the European Economic Community: Legal, Institutional and Economic Aspects* (Deventer: Kluwer Law, 1993) 101.

213 See Hoskins, M., 'EEC Banking Law: Plugging the Gaps' (1992) 1 Journal of International Banking Law 56, 58.

214 Major non-EU banks and investment firms were already established in the EU before the launch of the home country control programme. See Hoschka, T., *Cross-Border Entry in European Retail Financial Services: Determinants, Regulation and the Impact on Competition* (New York: St Martin's Press, 1993) 19–24. In addition, efforts for further harmonisation outside the EU have hardly been initiated

by the EU. For example, the requirements for the ownership of capital by banks, which have set standards for the capitalisation of banks observed in many countries outside the EU, have been worked out by the Basel Committee.

215 On the differences between EU and WTO/GATS rules applied for the localisation of financial services, see Dassesse, *op. cit.*, note 175, 473.

216 See Horn, *op. cit.*, note 5, 152; Thieffry, G. and Walsh, J., 'Securitisation: The New Opportunities Offered by Economic and Monetary Union' (1997) 12 JIBL 463.

217 ISD, Recital 31.

218 Here is where the role and work of international organisation, such as IOSCO, Basel and IASC, becomes extremely useful and important.

219 This mirrors the *de facto* view of the United Kingdom, confirmed by the recent Treasury's White Paper; see HM Treasury, *Realising Europe's Potential: Economic Reform in Europe* (White Paper, February 2002) 81.

220 This is also the belief of the Economic and Social Committee; see its *Opinion on 'Mutual Recognition in the Single Market'* (OJ C 116/14, 20 April 2001) 16.

6   The Case for a European Securities Regulator

1 European Commission, *European Governance: A White Paper* (COM(2001) 428 final, 12 October 2001) 5.

2 See, for instance, the Reports originated from discussions among the FESE and the Wise Men Group, chaired by Alexandre Lamfalussy: FESE, *Report and Recommendations on European Regulatory Structures* (September 2000); Committee of Wise Men, *Initial Report on Regulation of European Securities Markets* (9 November 2000, hereinafter 'Initial Wise Men Report').

3 See Goodhart, C. *et al.*, *Financial Regulation: Why, How and Where Now?* (London: Bank of England, 1998) 150.

4 The issue of enforcement will be examined later in Chapter 7, Section C.6.3.

5 The wording of Article 5 of the EC Treaty (former Article 3b) invites such an economic analysis; to justify the exercise of powers by European Community institutions, 'the scale or effects of the proposed action' must be taken into account.

6 See, for instance, Lomax, R., 'Supervision in the Single Market' (1993) 3 Central Banking 36, 39. On the political feasibility of centralised regulation as well as on the possibility of dealing effectively with *sui generis* problems of international finance, see Cranston, R., *Principles of Banking Law* (Oxford: Oxford University Press, 1997) 116.

7 See, for instance, Kenen, P., *Economic and Monetary Union in Europe: Moving beyond Maastricht* (Cambridge: Cambridge University Press, 1995) 32–5; Eichengreen, B., *Should the Maastricht Treaty be Saved?* (Princeton: Princeton University, 1992) 42–4.

8 The principle of attribution of conferred powers to the Community has been confirmed by the SEA, Article 32, incorporated in Article 5 EC Treaty.

9 'Implied powers', in their widest formulation, were invoked by the ECJ in *Commission v Germany*. The Court held that, whenever a provision of the Treaty confers a specific task on the Commission, that provision must also be regarded, by implication, as conferring on the Commission, within some limits, 'necessarily and per se the powers which are indispensable in order to carry out the task'. See Joined Cases 281, 283 to 285 and 287/85 *Commission v Germany* [1987] ECR 3203, Paragraph 28.

10 See Kirchhof, P., 'The Balance of Powers between the National and European Institutions' (1999) 3 ELJ 225, 234.
11 See Article 5 EC Treaty (former Article 3b). The positive concept of subsidiarity represents the possibility or even the obligation of interventions from the Community, both aiming to fulfil and enhance human life. *Per contra*, as seen before, negative subsidiarity refers to the limitations of competences of the Community in relation to its Member States; see Endo, K., 'The Principle of Subsidiarity: From Johannes Althusius to Jacques Delors' (1994) 6 Hokkaido Law Review 553.
12 See Lang, J., 'European Community Constitutional Law: The Division of Powers Between the Community and the Member States' (1988) 2 Northern Ireland Legal Quarterly 209.
13 However, for a national court's different view, see Case 2 BVR 2134/92 & 2159/92, *Manfred Brunner v The Treaty on European Union* [1994] 1 CMLR 57. The German Federal Constitutional Court held that any measure based on a wide interpretation of the Community's implied powers would not have binding effect in Germany. It referred to the interpretation of Article 308 EC Treaty (former Article 235), which 'may not have effects that are equivalent to an extension of the Treaty'.
14 Case 300/89 *Commission v Council* [1991] ECR 2867, better known as the 'titanium dioxide judgement'. For a detailed analysis of the case, see Barents, R., 'The Internal Market Unlimited: Some Observations on the Legal Basis of Community Legislation' (1993) 30 CMLRev 85, 87 *et seq.*
15 On this question, see Arnull, A., 'Does the Court of Justice have Inherent Jurisdiction' (1990) 27 CMLRev 683.
16 See Barents, *op. cit.*, note 14, 87–8.
17 See Case C-377/98 *Netherlands v Parliament and Council* [not yet reported] Paragraph 32.
18 McDonald, F. and Dearden, S., *European Economic Integration* (Essex: Longman, 3rd ed., 1999) 29.
19 *Ibid.*
20 The Economic and Social Committee shares this view; see its *Opinion on 'Mutual Recognition in the Single Market'* (OJ C 116/14, 20 April 2001). *Per contra*, the United Kingdom clearly favours mutual recognition over harmonisation; see HM Treasury, *Realising Europe's Potential: Economic Reform in Europe* (White Paper, February 2002) 81.
21 This has recently been the clear position of the Commission; see European Commission, *Better Lawmaking 2000* (COM(2000) 772 final, 30 November 2000) 6.
22 Hadjiemmanuil, C., *The European Central Bank and Banking Supervision* (London: Centre for Commercial Law Studies, 1996) 44.
23 The third paragraph states that 'any action by the Community shall not go beyond what is necessary to achieve the objectives of this Treaty'; see also the *Protocol (No 30) on the Application of the Principles of Subsidiarity and Proportionality Annexed to the Treaty of Amsterdam 1997*, Paragraph 6, which states that 'the Community shall legislate only to the extent necessary'.
24 See Case 71/76 *Thieffry* [1977] ECR 765, Paragraph 13; Cases 62/81 and 63/81 *Seco v Evi* [1982] ECR 223, Paragraph 8.
25 See Section C.2.
26 See, for instance, Davies, H., *Euro-Regulation* (European Financial Forum Lecture, Brussels, 8 April 1999); Hopt, K., 'Special Issue on the Economic Law of the Member States in an Economic and Monetary Union: Report' (1976) 13 CMLRev

147, 250; Avgouleas, E., 'The Harmonisation of Rules of Conduct in EU Financial Markets: Economic Analysis, Subsidiarity and Investor Protection' (2000) 1 ELJ 72, 84; Initial Wise Men Report, 26.

27   Case 9/56 *Meroni v High Authority* [1957–58] ECR 133, 157.

28   *Ibid.*

29   Case C-98/80 *Romano v INAMI* [1981] ECR 1241, Paragraph 20.

30   Case 45/86 *Commission v Council* [1987] ECR 1493, Paragraph 11.

31   For an analysis of these theories, see Barents, *op. cit.*, note 14, 100 *et seq.*

32   Case C-300/89, *op. cit.*, note 14, Paragraph 10; Case C-426/93 *Germany v Council* [1995] ECR I-3723, Paragraph 29.

33   See, *inter alia*, Case 45/86, *op. cit.*, note 30, Paragraph 12; Case 68/86 *United Kingdom v Council* [1988] ECR 855, Paragraph 51; Case C-62/88 *Greece v Council* [1994] ECR I-1527, Paragraph 10.

34   As a result of the stronger role of EU legislature in the process of integration and the addition of new powers, the number of such conflicts has considerably increased. See Ehlermann, C.D., 'The European Community, Its Law and Lawyers' (1992) 29 CMLRev 213, 216–17.

35   For more details, see Toth, A.G., *Oxford Encyclopedia of European Community Law: Vol I* (Oxford: Oxford University Press, 1990) 303–10; Emiliou, N., 'Opening Pandora's Box: the Legal Basis of Community Measures before the Court of Justice' (1994) 5 ELRev 488, 492–5.

36   Case C-202/88 *France v Commission* [1991] ECR I-1223, Paragraph 24.

37   Weiler describes Article 100a as 'the single most important provision of the SEA' for introducing majority voting in the Council; see Weiler, J., *The Constitution of Europe: 'Do the New Clothes have an Emperor?' and other Essays on European Integration* (Cambridge: Cambridge University Press, 1999) 68.

38   The first paragraph of this provision states that 'by way of derogation from Article 94 and save where otherwise in this Treaty, the following provisions shall apply for the achievement of the objectives set out in Article 14. The Council shall, acting in accordance with the procedure referred to in Article 251 and after consulting the Economic and Social Committee, adopt the measures for the approximation of the provisions laid down by law, regulation or administrative action in Member States which have as their object the establishment and functioning of the internal market'.

39   See Reich, N., 'Binnenmarkt als Rechsbegriff' (1991) Europäisches Zeitscrift fur Wirtschaftsrecht 203, 207.

40   See, for instance, Case C-155/91 *Commission v Council* [1993] ECR I-939, Paragraph 19. In its judgement, the Court stated that 'the mere fact that the establishment of functioning of the internal market is affected is not sufficient for Article 100a (sic) of the Treaty to apply. It appears from the Court's case law that resource to Article 100a is not justified where the measure to be adopted has only the incidental effect of harmonising market conditions within the Community'.

41   See Opinion of Advocate General La Pergola in Case C-271/94 *Parliament v Council* [1996] ECR I-1689, Paragraph 14.

42   See Ehlermann, C.D., 'The Internal Market following the Single European Act' (1987) 24 CMLRev 361, 382.

43   See Crosby, S., 'The Single Market and the Rule of Law' (1991) 16 ELRev 451.

44   Case C-350/92 *Spain v Council* [1995] ECR I-1985, Paragraphs 32–3.

45   See Case C-377/98, *op. cit.*, note 17, Paragraph 15; also, Case C-376/98 *Germany v Parliament and Council* [2000] ECR I-8419, Paragraph 86.

46 Article 308 provides that 'if action by the Community should prove necessary to attain, in the course of the operation of the common market, one of the objectives of the Community and this Treaty has not provided the necessary powers, the Council shall, acting unanimously on the proposal from the Commission and after consulting the European Parliament, take the appropriate measures'.

47 This point was clearly made in the *Edicom* case, which concerned the adoption of Decision 94/445/EC by the Council on the basis of Article 308. The ECJ annulled the Decision on the grounds that it was covered by Article 155 (former Article 129c), which should have formed the legal basis and not Article 308. Practically, this was important because the two Articles have different procedural bases. See Case C-271/94, *op. cit.*, note 41.

48 See Thieffry, G., 'Towards a European Securities Commission' (1999) 10 IFLR 14, 15.

49 Weiler, J., 'The Transformation of Europe' (1991) 8 Yale Law Journal 2403, 2445.

50 Opinion 2/94 *pursuant to Article 228(6) of the EC Treaty* [1996] ECR I-1759, Paragraph 30.

51 Thieffry rightly argues that the formation of the ESR falls within the scope of Article 308 on the basis that such a body is required to foster 'greater economic (...) cohesion', as is the wording of Article 2 of the Treaty; see Thieffry, *op. cit.*, note 48, 16–17.

52 Case 8/73 *Massey-Ferguson* [1973] ECR 897.

53 *Ibid.*, Paragraph 4.

54 Emiliou, *op. cit.*, note 35, 505.

55 The rationale for this trend may be traced to a main difference between a specific Treaty provision and Article 308 serving as the legal basis for the establishment of a new body: it may be alleged that the substantive range of its activities will tend to be narrower in the first case than in the second, because in the latter case the Council, acting unanimously on a proposal from the Commission and after consulting the Parliament, has a wide margin of discretion in determining the necessity of EU action in order to attain one of the objectives of the Treaty. See Lenaerts, K., 'Regulating the regulatory process: "delegation of powers" in the European Community' (1993) 18 ELRev 23, 43.

56 Thieffry, G., 'After the "Lamfalussy" Report: The First Steps towards a European Securities Commission (ESC)', in Andenas, M. and Avgerinos, Y. (eds), *Financial Market Supervision in Europe: Towards a Single Regulator?* (London: Kluwer, forthcoming 2003).

57 The EIB's Statute is drawn up as a Protocol (No. 10) annexed to the Treaty establishing the European Community. It forms an integral part of the Treaty (as provided for under Article 311 *et seq.*) and has the same legal value.

58 The ECB's Statute is also drawn up as a Protocol (No. 18) (ex No. 3) annexed to the Treaty.

59 Negotiations on the SEA began in June 1985 and the Treaty amendments entered into force in July 1987.

60 See Committee of Wise Men, *Final Report on the Regulation of European Securities Markets* (15 February 2001).

61 Danthine, J. *et al.*, *The Future of European Banking* (London: CEPR, 1999) 98; see also below, note 255.

62 Lenaerts, *op. cit.*, note 55, 42.

63 See Türk, A., 'The Role of the Court of Justice', in Andenas, M. and Türk, A. (eds), *Delegated Legislation and the Role of Committees in the EC* (London: Kluwer, 2000) 248.

64   For the different functions of agencies and committees, see Everson, M., 'Administrating Europe?' (1998) 2 JCMS 195, 198. The superiority of an independent body is obvious, as the latter would be 'largely shielded from explicitly political processes by their founding statutes, permanent staff, organisational independence, varying degrees of budgetary autonomy and direct networking with national administrators, whereas committees, born of a strong national desire to retain control over the setting and consequences of European regulatory norms, are more fluid in their composition and so deeply implicated in political processes that their status as "administrative" bodies is questioned'.

65   Haas, E. (1958), 'The Uniting of Europe', in Nelsen, B. and Stubb, A. (eds), *The European Union. Readings on the Theory and Practice of European Integration* (London: Macmillan, 2nd edn, 1998) 139–44.

66   *Ibid.*

67   Some scholars conclude that neo-functionalism failed to provide an adequate explanation of the process of European integration. See, for instance, Keohane, R. and Hoffmann, S., 'Institutional Change in Europe in the 1980s', in Keohanne and Hoffman (eds), *The New European Community – Decisionmaking and Institutional Change* (Boulder: Westview, 1991) 1–40; Moravcsik, A. 'Preferences and Power in the European Community: A Liberal Intergovernmentalist Approach' (1993) 4 JCMS 473, 478–80; Taylor, P., *International Organization in the Modern World* (New York: Pinter, 1993) 9.

68   For the opposite view see Kondgen, J., 'Rules of Conduct: Further Harmonisation?', in Ferrarini, G. (ed.), *European Securities Markets: The Investment Services Directive and Beyond* (London: Kluwer, 1998) 129. Kondgen believes that minimum harmonisation was designed to safeguard national autonomy and to preserve competition among Member States rules.

69   See Bratton, W. *et al.*, *International Regulatory Competition and Coordination* (Oxford: Clarendon Press, 1996) 35.

70   Majone, G., *Regulating Europe* (London: Routledge, 1996) 66.

71   Thieffry, *op. cit.*, note 48.

72   Scale economies may be defined generally as those benefits that result when the increased size of a single operating unit produces a single product, and reduces the unit cost of production. The theory of scope economies, on the other hand, states that the average total cost decreases as a result of increasing the number of different goods produced. Although the empirical evidence on economies of scale and scope is elusive, it appears that with recent technological improvements, relatively small-scale financial firms are likely to improve their cost and revenue efficiency by consolidating and achieving a larger size and scope of activities and by decreasing their compliance costs. There is an extensive literature on economies of scale and scope. See, generally, Pratten, C., *Economies of Scale in Manufacturing Industry* (Cambridge: Cambridge University Press, 1971); Chandler, A., *Scale and Scope: the Dynamics of Industrial Capitalism* (Cambridge: Belkman Press, 1990). For their influence on the European Single Market, see Owen, N., *Economies of Scale, Competitiveness, and Trade Patterns within the European Community* (Oxford: Oxford University Press, 1983); Emerson, M. *et al.*, *The Economics of 1992: The European Commission's Assessment of the Economic Effects of Completing the Internal Market* (Oxford: Oxford University Press, 1988); Holmes, P., 'Economies of Scale, Expectations and Europe 1992' (1989) 12 World Economy 525; European Commission, *Economies of Scale: Impact on Competition and Scale Effects* (London: Kogan Page, EarthScan, 1997).

73   Schmidtchen, D. and Cooter, R. (eds), *Constitutional Law and Economics of the European Union* (Cheltenham: Edward Elgar, 1997) 160.

74 See Majone, *op. cit.*, note 70. It could, thus, be also alleged that centralisation eliminates the negative effects of supervisory arbitrage.

75 Coase, R.H., 'The problem of social cost' (1960) 3 The Journal of Law and Economics 1, 15.

76 For similar or different categorisations of transaction cost, see Goodhart *et al.*, *op. cit.*, note 3, 150; Majone, *op. cit.*, note 70, 69–70; Alfon, I. and Andrews, P. *Cost–Benefit Analysis in Financial Regulation* (FSA Occasional Paper Series No. 3, September 1999) 16–19.

77 See Scharph, F., 'The Joint Decision Trap: Lessons from German Federalism and European Integration' (1988) 66 Public Administration 239.

78 On this issue, see Chapter 7, Section C.2.

79 See Annex II, Figure AII.2. This clearly supersedes any reduction in costs associated with home country control and mutual recognition, which may occur because of less conformity to technical regulations.

80 See Alfon and Andrews, *op. cit.*, note 76, 16.

81 Information equilibrium may be also enhanced by the transparency that a centralised structure promises. See Section C.2.3.

82 For a different view, see Bergh, R., 'The Subsidiarity Principle and the EC Competition Rules: The Costs and Benefits of Decentralisation', in Schmidtchen and Cooter, *op. cit.*, note 73, 168. Bergh argues that 'savings in search costs (thanks to legal certainty) accrue to export industry but are achieved at the expense of industries competing only in the home markets'.

83 Although it would be wrong to assume that all market actors share the same preferences, it seems that the only ones that will not generate gains from decreased legal cost are those who gain from costly law, notably lawyers. See Ogus, A., 'Competition between National Legal Systems: A Contribution of Economic Analysis to Comparative Law' (1999) 48 ICLQ 405, 410.

84 Rose-Ackerman, S., *Rethinking the Progressive Agenda: The Reform of the American Regulatory State* (New York: Free Press, 1993) 172.

85 Firms and consumers will be more supportive of the central regulatory body when they receive cheaper information, less burdensome administrative handling and more legal certainty.

86 Goodhart *et al.*, *op. cit.*, note 3, 154.

87 See Briault, C., *The Rationale for a Single National Financial Services Regulator* (FSA Occasional Paper Series No. 2, May 1999) 26.

88 See Deutsche Bank Research, *Regulation and Banking Supervision: Caught Between the Nation State and Global Financial Markets* (Frankfurt: EMU Watch No. 86, 29 June 2000) 4.

89 'Competitive neutrality' means designing a set of policies and legal arrangements ensuring that all individuals and organisations – public, for-profit, and non-profit – are treated in an equal manner in the bidding process. To the extent possible, all protections and special privileges that public units usually enjoy over private firms simply by virtue of public-sector ownership should be removed. The same should apply to the privileges that domestic firms usually enjoy over foreign ones.

90 See, for instance, ISD, Recital 2, which states: 'whereas firms that provide the investment services covered by this Directive must be subject to authorization by their home Member States in order to protect investors and the stability of the financial system'.

91 Hertig, G., 'Regulatory Competition for EU Financial Services' (2000) 2 Journal of International Economic Law 349, 365. Generally speaking, the ability of pressure

groups to influence decision-making differs across industries and subject matter. However, public choice teaches us that industrial groups will be more successful than investor groups. See Schmidtchen and Cooter, *op. cit.*, note 73, 165–6.

92   Ogus, *op. cit.*, note 83, 411–12.

93   Lee, R., 'Regulation of Capital Markets in the European Union', in Newman, P. (ed.), *3 The New Palgrave Dictionary of Economics and the Law* (London: Macmillan, 1998) 230.

94   On the issue of securities exchanges' consolidation, see Section 4.

95   Werner Seifert, for instance, chief executive of Deutsche Börse, is frustrated by the lack of progress so far; see The Economist, 'No SECs please, we're Europeans' (21 August 1999) 62. However, the formal approach of the Federation of European Securities Exchanges hardly moves in the same line; see *FESE Report, op. cit.*, note 2.

96   See generally, Stigler, G., 'The Theory of Economic Regulation' (1971) 2 Bell Journal of Economics 3. Peacock, A. *et al.*, *The Regulation Game* (Oxford: Basil Blackwell, 1984); Vickers, J. and Yarrow, G., *Privatization: An Economic Analysis* (Cambridge: MIT Press, 1988); Laffont, J. and Tirole, J., 'The politics of government decision-making: A theory of regulatory capture' (1991) 4 Quarterly Journal of Economics 1089.

97   Ogus, *op. cit.*, note 83, 412.

98   Before the crisis, 'lax prudential rules and financial oversight led to a sharp deterioration in the quality of banks' loan portfolios'; Fischer, S., *The Asian Crisis: A View from the IMF* (Paper presented at the Midwinter Conference of the Bankers' Association for Foreign Trade, Washington, 22 January 1998). There was excessive government ownership or involvement in banks, which resulted in too much 'connecting lending' with all the attendant dangers of concentration of credit risk and lack of arms-length credit decisions; Goldstein, M., *The Asian Financial Crisis: Causes, Cures, and Systemic Implications* (Washington: IIE, June 1998).

99   Crédit Lyonnais and Banco di Napoli are recent examples of public support to individual insolvency problems.

100   Majone, *op. cit.*, note 70, 71.

101   Goal independence implies the unilateral ability of the regulator to set its own policy targets and goals.

102   Considerations of efficiency and cost have generally led national authorities to the usage of the home language only. It remains a fact that most supervisors' Internet web sites do not yet provide all documents and legal resources in English.

103   See Taylor, M., *Twin Peaks: A Regulatory Structure for the New Century* (London: Centre for the Study of Financial Innovation, 1995) 15; Goodhart *et al.*, *op. cit.*, note 3, 156.

104   See Davies, H., *Building the Financial Services Authority; What's New?* (Travers Lecture, London Guildhall University Business School, 11 March 1999).

105   Edwards, G., 'Legitimacy and flexibility in post-Amsterdam Europe' in Boer *et al.*, *Coping with Flexibility and Legitimacy after Amsterdam* (Maastricht: European Institute of Public Administration, 1998) 139.

106   According to Snyder, legitimacy refers to the belief that a specific institution is widely recognised or at least accepted as being the appropriate institution to exercise specific powers; see Snyder, F., 'EMU Revisited: Are we Making a Constitution? What Constitution are we Making?' in Craig, P. and de Burca, G. (eds), *The Evolution of EU Law* (Oxford: Oxford University Press, 1999) 463.

107 See Chapter 7, Section B.1.

108 Taylor, *op. cit.*, note 103.

109 Schmidtchen and Cooter, *op. cit.*, note 73, 173.

110 Article 255(1) states that 'any citizen of the Union, and any natural or legal person residing or having its registered office in a Member State, shall have a right of access to European Parliament, Council and Commission documents'.

111 *Special report from the European Ombudsman to the European Parliament following the own-initiative inquiry into public access to documents* (OJ C 44/9, 10 February 1998).

112 For example, see Vos, E., 'Reforming the European Commission: What Role to Play for EU Agencies?' (2000) 5 CMLRev 1113, 1125.

113 In this way, the Securities Regulator should avoid the criticism of lack of transparency often targeted at the ECB.

114 In relation to judicial review, recent developments indicate that the ECJ would be prepared to loosen the strict *Meroni* requirements. In *Les Verts*, the Court had already elucidated that EU is based on the rule of law, thus permitting the Court to review the legality of all acts adopted by institutions. See Case 294/83 *Les Verts* [1986] ECR 1339, Paragraph 23. This decision should also apply to the Securities Regulator, irrespective of whether it would qualify as 'institution' or not. See Lenaerts, *op. cit.*, note 55, 46.

115 In banking, three committees are in place: the Banking Advisory Committee, the Groupe de Contact and the Banking Supervisory Committee of the ECB. In insurance, we have the Insurance Committee and the Groupe de Contact by the Conference of Insurance Supervisors. In securities, it should be noted that a High Level Securities Supervisors Committee was in place between 1992–2001. However, most of its functions have been undertaken by FESCO. Also, two Contact Committees, one for the listing and prospectus rules and one for UCITS, exist to facilitate harmonised implementation. Nevertheless, these committees have no comitology powers, which partially explains their weak influence. Recently, however, the Economic and Financial Committee proposed arrangements in line with the Lamfalussy framework for all financial sectors and the creation of separate Level 2 and 3 committees; see EFC, *Report on Financial Regulation, Supervision and Stability* (9 October 2002).

116 See Chapter 4, Sections C.3 and D.

117 In its session of 14 March 2001, the Parliament voted by 410 to 25 against the regime. Criticism is also crystallised in the compromise reflected in the Von Wogau report, which was voted on 5 February 2002; see EP *Report on the Implementation of Financial Services Legislation* (A5-0011/2002 final, 23 January 2002).

118 See, for example, the ESFRC statement in Chapter 4, note 63.

119 See Chapter 4, Section C.3.1.

120 See European Commission, *Financial Services and Progress: 3rd Report* (COM(2000) 692/2 final, 8 November 2000, hereinafter '3rd Progress Report') 4. The Commission admits that 'there are a number of serious concerns and the worry that without more effort in next few months the FSAP will fail to maintain sufficient momentum to achieve the ambitious 2005 deadline'; European Commission, *'Working together to maintain momentum': 2001 Review of the Internal Market Strategy* (COM(2001) 198 final, 11 April 2001) 4. See also Initial Wise Men Report, 23. The Committee is indeed concerned that the present system will not be able to deliver the FSAP on time.

121   The delay suffered in the genesis of the ISD, for example, illustrates the difficulties surrounding the liberalisation of financial markets in several Member States. The first proposal was submitted by the Commission in February 1989 and the Council finally adopted the Directive in May 1993.

122   Davies, H., *Introductory Remarks* (Speech at the Eurofi Conference, Paris, 15 September 2000).

123   Directives' provisions can be divided into two categories: (a) provisions that leave considerable discretion to Member States and supervisors to set out the detailed regulatory requirements and (b) provisions that allow less discretion. The disadvantage for the former is obvious; each Member State adopts its own standards and implementation methods. The problem with the latter is that, with the boom in securities market developments, the details of the Directives are often out-of-date and each Member State then needs to find its own legal solution. On the functions and the implementation process of directives, see Prechal, S., *Directives in European Community Law* (Oxford: Clarendon Press, 1995) 3 *et seq.*

124   This may lead to significant delay. See Avgerinos, Y., 'Essential and Non-Essential Measures: Delegation of Powers in EU Securities Regulation' (2002) 2 ELJ 269. In order to assist in the definition and interpretation of essential and implementing measures, the Committee for Economic and Monetary Affairs of the European Parliament has established a panel of financial services experts to provide independent advice on the measures set out in the Financial Services Action Plan. The capacity of this group, however, is merely advisory.

125   Characteristic is the paradigm of the draft Market Abuse and Prospectus Directives. In their first reading, the Parliament proposed 104 and 62 changes to the Commission proposal respectively. On the contrary, Council and Parliament agreed to the Regulation on IAS after a single reading.

126   If the average time allowed for the implementation of a Directive is added (up to 3 years) one can understand why legislation is often out-of-date by the time it becomes effective; see the latest Commission *Internal Market Scoreboard* (No. 9, 19 November 2001) 7, and Annex II, Figure AII.3.

127   See Chapter 5, Section C.1.4.

128   The recent 2001 Review of the Internal Market Strategy, *op. cit.*, note 120, 5, reveals that not only have key legislative proposals been delayed, but also progress in implementing existing Internal Market rules has been disappointing.

129   See Tison, M., *Conduct of Business Rules and their Implementation in the EU Member States* (Financial Law Institute WP 2000-14, Gent University, 2000) 4.

130   See Initial Wise Men Report, 24.

131   The precise meaning of the term 'directly applicable' of Article 249 EC has been the subject of debate among commentators. See e.g., Steiner, J., 'Direct Applicability in EEC Law – A Chameleon Concept' (1982) 98 LQR 229; Dashwood, A., 'The Principle of Direct Effect in European Community Law' (1978) 16 JCMS 229. However, the ECJ has signified that Member States should not pass any measure which purports to transform a Community Regulation into national law and thus obstruct its direct applicability; see Case 34/73 *Variola* [1973] ECR 981, Paragraph 10. Moreover, 'all methods of implementation, which would have the result of creating an obstacle to the direct effect of Community Regulations and of jeopardizing their simultaneous and uniform application in the whole of the Community, are contrary to Treaty'; see Case 39/72 *Commission v Italy* [1973] ECR 101, Paragraph 17.

132 Craig, P. and de Burca, G., *EU Law* (Oxford: Oxford University Press, 1998) 108.

133 *Ibid.*, 168.

134 See Case 50/76 *Amsterdam Bulb* [1977] ECR 137, Paragraph 33.

135 See Section C.7.

136 See, for instance, FESE Report, 12; Hopt, *op. cit.*, note 26; Levitt, M., 'Does Europe want a single market?' (2001) 4 The Financial Regulator 20, 24. Even standing against centralisation at the present stage, it is common belief that for the long term an ESR is a leading vision, given that a far more harmonised regulatory and legislative framework is accomplished.

137 See Avgouleas, *op. cit.*, note 26, 84.

138 See Joint Forum, *Supervision of Financial Conglomerates* (February 1999) 106.

139 See Deutsche Bank, *op. cit.*, note 88; also Breuer, R., *Convergence of Supervisory Practices – A Banker's View* (Paper presented at the Conference of European Banking Supervisors, Copenhagen, 20 November 2000).

140 See Dale, R., 'Reflections on the BCCI Affair: A United Kingdom Perspective' (1992) 26 International Law 949; Norton, J. and Olive, C., 'Globalization of Financial Risks and International Supervision of Banks and Securities Firms: Lessons from the Barings Debacle' (1996) 2 International Lawyer 301.

141 European Commission, *The Principle of Subsidiarity* (SEC(92) 1990 final, 27 October 1992) 1.

142 See, for instance, Kanda, H., 'Commentary 1 on Ruben Lee's Report No 1, Supervising EU Capital Markets: Do we Need a European SEC?' in Buxbaum, R. *et al.*, *European Economic and Business Law: Legal and Economic Analyses on Integration and Harmonisation* (New York: Walter de Gruyter, 1996) 206.

143 See, for instance, Ogus, *op. cit.*, note 83, 417.

144 Breuer, *op. cit.*, note 139.

145 On the limitations of self-regulation, see Chapter 7, Section C.5.2.

146 See the results of the 14th Meeting of the FSPG (27 February 2002) found at http://www.europa.eu.int/comm/internal_market/en/finances/actionplan/ 02-39.htm; see also European Commission, *Financial Services: Sixth Report* (COM(2002) 267, 3 June 2002) 4. On 9 August 2002, the European Commission adopted an amended proposal for a Directive on Prospectuses to be published when securities are offered to the public or admitted to trading. The original proposal was adopted in May 2001, then amended by the European Parliament in March 2002 and subsequently discussed by the Council.

147 See Initial Wise Men Report, 11.

148 For how market developments have influenced securities regulation and organisation in Member States, see Ferrarini, G., *Exchange Governance and Regulation: An Overview* in Ferrarini, *op. cit.*, note 68, 245 *et seq.*

149 See ECB, *Possible Effects of EMU on the EU Banking Systems in the Medium to Long Term* (February 1999) 12.

150 Between 1999 and 2002 only a core of operations had to be carried out in euro. The private sector will be convinced on purely economic grounds when the euro is available in physical form. The marginal cost of using a particular currency depends on how much it is used. Hence, a widely used currency has usually lower transactions cost.

151 See Hardouvelis, G. *et al.*, *EMU and European Stock Market Integration* (CEPR Discussion Paper 2124, April 1999) 33.

152 See Onado, M., 'Competition Among Exchanges or Financial Systems?' in Ferrarini, *op. cit.*, note 68, 228.

153 See Boland, V. and Guerrera, F. 'FSA staff brand iX plan a "nightmare"'
     (8 September 2000) FT 1.
154 Investment firms licensed in one market do not automatically receive a passport
     to operate in another Euronext country as well. They still have to comply with
     the ISD notification requirement and they continue to be subject to the frag-
     mented supervision and enforcement of the regulator of the home country; see
     Euronext, *Rule Book I* (30 July 2001) chapters 2 and 9.
155 ISD, Article 1(13).
156 ISD, Article 15(5).
157 It is a fact that some exchanges, such as Madrid and Athens, have no remote
     members; see European Commission, *Communication on Upgrading the Investment
     Services Directive (93/22/EEC)* (16 November 2000) 7.
158 See Tison, M., *The Investment Services Directive and its Implementation in the EU
     Member States* (Financial Law Institute WP 1999-17, Gent University, 1999) 32.
159 See Section C.6.
160 Clearing and settlement are the processes by which securities market transac-
     tions are finalised and are integral to the functioning of the financial system.
161 Giovannini Group, *Cross-Border Clearing and Settlement Arrangements in the
     European Union* (November 2001). A further report, examining possible develop-
     ments in the clearing and settlement architecture is scheduled to be produced
     by the end of 2002.
162 Recent developments confirm the trend towards consolidation. At the beginning
     of 2000, Luxembourg-based Cedel and Deutsche Börse Clearing (DBC) merged to
     create Clearstream International, only to be followed next year by the Euroclear
     Clearance System, which emerged from the merger of Brussels-based Euroclear
     and Paris' SICOVAM. Both mergers, however, were functional and not legal,
     since the two pre-existing structures remain. See Sáinz de Vicuña, A., 'The Legal
     Integration of Financial Markets of the Euro Area', in Andenas and Avgerinos,
     op. cit., note 56. Nevertheless, there remain a very substantial number of differ-
     ent national and international providers of these services. For example, in
     Europe, there are nineteen CSDs and two ICSDs providing various types of ser-
     vices and with various governance structures; see Giovannini Group, *ibid.*, 30.
163 The Depositary Trust and Clearing Corporation, the US umbrella organisation
     that brings together clearing and settlement for the US securities markets, shows
     that a single provider can work in the case of certain brokerage operations, such
     as trade confirmation, settlement and regulatory compliance; see Rosen, R.,
     'Clearing up Europe's Exchanges' (9 February 2001) FT 19.
164 Dalhuisen, J., 'What about a Single European Capital Market and its Regulation?'
     in Andenas and Avgerinos, *op. cit.*, note 56, 14.
165 See FESE, *Second Report and Recommendations on European Regulatory Structures*
     (January 2001) 6; Final Wise Men Report, 16.
166 See the Key Principles of the European Securities Forum at http://www.eurosf.
     com/key_principles.htm.
167 European Commission, *Clearing and Settlement in the European Union: Main Policy
     Issues and Future Challenges* (COM(2002) 257, 28 May 2002).
168 The Settlement Finality Directive (SFD) and the proposed Collateral Directive (CD)
     both contain provisions that represent an evolution from the principle that
     the applicable law should be that of the jurisdiction where a security is located.
     Instead, the security is to be treated as being located at the relevant register,
     account or system where it has been recorded; see SFD, Article 9(2) and draft CD,
     Article 10. However, the SFD and CD rules apply only in limited circumstances: the

SFD only to securities offered as collateral to central banks and to payment and settlement systems, and the CD only to securities offered as collateral. In its Communication, the Commission states that the ultimate solution for the divergence in the legal treatment of securities across the EU would require achieving a uniform legal treatment with the creation of a 'uniform securities code'.

169   As stated by the BIS, 'safe and reliable settlement systems are essential not only for the stability of securities markets they serve, but often also to payment systems, which may be used by an SSS or may themselves use an SSS to transfer collateral'; see BIS, *Recommendations for Securities Settlement Systems* (Consultative Report, January 2001) 7. Especially for risks in cross-border settlement, see Ferrarini, G., 'The European Regulation of Stock Exchanges: New Perspectives' (1999) 3 CMLRev 569, 592.

170   This need becomes now evident as the CESR and the ECB have joined forces to establish a working group, which will work on the drafting of common standards and recommendations for SSS and counterparties at European level; see CESR Press Release (25 October 2001) found at www.europefesco.org. In particular, they are considering the adoption of common standards for clearing and settlement entities in Europe, based on the G10 CPSS and IOSCO Recommendations and the standards of risk management developed by the European Association of Central Counterparty Clearing Houses (EACH). The CPSS-IOSCO Recommendations have been accepted globally by central banks and securities markets regulators as representing minimum standards for systems involved in the finalisation of transactions; see CPSS-IOSCO, *Recommendations for Securities Settlement Systems* (November 2001).

171   See Sáinz de Vicuña, A., *Legal Consequences of the Single Currency* (General Report at the FIDE Congress, Helsinki, 1–3 June 2000).

172   The divergences between technical market issues is not within the scope of this book. For such an assessment, see the first paper issued by the Giovannini Group, *The Impact of the Introduction of the Euro on Capital Markets* (July 1997).

173   The diversity, for instance, in the national implementation of Community Directives appears now as a non-quantitative barrier to a single currency market.

174   The first issue has been addressed by the previous section, whereas the third issue will be analysed in Chapter 7, Section B.1.

175   In the euro area, M&A across sectors have accounted for roughly 30% of all financial industry deals in terms of value over the past five years.

176   See ECB, *op. cit.*, note 149, 26.

177   European Commission, *Proposal for a Directive on the supplementary supervision of credit institutions, insurance undertakings and investment firms in a financial conglomerate and amending Council Directives 73/239/EEC, 79/267/EEC, 92/49/EEC, 92/96/EEC, 93/6/EEC, 93/22/EEC, and Directives 98/78/EC and 2000/12/EC of the Parliament and the Council* (COM(2001) 213 final, 24 April 2001).

178   However, the coordinator may be composed by more than one authority and on the basis of more than one criteria, which may confuse instead of facilitating supervisory arrangements; *ibid.*, Article 7.

179   Mayes, D. *et al.*, *Improving Banking Supervision* (Basingstoke: Palgrave, 2001) 61.

180   See Walker, G., 'Conglomerate Law and International Financial Market Supervision' (1998) Annual Review of Banking Law 287, 330.

181   See Chapter 8.

182   On the supervision of financial conglomerates in a global context, see the document released jointly by the Joint Forum on Financial Conglomerates, *op. cit.*, note 138.

183 European Council, *Regulation No 2157/2001 of 8 October 2001 on the Statute for a European company (SE)* (OJ L 294/1, 10 November 2001). The Regulation will enter into force on 8 October 2004.

184 It remains to be seen whether many financial companies will be transformed into an SE merely for the purpose of transferring their principal office and, thus, shopping their forum.

185 This means that, with growing cross-border exposures, failures in foreign activities constitute an increasing threat for the solvency of the entire financial firm and for the stability of the entire common market. See Mayes, D. and Vesala, J., *On the Problems of Home Country Control* (Bank of Finland Discussion Paper No. 20/98, 1998) 13.

186 Interpretation of Recital 26 of Regulation 2157/2001 leads one to the conclusion that the host country rules are still applicable: 'activities by financial institutions are regulated by specific directives and the national law implementing those directives and additional national rules regulating those activities apply in full to an SE'.

187 Duisenberg, W., *The Euro as a Catalyst for Legal Convergence in Europe* (Speech on the occasion of the Annual Conference of the International Bar Association, Amsterdam, 17 September 2000).

188 For a description of recent financial crises in Europe, see Benink, H., *The Future of Banking Regulation in Developed Countries: Lessons from and for Europe* (mimeo) 6.

189 For a comprehensive analysis, see Evans, H., *Plumbers and Architects: A Supervisory Perspective on International Financial Architecture* (FSA Occasional Paper Series No. 4, January 2000) 6.

190 Latter, T., *Causes and Management of Banking Crises* (Centre for Central Banking Studies Handbook No. 12, Bank of England, 1997) 36.

191 Bingham, Lord Justice, *Inquiry into the Supervision of Bank of Credit and Commerce International* (HMSO, October 1992, hereinafter 'Bingham Report').

192 The Bank of England, however, accepted Bingham's recommendations and proceeded to the establishment of a legal unit and a special investigation unit within it.

193 Namely, Articles 6–8; see *Three Rivers District Council v Governor and Company of the Bank of England* [2000] 2 WLR 1220, HL. The Court not only failed to refer the issue to the ECJ under Article 234 (former Article 177) EC Treaty, but also it failed to take sufficiently into account supervision developments in other jurisdictions. For an extensive and critical analysis of the comparative and community law aspects of the *Three Rivers* case, see Andenas, M., 'Liability for Supervisors and Depositors' Rights – the BCCI and the Bank of England in the House of Lords' (2001) Euredia 379.

194 See Bingham Report, Paragraph 3.19 *et seq*.

195 House of Commons, *Banking Supervision and BCCI: International and National Regulation* (Treasury and Civil Service Select Committee, 4th Report, London, 1992) ix.

196 See Bingham Report, Paragraph 2.70.

197 See Panourgias, L. and Andenas, M., *Euro, EMU and the UK Law* (Report submitted for the Euro-Spectator Project, April 2001).

198 House of Commons, *op. cit.*, note 195, 177.

199 The 'college' refers to working relationships between more than two sets of national supervisors with regard to a particular institution. With regard to the use of supervisory colleges, see Walker, *op. cit.*, note 180, 302.

200 See FESCO, *Report 1999–2000* (15 November 2000) 9. Also Kanda would be surprised if the EU were seriously considering the establishment of a European
   Securities Commission in the absence of preceding scandals; See Kanda, *op. cit.*,
   note 142, 205.
201 Walker, *op. cit.*, note 180, 327.
202 See Joint Forum, *op. cit.*, note 138, 92.
203 See Chapter 7, Section C.5.2.
204 Mayes and Vesala, *op. cit.*, note 185, 18.
205 *Ibid.*, 26.
206 For example, government efforts to restructure, rather than close down BCCI
   branch banks, were more extensive in countries, such as Pakistan, where BCCI
   dominated the market and was well linked with the political and economic
   establishment. Also, it seems that the United Kingdom's concern to protect
   depositors was secondary to the concern to safeguard the interests of the City of
   London as a citadel of finance capital.
207 Bingham Report, Paragraph 2.480.
208 The problem is that 'the use of crisis management instruments has traditionally
   been confined to banks, because *they are the most relevant from the viewpoint
   of financial stability*' (emphasis added). See Economic and Financial Committee, *Report on Financial Stability* (EFC/ECFIN/240/00, 8 April 2000, 'Brouwer
   Report') 22.
209 Mayes *et al.*, *op. cit.*, note 179, 3.
210 See ISD, Article 23.
211 Goodhart *et al.*, *op. cit.*, note 3, 155.
212 Forty five per cent of the responses to the Wise Men questionnaire on the regulation of European securities markets stated that the current arrangements for
   cooperation and mutual assistance between national supervisors are not sufficient. The main perceived shortcomings are differences in supervisory powers
   and duties, duplication of supervisory control, deficient channels for cooperation, excessive cost and lack of expertise and transparency. See Initial Wise Men
   Report, 34.
213 See the *Report by Singapore Inspectors on Baring Futures Singapore* (Financial
   Regulation Report, October 1995, hereinafter 'Singapore Report') On the contrary, the findings of the Bank of England Report were that the collapse was
   chiefly due to ineffective risk management and inadequate internal control. See
   Bank of England, *Report of the Board of Banking Supervision Inquiry into the
   Circumstances of the Collapse of Barings* (18 July 1995, hereinafter 'Bank of
   England Report') Chapter 13, Paragraphs 13.10–13.11.
214 Although the Barings case falls outside the ambit of the EU home country
   control system and the relevant Directives, similar elements of supervisory structures can be traced to the international context. The concept of 'lead supervisor', for instance, is internationally recognised in the Basel Concordat of 1983;
   see Chapter 3, Section D.1.
215 See Bank of England Report, Paragraph 13.58.
216 *Ibid.*, Paragraph 14.35.
217 See Singapore Report, Paragraph 15.41.
218 *Ibid.*, Paragraph 15.43.
219 Norton and Olive, *op. cit.*, note 140, 341.
220 Goodhart *et al.*, *op. cit.*, note 3, 40.
221 Centre for Financial Research, Cambridge, 20 February 1998.

222   IOSCO, *Guidance on Information Sharing* (November 1997); see also IOSCO, *Report on Cooperation between Market Authorities and Default Procedures* (March 1996).

223   The home authority may be reluctant to reveal unfolding problems, because it might fear that widespread knowledge risks market reactions that could actually take the problem further. In the same way, the home supervisor will merely receive information about problems in the host market second-hand.

224   National authorities maintain the right to refuse provision of information in instances where that transmission could violate public policy, sovereignty, national security or other essential interests.

225   In some jurisdictions, information that discloses the positions and funds of individual customers may not be available under relevant bank secrecy and similar laws.

226   FESCO, *Multilateral Memorandum of Understanding on the Exchange of Information and Surveillance of Securities Activities* (February 1999).

227   Article 4(3), for instance, requires that any request addressed to a supervisory authority should specify, *inter alia*, the following: (a) a description of the subject matter, the purpose for which the information is sought and the reason why this information will be of assistance, (b) a description of the specific information requested and the relevant Community law pursuant to which the authority discharges its responsibilities, (c) in case the request results from investigations of violations of any laws or regulations, a description of them and a list of the persons and institutions involved, and (d) whether the requesting authority is in contact with any other authority or law enforcement agency in the country of the requested authority.

228   According to Prati and Schinasi, supervisory practices vary considerably in the EU; see Prati, A. and Schinasi, G. *Will the ECB be the LLR in EMU?* (Paper presented at the SUERF Conference, Frankfurt, October 1998).

229   Mayes and Vesala, *op. cit.*, note 185, 16.

230   Norton and Olive, *op. cit.*, note 140, 342.

231   See Louis, J.V. *et al.*, *Banking Supervision in the European Community* (Brussels: University of Brussels, 1995) 60.

232   See Breuer, *op. cit.*, note 139.

233   See Gambetta, D., *Trust: Making and Breaking Cooperative Relations* (Oxford: Blackwell, 1988). See also, Chapter 5, Section C.1.3.

234   Metcalpe, L., 'Reforming the Commission: Will Organizational Efficiency Produce Effective Governance?' (2000) 5 JCMS 817, 829.

235   This was also the opinion of a Group of experts back in 1995, which suggested that *'the system of cooperation between authorities cannot be maintained without the setting up of a higher authority at Community level'*; see Louis *et al.*, *op. cit.*, note 231, 59.

236   Briault, *op. cit.*, note 87, 19.

237   See, e.g., Duisenberg, W., *The Future of Banking Supervision and the Integration of Financial Markets* (Speech delivered at the conference 'Improving integration of financial markets in Europe', Turin, 22 May 2000); ESFRC, 'The European Shadow Financial Regulatory Committee: a New Initiative' (1999) 2 JIBR 137, 140; Green, D., 'Enhanced Co-operation among Regulators and the Role of National Regulators in a Global Market' (2000) 2 JIFM 7, 12.

238   Lannoo, for instance, advocates a 'European Board of Financial Supervisors'; Lannoo, K., *Challenges to the Structure of Financial Supervision in the EU* (CEPS, 1999) 13.

239 Perpetrators of Internet securities fraud, for instance, can easily move both the location of their web sites and the target location of their fraudulent scheme from one jurisdiction to another, when they encounter difficulties in a particular jurisdiction; see IOSCO, *Securities Activity on the Internet* (September 1998) 37.

240 Similar concerns exist for banking and insurance services regulation and supervision; see *3rd Progress Report*, 13.

241 See Bolkestein, F., *An Uncertain Europe in the World of Upheaval* (Rand Europe Public Policy Lecture, Societeit De Witte, The Hague, 14 June 2002).

242 See Arlman, P., 'European Equity Markets after the Euro: Competition and Cooperation across New Frontiers' (1999) 2 International Finance 139, 146–7. FESE also points out that modernisation of regulation in Europe has to be accompanied by rapid agreement with the US authorities aiming at full and immediate reciprocity of securities market access; see *FESE Second Report, op. cit.*, note 165, 6.

243 See Woolcock, S., 'Competition among Rules in the Single European Market', in Bratton *et al., op. cit.*, note 69, 292.

244 Davies, *op. cit.*, note 122.

245 See the Commission's *White Paper on European Governance, op. cit.*, note 1, 26, advocating the EU's contribution to global governance. In June 2002, the Commission approved, as a follow-up to its White Paper, the consultation document: *Towards a reinforced culture of consultation and dialogue – Proposal for general principles and minimum standards for consultation of interested parties by the Commission* (COM(2002) 277, 5 June 2002). This document was, at the same time, a direct contribution to the *Action Plan for Better Regulation* (COM(2002) 278) and the Commission's new approach to impact assessment (COM(2002) 276), both of which the Commission adopted simultaneously.

246 Majone, G., 'Functional Interests: European Agencies', in Peterson J. and Shackleton M., *The Institutions of the European Union* (Oxford: Oxford University Press, 2002) 328.

247 See Lamfalussy, A., *Presentation on the Special Roundtable on the Findings of the Committee of Wise Men on the Regulation of European Securities Markets* (CEPS, 29 November 2000) (hereinafter 'CEPS Roundtable').

248 Davies, H., *Convergence of Supervisory Practice* (Speech delivered at the Banking Supervision Conference, Copenhagen, 20 November 2000).

249 Majone, G., 'Regulating Europe: Problems and Perspectives' (1989) 3 Jarhbuch zur Staats- und Verwaltungswissenschaft.

250 See Whittaker, A., 'A European Law for Regulated Markets? Some Personal Views' in Ferrarini, *op. cit.*, note 68, 270.

251 See Green, *op. cit.*, note 237, 10.

252 Brouwer Report, 14–15.

253 During the transition to the EMU, most governments, acting separately or through European institutions, showed a remarkable commitment to this goal, not only in words but also in deeds.

254 Breuer, *op. cit.*, note 139.

255 This is evident in the March 2001 IMF's plans to establish an International Capital Markets Department to enhance its surveillance, crisis prevention and crisis management activities; see http://www.imf.org/external/np/sec/nb/2001/nb0124.htm. See, also, the proposal for a World Financial Authority (WFA) in Eatwell, J. and Taylor, L. *International Markets and the Future of Economic Policy* (CEPA Working Paper No. 9, August 1998) 14 and in Alexander, K., 'The Need for Efficient International Financial Regulation and the Role of a Global Supervisor'

in Ferran, E. and Goodhart, C. (eds), *Regulating Financial Services and Markets in the Twenty First Century* (Oxford: Hart, 2001) 288. Finally, the Economist wonders who regulates firms like Citigroup, the world's largest and most diverse financial institution; see The Economist, 'The regulator who isn't there' (18 May 2002) 12.

256   Demarigny, F., Comment at the CEPS Roundtable.

7   Structure and Operation of the European Securities Regulator

1   Article 107(1) (former Article 106) EC Treaty.
2   At present, there are three Member States not participating in the single currency: Denmark, Sweden and the United Kingdom.
3   Article 107(3) (former Article 106) EC Treaty.
4   Article 112(1) (former Article 109a) EC Treaty.
5   Article 112(2) (former Article 109a) EC Treaty.
6   Article 107(2) (former Article 106) EC Treaty; for a legal approach to the ECB, see Zilioli, C. and Selmayr, M., *The Law of the European Central Bank* (Oxford: Hart Publishing, 2001).
7   On the question, whether the ECB constitutes a Community institution or not, see Dutzler, B., *OLAF or the Question of Applicability of Secondary Community Law to the ECB* (European Integration online Papers No 1, http://eiop.or.at/eiop/texte/2001-001a.htm, 2001) 7.
8   Gros, D., 'Delivering Price Stability in EMU: the European System of Central Banks', in Franke, H.H. (ed.), *Europäische Währungsunion: Von den Konzeption zur Gestaltung* (Berlin: Dunker & Humblot 1998) 356. The Council can only make minor technical amendments, but changes in ECB's powers or objectives requires Treaty amendment; Article 111 (former Article 109) EC Treaty.
9   Article 110(1) (former Article 108a) EC Treaty.
10 For some examples of ECB Regulations, see Thieffry, G., 'After the "Lamfalussy" Report: the First Step towards a European Securities Commission (ESC)?' in Andenas, M. and Avgerinos, Y., *Financial Market Supervision in Europe: Towards a Single Regulator?* (London: Kluwer, forthcoming 2003).
11 Article 110(2) (former Article 108a) EC Treaty.
12 See Leino, P., *The European Central Bank and Legitimacy: Is the ECB a Modification of or an Exception to the Principle of Democracy?* (Cambridge: Harvard Jean Monnet WP 1/01, 2001) 4.
13 Article 110(3) (former Article 108a) EC Treaty; see also Article 2 of the ECB *Regulation No 2157/1999 of 23 September 1999 on the powers of the European Central Bank to impose sanctions* (OJ L 264/21, 12 October 1999).
14 Statute, Article 34.3. See also Article 6(2) of the Council *Regulation No. 2532/98 of 23 November 1998 concerning the powers of the European Central Bank to impose sanctions* (OJ L 318/4, 27 November 1998).
15 Recommendations and Opinions are not included, since they do not produce legal effect; Article 230 (former Article 173) EC Treaty.
16 Article 234 (former Article 177) EC Treaty.
17 Article 237(d) (former Article 180) EC Treaty.
18 Editorial Comments, 'Executive Agencies within the EU: The European Central Bank – a Model?' (1996) 33 CMLRev 623, 629.
19 Article 108 (former Article 107) EC Treaty.
20 See, for instance, Magnette, P., 'Towards "Accountable Independence"? Parliamentary Controls of the European Central Bank and the Rise of a New

Democratic Model' (2000) 4 ELJ 326; Buiter, W., 'Alice in Euroland' (1999) 2 JCMS 181; Issing, O., *The Euro – Four Weeks After the Start* (Speech delivered to the European-Atlantic Group, House of Commons, London, 28 January 1999).

21 Both theoretical and empirical research supports the view that central bank independence is a desirable institutional device because it is associated on average with lower inflation and no lower growth. See Cukierman, A., *Accountability, Credibility, Transparency and Stabilization Policy in the Eurosystem* (mimeo, January 2000) 2.

22 See, for instance, Brentford, P., 'Constitutional Aspects of the Independence of the European Central Bank' (1998) 47 ICLQ 75, 108; Kirchgässner, G., 'Constitutional Economics and its Relevance for the Evolution of Rules' (1994) 47 Kyklos 321, 329.

23 European Ombudsman, *Annual Report 1996* (OJ C 272/1, 8 September 1997) 30. See also European Ombudsman, *Special Report to the European Parliament following the own-initiative inquiry into public access to documents* (OJ C 44/9, 10 February 1998).

24 See Special Report, *ibid.*, 4.

25 For the time being, even all voting records and motivations remain confidential. See ECB, *Rules of Procedure of the European Central Bank* (OJ L 125/34, 19 May 1999) Article 23.

26 ECB, *Decision of 3 November 1998 concerning public access to documentation and the archives of the European Central Bank* (OJ L 110/30, 28 April 1999) Preface.

27 The EP accepts the logic of delegation of powers to the ECB given by the Treaty and affirms its intention to *a posteriori* control its decisions; see Magnette, *op. cit.*, note 20, 327. The ECB, on the other hand has strengthened its relationship with the EP by attending hearings organised by the Parliamentary Committee on Economic and Monetary Affaires.

28 For such an analysis, see Chryssochoou, D., *Democracy in the European Union* (London: Tauris Academic Studies, 1998) 69.

29 The economic rationale lies in the perception that a pan-European monetary institution may be more effective than its national-level predecessors; see Oatley, T., *Monetary Politics: Exchange Rate Cooperation in the European Union* (Ann Arbor: University of Michigan Press, 1997) 143 *et seq.*; Gros, D. and Thygesen, N., *European Monetary Integration* (Harlow: Longman, 2nd ed., 1998) 261 *et seq.*; Frieden, J. and Jones, E., 'The Political Economy of EMU: A Conceptual Overview', in Frieden, J. *et al* (eds), *The New Political Economy of EMU* (Boston: Rowan & Littlefield, 1998) 168. The decision to complete the internal market lent strength to the belief long held by many Europeans that closely integrated national economies like those at the core of the EC have more to gain from exchange rate stability than from occasional realignments. It was argued that the EC countries could not reap the full gains of the internal market unless they banished the exchange rate risks and conversion costs arising from the use of separate national currencies; see Kenen, P., *Economic and Monetary Union in Europe: Moving beyond Maastricht* (Cambridge: Cambridge University Press, 1995) 9. The strongest statement of this view was made later on, in the European Commission's statement of the case of EMU, aptly titled 'One Market, One Money' (European Economy, 44). Concerns were also vividly put by Padoa-Schioppa, who warned against trying to pursue an 'inconsistent quartet' of policy objectives: free trade, full capital mobility, fixed exchange rates and independent national monetary policy. 'In the long run', he argued, 'the only solution to the inconsistency is to complement the internal market with

a monetary union'; Padoa-Schioppa, T., 'The European Monetary System: A Long-Term View', in Giavazzi, F., Micossi, S. and Miller, M. (eds), *The European Monetary System* (Cambridge: Cambridge University Press, 1988) 376.

30 See McNamara, K., 'Managing the Euro: The European Central Bank', in Peterson, J. and Shackleton, M., *The Institutions of the European Union* (Oxford: Oxford University Press, 2002) 168; Dyson, K., *The Politics of the Euro-Zone: Stability or Breakdown?* (Oxford: Oxford University Press, 2000) 260 *et seq.*

31 See Chapter 6, Section C.2.2.

32 A crucial difference is that decisions for the monetary policy are taken by the 12 Members of the EMU, while the Securities Regulator will be deciding for 15-plus (EEA) countries.

33 See Economic and Financial Committee, *Report on Financial Stability* (EFC/ECFIN/240/00, 8 April 2000, 'Brouwer Report') 6.

34 See Chapter 6, Section C.2.3.

35 Between 1 September 1929 and 1 July 1932, the value of all stocks listed on the New York Stock Exchange shrank from a total of nearly $90 billion to just under $16 billion, a loss of 83%; for details on the Great Crash, see Galbraith, J., *The Great Crash 1929* (Boston: Houghton Mifflin, 1997).

36 For an excellent historical description of the US securities market in the early twentieth century and the reasons that led to federal regulation and the establishment of the SEC, see McCraw, T., *Prophets of Regulation* (Cambridge: Harvard University Press, 1984) 162 *et seq.*

37 'Stock Exchange Practice': Hearings before the Senate Banking Committee (72nd and 73rd Congress, 1932–34). The purpose of the Stock Exchange Hearings, which lasted nine days, was to determine why these staggering decreases in securities values had occurred and to propose legislation to prevent another stock market crash. They also had an obvious political purpose. During the preceding twelve years, a majority of the country's voters had supported the *laissez-faire* economic policies followed by President Calvin Coolidge. The revelations of the Pecora Hearings were intended to diminish that faith and transform the national sentiment to a regulatory-reform ideology associated with President Roosevelt's New Deal; see Seligman, J., *The Transformation of Wall Street: A History of the Securities and Exchange Commission and Modern Corporate Finance* (Boston: Houghton Mifflin, 1982) 2.

38 The Pecora Hearings, the crash of the stock market, the around 8000 bank failures, the huge unemployment figures, the dismal picture for economic growth, the thousands of Americans who had lost their life savings through no fault of their own and a desire to prevent a total collapse of the banking system, led President Roosevelt to declare a national bank holiday and to draft new regulations to restore financial confidence and safety; see Gart, A., *Regulation, Deregulation, Reregulation: The Future of the Banking, Insurance and Securities Industries* (New York: John Wiley & Sons, 1994) 34. The Glass–Steagal Act required, *inter alia*, private banks to limit themselves either to receiving deposits or to providing investment services. As a consequence, the financial industry was divided into two by separating the business of receiving deposits and making loans (commercial banking) from that of underwriting or acting as a dealer or market maker (investment banking).

39 President Roosevelt stated: 'The new law will safeguard against the abuses of high-pressure salesmanship in security flotations. It will require full disclosure of all the private interests on the part of those who seek securities to the public. The Act is thus intended to correct some of the evils which have been so glaringly

revealed in the private exploitation of the public's money'; Roosevelt, F., *Public Papers and Addresses vol. 2* (New York: Random House, 1938) 213–14.

40 See Seligman, *op. cit.*, note 37, 39 *et seq.*

41 Roosevelt had already drafted Frankfurter as legal advisor and 'recruiting officer' for the New Deal; see Ritchie, A., *James M. Landis: Dean of the Regulators* (Cambridge: Harvard University Press, 1980) 40. Landis was Frankfurter's protégé, a unique academic scholar who became professor at the Harvard Law School at the age of twenty-seven. His advance thereafter was 'meteoric, almost unheard of', as Dean Roscoe Pound would concede; see Seligman, *op. cit.*, note 37, 61. On the interesting correspondence between Roosevelt and Frankfurter, see Freedman, M., *Roosevelt and Frankfurter: Their Correspondence 1928–1945* (Boston: Little, Brown & Company, 1967).

42 In addition to Landis, the team assembled by Frankfurter included two other former students, Thomas Corcoran and Benjamin Cohen, all to become later national heroes and symbols of the New Deal.

43 See Landis, J., 'The Legislative History of the Securities Act of 1933' (1959) 28 George Washington Law Review 29, 30–4; Moley, R., *The First New Deal* (New York: Harcourt, 1966) 306–15; Ritchie, *op. cit.*, note 41, 43.

44 For the history of the writing of the basic securities legislation, see Parrish, M., *Securities Regulation and the New Deal* (New Haven: Yale University Press, 1970) chapters 3–5; Bedts, R., *The New Deal's SEC: The Formative Years* (New York: Columbia University Press, 1964) chapters 2–3; Seligman, *op. cit.*, note 37, 39–100.

45 See Business Week (14 April 1934) 39.

46 Seligman, *op. cit.*, note 37, 97.

47 15 USC 78a *et seq.* (hereinafter, the '1934 Act'). The heart of the Act was Section 4, which created the SEC. Related sections empowered the Commission to enforce the new law and to assume jurisdiction over the 1933 Act. The new agency was to be composed of five commissioners appointed by the President, with the advice and consent of the Senate.

48 Loss, L. *Fundamentals of Securities Regulation* (Boston: Little, Brown & Company, 1983) 792.

49 See the SEC's web site, www.sec.gov.

50 After the adoption of the Gramm–Leach–Bliley Act of 1999, which repealed the Glass–Steagall barriers between commercial and investment banking, the SEC has also supervisory authority over banks and other financial institutions engaged in securities activities. For an analysis of the Gramm–Leach–Bliley Act, see Malloy, M., 'Banking in the Twenty-First Century' (2000) 25 The Journal of Corporation Law 789.

51 The term 'Broker' is defined in Section 3(a)(4) of the 1934 Act as a person 'engaged in the business of effecting transactions in securities for the account of others', while 'dealer' is defined in Section 3(a)(5) as a person 'engaged in the business of buying and selling securities for his own account'. It is important to emphasise that a large portion of US investment firms acts as both brokers and dealers. It is debatable whether Alternative Trading Systems (ATS) are legally treated as brokers-dealers; see *Muni-Action Inc.* (2000 Transfer Binder) FSLR (CCH) 77830 (13 March 2000). This case was invoked by a refusal of the SEC to issue a no-action letter to a web-based service that conducted one-time auctions for municipal bond issuers, rejecting the claim that the firm simply acted as a communications device for the transmission of investor bids and finding instead that it was certainly involved in the order-transmission process.

52   The registration process includes disclosure of specific information regarding investment policies, names, addresses and business experience of principal executives, business organisation and the like. Interestingly, as of 18 March 2002, investment advisers are able to register online, as online filings have become part of the Investment Adviser Registration Depository (IARD) programme developed by the NASAA and the SEC. Firms that have filed on the IARD system are able to register new representatives through the IARD system. The IARD system is intended to benefit regulators and the investment adviser industry because of the cost and time reductions from the elimination of paper filings. Investors should also benefit from easier access to information on investment adviser firms and their representatives.

53   Perhaps the most significant of these requirements is the SEC's net capital rule (15c3-1), which sets out the minimum standards of investment firm solvency based on the balance sheet. Rule 15c3-1 is among the longest and most complex of the SEC's rules.

54   15 USC 80a-1 *et seq.*

55   Besides SEC registration, investment firms must become members of a SRO before commencing business. The NASD and the registered national securities exchanges are all SROs.

56   Section 15(b)(7) gives the SEC the power to set standards of operational capacity, training, experience, competence and other qualifications for registered investment firms and their associated persons. The latter must pass SRO-administrated tests to ensure a basic level of expertise in the securities business; see Exchange Act Release No. 13629 (1977).

57   This is a very narrow exception. To qualify, all aspects of all transactions must be done within the borders of one State. Without SEC registration, no investment firm can participate in any transaction executed on a national securities exchange or the NASDAQ system.

58   Pub. L. No. 104-209, 110 Stat. 3416 (1996).

59   15 USC 77a *et seq.*

60   Such sanctions may be imposed in three types of circumstances: (a) if the SEC finds that the investment firm or the associated persons have committed a wilful violation of the federal securities laws or the rules and regulations thereunder or 'wilfully aided, abetted, counselled, commanded, induced or procured' such a violation by any other person, (b) if it finds that such a person wilfully made a false statement in any application for registration or report to the SEC, and (c) if it finds that such a person is subject to a 'statutory disqualification' – for example, that, he, she, or it has been convicted of a business-related crime within the past ten years or has elsewhere been enjoined from acting as a securities professional. In addition, however, to discipline for direct misconduct, Section 15(b)(4)(E) provides that investment firms and their associated persons may be disciplined merely for failing to supervise their employees with a view towards preventing such violations. It seems that adequate internal supervision and market discipline is a firm-wide responsibility, often requiring a more formalised compliance programme and comprehensive oversight by senior officials; see Task Force on Broker-Dealer Supervision and Compliance of the Committee on Federal Regulation of Securities, 'Broker-Dealer Supervision of Registered Representatives and Branch Office Operations' (1989) 44 Business Lawyer 1361, 1366 *et seq.* The SEC has indicated that it expects that those procedures must apply even to a firm's most senior personnel; see *Butcher & Singer Inc.*, Exchange

Act Release No. 23990, reprinted in FSLR (CCH) 84056 (13 January 1987); *Stein Roe & Farnham*, Advisors Act Release No. 1038 (24 September 1986).

61 Pub. L. No. 101-429, 104 Stat. 931, 15 U.S.C. 78a. On the features of this legislation, see Barnard, J., 'The Securities Law Enforcement Remedies Act of 1989: Disenfranchising Shareholders in order to Protect Them' (1989) 65 Notre Dame Law Review 32; Newkirk, T., McKown, J. and Corso, L., *The SEC's Enforcement Program under the Securities Enforcement Remedies and Penny Stock Reform Act of 1990* (American Bar Association Continuing Legal Education, 17 June 1994).

62 There has been some controversy about the legitimacy of giving such broad-based legal responsibility to what is essentially a private body; see *First Jersey Securities Inc. v Bergen*, 605 F.2d 690 (3d Cir. 1979), *cert. denied*, 444 US 1074 (1980); *Merrill Lynch, Pierce, Fenner & Smith v NASD*, 616 F.2d 1363 (5th Cir. 1980). The major substantive difference between the authority for SRO disciplinary proceedings and the authority for direct administrative enforcement proceedings by the SEC is that the jurisdiction of the latter does not encompass the SROs' ethics-oriented 'just and equitable' rules. When violations are found, courts tend to give the SEC a wide scope of discretion in choosing the appropriate penalty; see *Rizek v SEC*, 215 F.3d 157 (1st Cir. 2000).

63 Pan, E., 'The Case for a Single European Securities Regulator', in Andenas and Avgerinos, *op. cit.*, note 10. Pan argues that Europe already has a dominant securities regulator – the SEC – which influences to a great extent EU regulation. Accordingly, the Union's goal should be to bring into existence a regulator that can act as a counterweight to the SEC.

64 See Benston, G., 'Consumer Protection as Justification for Regulating Financial Services Firms and Products' (2000) 3 Journal of Financial Services Research 277, 278.

65 See Committee for the Study of Economic and Monetary Union, *Report on Economic and Monetary Union in the EC* (Luxembourg, April 1989, hereinafter 'Delors Report') Paragraph 62.

66 For example, the words 'European Central Bank' did not appear in the Delors Report. See Louis, J.V., 'A Monetary Union for Tomorrow?' (1989) 26 CMLRev 301, 311.

67 See, below, Section 5.2.

68 See EP, *Report on the Implementation of Financial Services Legislation* (A5-0011/2002 final, 23 January 2002) 15.

69 See Chapter 4, Section C.3.1

70 Bureaucracy means excessive and oppressive administration, which could inhibit innovation and could ultimately drive business away from European financial markets.

71 See Breuer, R., *Convergence of Supervisory Practices – a Banker's View* (Paper presented at the Conference of European Banking Supervisors, Copenhagen, 20 November 2000).

72 Although the formulation of a monetary policy is highly centralised within the ECB, its execution and operation is more broadly decentralised within the ESCB.

73 Larosière, J. and Lebègue, D., 'Bringing harmony to Europe's markets: Euro-zone states should hasten the integration of their financial systems' (14 September 2000) FT 17.

74 See FESE, *Report and Recommendations on European Regulatory Structures* (September 2000) 12.

75 See Committee of Wise Men, *Final Report on the Regulation of European Securities Markets* (15 February 2001) 18. Furthermore, one of the major institutional

problems facing the EU today is that the structure of the Commission has remained unchanged for more than forty years, and is proving increasingly inadequate to manage the growing complexity of its tasks; see Majone, G., 'Functional Interests: European Agencies', in Peterson and Shackleton, *op. cit.*, note 30, 323.

76   The Economist, *Scrapping over the Pieces* (9 March 2002) 67.
77   Articles 251 and 252 EC Treaty (former Articles 189b and 189c). This will remain even with the 'new' regime proposed by the Wise Men Committee, as the ESC's regulatory power is limited to non-essential implementing rules; see Avgerinos, Y., 'Essential and Non-essential Measures: Delegation of Powers in EU Securities Regulation' (2002) 2 ELJ 269.
78   Parliament and Council *Directive 2001/34/EC of 28 May 2001 on the admission of securities to official stock exchange listing and on information to be published on those securities* (OJ L 184/1, 6 July 2001) Article 108.
79   See European Commission, *Proposal for a Regulation on the Application of International Accounting Standards* (COM(2001) 80 final, 13 February 2001) Article 6.
80   The law-making process within the Council includes indirect democratic control through national parliaments.
81   See Chapter 6, Section B.2.
82   While regulators may not be in as good a position as private enterprises to design effective clearance and settlement systems, some oversight by the pan-European regulator might be helpful in achieving an efficient and workable pan-European securities market that is not fraught with systemic risk.
83   The no-action regime enables the SEC to interpret regulation in a changing market by providing guidance to market participants about the application of regulation of specific circumstances and, if appropriate, to grant relief if the market participant acts in accordance with the SEC's letter; see SEC Release No. 33-6253 (28 October 1980) FSLR 373, 1253 and No. 33-6269 (5 December 1980) FSLR 375, 1257.
84   For an analysis of different types of implementation activities, see Schäfer, G., 'Linking Member State and European Administrations – The Role of Committees and Comitology', in Andenas, M. and Türk, A. (eds), *Delegated Legislation and the Role of Committees in the EC* (London: Kluwer, 2000) 6.
85   The Bingham Report on the BCCI is explicit in that respect: 'the problem nonetheless remains that it is one thing to preach high supervisory standards and maybe another thing to practice them. The Treasury and Civil Service Select Committee has urged that the BIS should expand its role to encompass the monitoring of supervisory standards. This, plainly, is one possibility and other international bodies have been suggested as candidates to perform the task (...). It makes very good sense that supervision should be primarily conducted by the home supervisor, who is closest to the bank and best placed to monitor but if host supervisors are increasingly to rely on the home supervisor they must be reassured by some form of independent verification that the home supervisor is really doing its job'; Bingham, Lord Justice, *Inquiry into the Supervision of Bank of Credit and Commerce International* (HMSO, October 1992) 186.
86   See Chapter 6, Section C.3.2. In any event, the forthcoming ISD II is expected to solve many of the harmonisation problems.
87   'Progressive realisation' is the step-by-step approach proposed by the Delors Report in 1989 and adopted later for the three successive stages of the EMU and the creation of the ECB and the ESCB. See Louis, *op. cit.*, note 66, 315.
88   Mayes *et al.*, *Improving Banking Supervision* (Basingstoke: Palgrave, 2001) 80.

89 The actions of the ESR in this area may serve to alleviate the burden of reporting requirements for financial institutions, by harmonising the statistics and possibly replacing double reporting in several Member States, by single reporting to the ESSR.

90 See, for instance, Welteke, E., *Regulating European Financial Markets* (Speech delivered at the European Banking Conference, Frankfurt, 17 November 2000).

91 See Chapter 6, Section C.2.2.

92 See, for instance, Deutsche Bank, *Regulation and Banking Supervision: Caught Between the Nation State and Global Financial Markets* (Frankfurt: EMU Watch No. 86, 29 June 2000) 7.

93 The newly established European Company could serve as an example.

94 The hybrid system is not a new concept in European financial services. A similar regime has been recently proposed by the EP in the Huhne Report on the POP II Directive, which exempts from the scope of the directive issuers SMEs of national reach; EP, *Report on the proposal for a directive on the prospectus to be published when securities are offered to the public or admitted to trading* (A5-0072/2002, 27 February 2002) 32.

95 Market discipline is one of the three major elements adopted by the New Basel Capital Accord. The increased reliance on disclosure of information regarding risk assessment methods and capital adequacy calculations is intended to shift some of the role of regulation on to 'market discipline'. 'Meaningful disclosures inform market participants and facilitate market discipline'; see Basel Committee, *Overview of the New Basel Capital Accord* (Consultative Document, January 2001) 33. For the advantages of market discipline, see Caprio, G., *Bank Regulation: The Case of the Missing Model* (World Bank Policy Research WP No 1574, January 1996); Evanoff, D., 'Preferred Source of Market Discipline' (1993) 10 Yale Journal on Regulation 347. Minimum capital requirements and supervisory review process are the two remaining pillars that form the heart of the new Basel proposal. In a significant departure from the existing Capital Accord, new minimum capital requirements apply not only to market and credit risk as previously, but also to operational risk. Supervisory review, on the other hand, would allow regulators to adjust a bank's capital requirement in response to 'soft factors', such as the perceived quality of its internal risk assessment and would necessitate mechanisms that ensure comparable implementation across countries.

Self-regulation plays an increasingly significant role in highly technical areas of regulation, such as financial services, and offers a number of advantages; see Majone, G., *Regulating Europe* (London: Routledge, 1996) 23; Ogus, A., *Regulation – Legal Form and Economic Theory* (Oxford: Clarendon Press, 1994) 107. In the United States, for instance, the NASD registers member firms, writes rules to govern their behaviour, inspects their offices, books and records for violations of SEC regulations, and disciplines those that fail to comply, which is more efficient than direct governmental regulation.

96 Enron was perceived as a highly successful company and owed much of its initial success to deregulation, both in the gas and electricity and in a variety of other areas. More specifically, it was the product of reduced accounting regulation and supervision by the SEC. Inadequate accounting rules were partly responsible for the failure to disclose complex off-balance-sheet transactions and to uncover highly risky operations. Enron filed a petition for relief under Chapter 11 of the US Bankruptcy Code on 2 December 2001. Only then did market analysts react and shareholders and creditors became aware of its vulnerabilities.

For an initial reflection, see Padoa-Schioppa, T., *Reflections on Recent Financial Incidents* (Speech at the Third Joint Central Bank Research Conference on Risk Measurement and Systemic Risk, Basel, 8 March 2002). When Enron filed at the end of 2001, nobody expected there would be an even bigger bankruptcy within the next year. However, after the disclosure of a $3.9 billion accounting fraud, WorldCom, once the second largest long-distance telecommunications provider in the United States, filed for bankruptcy under Chapter 11 on 22 July 2002. On 27 June 2002, the SEC had filed a civil action in the federal district court in New York charging WorldCom with a massive accounting fraud totalling more than $3.9 billion. The SEC's complaint alleged that WorldCom fraudulently overstated its income before income taxes and minority interests by approximately $3.055 billion in 2001 and $797 million during the first quarter of 2002; see SEC, Litigation Release No. 17588 and Accounting and Auditing Release No. 1585 (27 June 2002). The sudden collapse of WorldCom deepened concerns about accounting, corporate governance and the quality of earnings; see Larsen, P. and Chaffin, J. 'WorldCom board agrees to file for bankruptcy' (22 July 2002) FT 1 and 27; The Economist, 'When something is rotten' (27 July 2002) 61–3.

97 Although there are differences, there were echoes of the 1930s when, in the aftermath of the Great Crash of 1929, Wall Street became public enemy number one; see Hill, A., 'Greed and fear return' (8 June 2002) FT 12; The Economist, 'The value of trust' (8 June 2002) 63.

98 The SEC has recently published a series of releases modifying, in a manner appropriate for the protection of investors, the requirements for including audited financial statements in registration statements under the Securities Act of 1933 and filings required by the Trust Indenture Act of 1939; see SEC Release Nos. 33-8070, 34-45590, 35-27503, 39-2395, IA-2018, IC-25464 and FR-62 (18 March 2002). Furthermore, on 20 June 2002 the SEC proposed rules to reform oversight and improve accountability of auditors of public companies, thereby enhancing the reliability and integrity of the financial reporting process. The proposed rules establish the framework for a Public Accountability Board (PBA), a system of 'private sector' (but not 'self') regulation that would not be under the control of the accounting profession. The structure is intended to supplement the SEC's oversight and enforcement efforts by expanding the opportunities to detect and remedy ethical lapses or deficiencies in competence, thereby complementing the Commission's enforcement efforts. The rules were based on months of extensive public input, including comments received during a series of SEC-sponsored Roundtables and the SEC's first Investor Summit. In order to receive additional public input, the rules remained open for comments for two months before being published in the Federal Register. Finally, on 13 February 2002 SEC Chairman Harvey Pitt asked the New York Stock Exchange (NYSE) to review its corporate governance listing standards. In conjunction with that request, the NYSE appointed this Corporate Accountability and Listing Standards Committee to review the NYSE's current listing standards, along with recent proposals for reform, with the goal of enhancing the accountability, integrity and transparency of the Exchange's listed companies. The proposals include a few gestures towards the corporate social responsibility lobby, such as the requirements that listed companies should publish corporate governance guidelines and a code of ethics on their websites. The main focus, however, has been on ideas for strengthening the role of independent (non-executive) directors, by demanding that a majority of the board consists of independent directors, that audit and remuneration committees be composed only of such directors, and that they meet each other and

company managers without the chief executive being present; see New York Stock Exchange Corporate Accountability and Listing Standards Committee Report (6 June 2002); The Economist, 'Designed by committee' (15 June 2002) 69–71.

99 See Jachtenfuchs, M., 'The Governance Approach to European Integration' (2001) 2 JCMS 245, 252.

100 For the pros and cons of incentive versus rule-based regulation, see Dhumale, R., 'Incentive v. Rule-Based Financial Regulation: A Role for Market Discipline', in Ferran E. and Goodhart, C. (eds), *Regulating Financial Services and Markets in the Twenty First Century* (Oxford: Hart, 2001) 66.

101 For an analysis on the costs and benefits of disclosure, see Basel Committee, *Enhancing Bank Transparency* (September 1998).

102 Regretfully, only investment firms engaged in *systematic* order-matching (ATS) are proposed to adopt these systems (emphasis added); European Commission, *Revision of ISD: Second Consultation* (25 March 2002) 24.

103 Mayes *et al.*, *op. cit.*, note 88, 171.

104 Tyco is a former New England electronics maker that has turned into a high-powered conglomerate. Its chairman and chief executive was forced to resign after allegations and charges of misuse of loans from the conglomerate and tax evasion; see The Economist, 'Taxing times' (8 May 2002) 57. WorldCom is the second largest long-distance telecommunications provider in the United States. For Enron and WorldCom, see *supra*, note 96.

105 See Proposed IAS Regulation, *op. cit.*, note 79.

106 European Commission, *A first EU response to Enron related policy issues* (Note for the informal ECOFIN meeting, Oviedo 12–13 April 2002). The Commission strongly promotes a strategy based on a principles-based approach to financial reporting, designed to reflect economic reality and so giving a true and fair view of the financial position and performance of a company. In this light, auditing standards, transparency and effective corporate governance are crucial to providing high quality audits.

   Various international *fora* are also studying the issues raised by Enron and other corporate failures. The March 2002 Financial Stability Forum meeting in Hong Kong discussed weaknesses in accounting and corporate governance. IOSCO has created a high-level subcommittee to assess accounting standards, disclosure and transparency practices, the role of ratings agencies, and the treatment of off-balance-sheet transactions. The Basel Committee on Banking Supervision is addressing banks' use of special purpose vehicles. The OECD plans to discuss corporate governance. Finally, the recent IMF Quarterly Report on Market Developments and Issues highlighted a number of weaknesses in accounting rules and their implementation, corporate governance, and lax market discipline; see IMF, *Global Financial Stability Report* (June 2002) Chapter II.

107 For a 'spectrum' of responses available to supervisors, see New Basel Capital Accord, *op. cit.*, note 95, 115.

108 See Articles 230 (former Article 173) and 232 (former Article 175) EC Treaty for other EU institutions.

109 Especially review competence *vis-à-vis* the acts of the ECB might be difficult to exercise, given the inherent complexities of monetary policy; see Leino, *op. cit.*, note 12, 14.

110 There is no provision that would permit states or individuals to claim that they have been affected in a discriminatory manner by an act of general application; see Dunnett, R., 'Legal and Institutional Issues Affecting Economic and

Monetary Union', in O'Keeffe, D. and Twomey, P. (eds), *Legal Issues of the Maastricht Treaty* (Bath: Chancery Law Publishing, 1994) 145.

111 Case 294/83 *Les Verts* [1986] ECR 1339, Paragraphs 23–5.

112 See European Commission, *Financial Services: Implementing the Framework for Financial Markets: Action Plan* (COM(1999) 232, 11 May 1999) 10. Indeed, Member States have declared their intent to cooperate on a cross-border basis by agreeing on the *Memorandum of Understanding on a Cross-Border Out-of-Court Complaints Network for Financial Services in the European Economic Area* (1 February 2001), which is based on the Commission *Recommendation 98/257/EC on the principles applicable to the bodies responsible for out-of-court settlement of consumer disputes* (30 March 1998). On 2 September 2002, the Commission launched a consumers' guide to FIN-NET, which aims to help European citizens to under-stand and use the FIN-NET network. The Guide gives consumers information about: (a) what to do if they have a complaint against a financial services provider in another Member State, (b) procedures for setting consumer financial services disputes out of court in the EEA, (c) how FIN-NET works, and (d) how to contact the national complaint schemes participating in the FIN-NET.

113 See the Financial Services and Markets Act 2000, Part IX, Section 132. FSMA 2000 received Royal Assent on 14 June 2000. 'N2', the date when the FSA assumed its responsibilities and powers under the FSMA, was 30 November 2001.

114 The procedure comprises both an administrative and a judicial stage. First, the Commission will send a reasoned opinion and then it will bring an action before the ECJ, if the Member State fails to comply with the opinion within the period laid down by the Commission.

115 *Opinion delivered pursuant to the second subparagraph of Article 228(1) of the Treaty* [1991] ECR I-6079, Paragraph 4. The ECJ did not find that an international agreement providing for the creation of a system of courts to interpret and apply the agreement's provisions was *per se* incompatible with the Treaty. However, under the agreement, the EEA Court would not subject to subsequent decisions of the ECJ, but the latter would only have an advisory role to the courts and tri-bunals of the EEA States. Hence, the ECJ concluded that the establishment of a EEA Court violated Community law.

116 FSMA 2000, Part VIII, Section 118(5).

117 *Wertpapierhandelsgesetz – WpHG* (v.26.7.1994, BGBl. I S.1750-60) Part 3, Sections 12 and 16(4).

118 *Strafgesetzbuch – StGB* (v.15.5.1871, RGBl. S. 127) Section 7(2)(1).

119 CESR-Pol, which has been created by the signature of the FESCO Multilateral Memorandum on the Exchange of Information of securities activities in January 1999, is composed of senior officials of each authority who are responsible for the surveillance of securities activities and the exchange of information. Its objective is to make cross-border information flows equally rapid as for a domes-tic matter and, by doing so, enhance the transparency, the fairness and the integrity of the European markets as a whole

120 See FESCO, *Market Conduct Standards for Participants in an Offering* (22 December 1999).

121 See, for instance, Green, D., 'Enhanced Co-operation among Regulators and the Role of National Regulators in a Global Market' (2000) 2 JIFM 7, 11. As Green puts it 'regulators do not exist in the abstract, floating above the national legal systems'.

122 See Council *Regulation No 1348/2000 of 29 May 2000 on the serving in the Member States of judicial and extrajudicial documents in civil and commercial matters*

(OJ L 160/37, 30 June 2000) and *Regulation No 1206/2001 of 28 May 2001 on coop-eration between the courts of the Member States in the taking of evidence in civil and commercial matters* (OJ L 174/1, 27 June 2001).

123 Council *Decision 2001/470/EC of 28 May 2001 establishing a European Judicial Network in civil and commercial matters* (OJ L 174/25, 27 June 2001).

124 Case 14/83 *Von Colson* [1984] ECR 1891.

125 *Ibid.*, Paragraph 23; Opinion of Advocate General Rozès, Paragraph I(3). Also, the so-called obligation of 'Community loyalty' expressed in Article 10 EC Treaty (former Article 5) is not specified in any detail, which lets us assume that it is an obligation of result rather than method.

126 In order to be effective, the measure must reinforce the value of the rule or principle infringed, and so reflect the gravity of the infringement and seek to deter further infringements. In other words, the measure must be deterrent, pro-portionate and comparable to sanctions applied to offences of the same gravity; See Opinion of Advocate General Rozès, *ibid.*, Paragraph I(4).

127 Case C-68/88 *Commission v Greece* [1989] ECR 2965, Paragraph 24.

128 See Harding, C., 'Member State Enforcement of European Community Measures: The Chimera of "Effective" Enforcement' (1997) 4 Maastricht Journal of European and Comparative Law 5, 22.

129 See Hertig, G., 'Regulatory Competition for EU Financial Services' (2000) 2 Journal of International Economic Law 349, 374

130 See Chapter 5, Section B.2.

131 For a balance of powers between EU institutions and national authorities based on the doctrine of separation of powers, see Kirchhof, P., 'The Balance of Powers between the National and European Institutions' (1999) 3 ELJ 225.

132 See new Basel Capital Accord, *op. cit.*, note 95, 30.

8 Consolidating Financial Supervision

1 Goodhart, C. *et al.*, *Financial Regulation: Why, How and Where Now?* (London: Routledge, 1998) 143.

2 In Europe alone, more than 1500 new cases of domestic groups engaged in bank-ing, securities and insurance activities have been reported since 1995; see European Commission, *Progress on Financial Services: 2nd Report* (COM(2000) 336, 31 May 2000) 5.

3 Carton de Tournai, G., 'A Few Reflections on Financial Conglomerates and Their Supervision', in Wymeersch, E. (ed.), *Further Perspectives in Financial Integration in Europe* (Berlin: Walter de Gruyter, 1994) 66.

4 The term 'financial conglomerate' means a group of companies under common control that engages in a range of different financial activities, which were or are traditionally kept separate by law or regulation.

5 See *Directive 83/350/EEC* (OJ L 193/18, 18 July 1983) and *Directive 92/30/EEC on the supervision of credit institutions on a consolidated basis* (OJ L 110/52, 28 April 1992), *Directive 98/78/EC on the supplementary supervision of insurance undertak-ings in insurance groups* (OJ L 330/1, 5 December 1998), and *post-BCCI Directive 95/26/EEC* (OJ L 168/7, 18 July 1995).

6 A recent proposal seeks to introduce specific prudential legislation for financial conglomerates and takes the initial steps to align the directives for homogeneous financial groups and for financial conglomerates in order to ensure a minimum equivalency in their treatment; see European Commission, *Proposal for a Directive*

> *on the supplementary supervision of credit institutions, insurance undertakings and investment firms in a financial conglomerate and amending Council Directives 73/239/EEC, 79/267/EEC, 92/49/EEC, 92/96/EEC, 93/6/EEC, 93/22/EEC, and Directives 98/78/EC and 2000/12/EC of the Parliament and the Council* (COM(2001) 213 final, 24 April 2001, hereinafter 'Conglomerates Directive').

7 Joint Forum, *Supervision of Financial Conglomerates* (December 1999).

8 Economic and Financial Committee, *Report on Financial Stability* (EFC/ECFIN/240/00, 8 April 2000, 'Brouwer Report').

9 'Homogeneous' groups of financial institutions are already covered by EU directives for specific prudential purposes: Directive 2000/12/EC relating on the taking up and pursuit of the business of credit institutions and Directive 93/6/EEC on the capital adequacy of investment firms and credit institutions provide for the consolidation of banking groups, investment firm groups and bank/investment firm groups, whereas Directive 98/78/EC on the supplementary supervision of insurance undertakings in insurance groups applies additional group supervision over insurance groups.

10 'Heterogeneous' financial conglomerate-type groups combining firms from the different sectors are merely covered to a limited extent and basically a comprehensive set of rules on their prudential supervision is lacking.

11 Conglomerates Directive, Article 7.

12 *Ibid.*, 4–5.

13 Briault, C., *The Rationale for a Single National Financial Services Regulator* (FSA Occasional Paper Series No. 2, May 1999) 15.

14 Meister, E., *How should regulatory and supervisory responsibilities be shared among the national functional regulators?* (Lecture held at the Multinational Banking Seminar, New York, 9 June 2001).

15 That is the case in Sweden, Denmark, Norway, the United Kingdom and, recently, in Austria. The *Finansinspektionen* was created in Sweden in July 1991 in response to actual and prospective market developments, including increasing integration both among different types of financial institutions and across borders. Similarly, the *Finanstilsynet* in Denmark (established in 1988) and the *Kredittilsynet* in Norway (established in 1986) supervise the banking, securities and insurance sectors. The new Austrian Financial Markets Supervision Act (*Finanzmarktaufsichtsgesetz*) establishing the Austrian Financial Market Authority (FMA) became effective as of 1 April 2002. In the global scene, Japan introduced a single regulator in June 1998, as did Korea in April 1998 with the new Financial Supervisory Service, and Iceland (the *Fjármálaesfirlit*) in January 1999. In 1987, the Canadian authorities merged banking and insurance regulation in the Office of the Superintendent of Financial Institutions (OSFI), while Hungary joined the list in April 2000, Latvia in 2001, and Estonia in 2002.

16 Consultation is underway in Germany, Ireland, Greece and Finland on government proposals to form a single financial services regulator. Also, Switzerland, Israel, Mexico and South Africa are among several countries considering moves towards a single regulator.

17 Briault, *op. cit.*, note 13, 5. See also, Briault, C., *Revisiting the Rationale for a Single National Financial Services Regulator* (FSA Occasional Paper Series No. 16, February 2002).

18 The text of the Act, its explanatory notes and the relevant Parliamentary debates can be found at www.fsa.gov.uk/fsma.

19 Although the FSMA has some 433 sections and 22 schedules, the final enactment provides only the framework, with a large part of the substance of the financial

reform left to secondary legislation. For the features of the legislation, see Alcock, A., *The Financial Services and Markets Act 2000: A Guide to the New Law* (Bristol: Jordans, 2000); Blair, M. *et al.*, *Blackstone's Guide to the Financial Services & Markets Act 2000* (London: Blackstone Press, 2001); Davies, H., 'Law and Financial Regulation' (1993) 4–5 JIFM 193; MacNeil, I., 'The Future for Financial Regulation: The Financial Services and Markets Bill' (1999) 62 MLR 725.

20 See Walker, G., *International Banking Regulation: Law, Policy and Practice* (London: Kluwer Law International, 2001) 247. The new agency was originally only referred to as New RO but was subsequently named the Financial Services Authority at its formal launch on 28 October 1997.

21 For an analysis on the history of the Bank of England, see Sir Clapham, J., *The Bank of England: A History* (Cambridge: The University Press, 1970); Giuseppi, J., *The Bank of England: A History from its Foundation in 1694* (London: Evans Bros, 1966); Schooner, H. and Taylor, M., 'Convergence and Competition: The Case of Bank Regulation in Britain and the United States' (1999) 20 Michigan Journal of International Law 595, 606 *et seq*. The central argument of Schooner and Taylor is the proposition that, even in the presence of globalised financial markets and the opportunities for rule competition brought in their wake, the financial regulatory system of the United Kingdom continues to be shaped for the most part by its prior history.

22 See Large, A., *Report to the Chancellor on the Reform of the Financial Regulatory System* (July 1997).

23 For earlier comments, see the interview with Alistair Darling, Labour's Spokesman on the City in 'Through the Looking Glass' (March 1996) 323 Euromoney 63–5. The new FSA was launched on 28 October 1997 by the Chancellor of the Exchequer. The first stage of the reform was completed in June 1998, when responsibility for banking supervision was transferred to the FSA from the Bank of England. In the interim, the Bank of England's powers to regulate banks have already been transferred to the FSA by virtue of the amendments made to the Banking Act 1987 by the Bank of England Act 1998. Then, the FSMA 2000 transferred to the FSA the responsibilities of several other organizations and transformed it to the 'broadest and most comprehensive financial regulator in the world'; see Davies, *op. cit.*, note 19, 193.

24 See Davies, H., *Why Regulate?* (Henry Thornton Lecture, City University, 4 November 1998).

25 Thieffry, G., 'After the "Lamfalussy" Report: The First Step towards a European Securities Commission (ESC)?', in Andenas, M. and Avgerinos, Y., *Financial Market Supervision in Europe: Towards a Single Regulator?* (London: Kluwer, forthcoming 2003).

26 See Lastra, R., *Central Banking and Banking Regulation* (London: Financial Markets Group, London School of Economics, 1996) 149.

27 See Fender, I. and von Hagen, J., *Central Bank Policy in a More Perfect Financial System* (ZEI Policy Paper B03, 1998)

28 In Greece, France, Spain, Italy, Ireland, Netherlands and Portugal the central bank functions as a supervisor as well, while in Belgium, Denmark, Germany, Luxembourg, Austria, Finland, Sweden and the United Kingdom it does not; see Chapter 4, Section C.2.

29 Beyond nationally, these questions become extremely important and at the European level, in the context of the functions of the ECB and the ESCB. The Statute of the ECB empowers it to conduct pan-European monetary policy, but leaves the exercise of banking supervision to national authorities.

30 Goodhart, C. and Schoenmaker, D., 'Should the Functions of Monetary Policy and Banking Supervision be Separated?' (1995) 4 Oxford Economic Papers 539, 545.

31 See Louis, J.V. *et al.*, *Banking Supervision in the European Community* (Brussels: University of Brussels, 1995) 56.

32 See Lastra, *op. cit.*, note 26.

33 Minimum reserves fall within the ambit of monetary policy, even though they have an influence on the liquidity of banks and thus on their prudential situation; see Louis *et al.*, *op. cit.*, note 31, 55.

34 Although in most central banks supervisors are usually kept physically separated from the rest of the staff for security and confidentiality purposes, important rescue decisions are taken at a strategic, policy-making level, where the general concern of the central bank is taken into account.

35 Goodhart and Schoenmaker, *op. cit.*, note 30, 554.

36 See Smits, R., *The European Central Bank: Institutional Aspects* (The Hague: Kluwer, 1997) 334; Moloney, N., *EC Securities Regulation* (Oxford: Oxford University Press, 2002) 893.

37 EC Treaty, Article 105(5) and Statute, Article 3.3.

38 Article 25.5 of the Statute states: 'The ECB may offer advice to and be consulted by the Council, the Commission and the competent authorities of the Member States on the scope and implementation of Community legislation relating to the prudential supervision of credit institutions and to the stability of the financial system'.

39 Article 5.1 of the Statute states: 'In order to undertake the tasks of the ESCB, the ECB, assisted by the national central banks, shall collect the necessary statistical information either from the competent national authorities or directly from economic agents. For these purposes it shall co-operate with the Community institutions or bodies and with the competent authorities of the Member States or third countries and with international organisations'.

40 Smits notes that Article 105(6) 'seems to imply a supervisory function separate from the competence of NCBs and other supervisory agencies. This may be read as a task alongside the supervisory tasks of these authorities as well as an overseeing role, more far-reaching than the coordinating one which the [ESCB] is to play from the outset'; Smits, *op. cit.*, note 36, 356.

41 Di Giorgio, G. and Di Noia, C., *Designing Institutions for Financial Stability: Regulation and Supervision by Objective for the Euro Area* (mimeo, November 2000); Lannoo, K., 'Challenges to the structure of financial supervision in the EU' (CEPS, 1999).

42 As the following paradigms suggest, this structure may have slight differences.

43 Elements of this system are traced in Italy, for example, where banks and investment firms are controlled by the central bank for systemic stability and prudential supervision and by CONSOB for conduct of business rules.

44 Goodhart *et al.*, *op. cit.*, note 1, 156.

45 Taylor, M., *Twin Peaks: A Regulatory Structure for the New Century* (London: Centre for the Study of Financial Innovation, December 1995).

46 An earlier paper of the Centre for the Study of Financial Innovation argued that the UK supervisory system had failed to keep up with the radical changes taking place in the financial services industry. Therefore, it proposed a new Financial Services Commission to take over the regulatory roles of the Bank of England, the Building Societies Commission and other regulatory bodies; see *UK Financial Supervision: A Blueprint for Change* (London: Centre for the Study of Financial Innovation, May 1994).

47 Di Giorgio, G., Di Noia, C. and Piatti, L., 'Financial Market Regulation: The Case of Italy and a Proposal for the Euro area', in Andenas, M. and Avgerinos, Y. (eds), *Financial Market Supervision in Europe: Towards a Single Regulator?* (London: Kluwer, forthcoming 2003).

48 Goodhart *et al.*, *op. cit.*, note 1, 159 *et seq.*

49 The ERF was set up informally on the Commission's initiative early in 2000 to meet the call from the Economic and Financial Committee. It comprises the Chairmen of the EU financial regulatory and supervisory groups: BAC, ECB Banking Supervisory Committee, Contact Group of banking supervisors, Insurance Committee, Conference of Insurance Supervisory Authorities, ESC and CESR.

50 Perhaps the British would be willing to abandon their traditional opposition to a pan-European authority, given that substantial gain was offered to them in exchange, e.g., its establishment in London.

51 Green, D., 'Enhanced Co-operation among Regulators and the Role of National Regulators in a Global Market' (2000) 2 JIFM 7.

52 ECB, *The Role of Central Banks in Prudential Supervision* (March 2001).

53 Goodhart and Schoenmaker, *op. cit.*, note 30, 539.

Epilogue

1 White Paper on Governance, 3.

2 Bolkestein, F., *The EU's Economic Test: Meeting the Challenges of the Lisbon Strategy* (Speech delivered at the 17th Annual State of the International Economy Conference, London, 19 November 2001).

References

Books

Alcock, A., *The Financial Services and Markets Act 2000: A Guide to the New Law* (Bristol: Jordans, 2000)

Andenas, M. & Avgerinos, Y., *Financial Market Supervision in Europe: Towards a Single Regulator?* (London: Kluwer Law International, forthcoming 2003)

Andenas, M., Gormley, L., Hadjiemmanuil, C. & Harden, I., *European Economic and Monetary Union: The Institutional Framework* (London: Kluwer Law International, 1997)

Andenas, M. & Türk, A., *Delegated Legislation and the Role of Committees in the EC* (London: Kluwer Law International, 2000)

Bedts, R., *The New Deal's SEC: The Formative Years* (New York: Columbia University Press, 1964)

Benink, H., *Financial Integration in Europe* (Dordrecht: Kluwer Academic Publishers, 1993)

Bernstein, P., *Capital Ideas* (New York: Free Press, 1992)

Bingham, Lord Justice, *Inquiry into the Supervision of Bank of Credit and Commerce International* (London: HMSO 1992)

Blair, M. *et al.*, *Blackstone's guide to the Financial Services & Markets Act 2000* (London: Blackstone Press, 2001)

Bratton, W., McCahery, J., Picciotto, S. & Scott, C., *International Regulatory Competition and Coordination* (Oxford: Clarendon Press, 1996)

Brenton, P. & Vancauteren, M., *The Extent of Economic Integration in Europe: Border Effects, Technical Barriers to Trade & Home Bias in Consumption* (CEPS WP No. 171, August 2001)

Breyer, S., *Regulation and Its Reform* (Cambridge: Harvard University Press, 1982)

Buchanan, J., *Liberty, Market and State: Political Economy in the 1980s* (Brighton: Wheatsheaf, 1986)

Buxbaum, R., Hertig, G., Hirsch, A. & Hopt, K., *European Business Law: Legal and Economic Analysis on Integration and Harmonisation* (Berlin: Walter de Gruyter, 1991)

Buxbaum, R., Hertig, G., Hirsch, A. & Hopt, K., *European Economic and Business Law: Legal and Economic Analysis on Integration and Harmonisation* (New York: Walter de Gruyter, 1996)

Campbell, D., *Financial Services in the New Europe* (London: Graham & Trotman, 1994)

Chalmers, D. & Szyszczak, E., *European Union Law, Volume II: Towards a European Policy?* (Ashgate: Aldershot, 1998)

Chryssochoou, D., *Democracy in the European Union* (London: Tauris Academic Studies, 1998)

Clapham, J., *The Bank of England: A History* (Cambridge: The University Press, 1970)

Cox, J., Hillman, R. & Langevoort, D., *Securities Regulation: Cases and Materials* (Gaithersburg: Aspen Law & Business, 3rd ed., 2001)

Craig, P. & De Burca, G., *The Evolution of EU Law* (Oxford: Oxford University Press, 1999)

Craig, P. & De Burca, G., *EU Law: Texts, Cases and Materials* (Oxford: Oxford University Press, 2nd ed., 1998)

Cranston, R., *Principles of Banking Law* (Oxford: Oxford University Press, 1997)

Cranston, R., *The Single Market and the Law of Banking* (London: Lloyd's of London Press, 2nd ed., 1995)

Cranston, R., *The Single Market and the Law of Banking* (London: Lloyd's of London Press, 1991)

Dale, R., *International Banking Deregulation: The Great Banking Experiment* (Oxford: Blackwell, 1992)

Danthine, J.P., Giavazzi, F., Vives, X. & von Thadden, E.L., *The Future of European Banking* (London: Centre of Economic Policy Research, 1999)

Dassesse, M., Isaacs, S. & Penn, G., *EC Banking Law* (London: Lloyd's of London Press, 2nd ed., 1994)

Davis, P., *Debt, Financial Fragility and Systemic Risk* (Oxford: Clarendon Press, 1995)

Den Boer, M., Guggenbühl, A. & Vanhoonacker, S., *Coping with Flexibility and Legitimacy after Amsterdam* (Maastricht: European Institute of Public Administration, 1998)

Di Giorgio, G., Di Noia, C. & Piatti, L., *Financial Market Regulation: The Case of Italy and a Proposal for the Euro Area* (Pennsylvania: Financial Institutions Center, 2000)

Dobson, W. & Jacquet, P., *Financial Services Liberalization in the WTO* (Washington: Institute for International Economics, 1998)

Duff, A., *Subsidiarity within the European Community* (London: Federal Trust for Education and Research, 1993)

Dyson, K., *The Politics of the Euro-Zone* (Oxford: Oxford University Press, 2000)

Edwards, F. & Patrick, H., *Regulating International Financial Markets: Issues and Policies* (Boston: Kluwer Academic Publishers, 1992)

Edwards, V., *EC Company Law* (Oxford: Clarendon Press, 1999)

Eichengreen, B., *European Monetary Unification: Theory, Practice and Analysis* (Cambridge: Massachusetts Institute of Technology Press, 1997)

Eichengreen, B., *Should the Maastricht Treaty be Saved?* (Princeton: Princeton University, 1992)

Engler, H. & Essinger, J., *The Future of Banking* (London: Pearson Education, 2000)

European Commission, *Economies of Scale: Impact on Competition and Scale Effects* (London: Kogan Page, EarthScan, 1997)

Evans, P., Rieschemeyer, D. & Skocpol, T., *Bringing the State Back in* (Cambridge: Cambridge University Press, 1985)

Fair, D. & Raymond, R., *Competitiveness of Financial Institutions and Centres in Europe* (Dordrecht: Kluwer Law International, 1994)

Ferran, E. & Goodhart, C., *Regulating Financial Services and Markets in the Twenty First Century* (Oxford: Hart, 2001)

Ferrarini, G., *European Securities Markets: The Investment Services Directive and Beyond* (London: Kluwer Law International, 1998)

Ferrarini, G., *Prudential Regulation of Banks and Securities Firms: European and International Aspects* (London: Kluwer Law International, 1995)

Franke, H.H., *Europäische Währungsunion: Von den Konzeption zur Gestaltung: Beihäfte zu Kredit und Kapital H.14/1998* (Berlin: Dunker & Humblot, 1998)

Freedman, M., *Roosevelt and Frankfurter: Their Correspondence 1928–1945* (Boston: Little, Brown & Company, 1967)

Frieden, J., Gros, D. & Jones, E., *The New Political Economy of EMU* (Lanham: Rowman & Littlefield, 1998)

Friedland, J., *The Law and Structure of the International Financial System: Regulation in the US, EEC and Japan* (Westport: Quorum Books, 1994)

Galbraith, J., *The Great Crash 1929* (Boston: Houghton Mifflin, 1997)

Gambetta, D., *Trust: Making and Breaking Cooperative Relations* (Oxford: Blackwell, 1988)

Gart, A., *Regulation, Deregulation, Reregulation: The Future of the Banking, Insurance and Securities Industries* (New York: John Wiley & Sons, 1994)

Giavazzi, F., Micossi, S. & Miller, M. (eds), *The European Monetary System* (Cambridge: Cambridge University Press, 1988)

Gilligan, G., *Regulating the Financial Services Sector* (London: Kluwer Law International, 1999)

Giovanoli, M., *International Monetary Law* (Oxford: Oxford University Press, 2000)

Giovanoli, M. & Heinrich, G., *International Bank Insolvencies: A Central Bank Perspective* (London: Kluwer Law International, 1999)

Giuseppi, J., *The Bank of England: A History from its Foundation in 1694* (London: Evans Bros, 1966)

Goldstein, M., *The Asian Financial Crisis: Causes, Cures, and Systemic Implications* (Washington: Institute for International Economics, 1998)

Goodhart, C. *et al.*, *Financial Regulation: Why, How and Where Now?* (London: Routledge, 1998)

Goodhart, C., *Money, Information and Uncertainty* (Cambridge: Massachusetts Institute of Technology Press, 1989)

Gros, D., *EMU and Capital Markets: The Institutional Framework* (Frankfurt: Institut für Kapitalmarktforschung, April 1998)

Gros, D. & Thygesen N., *European Monetary Integration* (Harlow: Longman, 2nd ed., 1998)

Hadjiemmanuil, C., *The European Central Bank and Banking Supervision* (London: Centre for Commercial Law Studies, 1996)

Hayek, F.A., *New Studies in Philosophy, Politics, Economics and the History of Ideas* (Chicago: University of Chicago Press, 1978)

Hazen, T., *The Law of Securities Regulation* (St. Paul: West Publications, 1996)

Hirst, P. & Thompson, G., *Globalization in Question: The International Economy and the Possibilities of Governance* (Cambridge: Cambridge Polity Press, 1996)

Hodges, M., Kirton, J. & Daniels, J., *The G8's Role in the New Millennium* (Aldershot: Ashgate, 1999)

Hoschka, T., *Cross-Border Entry in European Retail Financial Services: Determinants, Regulation and the Impact on Competition* (New York: St. Martin's Press, 1993)

Jeunemaitre, A., *Financial Markets Regulation: A Practitioner's Perspective* (Basingstoke: Macmillan Press, 1997)

Kapteyn, P. & Verloren Van Themaat, P., *Introduction to the Law of the European Communities* (Deventer: Kluwer Law International, 2nd ed., 1989)

Kenen, P., *Economic and Monetary Union in Europe: Moving beyond Maastricht* (Cambridge: Cambridge University Press, 1995)

Keohane, R. & Hoffman, S., *The New European Community – Decision-making and Institutional Change* (Boulder: Westview Press, 1991)

Keynes, J.M., *The General Theory of Employment, Interest and Money* (New York: Harcourt, Brace & World, 1936)

Kingdon, J., *Agendas, Alternatives and Public Policies* (Boston: Little, Brown & Company, 1984)

Lannoo, K., *Challenges to the Structure of Financial Supervision in the EU* (Brussels: Centre of European Policy Studies, July 2000)

Lannoo, K., *Does Europe need an SEC?* (Madrid: European Capital Markets Institute, November 1999)

Lannoo, K., *Challenges to the Structure of Financial Supervision in the EU* (Brussels: Centre of European Policy Studies, 1999)

Lannoo, K., *Financial Supervision in EMU* (Brussels: Centre of European Policy Studies, 1999)

Lastra, R., *The Reform of the International Financial Architecture* (London: Kluwer Law International, 2000)

Lee, R., *What is an Exchange? The Automation, Management and Regulation of Financial Markets* (Oxford: Oxford University Press, 1998)

Lastra, R., *Central Banking and Banking Regulation* (London: Financial Markets Group, London School of Economics, 1996)

Lipgens, W., Loth, W. & Milward, A., *A History of European Integration, Vol. 1, 1945–1947, The Formation of the European Unity Movement* (London: Clarendon & OUP, 1982)

Llewellyn, D., *The Regulation and Supervision of Financial Institutions* (London: Institute of Bankers, Gilbart Lectures on Banking, 1986)

Lo, A.W., *The Industrial Organization and Regulation of the Securities Industry* (Chicago: University of Chicago Press, 1996)

Loss, L. & Seligman, J., *Fundamentals of Securities Regulation* (Gaitherburg: Aspen Law & Business, 4th ed., 2001)

Louis, J.V. *The Euro in the National Context* (London: British Institute of International & Comparative Law, 2002)

Louis, J.V. *et al.*, *Banking Supervision in the European Community* (Brussels: University of Brussels, 1995)

MacDonald, R., *Consolidated Supervision of Banks* (London: Bank of England, 1998)

Majone, G., *Regulating Europe* (London: Routledge, 1996)

March, J. & Olsen, J., *Rediscovering Institutions* (New York: Free Press, 1989)

Marks, G., Nielsen, F., Ray, L. & Salk, J., *Governance in the European Union* (London: Sage, 1996)

Marsh, D. & Stoker, G., *Theory and Methods in Political Science* (Basingstoke: Palgrave, 1995)

Mayes, D., Halme, L. & Liuksila, A., *Improving Banking Supervision* (Basingstoke: Palgrave, 2001)

McCraw, T., *Prophets of Regulation* (Cambridge: Harvard University Press, 1984)

McCrudden, C., *Regulation and Deregulation: Policy and Practice in the Utilities and Financial Services* (Oxford: Clarendon Press, 1999)

Micklitz, H. & Weatherill, S., *European Economic Law* (Aldershot: Ashgate, 1997)

Moley, R., *The First New Deal* (New York: Harcount, 1966)

Molle, W., *The Economics of European Integration* (Alderscot: Ashgate, 4th ed., 2001)

Moloney, N., *EC Securities Regulation* (Oxford: Oxford University Press, 2002)

Morgan, G. & Knights, D., *Regulation and Deregulation in European Financial Services* (Basingstoke: Macmillan Press, 1997)

Newman, P., *The New Palgrave Dictionary of Economics and the Law* (London: Macmillan Reference, 1998)

Nielsen, P., *Services and Establishment in European Community Banking Law* (Copenhagen: DJOF Publishing, 1994)

Norton, J.J., *Yearbook of International Financial and Economic Law 1998* (London: Kluwer Law International, 1999)

Norton, J.J. & Andenas, M., *Emerging Financial Markets and the Role of International Financial Organizations* (London: Kluwer Law International, 1996)

Oatley, T., *Monetary Politics: Exchange Rate Cooperation in the European Union* (Ann Arbor: University of Michigan Press, 1997)

Oditah, F., *The Future for the Global Securities Markets – Legal and Regulatory Aspects* (Oxford: Clarendon Press, 1996)

O'Keeffe, D. & Twomey, P., *Legal Issues of the Maastricht Treaty* (Bath: Chancery Law Publishing, 1994)

Ogus, A., *Regulation – Legal Form and Economic Theory* (Oxford: Clarendon Press, 1994)

Paraskevopoulos, C., *European Union at the Crossroads* (Cheltenham: Edward Elgar, 1998)

Parrish, M., *Securities Regulation and the New Deal* (New Haven: Yale University Press, 1970)

Peacock, A., *The Regulation Game* (Oxford: Basil Blackwell, 1984)

Peterson, J. & Shackleton, M., *The Institutions of the European Union* (Oxford: Oxford University Press, 2002)

Porter, M.E., *The Competitive Advantage of Nations* (New York: Free Press, 1990)

Prechal, S., *Directives in European Community Law* (Oxford: Clarendon Press, 1995)

Rider, B. & Andenas, M., *Developments in European Community Law Vol. 1/1996* (London: Kluwer Law International, 1997)

Ritchie, A., *James M. Landis: Dean of the Regulators* (Cambridge: Harvard University Press, 1980)

Rosamond, B., *Theories of European Integration* (Basingstoke: Palgrave, 2000)

Rose-Ackerman, S., *Rethinking the Progressive Agenda: The Reform of the American Regulatory State* (New York: Free Press, 1993)

Schmidtchen, D. & Cooter, R., *Constitutional Law and Economics of the European Union* (Cheltenham: Edward Elgar, 1997)

Scott, H. & Wellons, P., *International Finance: Transactions, Policy and Regulation* (New York: Foundation Press, 8th ed., 2001)

Securities Association, *Investment Services Directive: A Commentary and Analysis* (London: Whitefriars Press, March 1989)

Seligman, J., *The SEC and the Future of Finance* (New York: Praeger, 1985)

Seligman, J., *The Transformation of Wall Street: A History of the Securities and Exchange Commission and Modern Corporate Finance* (Boston: Houghton Mifflin, 1982)

Servais, D., *The Single Financial Market* (Luxembourg: European Commission, 2nd ed., 1991)

Smits, R., *The European Central Bank: Institutional Aspects* (The Hague: Kluwer Law International, 1997)

Spulber, D., *Regulation and Markets* (Cambridge: Massachusetts Institute of Technology Press, 1989)

Steil, B., *The European Equity Markets: The State of the Union and an Agenda for the Millennium* (London: Royal Institute of International Affaires, 1996)

Stuyck, J., *Financial and Monetary Integration in the European Economic Community: Legal, Institutional and Economic Aspects* (Deventer: Kluwer Law, 1993)

Taylor, M., *Peak Practice: How to Reform the UK's Regulatory System: Implementing 'Twin Peaks'* (London: Centre for the Study of Financial Innovation, October 1996)

Taylor, M., *Twin Peaks: A Regulatory Structure for the New Century* (London: Centre for the Study of Financial Innovation, December 1995)

Taylor, P., *International Organization in the Modern World – The Regional and the Global Process* (New York: Pinter, 1993)

Toth, A.G., *Oxford Encyclopedia of European Community Law: Vol I* (Oxford: Oxford University Press, 1990)

Usher, J., *The Law of Money and Financial Services in the European Community* (Oxford: Clarendon Press, 1994)

Van Houtte, H., *The Law of Cross-Border Securities Transactions* (London: Sweet & Maxwell, 1999)

Vickers, J. & Yarrow, G., *Privatization: An Economic Analysis* (Cambridge: Massachusetts Institute of Technology Press, 1988)

Vittas, D., *Financial Regulation: Changing the Rules of the Game* (Washington: World Bank, 1992)

Walker, G.A., *International Banking Regulation: Law, Policy and Practice* (London: Kluwer Law International, 2001)

Wallace, H. & Wallace, W., *Policy-Making in the European Union* (Oxford: Oxford University Press, 4th ed., 2000)

Weatherill, S. & Beaumont, P., *EU Law* (London: Penguin Books, 3rd ed., 1999)

Weiler, J., *The Constitution of Europe: 'Do the New Clothes have an Emperor?' and other Essays on European Integration* (Cambridge: Cambridge University Press, 1999)

Wendell, F., *Issues Related to the Regulation of Broker-Dealers under the Investment Advisers Act and the Status of Investment Advisers under the Securities Exchange Act* (Washington: The American Law Institute, 1997)

Wymeersch, E., *Further Perspectives in Financial Integration in Europe* (Berlin: Walter de Gruyter, 1994)

Zilioli, C. & Selmayr, M., *The Law of the European Central Bank* (Oxford: Hart Publishing, 2001)

Articles

Abrams, C., 'The Investment Services Directive – Who Should be the Principal Regulator of Cross-Border Services?' (1995) 11 European Financial Services Law 317

Abrams, C., 'The Second Banking Directive and the Investment Services Directive: When and How can the Single European Passport be used for Cross-Border Services?' (1997) 10 European Financial Services Law 248

Ackerman, F., Mounts, D. & Thomas, D., 'Automated Compliance Systems' (1999) 1 Journal of Financial Regulation and Compliance 48

Adams, G., 'The Single Market in Financial Services – an Orwellian Approach' (1996) 3 European Financial Services Law 149

Alexander, K., 'The International Supervisory Framework for Financial Services: An Emerging Regime for Transnational Supervision' (2000) 1 Journal of International Banking Regulation 33

Andenas, M., 'Rules of Conduct and the Principle of Subsidiarity' (1994) 14 Company Lawyer 61

Andenas, M., 'Cross Border Cold-Calling and the Right to Provide Services' (1995) 8 Company Lawyer 249

Andenas, M., 'Directive on Deposit Guarantee Schemes Challenged' (1995) 1 Company Lawyer 18

Andenas, M., 'Current Developments: EC Law, IV. Insurance and Banking' (1996) 45 International & Comparative Law Quarterly 230

Andenas, M., 'Italian Nationality Requirement and Community Law' (1996) 17 Company Lawyer 219

Andenas, M., 'Financial Market Regulation and the Case Law' (1998) European Business Law Review 203

Andenas, M., 'The Financial Market and the Commission as Legislator' (1998) Company Lawyer 98

Andenas, M., 'Liability for Supervisors and Depositors' Rights – the BCCI and the Bank of England in the House of Lords' (2001) 3 Euredia 388

Arlman, P., 'European Equity Markets after the Euro: Competition and Cooperation Across New Frontiers' (1999) 2 International Finance 139

Armstrong, K., 'Integrating Law: An Introduction' (1998) 2 Journal of Common Market Studies 147

Arnull, A., 'Does the Court of Justice have Inherent Jurisdiction?' (1990) 27 Common Market Law Review 683

Avgerinos, Y., 'Essential and Non-Essential Measures: Delegation of Powers in EU Securities Regulation' (2002) European Law Journal 269

Avgerinos, Y., 'European System of Central Banks: Monetary Policy, Independence, Banking Supervision and Future Perspectives' (1999) 4 Journal of International Banking and Financial Law 144

Avgouleas, E., 'The Harmonisation of Rules of Conduct in EU Financial Markets: Economic Analysis, Subsidiarity and Investor Protection' (2000) 1 European Law Journal 72

Avgouleas, E., 'The Implementation of the Insider Dealing Directive in Greece' (1997) 4 European Financial Services Law 131

Barber, T. & Simonian, H., 'Germany's Financial Vision' (12 February 2001) Financial Times 20

Barents, R., 'The Internal Market Unlimited: Some Observations on the Legal Basis of Community Legislation' (1993) 30 Common Market Law Review 85

Barnard, J., 'The Securities Law Enforcement Remedies Act of 1989: Disenfranchising Shareholders in Order to Protect Them' (1989) 65 Notre Dame Law Review 32

Beckers, S., Rijckmans, L., Stam, Y. & Storm, S., 'Euronext: A Dutch Perspective' (2001) 7 Journal of International Banking & Financial Law 323

Benston, G., 'Consumer Protection as Justification for Regulating Financial Services Firms and Products' (2000) 3 Journal of Financial Services Research 277

Boland, V. & Guerrera, F., 'FSA Staff Brand iX Plan a "Nightmare"' (8 September 2000) Financial Times 1

Bradley, C., 'Competitive Deregulation of Financial Services Activity in Europe after 1992' (1991) 11 Oxford Journal of Legal Studies 545

Brentford, P., 'Constitutional Aspects of the Independence of the European Central Bank' (1998) 1 International & Comparative Law Quarterly 75

Buiter, W., 'Alice in Euroland' (1999) 2 Journal of Common Market Studies 181

Centeno, M. & Mello, A., 'How Integrated are the Money Market and the Bank Loans Market within the European Union?' (1999) 18 Journal of International Money & Finance 75

Clifford Chance, 'FSA Proposals for New Customer Classification Regime' (2000) 3 Journal of International Banking & Financial Law 103

Clifford Chance, 'Challenging Times for Exchanges' (1999) 10 Journal of International Banking & Financial Law 413

Clifford Chance, 'Commission Forms Forum Groups to Develop Action Plan' (1999) 11 Journal of International Banking & Financial Law 452

Coase, R.H., 'The Problem of Social Cost' (1960) 3 The Journal of Law and Economics 1

Conti, C., 'The Impact of New Technologies on the Financial Services Industry' (1997) 11 European Financial Services Law 284

Cremona, M., 'A European Passport for Investment Services' (1994) Journal of Business Law 195

Crockett, A., 'Market Discipline and Financial Stability' (2001) 10 Financial Stability Review 166

Crosby, S., 'The Single Market and the Rule of Law' (1991) 16 European Law Review 451

Dale, R., 'Regulating Investment Business in the Single Market' (November 1994) 4 Bank of England Quarterly Bulletin 333

Dale, R., 'The Regulation of Investment Firms in the European Union (Parts 1–2)' (1994) 10-11 Journal of International Banking Law 394

Dale, R., 'Reflections on the BCCI Affair: A United Kingdom Perspective' (1992) 26 International Law 949

Dale, R. & Wolf, S., 'The Structure of Financial Regulation' (1998) 4 Journal of Financial Regulation and Compliance 326

Dalhuisen, J.H., 'Liberalisation and Re-Regulation of Cross-Border Financial Services: Part I' (1999) 5-6 European Business Law Review 158

Dalhuisen, J.H., 'Liberalisation and Re-Regulation of Cross-Border Financial Services: Part II' (1999) 7-8 European Business Law Review 284

Dalhuisen, J.H., 'Liberalisation and Re-Regulation of Cross-Border Financial Services: Part III' (1999) 9-10 European Business Law Review 354

Dashwood, A., 'The Principle of Direct Effect in European Community Law' (1978) 16 Journal of Common Market Studies 229

Dassesse, M., 'The Regulatory Implications of the Location of Financial Services under EU Law' (2001) 10 Journal of International Banking & Financial Law 473

Davies, H., 'Law and Financial Regulation' (1993) 4-5 Journal of International Financial Markets 193

Deakin, S. & Slinger, G., 'Hostile Takeovers, Corporate Law and the Theory of the Firm' (1997) 24 Journal of Law and Society 124

Deane-Johns, S., 'Recent Developments in the UK and European E-Securities Framework' (1999) 2 Business Law Review 29

De Grauwe, P., 'Monetary Policies in the Presence of Asymmetries' (2000) 4 Journal of Common Market Studies 593

Demarigny, F., 'Disentangling the Single Market' (2000) 4 The Financial Regulator 32

Deutsche Bank Research, 'Regulation and Banking Supervision: Caught Between the Nation State and Global Financial Markets' (29 June 2000) 86 EMU Watch 1

Dimson, E. & Marsh, P., 'Calculating the Cost of Capital' (1982) 2 Long Range Planning 112

Eackhout, P., 'Recent Case-Law on Free Movement of Goods: Refining Keck and Mithouard' (1998) 2 European Business Law Review 267

Editorial Comments, 'Executive Agencies within the EU: The European Central Bank – A Model?' (1996) 33 Common Market Law Review 623

Edward, D., 'Establishment and Services: An Analysis of the Insurance Cases' (1987) European Law Review 231

Ehlermann, C.D., 'The European Community, its Law and Lawyers' (1992) 29 Common Market Law Review 213

Ehlermann, C.D., 'The Internal Market Following the Single European Act' (1987) 24 Common Market Law Review 361

Eichengreen, B., 'European Monetary Unification' (1993) 1 Journal of Economic Literature 31

Emiliou, N., 'Opening Pandora's Box: The Legal Basis of Community Measures Before the Court of Justice' (1994) 5 European Law Review 488

Endo, K., 'The Principle of Subsidiarity: From Johannes Althusius to Jacques Delors' (1994) 6 Hokkaido Law Review 553

Estrella, A., 'A Prolegomenon to Future Capital Requirements' (1995) 2 Federal Reserve Bank of New York Economic Policy Review 1

European Shadow Financial Regulatory Committee, 'The European Shadow Financial Regulatory Committee: A New Initiative' (1999) 2 Journal of International Banking Regulation 137

Evanoff, D., 'Preferred Source of Market Discipline' (1993) 10 Yale Journal on Regulation 347

Fell, P., 'The Single Passport – an Overview' (1994) 11 European Financial Services Law 176

Ferrarini, G., 'The European Regulation of Stock Exchanges: New Perspectives' (1999) 3 Common Market Law Review 569

Ferrarini, G., 'Towards a European Law of Investment Services and Institutions' (1994) 6 Common Market Law Review 1283

Galanopoulou, V., 'Recent Developments in Financial Services Regulation: A Good Example for the European Regulators?' (1999) European Business Law Review 408

Garzaniti, L., 'Single Market-Making: EC Regulation on Securities Markets' (1993) 3 Company Lawyer 43

Goodhart, C. & Schoenmaker, D., 'Should the Functions of Monetary Policy and Banking Supervision be Separated?' (1995) 4 Oxford Economic Papers 539

Green, D., 'Enhanced Co-operation Among Regulators and the Role of National Regulators in a Global Market' (2000) 2 Journal of International Financial Markets 7

Griffin, P., 'The Delaware Effect: Keeping the Tiger in its Cage: The Experience of Mutual Recognition in Financial Services' (2001) 3 Columbia Journal of European Law 337

Guericke, A., 'Deposit Guarantee and Investor Compensation Directives' (2000) 1 Journal of International Banking Regulation 61

Hadjiemmanuil, C. & Andenas, M., 'Banking Supervision and European Monetary Union' (1999) 2 Journal of International Banking Regulation 84

Haines, P., 'The Investment Services Directive – Progress to Date' (1995) 2 European Financial Services Law 30

Harding, C., 'Member State Enforcement of European Community Measures: The Chimera of "Effective" Enforcement' (1997) 4 Maastricht Journal of European and Comparative Law 5

Hatzopoulos, V., 'Case C-384/93, Alpine Investments BV v Minister van Financien, Judgement of 10 May 1995' (1995) 32 Common Market Law Review 1427

Hawkesby, C., 'The Institutional Structure of Financial Supervision: A Cost–Benefit Approach' (2000) 3 Journal of International Banking Regulation 36

Herranz, I.R., 'Distance Marketing of Consumer Financial Services' (2001) 16 Banking & Finance Law Review 303

Hertig, G., 'Regulatory Competition for EU Financial Services' (2000) 2 Journal of International Economic Law 349

Hertig, G., 'Imperfect Mutual Recognition for EC Financial Services' (1994) 14 International Review of Law and Economics 177

Hill, A., 'Greed and Fear Return' (8 June 2002) Financial Times 12

Hopt, K., 'Special Issue on the Economic Law of the Member States in an Economic and Monetary Union: Report' (1976) 13 Common Market Law Review 147

Hoskins, M., 'EEC Banking Law: Plugging the Gaps' (1992) 1 Journal of International Banking Law 56

Hudson, A., 'The European Netting Directive' (1996) 11 European Financial Services Law 309

Hunnings, N., 'Amending the EC Treaty: The Commission Proposals-II' (2000) 6 Perspectives on European Business Law 10

Jachtenfuchs, M., 'The Governance Approach to European Integration' (2001) 2 Journal of Common Market Studies 245

Jackson, H. & Pan, E., 'Regulatory Competition in International Securities Markets: Evidence from Europe in 1999 – Part I' (2001) 2 Business Lawyer 653

Jackson, P., 'Unified Supervision: The UK Experience' (2000) 3 The Financial Regulator 50

Jarvis, K., 'Does the Fiduciary Bell Toll?' (1996) 2 Company Lawyer 51

Joris, J.L., 'Will the European Company Work?' (2002) 2 International Financial Law Review 19

Kirchgässner, G., 'Constitutional Economics and its Relevance for the Evolution of Rules' (1994) 47 Kyklos 321

Kirchhof, P., 'The Balance of Powers Between the National and European Institutions' (1999) 3 European Law Journal 225

Krause, H., 'Germany Wins Compromise on EU Takeover Rules' (2001) 7 International Financial Law Review 18

Laffont, J. & Tirole, J., 'The Politics of Government Decision-Making: A Theory of Regulatory Capture' (1991) 4 Quarterly Journal of Economics 1089

Lambert, R. & Simon, A., 'An Ideal Regulatory Model for Dealing with Retail Financial Institution Runs and Failures' (2000) 4 Journal of Financial Regulation and Compliance 309

Landis, J., 'The Legislative History of the Securities Act of 1933' (1959) 28 George Washington Law Review 29

Landsmeer, A. & Van Empel, M. 'The Directive on Deposit-Guarantee Schemes and the Directive on Investor Compensation Schemes in View of Case C-233/94' (1998) European Financial Services Law 143

Lang, J., 'European Community Constitutional Law: The Division of Powers Between the Community and the Member States' (1988) Northern Ireland Legal Quarterly 209

Lannoo, K., 'A European Perspective on Corporate Governance' (1999) 2 Journal of Common Market Studies 269

Larosière, J. & Lebègue, D., 'Bringing Harmony to Europe's Markets: Euro-Zone States Should Hasten the Integration of their Financial Systems' (14 September 2000) Financial Times 17

Lasok, K.P., 'Freedom to Provide Insurance Services in the Light of the Co-Insurance Cases' (1988) Modern Law Review 706

Lastra, R., 'Lender of Last Resort' (1999) 2 International & Comparative Law Quarterly 340

Leleux, P., 'Corporation Law in the US and in the EEC' (1967–8) 5 Common Market Law Review 133

Lenaerts, K., 'Regulating the Regulatory Process: "Delegation of Powers" in the European Community' (1993) 18 European Law Review 23

Lenaerts, K. & Verhoeven, A., 'Towards a Legal Framework for Executive Rule-Making in the EU? The Contribution of the New Comitology Decision' (2000) 3 Common Market Law Review 645

Levitt, M., 'Does Europe Want a Single Market?' (2001) 4 The Financial Regulator 20

L'Heveder, C., 'The Investment Services Directive and its Implications for Participants in Europe's Financial Markets' (1996) 1 Journal of International Banking & Financial Law 5

Licht, A., 'Regulatory Arbitrage for Real: International Securities Regulation in a World of Interacting Securities Markets' (1998) 38 Virginia Journal of International Law 563

Llewellyn, D., 'Re-engineering the Regulator' (1996) 3 The Financial Regulator 21

Lomax, R., 'Supervision in the Single Market' (1993) 3 Central Banking 36

Lomnicka, E., 'The Home Country Control Principle in the Financial Services Directives and the Case Law' (2000) 11 European Business Law Review 324

Lomnicka, E., 'EC Harmonisation of Investor Compensation Schemes' (1994) 1 European Financial Services Law 17

Long, W., 'European Initiatives for On-Line Financial Services: Part 4' (2000) 3 Journal of International Banking & Financial Law 84

Long, W., 'European Initiatives for On-Line Financial Services: Part 1' (1999) 8 Journal of International Banking & Financial Law 324

Long, W., 'European Initiatives for On-Line Financial Services: Part 2' (1999) 9 Journal of International Banking & Financial Law 373

Louis, J.V., 'A Monetary Union for Tomorrow?' (1989) 2 Common Market Law Review 301

MacNeil, I., 'The Future for Financial Regulation: The Financial Services and Markets Bill' (1999) 62 Modern Law Review 725

Magnette, P., 'Towards "Accountable Independence"? Parliamentary Controls of the European Central Bank and the Rise of a New Democratic Model' (2000) 4 European Law Journal 326

Mahmood, S., 'Chinese Walls – An Evolutionary Process' (1999) European Financial Services Law 67

Majone, G., 'The Rise of the Regulatory State in Europe' (1994) 3 West European Politics 77

Majone, G., 'Regulating Europe: Problems and Perspectives' (1989) 3 Jarhbuch zur Staats- und Verwaltungswissenschaft

Malloy, M., 'Banking in the Twenty-First Century' (2000) 25 The Journal of Corporation Law 789

Marks, G. & Hooghe, L., 'Optimality and Authority: A Critique of Neoclassical Theory' (2000) 5 Journal of Common Market Studies 795

McVea, H., 'Financial Conglomerates and Conflicts of Interest: Resolving the Regulatory Dilemma' (1996) 47 Northern Ireland Law Quarterly 239

Metcalpe, L., 'Reforming the Commission: Will Organizational Efficiency Produce Effective Governance?' (2000) 5 Journal of Common Market Studies 817

Mohamed, S., 'A Single Regulator for the E.C. Financial Market' (2001) 8-9 Journal of International Banking Law 203

Mohamed, S., 'A Critical Assessment of the ECJ Judgement in Trummer and Mayer' (1999) 9 Journal of International Banking & Financial Law 396

Monney, P., 'Governing Globalised Businesses: Achieving New Business Models' (1999) 9 International Business Lawyer 366

Moravcsik, A. 'Preferences and Power in the European Community: A Liberal Inter-governmentalist Approach' (1993) 4 Journal of Common Market Studies 473

Moravcsik, A. & Nicolaidis, K., 'Explaining the Treaty of Amsterdam: Interests, Influence, Institutions' (1999) 1 Journal of Common Market Studies 59

Mwenda, K. & Fleming, A., 'International Developments in the Organisational Structure of Financial Services Supervision: Part II' (2002) 1 Journal of International Banking Law 7

Norton, J. & Olive, C., 'Globalization of Financial Risks and International Supervision of Banks and Securities Firms: Lessons from the Barings Debacle' (1996) 2 International Lawyer 301

Ogus, A., 'Competition Between National Legal Systems: A Contribution of Economic Analysis to Comparative Law' (1999) 48 International & Comparative Law Quarterly 405

Padoa-Schioppa, T., 'EMU and Banking Supervision' (1999) 2 International Finance 295

Philipe, H., 'Towards a Unified European Securities Market' (1997) 4 The Financial Regulator 11

Philippart, R. & Edwards, G., 'The Provisions on Closer Co-operation in the Treaty of Amsterdam: The Politics of Flexibility in the European Union' (1999) 1 Journal of Common Market Studies 87

Pollack, M. 'Delegation, Agency and Agenda Setting in the European Community' (1997) 1 International Organization 99

Pollack, M., 'International Relations Theory and European Integration' (2001) 2 Journal of Common Market Studies 221

Reich, N., 'Binnenmarkt als Rechsbegriff' (1991) Europäisches Zeitscrift fur Wirtschaftsrecht 203

Reich, N., 'Competition Between Legal Orders: A New Paradigm for EU Law?' (1992) 5 Common Market Law Review 861

Romano, R., 'Empowering Investors: A Market Approach to Securities Regulation' (1998) 107 Yale Law Journal 2359

Roth, W.H., 'EEC Treaty Article Fifty-Nine and its Implications for Conflicts Law in the Field of Insurance Contracts' (1992) 2 Duke Journal of Comparative and International Law 131

Roth, W.H., 'Case C-79/90 Manfred Säger v Dennemeyer & Co. Ltd.' (1993) 1 Common Market Law Review 145

Roth, W.H., 'Case C-233/94, Federal Republic of Germany v. European Parliament and Council of the European Union' (1998) 4 Common Market Law Review 459

Scharph, F., 'The Joint Decision Trap: Lessons from German Federalism and European Integration' (1988) 66 Public Administration 239

Schooner, H. & Taylor, M., 'Convergence and Competition: The Case of Bank Regulation in Britain and the United States' (1999) 20 Michigan Journal of International Law 595

Sherwood, A., 'The Impact of Electronic Trading on Regulatory Surveillance' (1997) 4 Journal of Financial Regulation & Compliance 299

Siebert, H. & Koop, M., 'Institutional Competition versus Centralisation: Quo Vadis Europe?' (1993) 1 Oxford Review of Economic Policy 15

Smits, R., 'Banking Supervision in the Monetary Union' (1999) 2 Journal of International Banking Regulation 122

Smout, C. & Barrass, J., 'International Regulatory Co-operation' (1996) 1 Financial Stability Review 44

Snell, J. & Andenas, M., 'Exploring the Outer Limits-Restrictions on the Free Movement of Goods and Services' (1999) 7-8 European Business Law Review 252

Steiner, J., 'Direct Applicability in EEC Law – A Chameleon Concept' (1982) 98 Law Quarterly Review 229

Stengel, A., 'Is Regulation Effective Enough to Combat Fraud?' (1998) 8 Journal of International Banking Law 276

Stigler, G., 'The Theory of Economic Regulation' (1971) 2 Bell Journal of Economics 3

Sun, J.M. & Pelkmans, J., 'Regulatory Competition in the Single Market' (1995) 1 Journal of Common Market Studies 67

Sykes, A., 'Regulatory Competition or Regulatory Harmonisation: A Silly Question?' (2000) 2 Journal of International Economic Law 257

Tanzer, G., 'Developing Uniform Standards to Allow a Global Passport for Mutual Funds – IOSCO's Role' (2000) 5 International Business Lawyer 229

Theil, R., 'The EC Investment Services Directive: A Critical Time for Investments Firms' (1994) 2 Journal of International Banking & Financial Law 61

Thieffry, G., 'The State of European Securities Regulation' (2001) 5 International Financial Law Review 15

Thieffry, G., 'Towards a European Securities Commission' (1999) 10 International Financial Law Review 14

Thieffry, G. & Walsh, J., 'Securitisation: The New Opportunities Offered by Economic and Monetary Union' (1997) 12 Journal of International Banking Law 463

Thorkildsen, T., 'Power to Draw up Conduct of Business Rules After the ISD' (1995) 15 Company Lawyer 102

Timmermans, C., 'How Can One Improve the Quality of Community Legislation?' (1997) 34 Common Market Law Review 1229

Tison, M., 'What is "General Good" in EU Financial Services Law?' (1997) 2 Legal Issues of European Integration 1

Tsebelis, G. & Garrett, G., 'The Institutional Foundations of Intergovernmentalism and Supranationalism in the European Union' (2001) 2 International Organization 357

Turing, D., 'General Principles of Risk Control' (2000) 2 Journal of International Banking & Financial Law 38

Usher, J., 'Financial Services in EEC Law' (1988) 1 International & Comparative Law Quarterly 144

Van den Bergh, R., 'The Subsidiarity Principle in European Community Law: Some Insights from Law and Economics' (1994) 1 Maastricht Journal of European and Comparative Law 337

Vives, X., 'Restructuring Financial Regulation in the European Monetary Union' (2001) 1 Journal of Financial Services Research 57

Von Rosen, R., 'Clearing up Europe's Exchanges' (9 February 2001) Financial Times 19

Vos, E., 'Reforming the European Commission: What Role to Play for EU Agencies?' (2000) 5 Common Market Law Review 1113

Walker, G., 'Conglomerate Law and International Financial Market Supervision' (1998) Annual Review of Banking Law 287

Warren, M.G. III, 'The Common Market Prospectus' (1989) 4 Common Market Law Review 687

Watson, J., 'International Co-operation in the Field of Financial Regulatory Enforcement: Part 2, The EU Approach' (2000) 1 Journal of International Banking & Financial Law 13

Watson, J., 'International Co-operation in the Field of Financial Regulatory Enforcement: Part 3, IOSCO and Transnational Regulatory Cooperation' (2000) 5 Journal of International Banking & Financial Law 157

Watson, J., 'International Co-operation in the Field of Financial Regulatory Enforcement: Part 4, The Current State of Play and the Future' (2000) 6 Journal of International Banking & Financial Law 187

Watson, J., 'International Co-operation in the Field of Financial Regulatory Enforcement: Part 1, The UK Approach' (1999) 11 Journal of International Banking & Financial Law 467

Weatherill, S., 'After Keck: Some Thoughts on How to Clarify the Clarification' (1996) 33 Common Market Law Review 885

Weiler, J., 'The Transformation of Europe' (1991) 8 Yale Law Journal 2403

Welby, J., 'Do Business Ethics Matter' (1992) 3 International Company and Commercial Law Review 46

Woolfson, P., 'Electronic Commerce and the Single Market in Financial Services in Europe: What Changes for Success?' (1997) 4 Journal of Financial Regulation and Compliance 306

Wouters, J., 'Conflict of Laws and the Single Market for Financial Services (Part I)' (1997) 2 Maastricht Journal of European and Comparative Law 161

Wouters, J., 'Conflict of Laws and the Single Market for Financial Services (Part II)' (1997) 3 Maastricht Journal of European and Comparative Law 284

Wouters, J., 'Rules of Conduct, Foreign Investment Firms and the ECJ's Case Law on Services' (1993) 13 Company Lawyer 194

Wymeersch, E., 'The EU Directives on Financial Disclosure' (1996) 2 European Financial Services Law 34

Zaring, D., 'International Law by Other Means: The Twilight Existence of International Financial Regulatory Organizations' (1998) Texas International Law Journal 282

Zavvos, G., 'Regulation of the European Securities Markets: The Challenges in the Post-Barcelona Era' (2002) 30 Kangaroo Group Newsletter

Zavvos, G., 'Banking Integration and 1992: Legal Issues and Policy Implications' (1990) 2 Harvard International Law Journal 463

Lectures and speeches

Bandilla, R., *Legal Consequences of the Single Currency* (Contribution to the FIDE Congress, Helsinki, 1–3 June 2000)

Becht, M., *European Disclosure for the Next Millennium* (Paper for CEPS Task Force, 7 December 1999)

Bolkestein, F., *The EU's Economic Test: Meeting the Challenges of the Lisbon Strategy* (Speech delivered at the 17th Annual State of the International Economy Conference, London, 19 November 2001)

Breuer, R., *Convergence of Supervisory Practices – A Banker's View* (Paper presented at the Conference of European Banking Supervisors, Copenhagen, 20 November 2000)

Camdessus, M., *Stable and Efficient Systems for the 21st Century: A Quest for Transparency and Standards* (Paper presented at the 24th IOSCO Annual Conference, Lisbon, 25 May 1999)

Crocket, A., *Banking Supervision and Financial Stability* (The William Taylor Memorial Lectures No. 4, 1998)

Davies, H., *EMU and Financial Markets: Winners, Losers and Regulators* (Paper presented at the Financial Times EMU Conference, London, 21 November 1997)

Davies, H., *Why Regulate?* (Henry Thornton Lecture, City University, 4 November 1998)

Davies, H., *Building the Financial Services Authority; What's New?* (Travers Lecture, London Guildhall University Business School, 11 March 1999)

Davies, H., *Euro-Regulation* (European Financial Forum Lecture, Brussels, 8 April 1999)

Davies, H., *Global Markets, Global Regulation* (Paper presented at the 25th IOSCO Annual Conference, Sydney, 17 May 2000)

Davies, H., *Introductory Remarks* (Paper presented at the Eurofi Conference, Paris, 15 September 2000)

Davies, H., *Convergence of Supervisory Practices* (Paper presented at the Conference of European Banking Supervisors, Copenhagen, 20 November 2000)

Duisenberg, W., *The ECB and the Accession Process* (Speech delivered at the Frankfurt European Banking Congress, 23 November 2001)

Duisenberg, W., *The Euro as a Catalyst for Legal Convergence in Europe* (Speech on the occasion of the Annual Conference of the International Bar Association, Amsterdam, 17 September 2000)

Duisenberg, W., *The Future of Banking Supervision and the Integration of Financial Markets* (Speech delivered at the conference 'Improving Integration of Financial Markets in Europe', Turin, 22 May 2000)

Duisenberg, W., *Financing in the European Capital Markets* (Speech delivered at the Waarborgfonds Sociale Woningbouw, Utrecht, 14 June 1999)

Dunnett, R., *The Transition to Stage Three: Impact on the Financial Markets* (Lecture given at the Workshop on Institutional Aspects of the EMU at King's College London, 26–27 January 1996)

Fischer, S., *The Asian Crisis: A View from the IMF* (Paper presented at the Midwinter Conference of the Bankers' Association for Foreign Trade, Washington, 22 January 1998)

Gemnill, G., *The Danger of Markets Collapsing* (Speech submitted at the conference 'The Role of Regulation in Global Financial Markets', City University Business School, London 13–14 July 2000)

Goodhart, C., *The Organisational Structure of Banking Supervision* (Financial Market Group Seminar, LSE, 30 October 2000)

Gretschmann, K., *The Subsidiarity Principle: Who is to do what in an Integrated Europe?* (Paper submitted to the Jacques Delors Colloquium, Subsidiarity: The Challenge of Change, Maastricht, March 1991)

Grundman, S. & Kerber, W., *Information Intermediaries and Extending the Area of Informed Party Autonomy – Securities and Insurance Markets* (Paper presented at the Conference 'Party Autonomy for the Internal Market', King's College, 11–13 May 2000

Ingves, S., *Assessing Financial Sector Soundness: The Role of the IMF* (Paper presented at the Conference of European Banking Supervisors, Copenhagen, 20 November 2000)

Issing, O., *The Euro – Four Weeks After the Start* (Speech delivered at the European-Atlantic Group, House of Commons, London, 28 January 1999)

Krantz, T., *The Danger of Price Fragmentation* (Speech delivered at the conference '24-Hour Securities Trading and the Growth of ECNs', London 9–10 November 1999)

Lamfalussy, A., *Presentation on the Special Roundtable on the Findings of the Committee of Wise Men on the Regulation of European Securities Markets* (Centre of European Policy Studies, 29 November 2000)

Louis, J.V., *The EMU, and After?* (Paper delivered at the Federal Trust Conference 'Consolidating EMU', London, 9 June 2000)

Meister, E., *How Should Regulatory and Supervisory Responsibilities be Shared Among the National Functional Regulators?* (Lecture held at the Multinational Banking Seminar, New York, 9 June 2001)

Norgen, C., *Securities Markets in the Information Age* (Address at the 26th Annual IOSCO Conference, Stockholm, 23–29 June 2001)

Padoa-Schioppa, T., *EMU and Banking Supervision* (Lecture at the London School of Economics, Financial Markets Group, 24 February 1999)

Padoa-Schioppa, T., *Securities and Banking: Bridges and Walls* (Lecture at the London School of Economics, 21 January 2002)

Padoa-Schioppa, T., *Remarks at the Roundtable: Mid-Term Review of Progress Towards European Financial Integration* (Brussels, 22 February 2002)

Padoa-Schioppa, T., *Reflections on Recent Financial Incidents* (Speech at the Third Joint Central Bank Research Conference on Risk Measurement and Systemic Risk, Basel, 8 March 2002)

Sainz de Vicuña, A., *Legal Consequences of the Single Currency* (General Report at the FIDE Congress, Helsinki, 1–3 June 2000)

Solans, E., *Financial Markets in the European Monetary Union* (Speech delivered at the 28th Annual Financial Markets Seminar, Valencia, 8 June 2001)

Spaventa, L., *Regulation for Financial Markets* (Speech delivered at the FESE European Financial Markets Convention, June 2000)

Stark, J., *The ECB and other European Institutions and the Future of the Euro* (Address at the 3rd Euro Capital Markets Forum, Amsterdam, 2 April 2001)

Summers, L., *Rising to the Challenge of Global Economic Integration* (Remarks to the School of Advanced International Studies, Washington DC, 20 September 2000)

Van Miert, K., *EU Competition Policy in the Banking Sector* (Speech delivered to the Foreign Bankers in the Belgian Bankers' Association, Brussels, 22 September 1998)

Vargas, F., *The Convergence of Banking Supervisory Practices* (Paper given at the Conference of European Banking Supervisors, Copenhagen, 20 November 2000)

Welteke, E., *Regulating European Financial Markets* (Speech delivered at the European Banking Conference, Frankfurt, 17 November 2000)

Wisbey, G., *The Challenge of Technology – Regulation of Electronic Financial Markets* (Speech delivered at the conference 'The Challenges Facing Financial Regulation', Cambridge, 6–7 July 2000)

Wyplosz, C., *Economic Policy Coordination in EMU: Strategies and Institutions* (Paper presented at the Deutsch-Franzosisches Wirtschaftspolitisches Forum, Bonn, 11–12 January 1999)

Zuberbühler, D., *The Financial Industry in the 21st Century* (Speech delivered at the Jubilee International Conference of Banking Supervisors, Basle, 21 September 2000)

Academic papers and electronic documents

Adonis, A. & Jones, S., *Subsidiarity and the Union's Constitutional Future* (Centre for European Studies Discussion Paper No. 2, Nuffield College, 1991)

Alexander, K., *The Role of the Basle Standards in International Banking Supervision* (ESRC Centre for Business Research Working Paper No. 153, Cambridge, March 2000)

Alfon, I. & Andrews, P., *Cost–Benefit Analysis in Financial Regulation* (FSA Occasional Paper Series No. 3, September 1999)

Benink, H., *The Future of Banking Regulation in Developed Countries: Lessons from and for Europe* (mimeo, 2000)

Briault, C., *The Rationale for a Single National Financial Services Regulator* (FSA Occasional Paper Series No. 2, May 1999)

Briault, C., *Revisiting the Rationale for a Single National Financial Services Regulator* (FSA Occasional Paper Series No. 16, February 2002)

Caprio, G., *Bank Regulation: The Case of the Missing Model* (World Bank Policy Research Working Paper No. 1574, January 1996)

Crooke, A., 'Securities Markets Attack EU Prospectus Reforms' (http://www.legalmediagroup.com, 9 September 2001)

Cukierman, A., *Accountability, Credibility, Transparency and Stabilization Policy in the Eurosystem* (mimeo, January 2000)

De Sousa, P., *Independent and Accountable Central Banks and the European Central Bank* (European Integration Online Papers No. 9, http://eiop.or.at/eiop/texte/2001-009a.htm, 2001)

Di Giorgio, G. & Di Noia, C., *Designing Institutions for Financial Stability: Regulation and Supervision by Objective for the Euro Area* (mimeo, November 2000)

Dutzler, B., *OLAF or the Question of Applicability of Secondary Community Law to the ECB* (European Integration online Papers No. 1, http://eiop.or.at/eiop/texte/2001-001a.htm, 2001)

Eatwell, J. & Taylor, L. *International Markets and the Future of Economic Policy* (Centre for Economic Policy Analysis Working Paper No. 9, August 1998)

Endo, K., *Subsidiarity and its Enemies: To what Extent is Sovereignty Contested in the Mixed Commonwealth of Europe?* (European University Institute Working Paper No. 2001/24, 2001)

European Shadow Financial Regulatory Committee, *The Regulation of European Securities Markets: The Lamfalussy Report* (Statement No. 10, Madrid, 26 March 2001)

Evans, H., *Plumbers and Architects: A Supervisory Perspective on International Financial Architecture* (FSA Occasional Paper Series No. 4, January 2000)

Fender, I. & Von Hagen, J., *Central Bank Policy in a More Perfect Financial System* (Zentrum für Europäische Integrationsforschung Policy Paper B03, 1998)

Gardener, E.P., *Theory and Practice in Banking Supervision: Some Reflections* (IES Institute of European Finance, Research Paper 86/2, 1986)

Goodhart, C., *An Incentive Structure for Financial Regulation* (LSE, Financial Market Group Special Paper No. 88, July 1996)

Goodhart, C., *Myths About the Lender of Last Resort* (mimeo)

Gruson, M., *Convergence of Bank Prudential Supervision Standards and Practices within the European Union* (Centre for Commercial Law Studies, Studies in International Financial & Economic Law No. 23, 1999)

Hall, B., *European Governance and the Future of the Commission* (Centre for European Reform Working Paper No. 5, May 2000)

Hardouvelis, G., Malliaropoulos, D. & Priestley, R., *EMU and European Stock Market Integration* (Centre of Economic Policy Research Discussion Paper No. 2124, April 1999)

Joerges, C., *The Market without the State? The 'Economic Constitution' of the European Community and the Rebirth of Regulatory Politics* (European Integration online Papers No. 19, http://eiop.or.at/eiop/texte/1997-01920htm, November 1997)

Karmel, R., *The Case for a European Securities Commission* (mimeo, 1999)

Kumar, A., *The Regulation of Non-Bank Financial Institutions* (World Bank Discussion Paper No. 362, 1997)

Latter, T., *Causes and Management of Banking Crises* (Bank of England, Centre for Central Banking Studies Handbook No. 12, 1997)

Leino, P., *The European Central Bank and Legitimacy: Is the ECB a Modification of or an Exception to the Principle of Democracy?* (Harvard Jean Monnet Working Paper No. 1/01, 2001)

Llewellyn, D., *The Economic Rationale for Financial Regulation* (FSA Occasional Paper No. 1, April 1999)

Mayes, D. & Vesala, J., *On the Problems of Home Country Control* (Bank of Finland Discussion Paper No. 20/98, 1998)

Niemeyer, J., *An Economic Analysis of Securities Market Regulation and Supervision: Where to Go After the Lamfalussy Report?* (Stockholm School of Economics Working Paper Series in Economics and Finance No. 482, December 2001)

Panourgias, L. & Andenas, M., *Euro, EMU and the UK Law* (Report submitted for the Euro-Spectator Project, April 2001)

Parti, A. & Schinasi, G., *European Monetary Union and International Capital Markets: Structural Implications and Risks* (International Monetary Fund Working Paper No. 97/62, May 1997)

Simpson, D., Meeks, G., Klumpes, P. & Andrews, P., *Some Cost–Benefit Issues in Financial Regulation* (FSA Occasional Paper Series No. 12, October 2000)

Steil, B., *Regional Financial Market Integration: Learning from the European Experience* (London: Royal Institute of International Affaires, 1998)

Stephan, P., *Regulatory Cooperation and Competition: The Search for Virtue* (University of Virginia School of Law, Legal Studies Working Paper No. 99-12, June 1999)

Shepheard-Walwyn, T., *The Future of Financial Services Regulation: Some Reflections from the Inside* (LSE, Financial Markets Group Special Paper No. 94, 1997)

Tison, M., *The Investment Services Directive and its Implementation in the EU Member States* (Gent University, Financial Law Institute Working Paper 1999-17, 1999)

Tison, M., *Conduct of Business Rules and their Implementation in the EU Member States* (Gent University, Financial Law Institute Working Paper 2000-14, 2000)

Tison, M., *Unravelling the General Good Exception: The Case of Financial Services* (Gent University, Financial Law Institute Working Paper 2000-03, 2000)

White, W., *What Have We Learned from Recent Financial Crises and Policy Responses?* (Bank of International Settlements Working Paper No. 84, January 2000)

Wymeersch, E., *The Harmonisation of Securities Regulation in Europe in the New Trading Environment* (Gent University, Financial Law Institute Working Paper 2000-16, July 2000)

Yataganas, X., *Delegation of Regulatory Authority in the European Union: The Relevance of the American Model of Independent Agencies* (Harvard Jean Monnet Working Paper No. 3/01, 2001)

EU institutions' documents

Committee for the Study of Economic and Monetary Union, *Report on Economic and Monetary Union in the EC* (Luxembourg, April 1989)

Committee of Wise Men, *Final Report on the Regulation of European Securities Markets* (15 February 2001)

Committee of Wise Men, *Initial Report on the Regulation of European Securities Markets* (9 November 2000)

Council of the European Union, *Memorandum of Understanding on a Cross-Border Out-of-Court Complaints Network for Financial Services in the European Economic Area* (1 February 2001)

Economic and Financial Committee, *Report on Financial Regulation, Supervision and Stability* (9 October 2002)

Economic and Financial Committee, *Report on Financial Stability* (EFC/ECFIN/240/00 – Final, 8 April 2000)

Economic and Social Committee, *Opinion on 'Mutual Recognition in the Single Market'* (OJ C 116/14, 20 April 2001)

European Central Bank, *Opinion of 16 November 2001 at the request of the Council of the European Union on a proposal for a Directive of the European Parliament and the Council on the prospectus to be published when securities are offered to the public or admitted to trading* (OJ C 344/4, 6 December 2001)

European Central Bank, *Opinion at the request of the German Ministry of Finance on a draft law establishing an integrated financial services supervision* (CON/2001/35, 8 November 2001)

European Central Bank, *Opinion at the request of the Austrian Ministry of Finance on a draft Article of the Federal law establishing and organising the financial market supervisory authority and amending the laws relating to banking, securities supervision, investment funds, equities funds, savings banks, building societies, mortgage banks, mortgage bonds, the IAPL, the stock exchange, insurance supervision, motor vehicle third party liability insurance, pension funds, capital markets, the Commercial Code, companies limited by shares, limited liability companies and the National Bank* (CON/2001/10, 25 May 2001)

European Central Bank, *The Role of Central Banks in Prudential Supervision* (March 2001)

European Central Bank, *Euro Area Securities Issues Statistics: July 2000* (20 September 2000)

European Central Bank, *The Institutional Framework of the European System of Central Banks* (ECB Monthly Bulletin, July 1999)

European Central Bank, *Rules of Procedure of the European Central Bank* (OJ L 125/34, 19 May 1999)

European Central Bank, *Possible Effects of EMU on the EU Banking Systems in the Medium to Long Term* (February 1999)

European Central Bank, *Assessment of EU Securities Settlement Systems against the Standards for their use in ESCB Credit Operations* (September 1998)

European Commission, *Report on the State of the Internal Market for Services* (COM(2002) 441 final, 30 July 2002)

European Commission, *2002 Review of the Internal Market Strategy* (COM(2002) 171 final, 11 April 2002)

European Commission, *Revision of ISD: Second Consultation* (25 March 2002)

European Commission, *Report on the Working of the Committees during 2000* (COM(2001) 783 final, 20 December 2001)

European Commission, *Economic Reform: Report on the Functioning of Community Product and Capital Markets* (COM(2001) 736, 7 December 2001)

European Commission, *Better Lawmaking 2001* (COM(2001) 728 final, 7 December 2001)

European Commission, *European Governance: Reviewing the Community Method* (COM(2001) 727 final, 5 December 2001)

European Commission, *Simplifying and Improving the Regulatory Environment* (COM(2001) 726 final, 5 December 2001)

European Commission, *Financial Services: Europe Must Deliver on Time: Fifth Report* (COM(2001) 712 final, 30 November 2001)

European Commission, *Internal Market Scoreboard No. 9* (19 November 2001)

European Commission, *European Governance: A White Paper* (COM(2001) 428 final, 12 October 2001)

European Commission, *Revision of the ISD: Open Consultation of Interested Parties* (24 July 2001)

European Commission, *Towards an EU Regime on Transparency Obligations of Issuers Whose Securities are Admitted to Trading on a Regulated Market* (11 July 2001)

European Commission, *Financial Services: Political Challenges: Fourth Report* (COM(2001) 286 final, June 2001)

European Commission, *Decision Establishing the Committee of European Securities Regulators* (COM(2001) 1501 final, 6 June 2001)

European Commission, *Decision Establishing the European Securities Committee* (COM(2001) 1493 final, 6 June 2001)

European Commission, *'Working Together to Maintain Momentum': 2001 Review of the Internal Market Strategy* (COM(2001) 198 final, 11 April 2001)

European Commission, *Communication on E-Commerce and Financial Services* (9 February 2001)

European Commission, *Unsolicited Commercial Communications and Data Protection* (Summary of Study Findings, January 2001)

European Commission, *XXXth Report on Competition Policy* (2000)

European Commission, *Communication on An Internal Market Strategy for Services* (COM(2000) 888 final, 29 December 2000)

European Commission, *European Company Statute: Commission Welcomes Political Agreement* (20 December 2000)

European Commission, *Towards an EU Directive on the Prudential Supervision of Financial Conglomerates* (MARKT/3021/2000, 19 December 2000)

European Commission, *Better Lawmaking 2000* (COM(2000) 772 final, 30 November 2000)

European Commission, *Communication on Upgrading the Investment Services Directive (93/22/EEC)* (COM(2000) 729, 16 November 2000)

European Commission, *Communication on the Application of Conduct of Business Rules under Article 11 of the Investment Services Directive (93/22EEC)* (16 November 2000)

European Commission, *Financial Services and Progress: Third Report* (COM(2000) 692/2 final, 8 November 2000)

European Commission, *Enhancing Democracy in the European Union* (SEC(2000) 1547/7 final, 11 October 2000)

European Commission, *Case No COMP/M.2004 Invescorp/Chase Capital Investments/ Gerresheimer Glas* (27 June 2000)

European Commission, *Progress on Financial Services: Second Report* (COM(2000) 336, 31 May 2000)

European Commission, *Reforming the Commission: A White Paper* (COM(2000) 200 final, 5 April 2000)

European Commission, *Communication on Strategic Objectives 2000–2005: Shaping the New Europe* (COM(2000) 154 final, 9 February 2000)

European Commission, *Freedom to provide Services and the General Good in the Insurance Sector* (C(1999)5046, 2 February 2000)

European Commission, *Economic Reform: Report on the Functioning of Community Product and Capital Markets* (COM(2000), 24 January 2000)

European Commission, *Institutional Arrangements for the Regulation and Supervision of the Financial Sector* (January 2000)

European Commission, *Risk Capital: Implementation of the Action Plan: Proposals for Moving Forward* (COM(1999) 493 final, 20 October 1999)

European Commission, *The Strategy for Europe's Internal Market* (COM(1999) 464 final, 5 October 1999)

European Commission, *Communication on the Mutual Recognition in the Context of the Follow-up to the Action Plan for the Single Market* (16 June 1999)

European Commission, *Financial Services: Implementing the Framework for Financial Markets: Action Plan* (COM(1999) 232, 11 May 1999)

European Commission, *Freedom of Establishment: Guide to the Case Law of the European Court of Justice on Articles 52 et seq. EC Treaty* (1 January 1999)

European Commission, *Freedom to Provide Services: Guide to the Case Law of the European Court of Justice on Articles 59 et seq. EC Treaty* (1 January 1999)

European Commission, *Report on the Operation of Certain Articles of the Investment Services Directive* (COM(1998) 780 final, 21 December 1998)

European Commission, *Financial Services: Building a Framework for Action* (COM(1998) 625, 28 October 1998)

European Commission, *Recommendation 98/257/EC on the Principles Applicable to the Bodies Responsible for Out-of-Court Settlement of Consumer Disputes* (30 March 1998)

European Commission, *The Impact of the Introduction of the Euro on Capital Markets* (II/338/97, July 1997)

European Commission, *Freedom to Provide Services and the Interest of the General Good in the Second Banking Directive* (SEC(97) 1193 final, 20 June 1997)

European Commission, *The Principle of Subsidiarity* (SEC(92) 1990 final, 27 October 1992)

European Commission, *Completing the Internal Market: White Paper to the European Council* (COM(85) 310 final, 28 June 1985)

European Commission, *Communication Concerning the Consequences of the Judgement given by the Court of Justice on 20 February 1979 in case 120/78* (OJ C 256/2, 3 October 1980)

European Commission, *Recommendation 77/534/EEC of 25 July 1977 Concerning a European Code of Conduct Relating to Transactions in Transferable Securities* (OJ L 212/37, 20 August 1977)

European Commission, *Second Report on Competition Policy* (1972)

European Council, *Resolution of 23 March 2001 on More Effective Securities Market Regulation in the European Union* (OJ C 138/1 of 11 May 2001)

European Ombudsman, *Special Report to the European Parliament following the Own-Initiative Inquiry into Public Access to Documents* (OJ C 44/9, 10 February 1998)

European Ombudsman, *Annual Report 1996* (OJ C 272/1, 8 September 1997)

European Parliament, *Report on the Proposal for a European Parliament and Council Directive on the Prospectus to be Published when Securities are Offered to the Public or Admitted to Trading* (A5-0072/2002, 27 February 2002)

European Parliament, *Report on the Implementation of Financial Services Legislation* (A5-0011/2002 final, 23 January 2002)

European Parliament, *Report on the Commission Communication on the Application of Conduct of Business Rules under Article 11 of the Investment Services Directive* (A5-0105/2001, 23 March 2001)

European Parliament, *Prudential Supervision in the Context of EMU* (Report 167.301, March 1999)

Giovannini Group, *Cross-Border Clearing and Settlement Arrangements in the European Union* (November 2001)

Giovannini Group, *The Impact of the Introduction of the Euro on Capital Markets* (July 1997)

Parliamentary Group of the Party of European Socialists, *Securities Markets: European Parliament is not blocking the Lamfalussy Process* (Press Release, 22 November 2001)

Sutherland, P. *et al.*, *Internal Market after 1992 – Meeting the Challenge: Report to the EEC Commission* (Brussels, 1992)

FESCO/CESR documents

CESR, *Proposed Standards for Alternative Trading Systems* (CESR/02-001, 14 January 2002)

CESR, *Standards and Rules for Harmonising Core Conduct of Business Rules for Investor Protection* (CESR/01-014, 18 October 2001)

CESR, *Draft Statement of Consultation Practices* (CESR/01-007b, October 2001)

FESCO, *Charter of the Committee of European Securities Regulators* (19 June 2001)

FESCO, *Standards and Rules for Harmonising Core Conduct of Business Rules for Investor Protection* (February 2001)

FESCO, *A 'European Passport' for Issuers* (20 December 2000)

FESCO, *Report 1999–2000* (15 November 2000)

FESCO, *Status of Implementation of the Standards for Regulated Markets* (25 September 2000)

FESCO, *Stabilisation and Allotment: A European Supervisory Approach* (15 September 2000)

FESCO, *The Regulation of Alternative Trading Systems in Europe: A Paper for the EU Commission* (September 2000)

FESCO, *Market Abuse: FESCO's Response to the Call for Views from the Securities Regulators under the EU's Action Plan for Financial Services COM(1999)232* (29 June 2000)

FESCO, *A 'European Passport' for Issuers* (10 May 2000)

FESCO, *Implementation of Article 11 of the ISD: Categorisation of Investors for the Purpose of Conduct of Business Rules* (15 March 2000)

FESCO, *Market Conduct Standards for Participants in an Offering* (22 December 1999)

FESCO, *Standards for Regulated Markets under the ISD* (22 December 1999)

FESCO, *Implementation of Article 11 of the ISD: Categorisation of Investors for the Purpose of Conduct of Business Rules* (November 1999)

FESCO, *European Standards on Fitness and Propriety to Provide Investment Services* (Press Release, 26 April 1999)

FESCO, *European Standards on Fitness and Propriety to Provide Investment Services* (2 April 1999)

FESCO, *Multilateral Memorandum of Understanding on the Exchange of Information and Surveillance of Securities Activities* (February 1999)

International organisations

Bank for International Settlements, *Recommendations for Securities Settlement Systems* (Consultative Report, January 2001)

Basel Committee, *Overview of the New Basel Capital Accord* (Consultative Document, January 2001)

Basel Committee, *A New Capital Adequacy Framework* (Consultative Paper, June 1999)

Basel Committee, *Supervision of Financial Conglomerates* (Joint Forum on Financial Conglomerates, February 1999)

Basel Committee, *Enhancing Bank Transparency* (September 1998)

Basel Committee, *Principles for the Supervision of Banks' Foreign Establishments (Concordat)* (May 1983)

Basel Committee, *Report to the Governors on the Supervision of Bank's Foreign Establishments (Concordat)* (September 1975)

FESE, *Second Report and Recommendations on European Regulatory Structures* (January 2001)

FESE, *First Report and Recommendations on European Regulatory Structures* (September 2000)

IOSCO, *Objectives and Principles of Securities Regulation* (February 2002)

IOSCO, *Securities Activity on the Internet II* (June 2001)

IOSCO, *Supervisory Framework for Markets* (May 1999)

IOSCO, *Securities Activity on the Internet* (September 1998)

IOSCO, *Objectives and Principles of Securities Regulation* (September 1998)

IOSCO, *Risk Management and Control Guidance for Securities Firms and their Supervisors* (May 1998)

IOSCO, *Guidance on Information Sharing* (November 1997)

IOSCO, *Principles for the Supervision of Operators of Collective Investment Schemes* (September 1997)

IOSCO, *Report on Enforcement Issues Raised by the Increasing Use of Electronic Networks in the Securities and Futures Field* (September 1997)

IOSCO, *Regulatory Cooperation in Emergencies: A Discussion Paper* (June 1996)

IOSCO, *Report on Cooperation between Market Authorities and Default Procedures* (March 1996)

National governments, regulators and exchanges

Bank of England, *Report of the Board of Banking Supervision Inquiry into the Circumstances of the Collapse of Barings* (London: HMSO, 18 July 1995)

Bundesaufsichtsamt für den Wertpapierhandel, *Annual Report 1998* (Frankfurt, 1999)

Commission des Opérations de Bourse, *The Freedom to Provide Services in the Area of Investment Services* (Report to the Comite des établissements de crédit et des entreprises d'investissement, 20 November 1998)

Euronext, *Rule Book I* (30 July 2001)

Financial Services Authority, *Complaints-handling Rules: Transitional Arrangements and Other Amendments* (Consultation Paper 99, June 2001)

Financial Services Authority, *Response to the Committee of Wise Men on the Regulation of Securities Markets* (27 September 2000)

Financial Services Authority, *The Supervision of EEA Banks* (30 September 1999)

Financial Services Authority, *Lead Supervision: The FSA's New Approach to the Co-ordination of its Supervision of Groups* (June 1999)

Financial Services Authority, *Financial Services Regulation: Enforcing the New Regime* (December 1998)

Financial Services Authority, *Differentiated Regulatory Approaches: Future Regulation of Inter-Professional Business* (October 1998)

Financial Services Authority, *Implementation in the UK of the EU Investor Compensation Directive* (August 1998)

HM Treasury, *Realising Europe's Potential: Economic Reform in Europe* (White Paper, February 2002)

House of Commons, *Banking Supervision and BCCI: International and National Regulation* (Treasury and Civil Service Select Committee, 4th Report, London, 1992)

London Stock Exchange, *Competing Market Mechanisms – Their Effect on the Rules of the London Stock Exchange* (Consultative Paper, September 1995)

Index